Carnegie Commission on Higher Education
Sponsored Research Studies

NEW DIRECTIONS IN LEGAL EDUCATION
Herbert L. Packer and Thomas Ehrlich

THE EMERGING TECHNOLOGY:
INSTRUCTIONAL USES OF THE COMPUTER
IN HIGHER EDUCATION
Roger E. Levien

WHERE COLLEGES ARE AND WHO ATTENDS:
EFFECTS OF ACCESSIBILITY ON COLLEGE
ATTENDANCE
*C. Arnold Anderson, Mary Jean Bowman,
and Vincent Tinto*

A STATISTICAL PORTRAIT
OF HIGHER EDUCATION
Seymour E. Harris

THE HOME OF SCIENCE:
THE ROLE OF THE UNIVERSITY
Dael Wolfle

EDUCATION AND EVANGELISM:
A PROFILE OF PROTESTANT COLLEGES
C. Robert Pace

PROFESSIONAL EDUCATION:
SOME NEW DIRECTIONS
Edgar H. Schein

THE NONPROFIT RESEARCH INSTITUTE:
ITS ORIGIN, OPERATION, PROBLEMS, AND
PROSPECTS
Harold Orlans

THE INVISIBLE COLLEGES:
A PROFILE OF SMALL, PRIVATE COLLEGES
WITH LIMITED RESOURCES
Alexander W. Astin and Calvin B. T. Lee

AMERICAN HIGHER EDUCATION:
DIRECTIONS OLD AND NEW
Joseph Ben-David

A DEGREE AND WHAT ELSE?:
CORRELATES AND CONSEQUENCES OF A
COLLEGE EDUCATION
*Stephen B. Withey, Jo Anne Coble, Gerald
Gurin, John P. Robinson, Burkhard Strumpel,
Elizabeth Keogh Taylor, and Arthur C. Wolfe*

THE MULTICAMPUS UNIVERSITY:
A STUDY OF ACADEMIC GOVERNANCE
Eugene C. Lee and Frank M. Bowen

INSTITUTIONS IN TRANSITION:
A PROFILE OF CHANGE IN HIGHER
EDUCATION
(INCORPORATING THE 1970 STATISTICAL
REPORT)
Harold L. Hodgkinson

EFFICIENCY IN LIBERAL EDUCATION:
A STUDY OF COMPARATIVE INSTRUCTIONAL
COSTS FOR DIFFERENT WAYS OF ORGANIZ-
ING TEACHING-LEARNING IN A LIBERAL ARTS
COLLEGE
Howard R. Bowen and Gordon K. Douglass

CREDIT FOR COLLEGE:
PUBLIC POLICY FOR STUDENT LOANS
Robert W. Hartman

MODELS AND MAVERICKS:
A PROFILE OF PRIVATE LIBERAL ARTS
COLLEGES
Morris T. Keeton

BETWEEN TWO WORLDS:
A PROFILE OF NEGRO HIGHER EDUCATION
Frank Bowles and Frank A. DeCosta

BREAKING THE ACCESS BARRIERS:
A PROFILE OF TWO-YEAR COLLEGES
Leland L. Medsker and Dale Tillery

ANY PERSON, ANY STUDY:
AN ESSAY ON HIGHER EDUCATION IN THE
UNITED STATES
Eric Ashby

THE NEW DEPRESSION IN HIGHER
EDUCATION:
A STUDY OF FINANCIAL CONDITIONS AT 41
COLLEGES AND UNIVERSITIES
Earl F. Cheit

FINANCING MEDICAL EDUCATION:
AN ANALYSIS OF ALTERNATIVE POLICIES
AND MECHANISMS
Rashi Fein and Gerald I. Weber

HIGHER EDUCATION IN NINE COUNTRIES:
A COMPARATIVE STUDY OF COLLEGES AND
UNIVERSITIES ABROAD
*Barbara B. Burn, Philip G. Altbach, Clark Kerr,
and James A. Perkins*

BRIDGES TO UNDERSTANDING:
INTERNATIONAL PROGRAMS OF AMERICAN
COLLEGES AND UNIVERSITIES
Irwin T. Sanders and Jennifer C. Ward

GRADUATE AND PROFESSIONAL EDUCATION,
1980:
A SURVEY OF INSTITUTIONAL PLANS
Lewis B. Mayhew

THE AMERICAN COLLEGE AND AMERICAN
CULTURE:
SOCIALIZATION AS A FUNCTION OF HIGHER
EDUCATION
Oscar Handlin and Mary F. Handlin

RECENT ALUMNI AND HIGHER EDUCATION:
A SURVEY OF COLLEGE GRADUATES
Joe L. Spaeth and Andrew M. Greeley

CHANGE IN EDUCATIONAL POLICY:
SELF-STUDIES IN SELECTED COLLEGES AND
UNIVERSITIES
Dwight R. Ladd

STATE OFFICIALS AND HIGHER EDUCATION:
A SURVEY OF THE OPINIONS AND
EXPECTATIONS OF POLICY MAKERS IN NINE
STATES
Heinz Eulau and Harold Quinley

ACADEMIC DEGREE STRUCTURES:
INNOVATIVE APPROACHES
PRINCIPLES OF REFORM IN DEGREE
STRUCTURES IN THE UNITED STATES
Stephen H. Spurr

COLLEGES OF THE FORGOTTEN AMERICANS:
A PROFILE OF STATE COLLEGES AND
REGIONAL UNIVERSITIES
E. Alden Dunham

FROM BACKWATER TO MAINSTREAM:
A PROFILE OF CATHOLIC HIGHER
EDUCATION
Andrew M. Greeley

THE ECONOMICS OF THE MAJOR PRIVATE
UNIVERSITIES
William G. Bowen
(Out of print, but available from University Microfilms.)

THE FINANCE OF HIGHER EDUCATION
Howard R. Bowen
(Out of print, but available from University Microfilms.)

ALTERNATIVE METHODS OF FEDERAL
FUNDING FOR HIGHER EDUCATION
Ron Wolk
(Out of print, but available from University Microfilms.)

INVENTORY OF CURRENT RESEARCH ON
HIGHER EDUCATION 1968
Dale M. Heckman and Warren Bryan Martin
(Out of print, but available from University Microfilms.)

*The following technical reports are available from the Carnegie Commission on Higher Education, 1947
Center Street, Berkeley, California 94704.*

RESOURCE USE IN HIGHER EDUCATION:
TRENDS IN OUTPUT AND INPUTS, 1930–1967
June O'Neill

MENTAL ABILITY AND HIGHER EDUCATIONAL
ATTAINMENT IN THE TWENTIETH CENTURY
Paul Taubman and Terence Wales

TRENDS AND PROJECTIONS OF PHYSICIANS
IN THE UNITED STATES 1967–2002
Mark S. Blumberg

AMERICAN COLLEGE AND UNIVERSITY
ENROLLMENT TRENDS IN 1971
Richard E. Peterson

MAY 1970:
THE CAMPUS AFTERMATH OF CAMBODIA
AND KENT STATE
Richard E. Peterson and John A. Bilorusky

PAPERS ON EFFICIENCY IN THE
MANAGEMENT OF HIGHER EDUCATION
*Alexander M. Mood, Colin Bell, Lawrence
Bogard, Helen Brownlee, and Joseph McCloskey*

The following reprints are available from the Carnegie Commission on Higher Education, 1947 Center Street, Berkeley, California 94704.

ACCELERATED PROGRAMS OF MEDICAL EDUCATION, *by Mark S. Blumberg, reprinted from* JOURNAL OF MEDICAL EDUCATION, *vol. 46, no. 8, August 1971.**

SCIENTIFIC MANPOWER FOR 1970–1985, *by Allan M. Cartter, reprinted from* SCIENCE, *vol. 172, no. 3979, pp. 132–140, April 9, 1971.*

A NEW METHOD OF MEASURING STATES' HIGHER EDUCATION BURDEN, *by Neil Timm, reprinted from* THE JOURNAL OF HIGHER EDUCATION, *vol. 42, no. 1, pp. 27–33, January 1971.**

REGENT WATCHING, *by Earl F. Cheit, reprinted from* AGB REPORTS, *vol. 13, no. 6, pp. 4–13, March 1971.**

COLLEGE GENERATIONS—FROM THE 1930s TO THE 1960s, *by Seymour M. Lipset and Everett C. Ladd, Jr., reprinted from* THE PUBLIC INTEREST, *no. 25, Summer 1971.*

AMERICAN SOCIAL SCIENTISTS AND THE GROWTH OF CAMPUS POLITICAL ACTIVISM IN THE 1960s, *by Everett C. Ladd, Jr., and Seymour M. Lipset, reprinted from* SOCIAL SCIENCES INFORMATION, *vol. 10, no. 2, April 1971.*

THE POLITICS OF AMERICAN POLITICAL SCIENTISTS, *by Everett C. Ladd, Jr., and Seymour M. Lipset, reprinted from* PS, *vol. 4, no. 2, Spring 1971.**

THE DIVIDED PROFESSORIATE, *by Seymour M. Lipset and Everett C. Ladd, Jr., reprinted from* CHANGE, *vol. 3, no. 3, pp. 54–60, May 1971.**

JEWISH ACADEMICS IN THE UNITED STATES: THEIR ACHIEVEMENTS, CULTURE AND POLITICS, *by Seymour M. Lipset and Everett C. Ladd, Jr., reprinted from* AMERICAN JEWISH YEAR BOOK, *1971.*

THE UNHOLY ALLIANCE AGAINST THE CAMPUS, *by Kenneth Keniston and Michael Lerner, reprinted from* NEW YORK TIMES MAGAZINE, *November 8, 1970 .*

PRECARIOUS PROFESSORS: NEW PATTERNS OF REPRESENTATION, *by Joseph W. Garbarino, reprinted from* INDUSTRIAL RELATIONS, *vol. 10, no. 1, February 1971.**

. . . AND WHAT PROFESSORS THINK: ABOUT STUDENT PROTEST AND MANNERS, MORALS, POLITICS, AND CHAOS ON THE CAMPUS, *by Seymour Martin Lipset and Everett C. Ladd, Jr., reprinted from* PSYCHOLOGY TODAY, *November 1970.**

DEMAND AND SUPPLY IN U.S. HIGHER EDUCATION: A PROGRESS REPORT, *by Roy Radner and Leonard S. Miller, reprinted from* AMERICAN ECONOMIC REVIEW, *May 1970.**

RESOURCES FOR HIGHER EDUCATION: AN ECONOMIST'S VIEW, by *Theodore W. Schultz, re-printed from* JOURNAL OF POLITICAL ECONOMY, *vol. 76, no. 3, University of Chicago, May/ June 1968.**

INDUSTRIAL RELATIONS AND UNIVERSITY RELATIONS, by *Clark Kerr, reprinted from* PRO-CEEDINGS OF THE 21ST ANNUAL WINTER MEETING OF THE INDUSTRIAL RELATIONS RESEARCH ASSOCIATION, *pp. 15–25.**

NEW CHALLENGES TO THE COLLEGE AND UNIVERSITY, by *Clark Kerr, reprinted from Kermit Gordon (ed.),* AGENDA FOR THE NATION, *The Brookings Institution, Washington, D.C., 1968. **

PRESIDENTIAL DISCONTENT, by *Clark Kerr, reprinted from David C. Nichols (ed.),* PER-SPECTIVES ON CAMPUS TENSIONS: PAPERS PREPARED FOR THE SPECIAL COMMITTEE ON CAMPUS TENSIONS, *American Council on Education, Washington, D.C., September 1970.**

STUDENT PROTEST—AN INSTITUTIONAL AND NATIONAL PROFILE, by *Harold Hodgkinson, reprinted from* THE RECORD, *vol. 71, no. 4, May 1970.**

WHAT'S BUGGING THE STUDENTS?, by *Kenneth Keniston, reprinted from* EDUCATIONAL RECORD, *American Council on Education, Washington, D.C., Spring 1970.**

THE POLITICS OF ACADEMIA, by *Seymour Martin Lipset, reprinted from David C. Nichols (ed.),* PERSPECTIVES ON CAMPUS TENSIONS: PAPERS PREPARED FOR THE SPECIAL COMMITTEE ON CAMPUS TENSIONS, *American Council on Education, Washington, D.C., September 1970.**

INTERNATIONAL PROGRAMS OF U.S. COLLEGES AND UNIVERSITIES: PRIORITIES FOR THE SEVEN-TIES, by *James A. Perkins, reprinted by permission of the International Council for Educational Development, Occasional Paper no. 1, July 1971.*

FACULTY UNIONISM: FROM THEORY TO PRACTICE, by *Joseph W. Garbarino, reprinted from* INDUSTRIAL RELATIONS, *vol. 11, no. 1, pp. 1–17, February 1972.*

MORE FOR LESS, HIGHER EDUCATION'S NEW PRIORITY, by *Virginia B. Smith, reprinted from* UNIVERSAL HIGHER EDUCATION: COSTS AND BENEFITS, *American Council on Education, Washington, D.C., 1971.*

ACADEMIA AND POLITICS IN AMERICA, by *Seymour M. Lipset, reprinted from Thomas J. Nossiter (ed.),* IMAGINATION AND PRECISION IN THE SOCIAL SCIENCES, *pp. 211–289, Faber and Faber, London, 1972.*

POLITICS OF ACADEMIC NATURAL SCIENTISTS AND ENGINEERS, *by Everett C. Ladd, Jr., and Seymour M. Lipset, reprinted from* SCIENCE, *vol. 176, no. 4039, pp. 1091–1100, June 9, 1972.*

THE INTELLECTUAL AS CRITIC AND REBEL: WITH SPECIAL REFERENCE TO THE UNITED STATES AND THE SOVIET UNION *by Seymour M. Lipset and Richard B. Dobson, reprinted from* DAEDALUS, *vol. 101, no. 3, pp. 137–198, Summer 1972.*

*The Commission's stock of this reprint has been exhausted.

New Directions in Legal Education

New Directions in Legal Education

by **Herbert L. Packer**

Jackson Eli Reynolds Professor of Law,
Stanford Law School

and **Thomas Ehrlich**

Dean and Professor of Law,
Stanford Law School

with the assistance of **Stephen Pepper**

Candidate for the J.D. degree,
Yale Law School

A Report Prepared for
The Carnegie Commission on Higher Education

MCGRAW-HILL BOOK COMPANY

New York   St. Louis   San Francisco   Düsseldorf

London   Sydney   Toronto   Mexico   Panama

Johannesburg   Kuala Lumpur   Montreal

New Delhi   Rio de Janeiro   Singapore

The Carnegie Commission on Higher Education,
1947 Center Street, Berkeley, California 94704,
has sponsored preparation of this report as a
part of a continuing effort to obtain and present
significant information for public discussion.
The views expressed are those of the authors.

NEW DIRECTIONS IN LEGAL EDUCATION

Library of Congress Cataloging in Publication Data

Packer, Herbert L

New directions in legal education.

1.   Law—study and teaching—United States.
I.   Ehrlich, Thomas, date   joint author.   II.
Carnegie Commission on Higher Education.   III.   Title.

KF272.P3   340'.07'1173   72-5311
ISBN 07-010047-0

123456789MAMM798765432

Contents

Foreword

Education in the law is increasingly regarded as a general education at an advanced level. Law school graduates move not only into the private practice of law but also into many other careers. As one result of this newly perceived status of legal education, applications to law schools are rising rapidly. Forty-three law schools responding to a Commission survey conducted by Richard E. Peterson of the Educational Testing Service reported an application increase of 51 percent between 1970 and 1971.

In this review of the conduct of law schools, the authors note that American law schools are now regarded differently by students than they once were, and they suggest some important changes. High on their list is the need for more diversity in American legal education and, especially, for alternatives to the prevailing model which emphasizes the case method. They also favor the expansion of the training and use of paraprofessionals within the legal profession, and changes in rules and procedures that would favor the use of paraprofessionals. Another major change they suggest is the reduction of total time required in school to prepare for a legal career. This could be accomplished either by reducing to three years the time required in college before law school or the reduction of law school training to two years. This suggestion is consistent with the more general recommendation of the Carnegie Commission that the time required for formal higher education be reduced in all fields. These proposals are offered on the basis of thorough investigation and deliberation by an eminently qualified group of experts.

Clark Kerr
Chairman
Carnegie Commission
on Higher Education

Preface

This study is an analysis of recent developments and future trends in the legal profession and of their consequences for legal education. It examines some structural problems of legal education and suggests changes to deal with those problems. By "structural," we mean those characteristics common to all law schools.[1] Our emphasis on structure does not mean that law schools should be immune to revisions in other aspects of their educational arrangements. Although structural changes will have a strong effect on all aspects of legal education, we think that curricular revisions must emerge from within an individual law school and must be tailored to the needs, abilities, and resources of that school. In consequence, this study does not focus on the details of law school curricula or of teaching methods.

We make no pretensions that this study is exhaustive. We do try to consider, at least briefly, the major issues that in our view are unique to law training as opposed to other areas in higher education. Each of those issues could be considered, with profit, in a separate volume. Further, several problems of critical concern to law schools and legal educators today are not here considered at all. The inadequate representation of racial minorities and women in law schools is perhaps the most important of these problems. We omit discussion of it here because, in our view, although it is a serious problem, it is not peculiarly related to legal education but endemic to all higher education. A word of further explanation may be in order.

We state categorically that there should be more women lawyers and lawyers from racial minorities in the profession. To meet the numbers problem, there must be: *(a)* encouragement to these groups

---

[1] For a list of these structural characteristics, see p. 24.

to consider law training, *(b)* adequate undergraduate training for them, and *(c)* money. In recent years, major steps have been taken to deal with the first of these matters, and some progress has been made with the last two. But much remains to be done.

The "research" on which this study is based did not include field studies, questionnaires, or opinion polls. Rather, our method consisted of asking the Advisory Committee to help frame some salient questions and then to suggest where the authors may have erred. In short, we tried to identify and think through the present and prospective problems of legal education.

Acknowledgments

We find it impossible to mention all the people who have aided us with this study. First, we give special tribute to our Advisory Committee members, who helped so much with our initial effort to define the issues. They subsequently gave us their reactions to our drafts. We sometimes reached conclusions at variance with what one or more of them thought, but we are most grateful to them. They are Charles F. Ares, dean of the University of Arizona Law School; Robert F. Drinan, S.J., former dean of the Boston College Law School and now a member of the United States House of Representatives; Abraham S. Goldstein, dean of the Yale Law School; Geoffrey Hazard, former director of the American Bar Foundation and now professor of law at Yale Law School; and Murray F. Schwartz, dean of the UCLA Law School.

If it were appropriate to dedicate this study, we would dedicate it to Bayless Manning, president of the Council on Foreign Relations and former dean of Stanford Law School. It was he who encouraged the Carnegie Commission to undertake this study; as his colleagues we owe him the debt of his inspiration and of his interest in the issues of legal education. His ideas are imbedded in this study.

We thank our colleagues at Stanford who helped by their interest in the problems of legal education and by their willingness to address those problems in a serious and constructive fashion. We are particularly grateful to Charles Meyers, Charles A. Beardsley Professor of Law at Stanford, whose work as chairman of the AALS Curriculum Committee suggested many of the proposals in this study; to Joseph Sneed, formerly professor of law at Stanford and now dean of Duke Law School, who as president of the American Association of Law Schools, was a leader in the move for constructive reform of legal education; and to Thomas Headrick, formerly assistant dean at Stanford Law School and now vice president of

Lawrence College, who helped to coordinate a study of the structure of legal education at Stanford in 1968–69 and who stimulated our thinking on many questions.

We benefited greatly from the suggestions of numerous students at Stanford Law School, particularly those who participated in a 1969–70 seminar on legal education and in the 1968–69 structural study. We thank particularly Richard T. Williams, Stanford J.D. 1968, who prepared an excellent bibliography on legal education, and Sally Schultz Neely, Stanford J.D. 1970, who helped us to organize materials and ideas.

Among those at other institutions who contributed to our work, we mention Paul Carrington of the University of Michigan Law School, Robert Gorman of the University of Pennsylvania Law School, Robert Stevens of Yale University Law School, and Preble Stolz of the University of California Law School at Berkeley. All have done much to make scholarship on legal education respectable.

Two other people were particularly helpful: Mr. Packer's former secretary, Joann Weber, who did much in many ways to keep this study alive; and our collaborator, Stephen Pepper, Yale Law School Class of 1973, who did much of the work that made this study possible.

Finally, we owe a special debt to Nancy and to Ellen.

H. L. P.
T. E.

March 1972

*New Directions
in Legal Education*

1. The Legal Profession: Past, Present, and Future

From the beginning of the nation, there have been strands of elitism and of populism both within the legal profession and with respect to public attitudes toward it. Nonetheless, the bar has generally reflected middle-class values and problems. As Willard Hurst puts it, "Over the years, the bar shared the prevailing religious, racial and national prejudices of middle-class Americans."[1]

In the early days of the Republic and up to the Civil War, the dominant subject of American practice was real property and commerce, and the dominant type of lawyer was the individual practitioner. After the Civil War, the emphasis shifted to problems attendant on the growth of American industry. The growth of industrial corporations and of railroads shifted the focus of practice in several ways. Practice began to be concentrated in large cities; large firms began to develop; by 1900 the "Wall Street firm" had established its pattern. The large firms of New York, Philadelphia, Boston, and later metropolitan centers in the Midwest and the West became the citadels of elitism in the practice of law as firms grew and served their corporate clients—industries, railroads, banks, and other financial institutions—more as counselors than as advocates in the courtrooms. At the same time, urbanization forced the general run of lawyers into the cities. The nonelite business was carried on mainly by individual practitioners and consisted primarily of commercial work—real property transactions, estates, and litigation involving disputes arising from the foregoing categories—plus personal injuries, divorce, and criminal work.

Meanwhile, another powerful influence was making itself felt. Government regulation of the economy was creating new fields

---

[1] Hurst (1950, p. 235). Hurst's book is by far the best source for the history of the American bar.

1

of practice. In the early years of this century, taxation, antitrust, labor relations, and government regulation of trade practices became important. The New Deal added to these a vast number of government administrative agencies, e.g., the Securities and Exchange Commission (SEC), the National Labor Relations Board (NLRB), the Federal Communications Commission (FCC), and the Civil Aeronautics Board (CAB). The states both led this development and followed suit with an increasing degree of public intervention in every aspect of the economy. All of this added greatly to the business of lawyers, although it contributed more to the growth of middle-sized and elite firms than it did to the everyday work of the average lawyer.

In 1966 over half of the 300,000 lawyers in the United States practiced in cities having a population of 200,000 or more, and just over half of the lawyers in private practice were individual practitioners, while in 1947 three-quarters were individual practitioners. The largest firms, located in New York, Washington, Chicago, Los Angeles, etc., may have as many as 30 or 40 partners and 100 employed associate attorneys. Income is apparently related to firm size. In 1965 the average annual net income for lawyers was about $10,000 (as compared to $7,000 for wage earners in the United States generally). The average for lawyers in partnership was $22,000. Partners in the large firms in the big cities probably average at least $30,000.[2]

The oddest thing about these developments is that up to the present, legal education and admissions to the bar and bar organization have combined to force the profession, at least on the surface, into a common mold, based largely on obsolescent patterns of practice. This has greatly inhibited the formal recognition (and sometimes even the perception) that lawyers, after all, are not members of a homogeneous profession. In Chapter 3, we will try to explain and account for this distorted perception of homogeneity. We believe that the supposed homogeneity is spurious and that the profession, including education for it, must respond to existing diversity and to the pressure for more and must acknowledge the need for specialization and the development of paraprofessional careers. These themes will recur.

There are today about 325,000 lawyers in the United States.

[2] The data in this paragraph are derived from the American Bar Foundation (1970).

Of these, over 200,000 are engaged in "private practice." Private practice, as we have suggested, takes diverse forms. And we have 40,000 lawyers working for the public at every level of government: federal, state, and local. These include a rapidly increasing sector of lawyers hired by agencies at various levels of government to represent the interests of certain private citizens. For example, the Office of Economic Opportunity employs over 2,000 lawyers to furnish legal services to the poor. And local government units and privately run Legal Aid offices employ many lawyers to serve as public defenders, primarily as counsel for "indigent" criminal defendants. About 10,000 lawyers serve as full-time judges. Business enterprises employ at least 30,000 lawyers as "house counsel." Over 2,500 lawyers teach full time, and about 1,500 more teach part time. Lawyers may also be insurance agents, stockbrokers, bank trust officers, and the like.

There has always been a preponderance of lawyers in elective public office, and many other lawyers hold nonlegal appointive positions. In 1970, 67 senators, a majority of representatives, and 4 Cabinet members were lawyers. Governors, mayors, school board members, aldermen, and their assistants are frequently lawyers. About one-quarter of all state legislators since 1900 have been lawyers. As members of what is preeminently a public profession, lawyers are often found in the roles of diplomat, university and foundation administrator, etc. Boards of trustees, both of public interest institutions (universities, foundations, etc.) and private corporations, frequently include lawyers.

One does not search long for prominent examples. Derek Bok, Kingman Brewster, Robben Fleming, and Edward Levi are university presidents who exercise broad influence both within and without their institutions, influence which we believe has deep roots in their legal education. The contribution to our public life, past and present, of lawyers like Elihu Root, Henry Stimson, and Dean Acheson is clear. What they all had in common was a kind of principled pragmatism that stamped everything they did as public men. To balance this observation it should be noted that one also does not search long for rather disreputable examples, lawyers at all levels of practice and belonging to all social classes who either lost or never received the "principled" element of their "pragmatism."

Glancing into the future, the following trends, predictions, and questions seem to us to warrant further exploration:

1   A cluster of fields in the law, new and old, seems to be expanding rapidly: criminal law, problems of poverty, problems of the consumer, issues concerning the environment, the restructuring of local government units, etc. Each of these brings with it the need for legal services. How are such services to be financed, and who will provide them?

2   Pressures are present and growing, from within and without, for new mechanisms and organizations of the profession: specialties within the law are growing, and so is pressure to accord them formal recognition. This brings with it the problems of licensing these specialties. There is growing pressure for and possibility of group legal services. How will these services be structured and financed?

3   Paraprofessionals are needed now, and the demand will certainly be greater with the development of group services and specialization. With these new mechanisms will come a decline in the battles over "unauthorized practice."

4   Educational arrangements will have to be made to accommodate the aforementioned developments. Who will train specialists and paraprofessionals? At what point on the educational ladder will these new forms of training come? Are the law schools equipped to deal with these questions, or will the response be purely spasmodic? Are we educating too many lawyers?

5   Several questions specifically confront the legal system and education: Can law adequately assimilate social science? Is there any prospect for the study of legal structures, for what we may call macrolegal structures? Can legal scholarship make a contribution? Is there a place in higher education for the study of law by laymen?

6   How are we to finance whatever appears to be the structure of legal education in the future?

We believe that the future of legal education is inextricably intertwined with the future of the legal profession, which in turn depends very much on the place of law and legal institutions in the future. The future is heavily clouded, and we lay no claim to a crystal ball. But we do think that a study of new directions in legal education will at least have to take account of our list of questions.

2. Some Aspects of the Future of the Legal Profession

There have been several stereotyped images of the lawyer in our culture. One is the image of the courtroom advocate participating in a kind of morality play; television has immortalized him. Another is the small-town lawyer advising his client; Arthur Train's Mr. Tutt epitomizes him. Then there is the Wall Street or Washington lawyer lifting his telephone and throwing his influence around; Ralph Nader has tried to make him notorious.

All these images reflect fragmentary aspects of reality. However, large aspects of current reality are at odds with these views. Contemporary reality includes general ignorance of the need for, scope of, and cost of legal services; inaccessibility of lawyers; and lack of communication between lawyers and the mass of their potential clients. There is a quiet crisis in the availability of legal services. Almost all developments in the law and the legal process move in the direction of increasing the need for legal services, yet those services are out of the practical economic reach of the major part of our population. This section is an attempt to provide a quick overview of the legal jobs that are going to need doing in the future and of some of the mechanisms that will probably develop to do them. This developing shape of our legal needs—what we shall call the *legal agenda*—covers a great deal of territory.

As the country grows steadily more urban, more postindustrial, and more service-oriented, it seems clear that the legal job will grow qualitatively as well as quantitatively. By the legal job we mean those tasks that appear to fall within the lawyer's competence. We do not mean that this work will necessarily be done by people who have been trained by legal education, as it has existed, and been admitted to the bar. Put another way, the legal job means, at a minimum, all the tasks that lawyers, *as architects of order* and *as advocates,* might do to help reconcile the interests of people

5

and of institutions. As *architects of order* we mean those who will help build the institutions and processes to service and accommodate our continuously changing social system. As advocates we mean people who represent interests. We do not exclude elected legislators, elected executives, and elected or appointed judges, to the extent that legal education tends to be a dominant element in preparing people for these positions. Such men are both architects of order and representatives of the "public interest." It would be futile (not to mention extremely shortsighted) to exclude representatives of the public interest from this discussion, for one man's public interest is simply another man's interest. Our emphasis will be on the advocacy of interests, whether one considers them public or private.

As a *necessary* response to the crisis in the availability of legal services we see a cluster of developments coming to make legal services more efficient and less expensive, and hence far more generally available. The development of sublegal and paralegal personnel, of group legal services, and of certified specialists are primary responses to the crisis. The bar will have to change several of its rules that now block the growth of these responses; one hopes that it will do so soon. Although these are certainly not the only responses that must come, they will probably be the most apparent as we survey the developing situation.

We may start our inventory of the legal agenda with the provision of services to "indigents" accused of crime. It has become increasingly clear from the now firmly established constitutional base that the necessary services include investigative services, expert witnesses, etc. It is therefore evident that the occupations involved in providing the necessary services include sublegal and paralegal occupations. While the constitutional meaning of indigence is presently quite restricted, we can see emerging a common acceptance of the category of *legal indigence.* In this category belongs the middle-class person who cannot afford to foot the bill for representation. We expect to see the emergence of a sense of obligation (although not necessarily in a constitutional sense) to provide legal services for such people. Just as we are now inured to the concept of medical indigence, so in the criminal field do we expect to see the concept of legal indigence appearing. We will have more to say later in this chapter about how this expansion to middle-class people can be financed. The scope of what we mean by *legal representation* is gradually expanding to include pretrial work, postconviction remedies, correctional services, and the various services required to help the ex-criminal find his way back into society, as well as quasi-criminal proceedings concerning, for example, mental health and juvenile delinquency. Thus, in this one example from the legal agenda we find extensions going along numerous axes: the kind of people who need representation, the kinds of representation they need, the diversity of what constitutes legal services, and the development of new careers to provide these services.

One can trace the beginnings of similar developments in civil matters also. Obviously, the legal agenda is not limited to litigation. Help in negotiation and counseling are needed in the myriad contract, tort, and property matters that make up the average man's contact with legal problems. Divorce and bankruptcy are two areas in which procedures will have to be streamlined, broken down into their component parts, and handled by a variety of specialists who may be largely sublegal and paralegal. This process has already taken place in the transfer of property (real and personal) both *inter vivos* and at death, and it is obviously coming along in personal injury matters, where one can see the seeds of a system in which not merely the insurance company but also the injured party will be represented by paralegal claim agents. Litigation is gradually giving way to negotiation, presumably by paralegals, as the chief means by which claims are settled.

Changes are probably coming in the substance of the rules that govern many of these transactions. There is a strong likelihood that either more state legislatures or Congress will pass legislation to replace the present negligence system for compensating victims of automobile accidents with a no-fault system that substitutes one's own insurer for a third party's liability insurer as the principal source of compensation.[1] This development is bound to have some effect on the incomes of that segment of the bar that litigates personal injury cases. The general estimate is that 15 to 20 percent of the revenue of the bar is derived from personal injury litigation. A no-fault arrangement for divorces is already here in one jurisdiction, California. Revisions in the law affecting the devolution of wealth from one generation to another—what lawyers refer to as probate work—are in the legislative hopper in several states. Such

---

[1] Massachusetts already has such a statute, based on the plan worked out by Professors Keeton and O'Connell (1966).

changes in substantive law affect what lawyers do; indeed, some of these changes are designed to reduce dependency on lawyers' services. Whether by design or not, the probable effect will be generally to reduce the need for the direct help of general legal practitioners and to increase the need for the planning, supervising, and help of the legal specialist. The effect on lawyers' jobs and income will obviously depend on how people react to changes in the way that the legal profession is organized.

One should add to this legal agenda such emerging interests as the environment, consumer protection, and privacy. Either through judicial decision or through legislation, there is a trend toward making it easy to bring lawsuits (and thereby to compel private settlements). We have in mind relaxed standing requirements, minimum liquidated damages, provision for attorneys' fees, aggregating claims, etc. To give one example, it has become possible as a matter of formal legal right for groups of people who suffer from air pollution to bring class actions against automobile manufacturers and, if they are successful, to recover a reasonable minimum of liquidated damages and attorneys' fees. (It should be noted here that there is a clash between such a policy of opening the courthouse door wider and the need to improve the machinery inside. Already the judicial system is sorely strained on both the civil and criminal side—too many hearings are being handled now, and cases take far too long. Something will have to be done to make the process speedier and more efficient if we are to make it easier to bring lawsuits.)[2]

Another development in the provision of legal services is the certification of specialists, which, it seems, cannot be long delayed, however strong a rear guard action the "organized" bar maintains. (This certification of specialists will also necessarily bring with it the growth of paraprofessional occupations, as will be discussed later in this chapter.)

These expanded legal services will probably be made available through a mixture of public and private institutions. If the legal agenda is to be made available to everyone, as it is already beginning to be to the poor, it will have to command a much broader constituency than the poor. Middle-class people simply will not put up the ante for the poor if their own needs are overlooked. A mixture of publicly supported agencies and tax gimmicks will be

[2] See Main (1970, p. 111).

necessary. The more affluent consumers of legal services will demand comprehensive prepaid legal assistance as their price for putting up the public money for legal assistance to those below or near the poverty level. The path that strikes one as being the most likely is group legal service, bought and paid for by the many institutions—corporations, universities, school systems, and other systems embracing public employees—whose employees will demand legal services. For example, a teacher will demand that when he has to negotiate with an insurance company to collect medical benefits he have as his representative a claim agent. Multiply that case by the millions of claims of various sorts that few can successfully assume the burden of undertaking at present, and the necessity for this form of countervailing power should become obvious. (It should be noted in passing that the additions to the legal agenda should make it possible for attorneys to profit from group practice and to encourage the development of certified specialties and of paraprofessional occupations.)

In short, to the extent that the legal agenda briefly sketched in this section develops, the stage is set for dramatic expansion of needed legal services and for equally drastic changes in the skills required to provide these services. This in turn has far-reaching implications for legal education.

The forms of providing both legal services and legal education are to an important degree prescribed by the organized bar through its Canons of Professional Ethics, its formal and informal ways of keeping its members in line, and its rules of admissions. Thus the response to the crisis in legal services we have been speaking of is dependent upon the bar and upon the legal system. Bastions of the organized bar will have to be modified: some of the fee-splitting limitations, advertising bans, and "unauthorized practice" prohibitions will have to go; specialization, paraprofessional and subprofessional occupations, and comprehensive, prepaid legal insurance will have to come. The concept and content of the education required for professionals functioning in such a new institutional context must be modified. As it now stands, too many of the young people who graduate from law school will not be able to put their skills to work usefully in the profession.

We do not mean to pose an essentially epistemological problem as the center of our inquiry, but candor requires the admission that central to our problem is knowing what we mean by the *legal profession*. On the one hand, our notion of what constitutes the legal profession will undergo changes. On the other hand, we may well be educating far too many *lawyers* in the old-fashioned sense of the term. It will require considerable changes in our consciousness of what the market is in order to allow the market to determine the size and shape of the legal profession. And without knowing whether either supply or demand is adequate, it is most difficult to speak of the future of legal education.

Since our views of what is meant by the *legal profession* are undergoing considerable change, we have to rely on present understanding, which tells us that we have today about 325,000 lawyers. This figure refers to people admitted to the bar. We think that a lawyer can and should be defined as a person who has had a law school education. This figure will, at the present rate of growth in the population of our law schools, almost double in the next 15 years. We tend to think that we can absorb this number of lawyers without straining our abilities. We would like to think that the growth in the legal agenda and the increasing diversity of the profession will result in an equilibrium at a higher level than we have today.

To establish such an equilibrium will obviously require that the profession redefine itself as a less homogeneous entity. There is very little doubt that, if left to its own devices in the face of a worsening supply-demand function, the bar will impose some additional restrictions on who is allowed to present himself as a lawyer and attempt thereby to discourage the entry of newcomers. If this "guild" response determines the number of lawyers, society will be the poorer for it.

Essentially, we need to free our minds of conventional images, such as the three sketched at the beginning of this chapter.

SPECIALIZATION AND CHANGES IN ORGANIZATION

As we have mentioned, specialization is already a fact in the legal profession: many, if not most, lawyers concentrate their practice in particular areas. Specialization may be by client (whether the government, or an individual corporation, or a particular industry such as drugs or automobiles), by locale (all the types of people in a confined area, such as a town or a neighborhood), by fields of legal doctrine (labor law, patents, probate, etc.), by tasks (negotiation, lobbying, litigation, etc.), or by institutional setting (the Federal Trade Commission, a particular court, legislature, etc.), among others. Such specialization is already part and parcel of the legal profession and is a fact.[3]

The most controversial aspect of specialization is the movement toward the certification of specialists in the law, somewhat as medical specialists are certified. Presumably certification would be accomplished by requiring a period of practice in the specialty and by an examination. In discussing specialization, it is important to be clear about the distinction between two basic functions of specialization. These are (1) making more efficient the high-volume type of transaction—collections, no-fault divorce, and the like—and (2) developing superior expertise in highly complex matters. The first of these is often expressed as a move toward paraprofessionalism. The second is often expressed as a move toward superspecialization. The first type of specialist seeks to do a job just as well as the general practitioner, but cheaper. On the other hand, the specialist in complex matters seeks to do a much better job than does the general practitioner, but at a higher price.

The issue in certified specialization is intraprofessional competition. The issue arises in the form of the prohibition against *advertising*. Lawyers who are specialists cannot band together to establish certification for their specialties because any disclosure of their certified status would be deemed a violation of the ban that the organized bar maintains against advertising. Certification of specialties would be an empty gesture unless (like physicians) lawyers were free to indicate their specialties in the yellow pages of the telephone directory, or at least within the bar itself as a device for facilitating referral. California has legitimated formal certification on an experimental basis, and other states are likely to follow soon.

Certified specialization of lawyers is only one means of making good legal services readily available to potential consumers. Another means is the banding together of potential consumers in a buyer's cooperative, known as group legal services. Group legal services involve establishing an attorney-client relationship through the medium of some group (a labor union, a corporation, an educational institution, or a government unit, for example), all of whose members agree to give their legal business to a firm or firms of

---

[3] See the good discussion of specialization and standardization in Johnstone & Hopson (1967).

lawyers. Such arrangements have been prohibited on the ground that they involve advertising, stirring up of legal controversies, and interference with the lawyer-client relationship. These prohibitions have been largely undermined by a series of recent Supreme Court cases that have announced that access to legal assistance is a constitutional right. Yet the opposition of state bar associations has so far largely prevented the amendment of the Canons of Professional Ethics to permit group legal practice. It seems to be only a matter of time before this opposition crumbles and affirmative rules allowing and regulating group legal arrangements are enacted. Rules of this type are indeed now in effect in California. The movement toward group legal practice seems more developed than the movement toward specialization, but the two will almost certainly have to move together.

To indicate how this is so requires a more detailed explanation of these two developments. As to specialization, the California experience is illustrative of both the problems in developing a specialization certification plan and the obstacles to securing the agreement of the organized bar to attempt trial of such a certification plan. A Committee on Specialization was organized in June 1966 and conducted a survey on specialization among the membership of the state bar in 1968. The committee submitted a final report on May 20, 1969, recommending that a pilot project (shortly to be described) be undertaken. At the 1969 meetings of the state bar the committee's proposed plan was defeated. The board of governors of the state bar promptly authorized a pilot project, which is now being carried out.

The results of the survey were as follows:

- Specialization is closely related to firm size, with 53 percent of solo practitioners specializing and over 80 percent of firms having more than 10 members specializing.

- Almost 75 percent of those polled expressed a desire to specialize in the future.

- About 75 percent expected a public benefit to result from certification of specialists.

- Sixty-six percent thought that certification would improve the public image of the bar.

- A small majority thought that the public needs a certification system to identify specialists.

- Almost 75 percent thought that the state rather than a national or local agency should do the certifying.

- Over 75 percent thought that a requirement of three to five years' experience should be exacted.

- Just over 60 percent favored an educational requirement. Of these, 46 percent favored a required curriculum, with 30 percent favoring administration by the Continuing Education of the Bar and only 16 percent favoring administration by a law school.

- Over 75 percent favored an examination for certification, and of these more than 60 percent thought that there should be both a written and an oral examination.

In spite of this generally favorable attitude:

- Slightly more than 50 percent thought that certification would harm general practitioners.

- Over 84 percent thought that one should *not* be restricted in his practice to his specialty.

- Over 86 percent thought that noncertified attorneys should not be excluded from practicing in certified fields.

These results are probably an adequate reflection of the present and somewhat ambivalent attitudes of the legal profession toward certification of specialists. The committee's proposed pilot project is carefully tailored to reflect these attitudes as expressed in the survey. While the pilot project does not spell out the educational details of the program but instead confides them to a proposed "Board of Legal Specialization," the program's most conspicuous features are *(a)* a requirement of five years in practice and *(b)* provision for a "grandfather clause" permitting practitioners with ten years of "substantial involvement" in a specialty to receive certification without examination. The final report of the committee concluded by making clear the connection between group legal services and certification of specialists.

The blockades to the development of certification of specialists and to group practice lie basically in the bar's Canons of Professional Ethics—the guiding rules of the profession, backed up by state law. One such blockade lies in the canons prohibiting the "unauthorized practice of law." The American Bar Association (ABA) first adopted Sharswood's *The Canons of Professional Ethics* in 1908 (before which the code of behavior was often unwritten and somewhat vague), with the principal additions coming in 1928. As Hurst (1950, p. 330) says, "[T]hey expressed a conscience which at its best was directed to the honorable relations between individuals, and which took little concern for the lawyer's role in his community." Put another way, one could say that the canons are built around the image of the known, accessible, small-town lawyer—an image that we believe is obsolete. The emphasis is upon independence and the lawyer's prime obligation to his client. The canons that stand in the way of group practice are generally those dealing with "unauthorized practice," "intermediaries," etc. These focus on the independence of the lawyer in pursuing his client's interest, which theoretically would be threatened by group practice.

We think that, notwithstanding resistance by elements in the bar, both group legal practice and certification of specialists are almost certainly coming. It may take a decade or a generation, but we must face the implications these developments will have for legal education. At the moment it is difficult to imagine what will happen because the law schools, our prime instruments for legal education, appear inappropriate vehicles for specialization as they now are. Law schools teach very little substance and offer perhaps even less "how-to-do-it" training; instead, they focus on various more general "skills," such as legal bibliographical research, legal reasoning, and "thinking like a lawyer." Moreover, today's law student is in no position during his years in law school to decide what area he would like to specialize in. Specialization begins only when the young attorney enters practice. In contrast, the certified specialization we are referring to here concerns basically "how to" knowledge and the practical expertise of experienced lawyers. Thus it would be incongruous with the genius of legal education as it has developed to "train" specialists in "how to" practice tax law, workman's compensation law, or criminal law, to cite the three examples selected for the California pilot project. Perhaps the law school could take students after several years of practice, but still the law school, as is, may be unprepared to teach such specialties.

Although the present situation of the law schools is ambiguous, we do not mean to express a judgment about whether law schools should or should not participate in the training of specialists. As we shall indicate later, the present third year of legal education may afford a transitional opportunity to offer specialty training to advanced students and to returning practicing members of the bar.

This might make it possible for law schools to allocate a portion of their resources for specialty training in a rational, coordinated way.

At least in the most populous states it appears that the organized bar itself is best suited to undertake specialist education. In California and New York the field has already been occupied by the Continuing Education of the Bar and the Practicing Law Institute, respectively. Directed as they are by practitioners and manned by a combination of practitioners and individual law teachers, these institutions probably deserve and will win the right to determine the curricula for most specialist training. Certainly law schools have a good deal that they might contribute to the continuing education of specialists. Some law schools already run summer institutes or evening classes for practicing lawyers. Since many state bars have neither the money nor the administrative structure to follow the California and New York models, they will have to form some sort of partnership with the law schools to accomplish this continuing education. At least for the "how to" sort of specialist training we are discussing here, however, law schools are presently ill equipped to assume the burden of planning and administering programs of continuing education. Their most appropriate role may well be to give an "academic" supplement to the great variety of present and potential continuing education programs, while the main burden falls on the bar itself.

PARAPROFES-
SIONALISM:
THE EMER-
GENCE OF
ALLIED
CAREERS

The paraprofessional is here already, giving tax advice, drafting real estate instruments, working on the probate of wills, administering trusts, investigating the facts of cases in litigation, negotiating and settling insurance claims. . . . The list could be expanded indefinitely. Although the distinction is often not clearly drawn, it is useful to distinguish between two types of paraprofessionals — the *sublegal* and the *paralegal.* We shall use the term *sublegal* to refer to occupations that are carried on under the direct supervision of a lawyer. By *paralegal* we refer to people who need not work (although they may do so) under the direct supervision of lawyers. *Sublegals* are typified by divorce specialists who follow assembly-line procedures in screening the uncontested divorces in a legal services office and preparing the necessary papers, all under the supervision of a lawyer. By contrast, the insurance claims adjuster is a *paralegal* specialist who may or may not work under the supervision of a lawyer.

Paralegals particularly incur the wrath of the organized bar and are either resisted by it under the rubric of "the unauthorized practice of law" or coexist under "treaties" that the organized bar has had to negotiate with such other professions as accountancy, banking, real estate, and insurance. However, with some exceptions, paralegals and sublegals share these characteristics: *(a)* they do work that in the past may have been performed exclusively or primarily by lawyers, and *(b)* they are not exposed to full legal education.

The movement to recognize the existence of paraprofessionals and to participate in their education and encourage their use comes from two quite disparate sources: the proponents of publicly supported legal services and private practitioners who practice in large firms, primarily in urban centers. An example of the first is the Legal Services Program of the U.S. Office of Economic Opportunity (OEO), which authorized the National Institute for Justice and Law Enforcement of the University Research Corporation to prepare a report entitled *Paraprofessionals in Legal Services Programs: A Feasibility Study* (hereafter cited as *Legal Services Paraprofessionals*). This report documents in detail the numerous uses that have actually been made of paraprofessional personnel in OEO offices. Divorce specialist, claims adjustor, case worker, investigator, and neighborhood worker are the sub- and paraprofessional roles discussed in detail. The report proposed institutionalizing these positions and developing training programs to fill them. Paraprofessionals could be trained to occupy a number of positions that depend only minimally or not at all on the supervision of a lawyer. As the primary rationale for developing training programs, *Legal Services Paraprofessionals* advances the economic problem of the heavy case load. This consideration is obviously of controlling importance when the issue is the unmet legal needs of the poor and the problem is viewed as one of providing legal services to the poor out of limited public funds.

In the case of overworked professional law firms the emphasis of the push toward paraprofessionalism is obviously quite different. They, too, have a strong interest in keeping costs down, not only to increase profits but also to make legal services available to great numbers of nonindigent persons who are presently precluded from receiving legal services because of high costs. However, law firms tend to stress the development of sublegal specialties and to underplay the role of the paralegal specialist. Their working model is the British solicitor's clerk. An example of this trend is the appointment in 1968 of a Special Committee on Lay Assistance for Lawyers (subsequently renamed the Special Committee on Legal Assistants) by the ABA. The chairman of the committee, H. Lee Turner, Esq., has been described as "the undisputed leader of this school of emerging thought" within the organized bar. In June 1971 Mr. Turner's committee published a draft report entitled *The Utilization of Legal Assistants by Law Firms in the United States: Liberating the Lawyer.* This report documents the fact that large and small firms throughout the country are now utilizing nonlawyers not only in office administration but also in connection with legal work in such areas as litigation and trusts and estates. It suggests that increased efficiency and productivity could be achieved by greater utilization of paraprofessionals in routine and repetitive tasks now performed by lawyers.

Oddly enough, in the substantial literature on paraprofessionals that has recently developed, inadequate attention has been paid to the legal training of paralegals who function outside of legal service programs. As mentioned previously these persons include insurance claims adjustors, real estate agents, and so forth. In addition, less traditional uses of paralegals deserve study. For example, one area in which the needs and the difficulties are equally obvious arises out of the situation of the criminal court dockets, which are greatly increased by the procedural requirements emanating from the Supreme Court's "due process revolution" and particularly by the *Miranda* rule that every person upon arrest is entitled to have what we shall call *legal representation.* It has been estimated that all the resources of the bar could be consumed by having attorneys counseling both the police and the arrestees about the *Miranda* rules. Is there not a case for having this counsel given by paraprofessionals? The difficulty, of course, resides in *(a)* the lack of disposition by police and prosecutors to have lay, adversary representation, and *(b)* constitutional questions about whether lay representation can pass constitutional muster. Both the need and the difficulty are clear. They illustrate a much more general need and difficulty. We must face the implications for the familiar adversary process in the assembly-line dispensation of what today passes for justice. Parole and mental health proceedings may well be other areas in which paraprofessionals can fill obvious gaps in our legal institutions.

It would lead us far astray from our immediate topic to do more than simply uncover problems such as these. Here we can go little further than stating that lay assistance is one of the only instruments even remotely capable of coping with the imminent breakdown in American justice. Our immediate question is what legal education can do to assist in the training of paraprofessionals.

We suspect that to the extent that paralegal and sublegal training is not undertaken *on the job* through apprenticeship programs, the bulk of such training will and should occur in the community colleges. The Special Committee on Legal Assistants, in its report *Proposed Curriculum for Training of Law Office Personnel,* recommends a two-year college-level program for the legal assistant and a four-year college-level program for the legal administrator. Each program would impart "an extensive knowledge of several fields of law" by requiring legal specialty courses in subjects such as trusts and estates and business associations (for nine quarter-hours of credit each). While this proposal seems to provide a sound model for training legal assistants, it does not appear to be the only sound model, and it is far too early in the development of the paraprofessional role to suggest the inappropriateness of other models. For example, a substantial demand may exist for paraprofessionals with bachelor's degrees. Also, to the extent that potential members of this labor force already have bachelor's degrees (for example, women who have recently graduated from college, college-educated mothers of school-age children, and unemployed aerospace engineers), or to the extent that particular colleges do not create training programs for paraprofessionals, it would seem desirable to have alternative training programs. Intensified programs of several months' duration might provide a suitable alternative for college-educated persons. In fact, at least two such programs have already begun. In addition, intensified programs may also be an appropriate means to upgrade experienced legal secretaries to paraprofessionals.

Another issue that should be left open at this time is whether the paraprofessional should be trained in one or several legal fields. The report *Proposed Curriculum for Training of Law Office Personnel* suggests the latter. However, legal services offices and law firms (especially large law firms) may prefer the former. And, while small firms may have insufficient volume in any one substantive area to employ a full-time paraprofessional specialist, part-time paraprofessionals or clusters of full-time paraprofessionals who contract out their services to numerous small firms are certainly a possibility. Of course the career ladder of the paraprofessional may be affected by whether he or she is a specialist or generalist, but even here it is not clear that the specialist would have fewer opportunities for advancement, either in terms of salary or responsibility.

In any event, the outreach of legal education will consist most appropriately of a combination of individual and institutional efforts to assist in the development of programs in other institutions. This assistance might take the form of advice regarding curriculum design and teaching materials. Also, some of our scarce academic resources will have to be devoted to working with people who will constitute the teaching corps for legal paraprofessionals (law professors themselves would seldom be involved in teaching the paraprofessional the required "how-to-do-it" skills). Whether this can be done better by lending academic talent directly to the community colleges or by developing within law schools programs of instruction for people who are interested in teaching in community colleges remains to be seen. Finally, law schools might also find, in settings such as clinical programs, opportunities to acquaint law students with the role and use of the paraprofessional as well as the potential impact of the paraprofessional on the legal profession and the delivery of legal services.

In the long run, the role of legal education depends, as much as on anything else, on how the bar itself reacts to the need for paraprofessionals. As the recent report of the American Assembly, "Law and the Changing Society" put it, once again emphasizing the close connection between legal education and the organized bar:

Innovations are needed in legal services offered all segments of the community. These should include . . . training and employment of subprofessionals and paraprofessionals acting, where appropriate, under the supervision and upon the responsibility of fully qualified lawyers. . . .

Law Schools, in cooperation with the organized bar, should consider the development of programs of education and training for sub-professional and paraprofessional personnel (American Assembly, 1968, pp. 6–8).

Let us conclude this section by suggesting what should be obvious to our nonlegal readers: paraprofessionals and subprofessionals can do their jobs *better* than the all-purpose lawyer. In part, the rationale for this statement applies also at the other end of the spectrum. The certified specialist, for precisely the same reasons, can do his job *better* than the all-purpose lawyer.

All too often this is not kept clearly in mind. The false unitary image of the legal profession forces upon both the lawyer and the public the impression that a lawyer is omnicompetent and exclusively competent to do legal tasks. Due to their common education, their common passing of "the" bar examination, and the lack of visible diversification (certified specialists or trained paraprofessionals), all lawyers, from the outside at least, appear qualified to do everything. We shall point out in Chapter 3 that, at least to date, the nature of legal education has been to train students in some basic fundamentals (analysis, legal theory, the general substantive map, etc.) only and that as a result the law school graduate generally is not competent to do *anything* very well. Experience is the real teacher of specific tasks, and, in the huge field of lawyers' work, the experience is always limited. Thus a lawyer is usually truly competent in a few areas only and minimally competent (perhaps often incompetent) in the rest. As a result specialists and paraprofessionals do their work better: "All day, every day, spent at the probate court filing papers makes a hell of a good filer." Trained divorce specialists will do a much better job obtaining uncontested divorces than will an all-purpose lawyer. Inevitably, the trends of specialization and paraprofessionalism will narrow the roles for — and the number of — generalist, all-purpose lawyers. Indeed, this process is well under way. We suspect that there will continue to be some place for the general practitioner, although a more elegant label may emerge for this counterpart of the internist in medicine. But we have no qualms in making the prediction that the jack-of-all-legal-trades will increasingly be viewed as master of none, and he will be increasingly uncomfortable — financially and otherwise — in that role.

3. *Legal Education:* *An Introduction to Its Problems*

Although the processes of legal education continue to produce "lawyers" to fill the present institutional roles calling for them, through methods that have worked and proved themselves consistently over the last 50 years, a feeling of malaise and discontent has been growing among students and faculty at the nation's elite[1] law schools. Feelings of malaise are probably endemic in the present stage of our culture. Although the emphasis of this study is necessarily on what is wrong with legal education, we must record our conviction that, taken as it operates at its best, legal education is a good thing.

We believe that the problems really do exist and that they are serious. Before one can understand this conclusion, however, one must have some familiarity with its context: the purposes of legal education, the processes by which it is currently carried on, and the way in which these processes came to be.

[1] The term *elite* requires some explanation. Of the approximately 125 law schools accredited by the ABA in the United States, within the profession about 25 are regarded as pacesetters. Rather than state our own conclusions about which law schools are, by any test, "elite," we will simply adopt the definition laid down by Warkov (1965) in his study for the National Opinion Research Center, *Lawyers in the Making.* Warkov and Zelan studied college students in their senior year and one year later who took the Law School Admission Test (LSAT) and subsequently entered law school. They classified the law schools that the students entered in terms of the students' scores on the LSAT. Stratum I schools were those ranking highest on the LSAT. Eight schools occupied Stratum I. They were described as being schools that are usually included in a layman's catalog of top national law schools. Sixteen schools were placed in Stratum II. They had the next highest LSAT scores for their entering class. The other hundred-odd law schools were placed in Stratum III. Without knowing the exact composition of Stratum I and Stratum II, we assume that it corresponds fairly well to our subjective estimate. Although Stratum I schools were described as belonging in a layman's catalog of top national schools, we believe that today such a catalog would contain at least 20 law schools, each one deserving to be considered an "elite" law school.

THE PURPOSES OF LEGAL EDUCATION Legal education on its most basic level is preparation for a profession, the "public profession of law." This factor is one of those at the core of the present problems in law, for often faculty—and very often students—have only a hazy idea of what *profession* means, and often these hazy ideas do not agree. A list of the characteristics of a profession, drawn from several sources, follows.

1 It possesses a highly complex body of knowledge that may be gained by a lengthy educational process.

2 Because of the complexity of that knowledge, it is largely incomprehensible to and untestable by the layman for whose benefit it is utilized.

3 Because the clientele is vulnerable, the professional owes his first duty to his client's best interests. The result is that all professions have a self-generated and self-enforced code of ethics.

4 Since the professional derives his livelihood from his work, this automatically involves him in a conflict of interests. He must subsume his self-interest to the best interests of his client.

This description would not be agreed to in all its points by many, but it at least gives us a framework in which to look at legal education. A listing of the characteristics that legal education seeks to imprint on its students will give us a more concrete framework from which to begin, but one must be careful. Both teachers and students are often unaware of such a list, and the connection between such an ideal and the real process of legal education may be tenuous. There have been many attempts to define the characteristics of the legal professional in greater detail. A recent example by former Dean Bayless Manning (1969*a*) follows.

Number 1. Analytic Skills By analytic skills, I refer to those special capacities of the lawyer to distinguish A from B, to separate the relevant from the irrelevant, to sort out a tangle into manageable sub-components, to examine a problem at will from close range or long distance, and to surround a problem, surveying it from many different perspectives.

Number 2. Substantive Legal Knowledge Every good lawyer knows some law, knows something of the general sea of substantive doctrine in which he works. In comparison with the entire legal universe, no lawyer, of course, knows very much law outside the single field or sub-field in which he has specialized. But every good lawyer can locate himself and his client's problem on the general map of substantive law.

Number 3. Basic Working Skills The first-class lawyer has at hand a bag of basic working skills. Most of his work involves the amassment of information and the skillful use of communication. The first-class lawyer knows how to write, how to use a library, how to be an advocate, how to listen, how to draft, how to interrogate, and how to find out what he decides he needs to know.

Number 4. Familiarity with Institutional Environment It is not enough for a lawyer to have thought a problem through, to know some law about it, and to be able to write a lucid document about it. The first-class lawyer is also familiar with, and able to operate effectively in, the institutional environment in which the problem arises. He must be able to deal with people, to negotiate around a table, to stand on his feet in a courtroom, and to unsnarl or cut his way through the red tape of courts, administrative agencies, legislatures and other legal institutional structures.

Number 5. Awareness of Total Non-Legal Environment By awareness of total non-legal environment, I refer to the first-class lawyer's ability to comprehend the non-legal environment of the problem at hand, to evaluate the impact that non-legal considerations will have upon the outcome, and to perceive the ways in which the knowledge and insight of non-lawyers can be mobilized and brought to bear. Every legal problem arises in its own unique setting of economic and political considerations, historical and psychological forces; each legal situation raises its own problems of data accumulation, ordering, and weighting. The legal process is a part of a vast surrounding social process; the first-class lawyer never loses sight of that larger picture, and he knows when and how to call upon accountants, psychiatrists, doctors, economists, market analysts, sociologists, statisticians, or others whose expertise can help him and his client.

Number 6. Good Judgment Difficult as it is to describe abstractly, all of us know in general what we mean when we say that "Lawyer X has good judgment" and all of us know that good judgment is a major distinguishing characteristic of the first-class lawyer.

Dean Manning's list includes the caveat that it speaks of the "educated first-class lawyer." It is probably fair to assume that his statement would gain general assent from most law teachers and students, at least as stating an ideal. Mystification and confusion enter the picture when teachers and students consider *how* this ideal is best effectuated in law school.

Legal education today has a unitary nature. As we have noted, legal education is inextricably bound to the profession, and the unitary nature of legal education is inextricably bound to the unitary standard for admission to the legal profession. Shortly we shall consider the somewhat fortuitous set of events that led to the present situation. Before looking at the areas in which differences occur, and without denying that there are wide variations in quality, we can say that all law schools are more alike than they are different. We do not claim that the elite law schools give the same legal education as those far down the list. But all share the same structural features and are bound by that structure. The graduates of all, in approximately the same proportion, enter the profession in the same way. We take the universal structural characteristics of law schools to be the following:

1   Their primary mission is the education of students for entry into the legal profession.

2   The faculties of none are primarily engaged in research.

3   None engages in undergraduate education.

4   None offers its professional degree (LL.B. or J.D.) in less than three academic years.

    In a later section of this chapter we shall describe in some detail what occurs within this structure. Whether or not it is an appropriate structure for accomplishing the goals we have previously listed in this chapter is one of the main questions we are addressing and one of the main doubts that is at the root of the malaise currently felt in the law schools. It is nonetheless *the* structure, a common product of a common history.

RECENT HISTORY OF LEGAL EDUCATION IN A NUTSHELL

Education, admissions policy, and organization wove together to form main strands in the character of the Bar in the United States.

(Hurst, 1950, p. 293)

If Hurst is correct, and we believe that he is, one cannot speak of legal education without also considering "admissions policy" and "organization." To understand the history of legal education we must also look at the role of bar organization and of the policy of regulating admission to the bar.

Jacksonian egalitarianism had succeeded by then [the Civil War] in eliminating all but the formality of admission to the bar. We abolished any requirement that a number of years be spent in training for the bar, either as an apprentice in a law office with supervision by a highly organized bar as in England or in Universities as on the Continent. There was no organized bar. What little training lawyers got, they were most apt to get studying in a lawyer's office. . . . Law schools started as a supplement to and then as a substitute for law office training (Stolz, 1971, p. 142).

Starting with the end of the Civil War, legal education and admission to the bar began to lose this populist character. The move to university-connected law schools began, accelerating rapidly around 1900. The primacy of Harvard guaranteed that the movement conformed to the Harvard pattern. (We will comment further on that pattern later.) The importance of the Harvard pattern for present purposes was that it ultimately became dogma that legal education should be full time, should take three years, and should be preceded by four years of undergraduate college education. This occurred despite the multiplicity of law schools, some operating as correspondence schools, that required, if anything, no more than a high school education. The requirements for admission to the bar, which were set by the several states, were typically silent about both the quantum of education and its character. Standards remained diverse, and the quality of the beginning lawyer was often poor.

Pressure for raising the requirements for admission to the bar came from many sources. One of the most important was the desire to emulate the results of Abraham Flexner's survey of medical education, commissioned by the Carnegie Corporation. Published in 1910, the survey had the dramatic and immediate effect of driving the inferior medical schools out of business and tying the remaining schools to universities. The number of medical schools dropped from 160 in 1899–1900 to 76 in 1929–30. The number of medical students rose absolutely but fell as a percentage of total population. The results of the Flexner report were hailed by the representatives of the organized bar as worthy of emulation in legal education.

The American Bar Association was founded in 1878 and, unlike the American Medical Association, which represented and still represents state and county associations, was and remains largely an organization of individual lawyers. By 1900 its membership included only 1.3 percent of the nation's lawyers; by 1920 it had grown to about 9 percent. Its leaders were impressed by the Flexner report. In 1913, the ABA's Committee on Legal Education, led by legal educators, wrote to the president of the Carnegie Corporation suggesting that a Flexner-like study of legal education be carried out. Carnegie accepted the suggestion, and A. Z. Reed, a non-lawyer, was appointed to carry on the investigation.

Mr. Reed's report, published in 1921, did not become another Flexner report. Today his excellent work still repays reading. The main body of the work, his history of legal education, is still considered definitive; his recommendations, however, were not followed. As Reed saw it, the issue was whether to improve the quality of the profession by forcing everyone into the mold of the Harvard graduate (four years of college followed by three years of full-time legal education) or to improve the quality by building a differentiated bar with some members trained to do some things and some trained to do others, with competence enforced by civil-service-type examinations for the various tracks. (Reed specifically recommended only two tracks: one for the graduate of the part-time or night schools and one for the more nearly omnicompetent Harvard-mold graduate.) The conflict, which was to work itself out within the Byzantine complexity of ABA politics, was between the "schoolmen"—the leaders of legal education and the "elite" members of the bar—who wished to drive the part-time and night law schools out of business (following the example of the Flexner report) and the representatives of those marginal schools and their partners, the bar examiners, who very much wished to stay in business.

In 1893 the ABA had formed its first standing committee, a Section on Legal Education and Admissions, open to anyone interested. At least in its first years this section was basically composed of and controlled by the schoolmen. At the initiative of this section (which was attempting to build a congenial constituency for its goals) the Association of American Law Schools (AALS) was formed in 1900. From the start the AALS imposed standards for membership. Member schools had to require that entering students possess a high school diploma and pursue a course of legal studies for at least two years. In 1905 this requirement was increased to three years. Until 1919, when the ABA was reorganized under a new constitution, a close relationship prevailed between the ABA section and the AALS. From the beginning the leaders of both moved vigorously to raise the standards for legal education and for admission to the bar, but they met setbacks and defeat at the hands of the general membership of the ABA.

In 1919, amidst "gloom and general despair," W. Draper Lewis of Pennsylvania laid out an aggressive, one-shot strategy to the AALS, the partial success of which was to shape legal education to the present day. Lewis and his allies saw that meetings of the ABA could be manipulated, that leadership was essential, and that the indifference of the bar to legal education could be an asset. They caused the ABA at its 1920 meeting to pass a resolution creating a special committee to study legal education and report at the 1921 meeting. The most important element in this strategy was to choose the right leader. The choice fell upon Elihu Root, former Secretary of State, past president of the ABA, an elder statesman in his seventies. The Root committee produced a compromise that sailed through the 1921 meeting of the ABA. (Significantly for potential debate at that meeting, it was held before Reed's report had been generally circulated. The Root committee had had access to the first copies, however.) The main elements of the compromise were as follows:

1   Before admission to the bar of any state a candidate should be required to have:

    (a) graduated from a law school complying with certain standards, and

    (b) passed an examination by public authority determining his fitness.

2   A certified law school should require three years of full-time legal education or the same number of hours in part-time study over a longer period.

3   The Council on Legal Education and Admission to the Bar should certify which law schools have complied with the applicable standards, and should publish from time to time the names of those that do and do not comply with the standards.

Reed's recommendation for a differentiated bar was passed over with little consideration (except, perhaps, within the Root committee). In the debates the committee implied that its recommendations were in line with Reed's, although they were not. The ABA resolution had no legal effect, of course. It took some time, plus the Depression, to persuade the states to adopt the ABA requirements. By the beginning of World War II, all but a few states required two years in college plus three years of full-time legal education or its part-time equivalent as preconditions for admission to the bar. At the same time, bar examinations became an almost universal requirement. The main exception was that some states, largely in the South, gave a "diploma privilege" to the graduates of certain law schools within the state. Admission following apprenticeship almost disappeared. The triumph of the ABA in persuading the states was almost complete. The membership of the AALS tended to correspond to the law schools having ABA approval, although membership in the AALS has been somewhat more selective.

And so it was that organization, admission, and legal education assumed the dimensions that they have today. Like it or not, law schools all share the structural characteristics we have listed. Our unitary legal education is inextricably bound up with our unitary standard for admission to the legal profession. It is profitless to argue about which is the cause and which the effect. The ABA standards, the formally undifferentiated character of the bar, the unifying effect of Langdell's "case system" discussed below—each is both cause and effect of the others. In an increasingly national society the unitary structure of legal education develops a certain common culture among lawyers, a culture that, it can be argued, is an important base for the profession. We will suggest, however, that the culture could be preserved without the rigid maintenance of formal unity. The ABA laid a pattern in 1921 that still determines legal education. Reed felt that legal education should not be exclusively patterned on the Harvard mold; the schoolmen disagreed, and it was they who successfully maneuvered the 1921 meeting.

COMMON STRUCTURE AND GOALS We can now move on to inquire how law schools use their common structure to reach the goals we have discussed. Most schools have what amounts to a common curriculum in the first year. The basic subjects are civil procedure, contracts, property, and torts. In many schools it has been found desirable to include some subjects in public law in the first-year curriculum: administrative law, constitutional law, and criminal law. Frequently a first-year course—typically called Legal Method, Introduction to Law, or Legal Process—is designed to give the beginning student a synoptic view of law and legal institutions. Most schools also offer first-year instruction in legal writing. Usually the first-year curriculum is entirely prescribed.

In schools whose ratio of students to full-time faculty does not exceed 25 to 1, most instruction in the first year is carried on through the case method, in which the instructor assumes a Socratic role. The case method developed by Langdell at Harvard before the turn of the century consists of studying the decisions of appellate courts. In the Socratic stance the teacher asks questions, engaging the class or a few of its members in a dialogue. Although the Socratic custom is often honored in the breach, it is still the model and the characteristic method of first-year legal education. The instructor does not lecture; among law teachers *lecture* has been a dirty word.

The Socratic method has worked pretty well in the first year. At some of the leading schools, the average size of a first-year class exceeds 100, and the excitement and the intellectual interest of the average well-taught first-year class has to be seen to be believed. The learning curve for first-year students is typically steeply pitched, and the élan of students undergoing their initiation in the first few months of law school, at full-time schools, has been truly extraordinary, at least until the last few years. By contrast, the students at part-time schools, who are usually older, have a much less exciting time during their first year. Typically, although their first-year curriculum virtually duplicates that in the national and regional schools, minus such "frills" as legal writing and courses in law and legal institutions, the method of instruction tends to be straight lecturing. The emphasis is much more on knowing the rule rather than, as is the case with the stronger schools, on analysis and method.

Taking the run of national and regional full-time, university-connected law schools as a unit, a visitor could sit blindfolded in, say, a first-year torts class in any one of them with some assurance that he would not be able to tell whether he was at Harvard, Yale, Columbia, Chicago, Stanford, or East Cupcake. The level of the dialogue might be higher or lower, depending on the quality of the students and the instructors, but aside from that factor our hypothetical blindfolded visitor could not come within a thousand miles of locating the school. This is far more the strength than the weakness of the first year in American legal education, for here lawyers obtain their common cultural base. Regional differences play little part; law schools, whether they advertise themselves as "national" or not, try to teach the entering student not The Law of a given jurisdiction but rather The Approach to doctrinal analysis and method.

From Dean Manning's list of the attributes of an educated first-class lawyer (pages 22–23), the first year in law school is intended to achieve, in substance at least, items one and two, analytic skills and substantive legal knowledge, and to give a good working introduction to substantial portions of three and four, basic working skills and familiarity with institutional environment. Generally it is believed the effort is moderately successful.

We are beginning to hear, however, serious and intense complaint and criticism concerning other effects of the first year. The class atmosphere is said to be a hostile one, with the hostility directed from the icily distant teacher toward the student on the spot. Law professors as a group tend to be extremely intellectual and extremely verbal, very often to the point of ignoring the emotional and connotative level of communication. In any case the student may suffer a severe loss in self-respect and possibly even an identity crisis. This result of the case-Socratic method of teaching is usually rationalized by explaining that the method is meant to acclimate the students to "legal reasoning" or "thinking like a lawyer." It is difficult, however, to see the relationship between the psychic damage and these stated goals, and one often gets the feeling that the recitation of "thinking like a lawyer" has become more a talismanic justification for what is going on than an articulated educational program. Some would retort that phrases such as "loss of self-respect," "identity crisis," and "psychic damage" have likewise assumed a talismanic role.

In addition to criticisms of the emotional result of the Socratic method we now hear claims that the process does damage to the student's intellectual initiative and imagination. The limits of the discussion are totally controlled by the teacher: his assumptions frame the discussion; his questions are considered. The student, it is claimed, is conditioned to work in a "given" framework, not to construct his own. Most law teachers would sympathize more with the emotional factor criticism than with the intellectual one.

These concerns apart, the first year for most students remains an exciting, agonizing, challenging, intellectually eye-opening experience. Although the learning curve perhaps ceases its rapid rise after the first semester, the first year is still generally considered a pedagogic triumph. It is probably no accident that first-year teaching assignments are eagerly sought and that the cream of any faculty tend to teach first-year classes. If, as we have stated, the first four of Dean Manning's six attributes should be imparted in whole or in part during the first year, how do the second and third years of legal education, aside from further refining these items, seek to achieve the others, awareness of the total nonlegal environment and good judgment?

One has to be very guarded in making statements about the curriculum beyond the first year. Most of what we may call the "bellwether" schools have abandoned, over the past decade, curricular rigidity after the first year. Generally speaking, their students are free to take whatever they wish in the second and third years. There has been a general movement toward seminars and other forms of small-group instruction in the latter part of a law school career. There has also been a strong trend to encourage (or even require) written work. Until recently such work usually took the form of the student-edited law reviews, which remain the unique law school experience for those few students who are lucky enough to "make law review." Selected primarily on the basis of their first-year grades, students who make law review join an elitist institution, a pure example of meritocracy that probably represents the best form of education for the "best" students. Recently there has been a tendency to open the law review to those students who do not make it in the ordinary way by permitting them to write their way onto the law review through the medium of papers prepared for seminars. In some schools selection is no longer based upon grades at all but only upon such a submitted written piece.

Another trend has been the encouragement of joint work, usually of a basic character, between disciplines: law and sociology, law and psychiatry, law and business, law and just about anything. Sometimes this involves work toward two degrees, e.g., the J.D. and the M.B.A., or the J.D. and an M.A. in political science. In these programs the student takes both law courses and courses in his special field of interest.

Still another new trend has been the move toward "clinical" programs. This movement owes much to a program financed in its initial stages by the Ford Foundation. The organization, by a grant from the foundation, of the Council on Legal Education for Professional Responsibility, Inc. (CLEPR), under the direction of William Pincus, formerly the Ford Foundation's program officer in the field of legal education, has stimulated the development of clinical programs. So far their arena has been primarily criminal defense offices and poverty-related neighborhood legal-aid offices. We will have more to say about this development in Chapter 6. It is enough to note for purposes of this *tour d'horizon* of law school curricula that the development of clinical programs has helped to take up the slack of the second and third years.

Aside from the impact of these trends, the second and especially the third years of law study still strike most students as too often simply more of the same and a bore. Already in the first year many students find the effort to be "Socratic" with 75 to 100 people in a class very questionable, and in the last two years what rapidly becomes a watered-down version of the Socratic technique is deadly. Most courses are treated as introductory or survey, and the tedium of the case method continues. (Since the necessary analytical techniques have been learned by the first year, or shortly thereafter, and since the Socratic method is an immensely wasteful way to impart information, some teachers are not sure that they teach anything at all in the last two years.) Taxation, trusts, corporations, and whatever march by appearing exactly alike. Most schools provide little opportunity for specialization or in-depth study. No law faculty has succeeded in revamping the second and third years to eliminate the tedium. However ingenious the efforts have been, it is still the verdict of students (and perhaps the private conviction of many if not most law teachers) that the last two years of legal education leave much to be desired. The plain fact is that large classes after the first year (and sometimes even then) tend to be an academic wasteland. Students not only cannot be made to drink, they cannot even be led to water.

In spite of all this, their teaching performance (particularly in the first year) remains the great merit of law teachers. We must admit, however, that their research output is rather slight. Legal writing has tended, until very recently, to be primarily doctrinal and to be based mainly on research in the law library. To the extent that law teachers have written, their books have tended to be treatises (often multivolume) on doctrinal subjects. Their articles, published in the 80-odd law reviews, have been treatments of less general legal problems, again purely from a doctrinal, analytic standpoint. The reasons for this heavily focused unproductivity are manifold, relating both to the financial structure of the law school and its double nature as professional school and graduate academy. We will canvass these problems at length in Chapters 6 and 7.

There is, however, a good deal of ferment on this front. Most law teachers have given primacy to the teaching function, but this is beginning to change. Many, influenced primarily by the behavioral sciences, have tried to go outside the library and to conduct empirical research on how law actually operates. This trend goes hand-in-hand with the developing interest in law and _____. One can fill in the blank with whatever behavioral science—economics, sociology, psychology—happens to interest one or at least is thought to hold the key to an understanding of one's field of interest. Many people, enchanted by what they conceive to be the rigor of the behavioral sciences, have sought to wed them to such emerging specialties as urban law, poverty law, correctional law, and (most recently) environmental law. Others, perhaps "turned off" by what they see as the tendency of the behavioral sciences to work for rigorous solutions to trivial problems, see law as a humanistic subject and tend to turn their interests to such fields as history and philosophy, seeking through them better insights into the role of law. This group of humanists, if *group* is the right word, probably represents a minority among serious legal scholars.

Whether their bias is scientific or humanistic, most serious legal scholars have abandoned the production of treatises, the compilation of teaching materials (a very common art form among legal scholars), and the writing of doctrinal articles in law reviews. In place of these art forms, scholars are now turning to art forms for which law schools, plagued as they are by the absence of support for research, are almost totally unprepared, be they empirical studies or humanistic studies.

Looking over these trouble spots we see that students are often unsure of what being a professional means, and when they find out they are often disappointed. There is a conflict between the view of the lawyer as a hired gun and the view that students attend law school to get their tickets as social reformers. Both views, of course, are somewhat spurious, but they each reflect enough reality to be responsible for conflict. Students often find their teachers remarkably vague and inarticulate about the purposes of law school.

Law teachers often *are* confused about legal education and the form that it has been forced to take by the interplay of bar admission requirements, professional organization, and the law schools.

They are unclear about the goals of the second and third years of legal education. They are often frustrated in their scholarship and uncertain about their professional and academic roles. Increasingly disappointed and impatient students interact with increasingly frustrated and confused teachers and emerge with a patchwork professional education and an ambivalent view of themselves as professionals.

Although the idea of malaise is not the center of this study, as we progress, its intellectual causes will never be far from the center of the stage. Our overall recommendations will be found to be in the main responsive not merely to this malaise but also to what we believe to be the central intellectual and academic illness of our times.[2] We believe *secularization* to be the prime intellectual cause of the contemporary malaise in legal education. In the following paragraphs, we will first try to define secularization.[3] We will then try to explain why secularization should have come to be a vexing problem at this precise moment in the intellectual history of the law itself.

Over the past 200 years law has undergone the process of becoming viewed not as a sacred mystery but as a science. The process starts with Sir William Blackstone, whose *Commentaries,* published during the eighteenth century's Enlightenment, was the first book by an English-speaking scholar to mark the law indelibly with rationalism. Then, in the second half of the nineteenth century, C. C. Langdell, as dean of the Harvard Law School, was tremendously influential in establishing the view that law was an inductive science that could only be studied by academics who could extract principles from the decided cases. During the half-century 1870–1920 law came to be regarded as an academic science. Stirrings of rebellion against the Langdellian dogma came during the next 20 years, mainly from people whom we now call the Legal Realists. They were responsible for two achievements, one negative and one positive. They demolished much of Langdell's case method by showing that law is not in the main a set of principles but is largely a prediction of what decision makers will do. And they tried to make law more useful by converting it into a technological study

[2] In particular, see Chapter 6.

[3] This explanation draws heavily upon Woodard (1968). This important article is reprinted as Appendix B.

that could be wedded to the behavioral sciences. Much of the foregoing is an oversimplification. But today we live in a post–Legal Realist world in which we are trying to carry the lessons of the Legal Realists a stage further.

The dilemma that the Legal Realists uncovered can be stated in several different ways. We prefer to state it as questions: How can a study that is nonscientific be viewed as a technology when it does not rest on a body of scientific knowledge? Or, if it is an art, is law merely a set of means without any goals? Legal education today stands somewhere between the social engineering that the Realists viewed as its proper role and an as yet undefined preoccupation with social policy.

Social policy to what end, one asks? Students come to law schools these days amidst criticism that our legal institutions and processes are not merely inadequate but are based on faulty premises. The general outcry against our legal institutions and processes paints a picture of the prevalence of injustice that is even worse than the reality. Attacks from both the Right and the Left define these injustices in terms of social goals. These attacks inevitably take their toll on law students and faculty members, who have been taught either to regard law as independent of goals or dependent on widely shared implicit goals. The lack of consensus about social policy causes the malaise of which we have spoken. In an era of stress such as the present one malaise is probably unavoidable. But some of it is, we believe, misconceived. Many academic lawyers are contributing valiantly to the attack on our social problems. Students often do not see these contributions but stress instead the irrelevance of much that is discussed in the classroom. In so doing, they are truly the heirs of the Legal Realists; they either know what The Goals of The Law are or they want to be told what The Goals are. In either event, their concern is with How, not with Why. Dogmatic statements about The Goals inevitably misconstrue the relationship between means and goals at many different levels of abstraction. Law, we assert, is not a science but an art, a craft.

We agree with Professor Woodard that the higher goal of the law is justice, a goal that is never quite achieved. We assume that he would agree with us that making justice the goal is much too abstract to serve any real function. He does make the useful statement that the law school curriculum can and should promote attention to justice in three ways:

First, by serving the needs of private individuals (the "practical aspect"); second, by dealing with problems too complicated or too far reaching to be resolved on a piecemeal basis (the "collective aspect"); and third, by encouraging speculation about the nature and role of law in any of its variegated forms (the "philosophical, or theoretical, aspect") (Woodard, 1968, p. 737).

Law school curricula have so far focused largely on what Woodard calls the practical aspect. We believe that much more attention needs to be paid to the collective aspect, both in the curriculum and in legal scholarship. And, we think that it is time for legal educators to pay more attention to a broader and more philosophic inquiry into the law.

4. Clinical Education: A Testing Case for Legal Education?

The present shape of the legal profession and probable future developments have been briefly sketched in the previous chapters. The development of legal education into its present structure and our short description of the present process of legal education were presented in Chapter 3. Now we have reached the point of considering new developments in legal education, their value, and the prospects for the future of legal education. Although the structure has remained the same, within that structure legal education has been constantly changing. Even though they may not understand the nature of the malaise, acting on the premise that one can know that an egg is rotten without tasting it, faculty and students are rapidly proposing solutions. In response to the discontent there is these days a good deal of talk about fundamental, overall change, a total curricular and methodological revolution in legal education. Apocalyptic solutions to largely misunderstood problems are hardly promising. The principal area in which misunderstood problems tend to yield easy answers is in the idea that law students should learn by doing, should get out of the sterile air of the classroom into the vital atmosphere of functioning legal institutions. The current shibboleth is "clinical education."

Three reasons help to account for the current popularity of clinical education. First is the urge, by no means confined to law schools, that education should become more "relevant" to perceived social needs and should contribute to providing better legal services for the poor and other unrepresented groups in society. Second, clinical education lends itself to being a *separate* activity; it is by nature *removed* from the law school and up to the present has been essentially extracurricular. Thus small clinical programs can be added "on the side" to the curriculum, necessitating no fundamental changes in the life of the law school nor, more significantly, in the lives of most of the faculty. The third reason is the existence of the Council on Legal Education for Professional Responsibility, Inc. (CLEPR), a philanthropic organization funded by the Ford Foundation. CLEPR has been making small grants to law schools for experimental clinical education programs. CLEPR grants usually last only from six months to a year and thus do not provide permanent funding for any ongoing program. Nevertheless the existence of this funding and proselytizing organization, combined with the interest of students, has been enough to get at least a foot, and maybe even a good portion of the leg, through the door. Through this outlet the force created by the feelings of dissatisfaction and unease at the nation's law schools is being channeled. As one observer has put it, "clinical training within an academic context is a proposal whose time has come in American higher education. . . ."[1] Clinical education is happening on a small scale. The question for us remains: Is this the best direction for legal education to be moving in?

Clinical education refers to learning by doing: teaching a law student by having him actually perform the tasks of a lawyer. As we have described it, conventional legal education consists of (1) relatively large classes that engage in analyzing "cases" (usually the opinions of appellate courts) by the Socratic method (the teacher asking questions, the students answering); (2) seminars on topics quite removed from those treated in large classes and utilizing a diversity of materials; and (3) independent research, mainly on or for the law review. We shall say more in the next chapter about some other new directions for law school curricula. Traditionally, anything other than the classifications mentioned above had to be *extra*curricular. It is against this background that one must examine clinical education and the claims made for it.

Active participation is fundamental in clinical education. As more and more programs develop, a definition for clinical education runs into the ambiguities inherent in the phrase "the tasks of a lawyer," given the variety of tasks lawyers now perform. A broad definition of what clinical education means is participation or observation outside the formal structure of the law school. In this sense, the term includes observation, either casual or systematic, of some legal or social institution (e.g., a prison, a hospital, a court, or an adminis-

---

[1] Kitch in *Clinical Education* . . . (1969). This volume, prepared from papers cosponsored by the University of Chicago Law School and CLEPR, gives a good overview of the issues in clinical education.

trative agency) and participation in one of the roles within such an institution. It also includes simulation of some legal role (interviewing, negotiation, etc.). Some people, like the officers of CLEPR, insist the only true version of clinical education is the real-life element of the lawyer-client relationship: "The clinical component is that in which the professional actually performs a specialized service for the person who needs his specialized skill. It is the practice of the profession as a student under faculty supervision" (Pincus, 1970). By this definition instruction outside the classroom is within the ambit of clinical education only when the student is performing some real professional task for a client who needs legal services.

Whatever the definition, the term *clinical* is in origin an analogy to medical education. The analogy is not particularly apt, however, for in law there is no analogue to the hospital, and hence none to the teaching hospital. There is no institution in the legal order that dispenses, even to the limited extent of the teaching hospital and clinic, all services. This fact alone diminishes the allure of the clinical concept in law.

There are three axes along which one can evaluate clinical education. They are *involvement,* the extent to which the student is exposed to the experience; *supervision,* the extent to which the student is supervised by a responsible person; and *academic integration,* the extent to which the experience is blended with other aspects of the student's program. At one extreme, involvement may be total for a fixed period. At the other, it may be for only a few hours per week. Supervision may be very erratic, or it may be very purposeful. Academic integration may be very close, as when the experience is linked to an ongoing class, or it may be very loose, as when the student is told that he must somehow integrate the experience with the rest of his education, perhaps by writing a paper *(How I Spent My Summer in a Poverty Office).*

The goals pursued in the clinical legal education movement are diverse and not always complementary. Along the wide spectra of involvement, supervision, and academic integration, clinical programs can pursue highly diversified goals. To answer the question of whether clinical education should become a dominant form of legal education, we think that the following questions must first be answered: (1) Does it increase the availability of legal services? (2) Does it have a substantial input back to the rest of the law school program? (3) Does it improve or add to the student's skills? (4) Does it add to the student's experience and understanding of

society? (5) Does it add to the student's professional responsibility?
(6) If the answer to any of the first five questions is a qualified affirmative, how does clinical education compare in cost with other
forms of legal education?

The provision of legal services
"One day we were sitting and talking about the whole question of
legal service and legal education, and whether there is a connection,
or should be. . . . [T]here was something that ought to be done to
put the law schools together with the provision of legal services and
legal aid, particularly."[2] The objective of providing legal services
apparently was a basic one in the early days of the modern clinical
education movement, for here William Pincus, president of CLEPR,
was speaking of the founding of CLEPR's forerunner, the Council
on Legal Clinics. This objective continues today. The preamble to
the ABA model student practice rule includes the statement that
"as one means of providing assistance to lawyers who represent
clients unable to pay for such services . . . the following rule is
adopted."[3] Apparently it is felt that students represent a great
reservoir of untapped legal service potential and that they can provide a significant contribution to our legal services crisis. Certainly
the students have a great deal of time and energy to devote to the
area; many of them have a great desire to do so, and most of them
have a modicum of legal knowledge and expertise. The question
remains, however, whether clinical legal education is a successful
method for transferring this resource from a potential to an active
state.

The axis of involvement seems to be extremely important in the
question of legal services: when students work full time, undis-
tracted by the normal demands of the curriculum, they can be of
far greater value than when they can give only part-time attention,
interrupted by classes, examinations, vacations, etc. The axis of
supervision is also significant: when students are essentially unsupervised there is a great danger that inferior service will be
given (magnified when students have the distractions of regular
classes). On the other side, the chore of supervision eats up the
time of the supervisor; it is a demand which the supervisor often

[2] Unpublished transcript of an interview with William Pincus, in the authors'
files.
[3] Quoted in *Clinical Education* . . . (1969, p. 15).

finds excessive and which lowers his effectiveness to the clients. With the exception of the vague upgrading pressure the presence of students in the process might provide, on balance it remains very problematical whether students are an economical source of legal services. Aside from anecdotal reports, we know of no work that can be said to have demonstrated that law students are such a source.

The educational input back to the rest of the law school program
This second goal of clinical legal education is not nearly as problematical. A clinical education program seems to provide a great educational input back to the law school in the form of greatly heightened student interest and motivation in their studies, including the traditional classes. Time after time this theme was echoed at the Institute on Curriculum Reform and Clinical Education held at the University of Southern California in November 1970. "They [the students] just come back much better students." As Dean Goldstein at Yale has said, "It has seemed to me in the past that clinical education is most effective when it takes students who are turned off in a variety of ways and makes concrete for them a lot of very abstract things. And for many of them it turns them back into the academic exercise in a very, very effective way."[4]

Although this was perhaps not one of the main objectives of clinical education, it is certainly one of the principal benefits. Almost anywhere along our three axes, from the briefest involvement to a total involvement, integrated with class or not, this phenomenon occurs frequently. The reaction is not, of course, unanimous. The favorable effect, while clearly a benefit of clinical education, can hardly by itself automatically justify clinical programs. Rather, one would be led first to look with a very critical eye at the apparent defects in a curriculum that seems to need so badly a transfusion of motivational energy. In justifying university professional clinical education William Pincus (1970) has remarked:

Educators tend to overlook the corrosive effect of so much confinement to the campus on the human personality. The student's role is passive. He is locked away from the rest of the world in the sense that he is a con-

---

[4] Unpublished transcript of a conference with Abraham S. Goldstein, in the authors' files.

sumer and not a producer of goods, services, or even ideas. He reaches and passes well into adulthood still being spoon-fed from various sources, and most especially by the university and its faculty whom he sees more than anyone except his fellow students. At most the student may have an occasional opportunity to become an observer in some field of experience. He fails to find anything that is peculiarly his as a contribution to the world. He suffers from an increasingly poignant sense of lack of fulfillment. A fundamental part of the student's personality is retarded in its growth— that part which takes us through life with at least that small sense of security which comes from the knowledge that we can do something of consequence to others in the larger world.

Clearly clinical education is one cure for the symptoms of this problem. The student finds the clinical experience a breath of fresh air after years of study and, with a lungful, he can return for awhile to the classroom and library and again find relevance and excitement in his studies. The motivational input back to the traditional educational system is certainly a valuable side effect of clinical education.

Skills training

Skills training is often put forward as the crux of the matter in clinical education. "How can you call it law school if it doesn't teach its students how to be lawyers?" To the practicing bars, law schools are notorious for sending them young men who do not know how to practice law. Legal education today puts very little emphasis upon "practical" skills, offering training only in reading, occasional writing, and sometimes speaking. One list of the additional possible skills to be gained by clinical education includes client interviewing and counseling, fact gathering and sifting, legal research into specific problems, decision making about alternative strategies, negotiation, application of canons of ethics to specific cases, advocacy before tribunals, "packaging" a business arrangement or community development project, etc. In clinical education these skills are supposedly gained by being practiced—real skills in real situations. Most programs provide either for supervision by an experienced attorney or faculty member or for advanced preparation and instruction on the types of problems supposedly encountered.

Unfortunately, however, "the doing of tasks requiring skills does not equal the learning of them. It is just as possible to learn bad as good habits from experience" (*Clinical Education . . . ,* 1969,

p. 13). In fact, the pressures of real life, as opposed to simulation, seem to make for a bad learning situation. Close supervision seems to be a real sine qua non for skills training. Although it is a necessary requisite for success, it does not even come close to guaranteeing success, as those who have tried to "teach" a skill can attest.

Skills training has not been a main emphasis of law schools traditionally. The main emphasis has been to teach various qualities of mind, "thinking like a lawyer," that provide a sound foundation upon which the student can build his professional skills when he begins practice. If we want to move skills training into a more significant part of law school education (a hotly controverted issue), clinical education does not appear to be the only way of doing so, or even, perhaps, the most effective way. Current changes in curricula and methods, such as simulation, may do just as well.

Experience and understanding of society
This nebulous goal refers to the fact that law students often come from a narrow middle-class background and that to understand the problems of law, societal institutions, and poverty they need some real experience of what poverty actually is and means. The implication is that without firsthand experience of the "nitty gritty" a student cannot gain real knowledge. It is questionable, however, whether exposure leads to understanding or merely to strong feelings. We detect in the rhetoric of the proponents of clinical education a strong messianic note, not merely about clinical programs but about the effectiveness of clinical programs in dealing with some of this country's most pressing problems. If one considers the contribution of clinical programs to be at best marginal, one would like to have the opportunity to discuss the intellectually interesting means/ends problems of changing the structural characteristics of society with students who have become emotionally sensitized to the problems of the poor through participation in clinical programs. That is in a way a plea for equal time to which the proponents of clinical education have not responded. Absent this element of intellectual rigor, we doubt whether the students who are sensitized by their clinical education experience are assured of being "put through the wringer" on the underlying issues. Since we are by nature and by training people who place a strong value on intellectuality in legal education, we think that this goal of clinical education is incomplete unless steps are taken to assure that, in addition to experience, intellectual goals are served.

The development of professional responsibility

This last category of objectives for clinical education brings us once again into the center of the problems in contemporary legal education. When learning by doing, as we have pointed out, it is just as easy to learn bad habits as good ones, and this appears to be true in the area of professional responsibility.

Two categories of students need special attention in this context. First, many students who for years have had the upward mobility aspects of higher education emphasized to them again and again look to law school and the legal profession as simply another step toward "making it" in material terms. The service component of the profession is something they have never been forced to think about. Such an attitude is not new and for years has been partially responsible for giving the profession the bad reputation it has among much of the populace. Second, the activist-oriented students, often after being disappointed at reform efforts of various sorts as undergraduates, come to law school essentially to become "first-class citizens," to get their tickets to become social reformers. These students envision themselves as lawyers, but without clients, and, as is becoming clear, that is a dangerous stance. Clinical education is seen by many as a way to bring to the minds of students of both these types, as well as others, the meaning of professional responsibility in its most basic sense.

It is probably for this reason that CLEPR, for example, insists on its narrow definition of clinical education, demanding that the lawyer-client relationship be included.

Clinical education, in its confrontation with the individual's share of the world's headaches, humanizes the educational process. It teaches that while the professional's intellect dissects the larger problems and places the individual's plight in the larger setting, the professional's dedication and skill also has to be used in solving the individual's problems for the sake of the individual and not for the sake of the answer to the big problems. . . . He [the student] learns through the insistent demands of another personality the necessity of placing restraints on his own leanings: to work out approaches that are suitable to more than his own inclinations, to repress the arrogance which would dictate answers for others (Pincus, 1970).

While agreeing with the direction of this sentiment, we feel that broader applications of the "clinical" concept than simply the lawyer-client relationship could also serve the purpose—a legislative internship, for example. A student serving a legislative internship can act in various capacities. Sometimes he serves as a personal aide to a legislator, assisting him with his day-to-day business, researching, evaluating, etc. Sometimes he aids committees or individuals. Often serving on a team with fellow students, he drafts legislation.

More than any of the other objectives listed, we feel that the development of professional responsibility is necessary for contemporary legal education. Nonetheless it is far from certain whether clinical education can reach the goal. The uncertainty and spottiness of clinical programs—particularly with regard to supervision—frustrates doing so. Despite our skepticism, we have an open mind on this issue.

On another issue, we are not equally open to persuasion. Given the fact that many clinical programs involve service to poverty-stricken clients, we are adversely impressed by what has become general knowledge—that such programs involve much repetitious, intellectually low-level work and that few law students gain from it a commitment to professional responsibility.

Cost

Clinical education, if it is properly supervised, costs more than "conventional" legal education, primarily because a teacher in a clinical setting can generally supervise fewer students than in a classroom setting. As one critic (*Clinical Education . . . ,* 1969, p. 21) has put it:

The central dilemma here is that the special quality that distinguishes a clinical education program from the experience of practice is supervision. But if there is to be good educational supervision it is costly. To start with, the ratios must be smaller. Where a teacher can teach 60 or more students in the classroom, 20 seems to be about the upper limit for supervision by a single clinical teacher. Secondly, the clinical teacher will not enjoy many of the non-monetary benefits that have helped to attract law teachers to academic life. As in practice, the clinical professor will have the responsibilities of affording client service. He must invest in the problems of his clients the continuing emotional and intellectual energy of the practitioner. In addition he will have the special responsibility of a teacher: to convert the experience into a beneficial one for the student participants. If the program has an ongoing service component, often necessary to assure the needed variety of cases, long vacations will probably be impossible. In the program he will be called upon daily to perform demanding legal tasks which are highly rewarded in practice.

In conclusion, we are dubious about the relative merits of clinical education given its high costs. Our concerns center around this proposition: we doubt that clinical education is *the* solution that many of its proponents claim it to be or that it should be *the* dominant trend of legal education in the future. We are also concerned that an anti-intellectual tendency of clinical education will offer an allure to students and to some faculty members who seek "relevance" at any price. We do not see clinical education as *the* testing case for the legal education of the future. While we believe that clinical education has a useful role to play in legal education, its role is not unique. We prefer to think that the path of improvement lies in experimentation with many modest ideas, one of which is clinical education. We will canvass some of the others in the next chapter.

5. A Diversity of New Directions: A Review of the Carrington Report

One of the most important contributions in 50 years to the study of legal education is the far-reaching report to the Association of American Law Schools entitled *Training for the Public Professions of the Law: 1971*,[1] issued after much preliminary debate on September 7, 1971. The text of that report is appended as Appendix A. We will examine it here in some detail both because of its inherent importance in the field of legal education and because it provides an excellent vehicle for reviewing our own views. The report is the work of a committee of the AALS consisting of a number of innovative legal scholars who have been interested for many years in problems of the legal profession and legal education. Professor Paul Carrington of the University of Michigan School of Law was chairman of the committee and the major force in designing and drafting the report.

The format of the report consists of a model course announcement, including a set of curricula, and a rationale for the announcement. The model, it is explicitly stated, is not designed for adoption in toto by any law school. Rather, this pedagogic device was adopted, one infers, for three reasons, one explicit and two implicit. The explicit reason is that the details of the model are given for the purpose of illuminating the report's conclusions and for stimulating focused discussion. The first implicit reason is that the report is the product of a committee on curriculum set up by the AALS. The association is an organization of law schools to which almost all law schools belong. Its member schools vary a good deal in quality and in aspirations. Like many of its committees, this one is dominated

---

[1] The title was deliberately chosen to commemorate the work of Alfred Z. Reed (see Chapter 3), which was published in 1921 by The Carnegie Foundation for the Advancement of Teaching.

by faculty members from the elite schools. Since the association is the only forum available to academic lawyers, and since it is not an association of individual scholars as are the American Historical Association, the American Political Science Association, and the American Sociological Association, its sponsorship of this report puts considerable handicaps in the way of adoption of the report. At meetings of the association, each member school has one vote. The second implicit reason is that this format is congenial to the habits of thought of academic lawyers. The appearance of concrete proposals appeals to them more than the sort of general, abstract report that scholars in other disciplines would find congenial.

The report does start out with a general statement of objectives. These are stated as follows:

1   Legal education should offer training that is coherently related to the varied demands of the public for legal services and to the varied ambitions of a wider array of students.

2   The attainment of that objective requires that each member school re-examine its program, and each unit of instruction within it, to determine whether the costs in human and financial resources are fully justified by the benefits obtained in service to such varied educational goals.

3   Each member school should consider the extent to which its instructional offering ought to relate to such diverse goals as:

(a)   training individuals for general practice as lawyers;

(b)   training lawyers desiring special competence in particular fields of practice;

(c)   training scholars capable of interdisciplinary research;

(d)   training individuals for careers in the delivery of legal services as members of allied professions;

(e)   training about law for students motivated by intellectual curiosity, by uncertainty of career goals, or by career goals in other disciplines.

To the extent that each is deemed to be an appropriate goal of a particular school, its offerings should be coherently related to such goals.

4   In pursuing such goals, schools should not be inhibited by received limitations which do not relate to function. Specifically, schools should not be bound by the traditions that:

(a)   all graduates must be trained to omnicompetence;

(b)   all schools must pursue the same general goals;

(c)   most courses or units of instruction must be centered on a core of doctrine and serve the usual function of training students "to think like lawyers";

(d)   all students must have prolonged undergraduate training;

(e)   students cannot attain their first degrees in law without three years of study within the walls of a law school.

5   In order to encourage such re-examinations and to foster diversity among member schools, the Association should conduct a re-examination of the existing standards of the Association to consider the extent to which they impede better service to the public and to students.

These generally stated conclusions are consistent with what has so far been stated in this study. As we go through the Model Curricula, our inquiry will be to what extent the work of the authors of the Carrington Report accords with what we think is going on in the law school world (or what we would like to see going on in that world). The generally stated conclusions are, we believe, fairly representative of the views of many legal educators today. It remains to be seen over the next few months and years how much agreement there is with the details of the Model Curricula.[2] In a sense, that is less critical than is the ability of the report to marshal general support among the members of the legal teaching profession.

The first model is of what the authors call a Standard Curriculum.[3] It is designed to replace the curriculum that prevails in most law schools today as a method of educating "lawyer-generalists." The first year is entirely prescribed. Aside from some relabeling, the courses bear a strong resemblance to what is taught today in many law schools. It would have been an advantage if the authors had clearly identified changes from what exists today instead of simply changing all the labels. One clear change is a first-year course in legal advocacy, which combines in a one-semester course

---

[2] Before turning to the models in detail, one should note a major difficulty in organization. The models are preceded by explanatory comments and are followed by a statement of rationale. We cannot imagine what led the authors of the report to adopt a scheme of organization that places such extraordinary obstacles to understanding. In what follows, we have combined the preliminary comments and the rationale with discussion of each Model Curriculum. We shall identify the page numbers of the preliminary comments, the descriptive text of the model, and the rationale.

[3] Pp. 8–11, 16–23, 37–50.

much of the old course in civil procedure plus elements of the basic course in torts. "Attention is also given to a comparison of the social utility of the adversary process and the alternative methods of claims management through private or social insurance which have evolved for the compensation of some of the losses otherwise subject to adversary litigation" (p. 17).

Much of the present content of the courses in civil procedure and torts would undoubtedly be lost through this shift in focus, which sounds like more than a simple reshuffling of old material. Whether it can be done without losing much of the old-time learning is dubious. Yet we would be enthusiastic to see an attempt made along the lines suggested. It sacrifices substantive knowledge in an effort to achieve a broad view of this area of risk allocation. We doubt that the Socratic method would be very useful in teaching a systems approach to the problems of risk allocation and procedure. The fact that some law professors are willing to make the effort to change their approaches may indicate that a new departure is possible. Experimentation by a few schools should supply a limited answer to the question of whether "success" is possible. Given the great diversity of law teachers and their varying abilities and backgrounds we would think that this effort may well be typical of what the Model Curriculum makes possible. Its details are designed to liberate individual law teachers to rethink their approaches.

The first-year curriculum, in particular, is designed to assist in the education of the generalist. Given the diversity of possible approaches, we do not think that experimentation with this aspect of the Model Curriculum would be likely to lead to a unitary curriculum in the immediate future. On the contrary, experimentation with some aspects of this Standard Curriculum would probably result in greater diversity than we have now. Would law students thereby lose the common cultural base that they have today? We doubt that because law teachers will presumably continue to be people who have the same cultural base, at least until a new generation of teachers is educated. Even if the content of the common first year is eroded, we do not anticipate that greater diversity would materially affect the common culture of law students.

We agree with the authors of the Carrington Report that a new look is needed at the goals of the first year. Like them, we believe that more than a cosmetic change or a relabeling is required. The first year is crucial because, as we have emphasized earlier, that is when the student forms his ideas of the law. The great merit of the report is to give much greater emphasis to what might be called macroissues, as opposed to microissues, of doctrine. Any variation of the Model Curriculum would focus the attention of faculty members and hence of students on these macroissues. Whether this change of focus can be managed without sacrificing the training in legal analysis that dominates the first year is a good question. We see no answer, but we hope that a few schools will make the effort.

The post-first-year curriculum is organized under two headings: intensive and extensive. Intensive instruction is given to small classes with limited enrollment, going into considerable detail on relatively narrow topics. Extensive instruction, on the other hand, involves subjects that are taught on the basis of a syllabus by lecture or by some audiovisual method and requires the student to submit to an examination of his knowledge. The lists of topics for these two types of instruction reveal very little of what criteria might be used to delineate the difference between intensive and extensive instruction. As we interpret this classification, intensive instruction follows basically the model of the seminar; extensive instruction involves large groups.

In the discussion of intensive instruction, the authors of the report deliver themselves of some highly critical observations on clinical education (pp. 41–42). Their criticisms are centered on the narrow definition espoused by CLEPR (see Chapter 4). This feature by itself has been responsible for much of the controversy that has attended the Carrington Report and has been used, so it seems to us, as a basis for an attack on a closely related feature of the report: the proposal that the basic professional degree be attainable in two years of study. In calling it the two-year proposal, we are oversimplifying. In fact, the report does not categorically state how much time legal education should consume. Given the degree requirements stated, the authors assert that "some students will be able to complete it (the Standard Curriculum) in two years while most will complete it in less than three" (p. 44). In support of shortening the time required for legal education, the authors cite the need for greater availability of legal services and the desirability to that end of reducing current time-serving requirements. They also cite the desirability of placing more of the burden of professional education on postdegree training. They denigrate the assumption that acquiring a store of information is the principal value of legal education. They view present reliance on the case method as "a precious elaboration of details of little value to the generalist." Finally, they denounce the idea that the three-year requirement is necessary to maintain the level of professional income. We discuss the issue of a two-year professional degree in Chapter 8.

The next major proposal is an Advanced Curriculum.[4] This is both a holding operation and the basis for devoting some of the law school's resources to post-J.D. specialized training. As a holding operation, the Advanced Curriculum serves as a way for students to meet the present time-serving requirements imposed by the bar. The model includes a bar review course, which is contrary to the present standards of the Association of American Law Schools. Like the authors, we see no reason why law schools should consider providing this service to students beneath their dignity.

The education of part-time students should no longer be viewed as contrary to a law school's ethos. We favor the report's position in favor of postdegree training. Given the variety of institutes, summer programs, and the like already being given by many law schools, we see this additional step as being in the best interests of the law schools and of the legal profession. We join the authors of the report in concluding:

The credentials awarded should be adequate to reinforce the awareness of professional achievement, but not so tinseled that they become yet another set of funeral beads to be won in the "credentials race." The law school need not enlarge its unsought position as a gatekeeper to professional status by an attempt to certify competence in the fashion of public licensing authority. But there is no reason why the law school specialist examination cannot co-exist with certification systems.

Another proposal in the report is an Open Curriculum, one element of which is a program of instruction about law for undergraduates. We discuss this in Chapter 6. The other feature of the Open Curriculum contemplates the emergence of paraprofessional careers, which the report terms *Allied Professions*.[5] We have discussed this topic in Chapter 2. This feature has given rise to controversy that has centered on the objection of certain minority representatives that setting up allied professions will induce minority students to become second-class citizens. As stated by the authors:

[4] Pp. 11–13, 24–26, 51–55.
[5] Pp. 14–15, 31–34, 62–68.

The second and third responses come from women and members of minority groups who are quick to see the proposed programs as a thinly disguised "tracking" system, which will consign blacks, Chicanos, and women to second class careers in the delivery of second class services to poor clients.

The authors give this response, with which we agree:

The real alternatives for those who would be affected is a career outside the law (or perhaps no career at all) and a choice between no legal service or service that is beyond their means. The hostile reaction is reinforced by the romantic illusion of a unitary bar. The illusion is produced by the fact that all lawyers are now trained for the same length of time in the same way; this provides an egalitarian appearance which is false, as anyone familiar with the bar can attest. The maintenance of the illusion of equality has ill-served the public. It has prevented useful careers from developing and it has caused services to be more expensive than they need to be. Certainly, the choice to be faced is not ideal. The Model is not insensitive to the emotional discomfort of those who would perform as members of the new professions. But it recognizes that such suffering will have to be borne if the real interests of the people are to be served.

In addition, we would say that if some new careers are deemed possible, why should law schools be exempt from exploring them? The argument that law schools should not dirty their hands with matters of this sort is, we believe, essentially an argument that law schools should not take part in any movement that may have the effect of restricting either the number of lawyers or the net income of lawyers. We view this argument as another manifestation of the guild view toward the legal profession that we have already indicated we oppose. We think that only a few law faculties will want to devote resources to developing paraprofessional careers and that the principal burden of providing instruction will have to fall on community colleges.[6] Nonetheless, we do see a kind of leadership role that a few law teachers should be able to perform.

This cursory review of the Carrington Report has indicated, we hope, its tendency toward creative innovation. It is basically, as its authors themselves state, a conservative document. It is lawyer-like in the best sense. We would like to quote its last two paragraphs,[7] which give its conservative flavor:

[6] See, especially, such publications of the Carnegie Commission on Higher Education as *Less Time, More Options* (1971).

[7] For the benefit of those who will not read the full report.

Radical as some features of the Model may seem, it is conservative in two important respects. The first is that the Model abides what it regards as the appropriate jurisdictional limits of curriculum planning. It does not presume to express any grand design of the society in which we should live, but meets the social issues only when they intersect with the educational mission of facilitating the attainment of individual goals by students and teachers. In this respect, the Model assumes that a law school is not equipped with a suitable process for identifying the ultimate goals of society. It also assumes that no institution committed to inquiry should attempt firm conclusions because to do so would impair its receptivity to other ideas. It expresses the faith that the university law school can best serve by continuing the tradition of the university as a harbor for reason, tolerance, and speculation. It expresses skepticism that a law school can be effectively used as a means of altering the goals of the larger society. In this respect, it assumes that those changes which might be accomplished through the use of the law school curriculum could be accomplished at least as effectively by other means. It should be conceded that this is a debatable conservatism. Thomas Jefferson, for example, planned his University law school as a school for Whigs, as an incubator for generations of like-minded Jeffersonians. In resisting this kind of manipulation, the Model can fairly claim to be more Jeffersonian than Jefferson.

The Model's second conservatism is that it expresses faith in the institutions of legal education and in the tradition of rigorous rationality which have been their pride. Indeed, it seeks to turn that tradition on itself. In an effort to "think like a lawyer" about the problems of legal education, the Model warmly embraces tradition; it celebrates more than it changes.

6. The Law School in the University

We regard the current state of legal education as having much in common with the intellectual plight of our universities generally. We have indicated at the end of Chapter 3 how secularization has led to much muddled thinking about the law. The rational study of values, or ends, has been viewed as off limits to most scholars. Academicians who do not trouble themselves to analyze ends are technicians who, concerning themselves solely with means, may produce useful work that tends to be trivial. Nowhere other than in law is it so crucial for scholars to pay attention to ends, since it is only through the interaction of means and ends that a system of law can attain any ends. The rational study of ends, which is to say of values, is a very difficult enterprise. Yet it is essential that scholars begin to make an effort to study the means/ends interaction of the problems in which they are interested. No discipline more than law invites scholars to make this effort.

Legal scholars have not been at the center of intellectual ferment in the universities. But they have managed to contribute a good deal to the general education of students. No field of study in American universities has been so much a general-purpose field as law has been. Whether this primacy will continue depends, we believe, on how well legal education manages to respond to the challenge that is afforded by the rational study of values in a means/end relationship. We shall discuss the prospects for legal education's meeting the challenge to strengthen itself as *the* general-purpose field of study in American universities under three headings: the general-purpose degree, scholarship about law, and undergraduate instruction in legal processes and institutions.

LAW AS A GENERAL-PURPOSE DEGREE

"If there be one school in a university of which it may be said that there students learn to give practical reality, practical effectiveness to vision and to ideals, that school is the school of law."

(Llewellyn, 1971, p. 34)

While Llewellyn's dictum, deriving as it does from the heyday of Legal Realism, gives great prominence to means as opposed to ends, it characterizes the role of the professional study of law in universities in this country during the past hundred years. Let us examine how the new direction in law schools will fortify the continuation of this tradition. At the risk of anticipating much that we shall say later in this chapter, law is now recognized by most teachers of law to be a multidimensional phenomenon—historical, philosophic, psychological, social, political, economic, and religious. As these currents come to be more fully reflected in legal curricula, the study of law will become an increasingly stronger integrating study in which other disciplines come to be a part.

Similarly, law teachers will continue to be viewed as useful models of how a person can contribute to useful social reforms. Faculty members engage in public service activities that may include writing briefs in cases that raise an issue that affects the public; helping to draft legislation for a legislature, for an executive officer of government, or for one of the many organizations that sponsor legislation (such as the American Law Institute); arbitrating disputes; or doing background studies for official agencies. These activities endow the law teacher with experience that he can then transmit to his students. To this tradition we ascribe much of the credit for the good repute of legal education as a kind of "advanced general education." We assume that if the demand for "relevance" continues in higher education, the law schools will be in an excellent position to maintain their primacy as offering advanced general education without sacrificing their intellectual rigor. Demand for such education is evidenced by the fact that in the past three years the number of persons taking the Law School Admission Test, the best index of interest in legal education, has almost doubled. In the same period, total law school enrollment increased by about 30 percent. There seems little reason to doubt that much of the increase in interest is due to the allure of law as the generalist's entry into careers that offer an opportunity to contribute to the making, the execution, or the reform of social policy. While today's enthusiasm for legal study may not be enduring, we suspect that it is more than a temporary fad. The president of the ABA recently suggested that more and more graduating law students may find their way into "other pursuits" as opposed to becoming practicing lawyers. We cannot make any such prediction. But there is a good deal to be said for the proposition that legal education may come to be an advanced general education for students who are unsure about what professional role they want to occupy.

THE ROLE OF SCHOLARSHIP The much-heralded marriage of law and the behavioral sciences has not yet taken place, despite the encouraging noises that some enthusiasts have been making. On the whole, we are not disappointed that the courtship has not resulted in a permanent union. Scholarship in law has, it is true, not achieved the quantitative precision that is characteristic of such disciplines as economics or psychology. While scholarship about law is not as precise, neither is it trivial. The worst aspects of journeyman work in the behavioral sciences—triviality and irrelevance—are reflected, in our opinion, in the headlock that the Ph.D. puts on higher education.[1] We are delighted that legal scholarship has so far escaped this headlock.

Law is not, we think, a science; it is an art and a craft. However, it badly needs to be broadened to include the insights of the best behavioral sciences as, in the words of the Carrington Report, it supplements the "intuitive, prudential values which the profession brings to official decision-making" (p. 56). Changes such as those that the Carrington Report advocates in the curriculum require that law teachers retool themselves to incorporate a broadly based familiarity with aspects of the behavioral sciences into their teaching. That effort, we think, must precede any massive attempts to use the insights of allied disciplines in legal scholarship. Assuming that legal scholarship remains the preserve of law teachers, we see no escape from the conclusion that only by affecting their teaching and what is taught to the next generation of law teachers (who are mainly today's law students) will legal scholarship become more broadly based. The trend is already under way. The youngest generation of law teachers today does not merely have a general legal

[1] For an intemperate view of the Ph.D., see Packer (1970).

education. These teachers have studied at an advanced level such fields as economics, psychology, history, and philosophy. (Indeed, several law schools now have on their faculties people who have advanced degrees in allied disciplines and not in law.)

One direction that we think legal scholars are now exploiting is the interdisciplinary study of what Professor Alfred Conrad (1971) has called *macrojustice*. This is the study, from the point of view of such new disciplines as systems analysis, of how the institutions for dispensing justice might be improved. The organization of the legal profession itself is ripe for this kind of study.

One might easily multiply examples of problems that can be studied with the aid of knowledge or methods borrowed from allied disciplines. The Carrington Report, in advocating a program for research instruction (pp. 56–57), stresses the importance of interdisciplinary work. As one example, we believe that legal scholarship can add a good deal to the study of the university as a social system. Given the myriad problems that universities now face, shouldn't this become a priority item for study by interdisciplinary groups? Since charity is said to begin at home, we strongly push the idea that legal scholars should take the lead in formulating and studying problems that affect the universities.

Legal scholarship in this country has passed through two phases. The first was a Langdellian search for scientific principles that could be gathered by an inductive process through analysis of appellate decisions. In the second phase, legal scholarship concentrated on getting the answers to questions about means of achieving objectives through methodological broadening of the scope of inquiry to center on the facts of the real world. This phase, which we may call the Legal Realist phase, ran into the dead end of being concerned only with means to the exclusion of ends. It made lawyers into mere technicians. The challenge now is to bring the study of law into a position in which it focuses on the goals for which its techniques are used. Adding the broadening of the second phase to the search for principles of the first phase can result in the study of means/ends relationships. This is where allied disciplines can contribute to making law a discipline more receptive to ideas from other fields. Thereby, we hope that law will be enabled to take its rightful place not as a science but as an art that is supported by a distinctive craft. Another way of stating this direction is to say that legal scholarship can become what some law professors are in the university today—capable of addressing themselves to any problem that has a social context.

THE ROLE OF LAW IN UNDERGRADUATE EDUCATION Law in this country has been for the past hundred years a subject for *postgraduate* and *professional* instruction because of developments that have already been described. This was not true previously, nor is it now true in most other Western countries. As the Harvard model became *the* model for American legal education, a hole was left in the undergraduate curriculum: law is not part of the undergraduate curriculum in most universities.

Many people believe that a democratic society is particularly dependent on a general understanding of law. Yet even educated citizens seem to consider law an arcane craft whose secrets must remain a mystery to them. Graduates of our colleges are fundamentally ignorant about legal processes and institutions. There is at present no place in the undergraduate liberal arts curriculum where a student can remedy this deficiency.

There are, of course, many individual courses that have something to do with law. Constitutional law and international law, offered by the political science department, are the most common. Courses in business law are part of most undergraduate programs. Sociology departments sometimes offer a course in law and sociology, and anthropology departments may include law and anthropology, but these are generally courses in sociology and anthropology, not law. Some universities offer a course, often denominated Law and Society, that tries to introduce students to the legal process. But few of these courses go far toward exposing students to the norms and institutions of the American legal system, let alone the legal systems of other nations.

The Carrington Report offers a Model Curriculum for undergraduates.[2] The report advances a threefold rationale for such a curriculum:

1 the desirability of using the legal setting as a matrix for intellectual inquiry about such pervasive issues as "the tension between stability and change, freedom and security, history and logic, ideal justice and justice in practice" (p. 59);

2 the increasing importance of law to citizens in our society;

3 an opportunity for students to test their interest and capacity, a kind of "headstart" reason.

[2] Pp. 13, 27–31, 59–61.

While we recognize that the citizenship reason is also appealing, we would stress the intellectual rationale. While many would view the "headstart" reason as justifying the effort, we think that this reason is at best speculative.

A course taught or designed by an academic lawyer and making use of basically legal materials can accomplish two valuable educational objectives. First, it can convey knowledge and understanding about law as fact and artifact — a picture of law as institutions and processes and its various ways of functioning. Second, it can convey insight into and practice in various useful methods of thought — an introduction to some of the attributes we associate with a good lawyer. As Paul Freund (1968, p. 110) has put it in prefacing his own list of valuable traits academic lawyers can impart to undergraduates:

The art is to hold the legal materials in a double focus: to see them as significant for their own sake, developments in the rationalizing of certain areas of human experience and also as exemplification of the rational process itself, with a wider significance for the developing intellectual style (to use a too pretentious phrase) of the student.

The study of law as fact and artifact focuses the student's attention on the conception of a legal system: who operates in it, how they function, what impact they have, how the system changes, the impact the system has on other elements of our society, and vice versa. Here the effort is to give the student an idea of law as a social process, the functions it performs, the institutions involved, and how changes take place. It gives at least an introductory idea of the structures and processes involved in society's efforts to shape and organize individual and group behavior — a view of law as an ordering process.

The study of law as methods of thought focuses on several complex rational processes. Involved are the abilities to analyze the significance attributed to verbal signals and messages; to employ communication as a planning and control mechanism; to capture the consequences of courses of action; and to digest and synthesize as well as break a problem into components and reassemble it. Studying law with this focus gives students exposure to a method of thought involving values and value choices tied directly to the making of decisions that result in action, and it is in this respect different from those focuses generally used in the social and natural sciences.

As these two areas of focus combine the student is given an insight into practical questions of order and disorder in human experience. The undergraduate generally derives no understanding of the ways in which men actually reach decisions of the kind that form a framework for future human relations and dealings. In a double-focus study of law this gap can be filled. A study of law opens up questions of how social ends and means interact and reveals the complications involved in attempting to create or re-create the ongoing, working institutions of a society. Theory and practice meet and interact. Values, ends, means, information, and theory all intersect. Such a study of law is not so much another discipline as an education in the relation of specific social problems to various sources of knowledge and modes of thought.

SUMMARY   In this consideration of the role of law schools in their universities, we have suggested that legal education already is a form of general-purpose, advanced higher education, that in it there is a need for promoting scholarship in macrojustice, and that there is a great potential value in law as a humane study for undergraduates. Extrapolating from these particulars, there is a need for the study of law which is not rigidly linked to professional study and which works closely with other academic disciplines. To quote what Robert M. Hutchins (1934, pp. 511, 518) said nearly 40 years ago: "And gradually, very gradually, the law might once again become a learned profession."

7. Financing Legal Education

The problems of financing legal education deserve a lengthy separate study of their own.[1] The question is important. The chief constraint on reform of legal education is that since it is now so cheap, almost all reforms that we have considered will raise unit costs. The question is complicated. Private and state law schools have disparate mechanisms of providing funds. The cost structures and revenue possibilities of nationally prominent schools differ from those of regional or urban schools. The independent law schools differ from those that are part of larger university structures. All have different needs and opportunities. These aspects of diversity are only the beginning, for if legal education follows the pattern we urge in this study and which we believe is now under way, law schools will cease to have even structural similarity. Legal education will be spread over many levels, from paraprofessional to superspecialist, and law schools themselves will specialize in various ways.

A full study of the financing of legal education would have to explore each of these dimensions, both as they exist now and as they are likely to develop. We can make only a preliminary appraisal of the problem and suggest a few possible solutions. Our focus will be a composite model of the law school. At times we shall speak in terms of the private, university-related law school. It is this institution that is now in the most financial trouble. With only minor qualifications, however, what we say applies to state-supported law schools as well.

Traditionally, legal education has been inexpensive relative to other types of graduate education. As a result, it has developed

---

[1] We have in mind something along the lines of *Financing Medical Education* by Rashi Fein and Gerald Weber (1971)—a study specifically of financing done by experts both in financing and medical education.

neither constituencies nor mechanisms to provide substantial financial support. This tradition of low funding lives on into an age in which legal education has changed and become much more expensive. Moreover, if legal education is to be viable in the future it will become even more expensive. Many influential people now have a concept of legal education that is inconsistent with the developments that we have sketched in this study. Costs are rising, not just the costs of traditional legal education but also the costs of developing new directions. At the moment new revenues to meet these rising costs have not been found. Substantial sources must be developed and stable mechanisms built for the financing of legal education in the future.

THE TRADITION

Law schools are run "on the cheap." Law schools in this country were once proprietary profit-making institutions. Some of them are still treated by university administrators as if they were proprietary schools franchised to use the name of a university (as many of our oldest and most prominent law schools originally were). Law students are expected to pay a high tuition, and the cost of their education is expected to be inexpensive. Law schools in general remain to this day effectively self-supporting.[2] Indeed, one suspects that at the less well-endowed private universities the law school subsidizes the more costly parts of the university. The traditional model of the law school can operate in such a way due to very large classes, the limited nature of the library demands, the narrowly professional educational aspirations of the students, and a concentration on teaching rather than research by the faculty. Most graduate departments usually have a faculty-student ratio of approximately 1 to 5, and medical schools function at 1 to 2 or 1 to 1; legal education functions normally at 1 to 20 or worse. Harvard Law School, for example, has a full-time faculty of about 65 and a student body of 1,750 — or a 1 to 27 ratio. Under the Harvard model for case method teaching, the ratio of students to teachers was very high; the cost of materials was low; no great research efforts were expected of faculty members (and if expected, certainly were not supported); students were expected to be able to pay the full cost of what they received; and nothing changed very much. New

[2] See Stevens (1969) for an excellent discussion of the financial aspect of legal education as well as interesting insight and source material for all the issues we have been discussing. We have relied upon it heavily in this chapter.

courses and materials were developed glacially. For most of those who should be concerned with legal education, particularly the present bar, this image remains dominant. National and local and public and private law schools alike are not considered in need of funds.

The lack of outside support for scholarship or "research" (a term that we dislike but will adopt because of its general use) at law schools is just one example of the problem, though a dramatic one. At Stanford University in a recent year total university expenditures for research amounted to more than $37 million; of that amount more than $10 million was devoted to medical research— and less than $20,000 was attributed to legal research. These research ratios are nationally typical.

Legal education receives only marginal foundation support and essentially *no* support from the federal government. In these respects it is unique in American higher education. In fiscal 1966–67, the Yale Law School, with a total budget of about $2.2 million and some 600 students, received a *de minimus* amount from the federal government and nothing whatever from the state; in the same year the Yale Medical School, with a total budget of about $23 million and some 400 students, received about $14.3 million from the federal government and about $1.1 million from the state government. The Yale budget is among the very highest for law schools on a per-student basis. Tuition at such elite schools may cover only half or even less of the real costs of a student's education. At Stanford, for example, a student's legal education has to be subsidized by about $7,000, assuming that he pays full tuition, or by an average annual subsidy of about $1,460. Law schools *still* are run "on the cheap." And that fact is a strait jacket that can do great damage in the near future.

IS ANYBODY INTERESTED? Bayless Manning (1969*b*) has best described the dilemma the law school faces as it searches for funds:

In appearance (and in a sense in fact) the financial difficulties of legal education stem from a shortage of interested supporting constituencies.

In a modern university, the physical science departments and engineering schools are heavily supported by the National Science Foundation and federal research grants and contracts. Law schools never receive these grants and contracts.

Medical schools today operate only because of massive direct federal aid and would close their doors at once if that aid were not provided. Legal education receives no federal support.

Testamentary bequests from a wide public form a major basis of funding for many parts of the modern university, again including medicine. Bequests rarely come to law schools and almost never from anyone but lawyers.

University programs for religion, music, the fine arts and the performing arts are able to rely in considerable measure on their own special constituencies of enthusiasts. Law schools have no such outside constituency.

The social sciences have been major beneficiaries of the development of large-scale, professionally staffed foundations. Except in the one area of international legal studies, in which the Ford Foundation has been helpful, law schools have received little foundation support.

Business schools and engineering schools are able to draw on major sources of corporate giving. Law schools so far have been almost wholly unsuccessful in appealing to the board room.

The disinterest of nonlawyers in the problems of our law schools is neither surprising nor a ground for fair criticism. Nonlawyers assume that the Bar, as a learned profession, is interested in its own education, is generally well-to-do, is able to look after its own and presumably is doing so.

But the fact is that the Bar by and large provides almost no financial support for legal education, has only the remotest idea of what is happening inside the law schools, is unaware that they are in financial trouble and does not know why. . . .

We have described the isolation of legal education from the practicing bar. Despite many changes, those already made and those imminent, lawyers generally believe legal education functions much as it did 40 years ago. They are unaware of the inadequacy of running legal education "on the cheap." Thus there are no constituencies and no mechanisms for funding legal education. The necessity for funding will soon be reaching a crisis point.

THE CHANGING COSTS OF LEGAL EDUCATION Two factors are combining to cause the current crisis in financing legal education. The first is the general depression that has come to all higher education in the present decade.[3] The second cause includes the changes that have taken place in law schools without an alteration in the traditional structure of legal education. In

[3] See Cheit (1971) for a revealing discussion and survey.

many ways these shifts have been substantial, and they have been expensive. Developing under the guise of the old structure, however, they have often not been noticed and are already suffering from underfunding. This problem will be greatly exacerbated by the substantial changes in both the structure and content of legal education that we have been recommending throughout this study.

To many of our readers who are academic lawyers our recommendations will come as no surprise. Most of our ideas are not new, and the pressure for them is high at many institutions. As we have emphasized, the law school is underfunded in relation to the rest of the university. And yet the university itself has reached a state in which it cannot continue to finance its operations. Costs are rising much faster than income, and there appears to be no relief in sight. Law schools will thus find it difficult to maintain even their present underfunded status.

Professor Cheit, in his study for the Carnegie Commission entitled *The New Depression in Higher Education* (1971, p. 9), reports that at certain selected institutions expenditures for departmental instruction and research have for several decades risen "at the remarkably constant (compound) annual rate of $7\frac{1}{2}$ percent, per student. Inflation accounted for only about one-fourth of this increase." This $7\frac{1}{2}$ percent per-student annual increase will probably continue throughout the coming decade. Twenty-seven percent of the institutions in Professor Cheit's study were in financial difficulty by his definition. At these schools, educational and general expenditures grew even faster: at the compound average annual rate of 9.5 percent per student. There is no reason to believe that law schools, even remaining essentially stagnant, would have a significantly lower cost increase. Thus even if the tradition of education "on the cheap" were not changing, law schools would be in serious financial trouble.

The problem is more serious because that tradition *is* changing. Legal education, even at schools where the structure has not changed, no longer fits the classic model. Many new areas of law have developed. A modern curriculum includes courses that were unimagined in the classical Langdellian era. American law has undergone a process of subproliferation. The traditional category of property has splintered into zoning, land-use control, urban renewal, real estate financing, water resources, oil and gas, conservation, and many other subcategories. All this development is reflected in the curriculum. Many long-ignored areas of the law have undergone similar development. One need only mention criminal law, with its splintering into numerous varieties of criminal procedure, such as law affecting the police, correctional law, juvenile law, and so on. This development has spawned many courses in the curriculum. There is far more law being generated today than in a less complex world. A nation of 200 million people who litigate more and are subject to much more government regulation, who have many more governing agencies and more tribunals that insist on printing everything, and who have more legislatures that are not hesitant to legislate all combine to produce a society that is very heavily dependent on lawyers. For a law professor today to stay on top of his heavily subdivided field requires a degree of attention, a variety of inquiry, and a degree of specialization unknown in yesterday's law school world.

These are not the only changes from the traditional model. The career goals of law students are far more diverse than they used to be. The clinical education movement appears to be gaining momentum, and scholarship by both faculty and students is taking up a much larger share of time than it used to. The institutional and moral impetus behind these movements is indeed so strong that the strongest present inhibition to their fulfillment is their cost. The changes have already occurred within the old structure; at the same time, the continuation of the old image has prevented even the development of possible supporting constituencies. And the new developments themselves have not yet even taken place at the less well-financed law schools. The money to maintain or develop these new directions is an added expense the law schools are going to have to finance in the coming years.

If there are to be fundamental changes in the structure of legal education that go beyond the current developments at leading law schools, the costs of legal education will increase even more. We have discussed the need to dismantle the unitary mold of legal education. We have talked of specialization in subject matter both within the law school and among various law schools. We have discussed the desirability of fundamental curricular and teaching materials reforms. New career paths at all levels—paraprofessional, professional, superspecialization, and academic—are needed developments. We consider in the next chapter changing the length of law school education and providing for multiple curricular tracks to serve the interests of different kinds of students. All these will be expensive. Scholarship is expensive. And, at perhaps the most fundamental level, student-teacher ratios in many areas of legal education are going to have to go down drastically. That is expensive. All these things will be expensive. Many of them are already taking embryonic shape. But the funding for them is largely absent.

Thus, in a way, we are whistling in the wind in discussing reforms in legal education. In all probability we are, for the short term at least and maybe longer, entering a time of depression in higher education. Even before that depression, law schools were too poor to innovate, even when the ideas and justifications for them were available and clear. The *Journal of Legal Education* is a graveyard of ideas that died or were stillborn because their authors never considered the traditional financial limitations on law schools.

THE AMOUNT Legal education will remain a relatively inexpensive effort. Law schools will not have large demands for expensive equipment or instrumentation (although the demands for them will be higher than they are now). Law schools are small—there are only about 3,000 full-time law teachers in the country—and even to double the size of the faculty does not involve great numbers. An increased national investment in legal education of $100 million would double the present aggregated budget of our law schools. Doubling our annual expenditures represents a very modest goal. The absolute amount needed, in relation to, say, medicine, is thus very small. It only seems huge when one realizes the present paucity of sources.

WHERE CAN THE MONEY COME FROM? Financing legal education for the future is not going to be a simple task given the almost complete lack of present funding sources. We contemplate three important potential sources for legal education funding: (1) the development of various supporting constituencies, (2) the development of institutions to facilitate and rationalize individual student borrowing, and (3) the development of mechanisms for institutional borrowing. The three are not separate, and in many ways each will depend upon and be part of the others. Thus the supporting constituencies will be the potential backers of borrowing. Each source and device deserves a separate description here, and each will have to be developed separately in most cases.

The constituencies

First: the legal profession itself

If every graduate of a law school were to take it upon himself, when and as his economic circumstances enable him to do so, to pay into his law school an amount equal to the difference between the cost of educating one law student and the tuition rate—and thereby make it possible for a student to receive a legal education as someone made it possible for him to receive a legal education—that step alone would go far to meet the financial problems facing our law schools (Manning, 1969*b*, p. 1127).

Such support for legal education does not now exist among the legal profession. Many law schools are now emphasizing restoration of the subsidy that law students now receive in their alumni giving programs. There is, we believe, an obvious need for each law school to develop statistics on its subsidy and to emphasize it through publicity.

Second: employers of law school graduates   Each young graduate from a first-rate law school hired today by a law firm or corporation represents a valuable asset. That asset will not only be converted into a high income for the graduate involved; it will also generate income for the employer. These employers are in the business of marketing legal services, and they cannot perform it without a supply of young lawyers. Thus it would not seem unreasonable to attempt to educate them in the need for funds and then solicit from them funds for the support of legal education.

Third: major gifts from lawyers   Few lawyers have ever made law schools a significant beneficiary of their philanthropies. Many lawyers are in a financial position to give significant gifts. Occasionally such gifts are made, and without them privately financed legal education would long since have disappeared. They are rare, however. A major effort at educating the bar in the problem can help.[4]

Fourth: gifts from nonlawyers   It is often possible for a lawyer counseling a client to suggest a charitable institution as a beneficiary. Every major university regularly receives a flow of gifts, usually testamentary, resulting from suggestions made by lawyers. It is surprising that very little of this financing is addressed to the

---

[4] The recent establishment of a Center for the Advance of Legal Education may be an important step in this direction.

needs of the law schools. That may be because of the lawyer's reticence to talk about his own corner of the university. But the lack of gifts to legal education is probably the result of the bar's lack of awareness of the financial problems facing law schools.

The public is generally unaware of the relationship between legal education, legal research, and the social order. Medical schools have done a far better job of educating the general citizenry. If and when the public becomes aware of the importance of legal education and research to the basic functioning of society, sizable gifts may begin to come to the law schools in significant numbers.

Fifth: corporate giving   Business every day places its reputation and its success in the hands of lawyers. Business has to have well-trained lawyers. The corporate world draws heavily upon the legal profession to man its management. There is, we submit, just as strong an argument supporting corporate giving to legal education as presently exists for business schools. The business community cannot be unconcerned about the state of the society, and a healthy society is going to depend upon healthy legal institutions, which depend directly upon legal education. Here again the problem will be one of communication and informing the relevant parties of the actual situation.

Sixth: foundations   The nation's law schools stand in need of a substantial, privately funded foundation for legal education and research. A new foundation could be invaluable (1) in providing pilot funding for innovations in legal education; (2) in supporting deserving research projects; and (3) in serving as a clearing-house, intelligence-gathering unit and as a communications network for legal education. There are a few foundations, such as CLEPR, that have a very limited function. But no foundation exists to serve the general needs of legal education.

Seventh: federal support   Up to now, there has been *no* federal support for legal education. We believe that help is essential. It must be provided through mechanisms that ensure freedom from political intrusion, for law is intimately related to politics and political controversy. One form of support will be through the types of loan programs we shall describe shortly, particularly student loans, but at least three other important possible avenues exist.

(*a*) The Carnegie Commission of Higher Education (1968, 1970) has recommended a system of federal scholarships to students, linked with both a direct subsidy to the university the student attends and student access to a national loan program. This is essentially a GI Bill model. We strongly approve of these recommendations in relation to law students.

(*b*) Project support is the traditional form of federal assistance to higher education. Over the past decade much of higher education has been transformed by grants and contracts to specific professors for research in certain areas. The disadvantages of this type of aid are numerous: private fiefs may develop; an institution relying greatly on such funds may find it impossible to plan or control the direction of its own growth; the search for new knowledge on subjects that scholars deem important may be transformed into a search by scholars for subjects that bureaucrats deem important; a few prominent universities may gain most of the money because their salaries and prestige draw the researchers who have the grants or contracts. These dangers are real, but they can be met, and their reality should not blur the plain fact that legal education and legal research could profit greatly from an extension of project support to law schools. The National Science Foundation and the National Endowment for the Humanities have already evinced their willingness to help out. Unfortunately these institutions do not support the kind of projects that we visualize as being particularly appropriate for legal scholarship. Large-scale federal support for macrojustice projects may require a redefinition of existing support institutions.

(*c*) Block grants provide for lump sum payments directly to universities according to a specific formula. This arrangement avoids the dangers of project support. But block funding also has drawbacks: it is often unreliable, and it is more likely to help all schools a little bit rather than providing major opportunities for some. From the viewpoint of many law schools, however, this source could be extremely helpful.

The development of any of these seven constituencies of support would obviously be a significant gain for legal education. With the exception of federal scholarship support, however, it is unlikely that these constituencies will provide more than fringe support for much of the progress that must be made at most schools. They could support various areas of new research, help the growth of various special programs, and offer some support to tide over some law schools as they are. For the bulk of funds necessary to change the structure of legal education, however, these constituencies will probably remain inadequate even if developed. New structures for financing legal education must be devised at the same time that we are developing the new structure of that education itself. In our view, much of the new funding for legal education should come through new mechanisms for student borrowing and for institutional borrowing.

Student borrowing

Most graduate schools in areas other than law offer grants covering both tuition and living expenses. Law schools have never offered much to their students in the way of support.

Traditionally, law students have been expected to pay their own way, to be wealthy, to work, or to borrow. Tuition at private schools, however, is beginning to push toward $3,000 per year (and that does not include costs for living, books, and transportation). Recently the rock-bottom cost of a year at the good private law schools has been approximately $4,500. State schools are beginning to turn toward the imposition of tuition, and their students must now incur high living costs and costs of books. Given these expenses, no law student, at least at a private school, can possibly finance the expenses of his education out of his current earnings. Limiting access to law schools to those who can afford it (i.e., the wealthy) is a prospect that has come into justifiable disfavor. Student borrowing is the remaining option.

Legal education is an investment. On the average, that investment has a high return in the form of substantially heightened lifetime income. Loan programs now exist at some schools, but in most cases payment must begin within one year after study has ceased, and the loans must be paid off within five to ten years. This leaves little breathing room for the beginning of payments and can be quite a burden on the early years of a career. This problem is particularly serious for the increasing numbers of law students who have been forced to borrow for their undergraduate education as well as for law school and who graduate as lawyers with over $10,000 of debt. Such a debt load can drastically limit the career opportunities from which a graduate can choose. This situation will become more common as tuition increases and the student-aid resources of most universities decrease. In a time when we are trying to extend access to legal services to the lower and middle classes, and when it is often the very students we are discussing who are providing the impetus for that attempt, such a limitation on career choices is unfortunate. (Worse still, to the middle- and lower-class students involved, it often seems like little less than an insidious combination of forces pushing them toward service of specific interests—employment with the large, high-paying corporate law firms.)

Even given these problems, we are convinced that students' payments to their law schools for their professional education can and should be a greatly expanded source of revenue for those schools. That revenue can only come, however, out of the students' professional earnings after graduation. If the schools are to receive the funds for current educational purposes, those funds must be borrowed and repaid by the students over time. Even if federal scholarships along the lines we propose are established, law schools—and particularly the private ones—must establish rational arrangements for these students to finance a higher share of the higher costs of legal education out of their professional earnings.

An initial problem in creating new student loan programs is that many people are very reluctant to go into debt to finance their higher education. This reluctance, however, is being overcome as more students graduate from college with the experience of loans already behind them and as the financial crunch on the universities lowers their ability to provide grants to their students.

The much more complex issues in this area concern the choices among the infinite variety of different mechanisms that can be used in the loan programs. Three interrelated variables deserve mention, with recognition that the particular problems of each school require a substantial amount of hand tailoring. First, a loan program might be undertaken by an individual school acting alone, by a consortium of law schools acting together, by a consortium of professional schools within a single university or within a cluster of universities, by an entire university or group of universities, or by some even broader arrangement. Second, the working capital for the program might come from a single private entity, such as a bank or insurance company, from a consortium of such entities, from federal or even state sources, or from some combination of private and public funds—perhaps private borrowing with limited public guarantees. Third, the terms on which students might borrow could vary in several critical respects. All the variables in use for conventional loans are possible. Further, the contingency of future earnings might be taken into account in one or both of two ways. On the one hand, the *rate* of repayment might depend, at least in part, on a student's future earnings.[5] On the other, the actual *amount* of payment might vary with a student's future earnings.[6]

We do not propose any particular program for all law schools, or even for all private law schools. Indeed, we expect that some experimentation in program arrangements is probably desirable, though we recognize the advantages of leverage and risk-spreading that can be gained by pooling arrangements. In all events, detailed studies of possible arrangements are beyond the scope of this study. We are certain, however, that substantial student borrowing programs *must* be a major part of the future financing structure of legal education.

Institutional borrowing

Direct institutional borrowing, at least for private universities and law schools, also appears to us to be a promising, and presently neglected, avenue for funding. Although this path is perhaps most promising on a large scale, with the parent university doing the borrowing, we see no reason why established law schools should not also take advantage of the opportunities offered by borrowing. Borrowing at the pace-setting private universities has been a dirty word. This appears to be an unjustifiable position. Why, to take the simplest possible case, cannot University X or Law School X obtain from a bank or consortium of banks a line of credit? Just as the railroads do, the university could pledge some designated asset as collateral. So long as interest payments are kept up, there should be no difficulty in refinancing the principal of the loan. One would also suppose that the university or law school should be entitled to the prime rate of interest.

There is one important additional factor. Interest payments to the extent forgone would be deductible as charitable contribu-

---

[5] E.g., a student borrows $1,000 and must repay $1,000 plus fixed interest, but repayment will be deferred in any year in which his earnings are less than $10,000 or will be based on 0.4 percent of his earnings between $10,000 and $20,000 and 0.6 percent of his earnings above $20,000.

[6] E.g., a student borrows a given amount and repays with a certain percentage of his income (say 0.4 percent per thousand dollars of debt) over a fixed number of years (say 35). Over time those with high incomes pay much more than their debt plus interest, while those with low incomes pay less. From the aggregate of experiences the fund revolves.

tions by the lender, be it a bank, an insurance company, or any other institutional lender. Taking this factor into account, the interest cost to universities might be extremely low. Even if substantial interest payments are required, the opportunity costs of deferring expenditures are often even greater.

One can take the argument at least one more step. Why just borrow in the money market? Why not issue bonds and make them available to the public? To carry the argument still another step, might not legislatures be willing to extend the tax-exempt privilege to private institutions? The legal problems of such a step are multifarious. But is it pure utopianism to look forward to the day when private universities, according to their respective credit standing, might be able to take advantage of the privilege to issue tax-exempt bonds?

The most modest use of institutional borrowing would be as a mechanism to facilitate student borrowing. We recommend this as a first step for those universities and law schools that are interested in the idea of institutional borrowing.

CONCLUSION   Previous chapters have underscored the problems of legal education, the relationship between legal education and the provision of legal services, and the importance of those services to the health of our entire society. The future development of legal education will depend directly on the provision of substantial new funding. We have pointed out the almost total absence of existing sources. We have also outlined some of the needed and possible future sources. Ultimately, we see *borrowing,* backstopped by the federal government, as the prime source of funds. The development of the other constituencies and mechanisms that we have discussed is also essential.

8. The Length of Higher (Legal) Education: Some Interim Proposals

The constraints of the present require that we deal with the present rather than venture to predict the future shape of higher legal education. We therefore must assume that legal education will remain, for the present, postbaccalaureate. There does not seem to be any reason, however, why it has to take seven years for all students. Within the present structure, two modest changes are possible that can reduce the time spent in higher education by either one or two years:

(1) Reducing the minimum prebaccalaureate time to three years

(2) Reducing the minimum time spent in law school to two years

We think that both should become options for some students at some schools.

THREE YEARS OF COLLEGE At the present time, most students take four academic years for their baccalaureate degrees and three academic years for their law degrees. The current ABA standards do not require seven years. Both the ABA and the AALS permit a student to enroll in law school after three academic years in college. The overwhelming majority of students now in law schools take their baccalaureate degree before they begin law school. We have had some experience with undergraduates who come to law school after three years. Our experience leads us to believe that three years of college are enough for many students.

The credential of the B.A. appears to mean a good deal to students. It could be conferred at the end of the first year in law school, as has long been done under the "professional option" sequence at many universities. Alternatively, the minimum time-serving requirement for the baccalaureate degree can be reduced to three years. We are emboldened to consider this possibility because that conclusion has already been reached by the Carnegie Commission (1971).

The four-year baccalaureate persists partly because of the dogma of the major. The most common rationale is that the first two years are for "general education" and the second two years for "concentration." This pattern may suit students who know what careers they intend to pursue. Those students who intend to take advanced work in a field represented in the undergraduate curriculum ("academic" as opposed to "professional" fields) may fit this pattern. By majoring in a subject they get a kind of head start on their graduate work. Aside from this advantage for a minority of students, the rationale for a major is extraordinarily diffuse, as witness the trend toward interdisciplinary majors and "do-it-yourself" majors.

The law student, *par excellence,* requires a general education. Law faculties have rightly been most reluctant to prescribe the ingredients of that general education. *A fortiori,* they have been reluctant to prescribe a major. A basic ability to read, write, and speak the English language is, we think, the principal preparation that law students require. Francis Bacon was right about the qualities that attend these activities. We additionally recommend some study of economics (which is the social science most directly applicable to law), history (for its liberating perspective), and a "hard" science (for its example of how scientific knowledge is pursued). This list resembles the distribution requirements that typically attend the years of general education.

We recommend that law schools allow undergraduates to be admitted following three years of study. This means that the practice presently observed in some universities of permitting undergraduates from one's own university to enter after three years should be extended to all undergraduates. Our recommendation will require a change in the kind of publicity given by law schools to their admissions requirements.

TWO YEARS OF LAW SCHOOL The time for completing one's legal education has been firmly fixed at three years by the combined weight of the ABA and the AALS. In our opinion this absolute requirement for all students at all law schools is unfortunate and unjustified. Two years of law school would today be adequate for many students. No persuasive educational rationalization for the three-year period ever seems to have been given. One first encounters such a time period in the early apprenticeship requirements.[1] Under the pressure of Jacksonian democracy these long waiting periods disappeared, however. The period reappeared in 1878 when Harvard, under Langdell, was the first school to require three years of legal education for a degree. Langdell apparently never explained why he thought three years was proper. Finally, at the remarkably determinative ABA meeting of 1921 (the political preparations for and importance of which we described in Chapter 3), where the Harvard model was engraved as *the* structure for legal education, three years was given an official stamp of approval. The requirement was, over the years, adopted by the states. Langdell felt that law was a science with certain "fundamental principles" that had to be mastered. Presumably he and his followers believed that three years was the amount of time necessary to satisfactorily learn these principles. As law became more complex pressure started for a four-year curriculum. During the 1920s a number of schools considered the possibility, as they did shortly after the Second World War. Now, however, with the incredible growth of law in amount and complexity, few believe that the science and/or fundamental principles of law can be learned in three, four, or five years. The justification for Langdell's method has changed completely.

The original theory was that because a few basic principles underlay the whole law, students could thus be taught the whole body of important doctrine. As the schools had more experience of the time cost of the case method, and became more aware of the protean reach of modern law, the rationalization of the case method changed. . . . The claim now was that the case method best served to train men in a sound and efficient technique for bringing to bear on a problem of counseling or advocacy the principles and rules to be found in reported decisions. The case method provided not so much a map to point the road over rough ground, as a compass by which to take bearing, and an axe with which to hack through the underbrush (Hurst, 1950, p. 265).

Many results of this pattern, as we described in more detail in Chapter 3, have been unfortunate. Now that no attempt is actually

---

[1] For example, in a requirement that is curiously similar to the present one of four years of college and three years of law school, Maine, from 1821 to 1837, by act of the Legislature, required "seven years in the acquisition of scientific and legal attainments, of which at least three years with a counsellor-at-law" (Reed, 1921, p. 84).

made to teach the students very much of the doctrine of the subjects they study, they are taught over and over again in the variously named classes the same method to use in hacking "through the underbrush." They have usually learned the method after one or, at most, two years. Although never fully justified, and less so now than before, the three-year requirement, through the Harvard model, the ABA recommendations of 1921, and the state bar rules and laws that followed, is entrenched in contemporary legal education.

Our recommendation on this score is addressed to the organized legal profession. It is that the legal profession should take the steps necessary to reduce the present minimum requirement from three years to two. In what follows, we shall discuss the considerations that individual law faculties should take into account in deciding, assuming that this structural change is made, whether they should continue to offer a three-year degree or should offer a two-year degree or should offer an option of either. Our conclusion is that most law schools during the transitional period that attends the structural change should offer the option of either a three-year or a two-year degree. We believe that, if the structural change is made, most law schools will need a period to experiment with both options.

Legal education faces two choices today: either (*a*) diversify the three years so that the student acquires the rudiments of an understanding not merely of what has hitherto been understood as "the law" but of the interrelations of social knowledge with the law or (*b*) reduce the minimum time-serving requirement to two years with a resulting emphasis on doctrinal analysis. The first alternative is very alluring; the trouble is that no one has been able to say in any detail how such a curriculum relates to the practice of law. The second alternative may have the unfortunate consequence of making the curriculum more rigid than it is at present. If law faculties stick to the present conception of what the law student needs to learn, there is certainly some reason to fear that shortening the time will have this consequence. In the absence of any agreed-upon position about the content and the method of curricular change, there is certainly a good deal to be said for taking *for the present* the conservative position of retaining the three-year minimum and permitting a period of further experimentation about the curriculum. The fact that the Carrington Report did not take this position both moves us toward the two-year position and reinforces our doubts as to whether law schools are now in a position to make this structural change.

We believe that some of the elite schools are ready to press for this structural change. In them we see most clearly that the conditions for shortening the minimum time are present. In their first year they now teach very successfully what is currently the main component of legal education: the method and the rationality of the professional. It is also in these schools that the added elements of legal education come nearest to being present. If the elite schools are ready to make the change, cannot one assume that others will very rapidly make the necessary adjustments to permit them to comply? This "trickle down" theory of how education makes adjustments may well be justified by history (although we cannot really claim to have studied that issue). The elite schools are probably in the best position both to shorten their minimum time to two years and to benefit from having three years with which to experiment. It will be recalled that by *elite* we mean the top 25 law schools. Given that critical mass, we think that the case both for structural change and for no immediate structural change is strengthened.

A special ABA Committee of Accreditation recently proposed significant revisions in the minimum standards to qualify as an "accredited" law school.[2] ABA accreditation is currently accorded only to law schools that require three years of legal education for the first professional law degree. The new proposal, however, would allow a law school "to establish a course of study that will permit a

---

[2] A few words on the subject of accreditation may be helpful for some readers. Regulations for admission to the bar are completely controlled by each individual state, and the state legislature and Supreme Court (depending on the jurisdiction) set the state's rules. In most states, attendance for three years at a law school accredited by the ABA is a prerequisite for admission to the bar. The governing council of the ABA Section on Legal Education and Admissions to the Bar is charged with the power and responsibility, subject to approval by the ABA House of Delegates, to grant or withhold ABA accreditation to law schools. The standards applied by the council for accreditation were drawn up in 1921. Since then a substantial body of informal interpretations of these criteria has been developed by the council. The AALS also operates its own accreditation procedures, and some states look to the AALS in determining which law schools are "accredited." Finally, in a few states — California, for example — the state bar association, acting by authority delegated by the state Supreme Court or the state legislature, undertakes to accredit law schools within the state. In general, the accreditation standards applied in these three forms tend to approach a single norm, with the standards of the AALS being somewhat more stringent than those of the ABA.

full-time student to qualify for the first professional law degree by satisfactorily completing not less than 900 class hours during not less than sixty weeks of instruction extending over a period of not less than twenty months." Such a course of study would have to be specifically approved by the governing council of the Section on Legal Education and Admissions to the Bar of the ABA. It almost certainly will require some time — perhaps several years — before this proposal clears the necessary hurdles within the ABA and then the states themselves. Many, in and out of law schools, will no doubt raise troubling questions:

- Will law schools generally, or at least some of them, eliminate the liberal, cultural courses in favor of a rather rigid program?
- What will be the actual impact of the two-year option?
- Will all law schools immediately adopt the option?
- Will all the best students opt for the two-year degree? Or will some of those students stay on for specialized training in a third, or perhaps even a fourth, year? What about other students?
- To what extent will the two-year option increase the flow of new lawyers into the market? As we have already indicated,[3] the numbers of lawyers in this country will dramatically increase over the next decade without any change in the length of legal education. Will the two-year option make a problem of oversupply even more serious? Or does it rather point to a solution for the serious lack of legal services in many sectors of our society?
- Will many law schools, particularly the state-supported ones, feel compelled to increase the number of students admitted in their first- and second-year classes to offset those who decline the option of remaining for a third year? Or will the two-year option offer a real opportunity for law schools to move toward better third-year instruction with a better student-faculty ratio?

These are just some of the questions that a shift to a two-year professional degree will occasion. We do not pretend to have the answers to these questions. But we are convinced that the case has been made for the bar to reduce its three-year standard to a two-year standard. We do not say that all law schools should immediately adopt a two-year option, and we certainly do not suggest that the option should be available to all students. We are convinced that for many law students the marginal benefits of a

[3] See the discussion in Chapter 2.

third-year legal education are outweighed by the cost of that year. Even more important, we are convinced of the need for experimentation and diversity among law schools and the education that they provide. The introduction of a two-year option can lead to increased diversity (though it carries with it the danger of precisely the reverse).

If two years is better than three, some may say, why not eighteen months or even less? We do not pretend that two years is a perfect solution for all students. Rather, we believe that it is probably about the minimum in which students can be reasonably expected to obtain a fair understanding of both the working skills of a lawyer and the general contours of the substantive legal terrain. We would expect some schools to adopt comprehensive examinations or other mechanisms to determine qualification apart from successful completion of a specified number of courses. Other schools, we suspect, will continue to rely on the customary course unit requirements. In all events, we would expect the availability of the two-year option to trigger in most law schools a major review of their curriculum. This in itself is a strong argument for the option.

DIVERSITY Our willingness to advocate structural change is increased by our conviction that the unitary bar is crumbling. If the delivery of legal services comes at all close to resembling our forecast in Chapter 2, today's picture of what law schools are will also change. Although all will continue to provide a generalist's education, individual schools will have a number of options. For example, School A may become either its state's or its region's or the nation's center for training specialists in field X. School B need not supinely imitate School A. It may become a center for field Y, or it may decide that it will not offer any specialized training. School C may become a center for the advanced education of interdisciplinary scholars; it may become a kind of center for educating aspiring law teachers or scholars. Given sufficient differential resources, we would expect different schools to move along different tracks.

The possibility of permitting students to "stop out" (to use a phrase already popularized by the Carnegie Commission) can add a good deal of flexibility to the ways in which law schools educate. Specialist training will almost certainly have to be interjected into the individual student's career rather than be an element of preparation for his career. Part-time education should be possible for paraprofessionals who aspire to become generalist professionals or specialists. Changes to careers in scholarship and in teaching likewise may become possible by stopping out. Or a law student may simply decide to continue his education beyond the point required for the generalist and become a career scholar and teacher. We hope that degrees as marks of credentials will not proliferate. It would in our view be enough if law schools were to offer the degrees indicated below:

- J.M. (or M.A.)—for one year of law study, normally combined with study of a different discipline
- J.D.—the normal generalist's first law degree
- J.S.D.—an advanced degree (after the J.D.), for a substantial scholarly contribution

In this study of new directions in legal education, our major recommendation for the future can be summed up in one word: *diversity.* We are convinced that over the next generation our nation's law schools will increasingly diversify. This is as it should be. Legal education has, for too long, been in the grip of a single model. The process of remodeling is well under way— not by discarding the old patterns completely but rather by building on those patterns where new development is called for. We expect that some schools with limited financial resources will concentrate the expenditure of those resources in a few areas in order to maintain the highest standards of educational excellence in those areas. Other more well-endowed schools may continue their past practices of broad curricular coverage. But even these schools, we suspect, will try different approaches and different techniques in legal education. All this is to the good. As we have tried to show, for example, in our discussion of clinical education, at least until we have far more evidence than is now available, no single schema should be imposed on law schools and all students. Rather, a diversity of approaches can yield—over time—real evidence on which to make considered judgments.

Our support for the structural changes in degree programs that we have proposed are thus one dimension of our more general appeal for diversity. In our view, it will be a better allocation of resources with a better production of legal talent if some students attend law school for two years, some for three, and some for four or even more. Similarly, we would expect the development of different curricula at different schools and, we would hope, sufficient exchange between those schools for continuing insights into what works in what educational contexts.

In the end, of course, a law school's strength is not in the structure of its programs or even in the substance of its courses. Rather, a law school's strength is in the capacity of individuals on its faculty to shape their own careers and their own views of what legal education is all about. That capacity, when reinforced by mutual respect, ensures that a law faculty can make a contribution to the development of legal education. At all costs, that capacity should be protected.

Suggestions for Further Reading

We present here, arranged by chapter, a collection of generally available works that anyone interested in the subject of legal education ought to read.

1 **Hurst, James Willard:** *The Growth of American Law: The Lawmakers,* Little, Brown and Company, Boston, 1950.

2 **Johnstone, Quintin, and Dan Hopson:** *Lawyers and Their Work,* The Bobbs-Merrill Company, Inc., Indianapolis, 1967.

 Schwartz, Murray L.: "Changing Patterns of Legal Services," in Geoffrey C. Hazard, Jr. (ed.), *Law in a Changing America,* The American Assembly, Prentice-Hall, Inc., Englewood Cliffs, N.J., 1968.

 "Symposium on Legal Paraprofessionals," 24 *Vanderbilt Law Review* 6, 1971.

3 **Currie, Brainerd:** "The Materials of Law Study," printed as an appendix to the Carrington Report, which is reprinted as Appendix A to this study.

 Prelaw Handbook, The Official Guide to Law Schools, prepared and published by the Association of American Law Schools and the Law School Admission Test Council, 1971–72.

 Stolz, Preble: "Training for the Public Profession of the Law (1921): A Contemporary Review," printed as an appendix to the Carrington Report, which is reprinted as Appendix A to this study.

4 *Clinical Education and the Law School of the Future,* cosponsored by the University of Chicago Law School and the Council on Legal Education and Professional Responsibility (CLEPR), 1969.

5 Association of American Law Schools: "Training for the Public Professions of the Law: 1971," curriculum study project, reprinted as Appendix A to this study.

6 Currie, Brainerd: "The Place of Law in the Liberal Arts College," 5 *Journal of Legal Education* 428, 1953.

  Introductory essay by Bayless Manning and contributions by Harry Kalven, Jr., David F. Cavers, Abraham S. Goldstein, and Alex Elson in Geoffrey C. Hazard (ed.), *Law in a Changing America*, The American Assembly, Prentice-Hall, Inc., Englewood Cliffs, N.J., 1968.

  Levi, Edward H.: "The Political, the Professional, and the Prudent in Legal Education," 11 *Journal of Legal Education* 457, 1959.

  Woodard, Calvin: "The Limits of Legal Realism: An Historical Perspective," 54 *Virginia Law Review* 689, 1968, reprinted as Appendix B to this study.

7 Manning, Bayless: "Financial Anemia in Legal Education," *American Bar Association Journal,* December 1969.

References

American Assembly: *Report on Law and the Changing Society,* Center for Continuing Education, University of Chicago, March 14–17, 1968.

American Bar Foundation: *The Legal Profession in the United States,* rev. ed., Chicago, 1970.

Association of American Law Schools: "Training for the Public Professions of the Law: 1971," *Proceedings,* 1971 annual meeting, part one, sec. II, 1971.

Carnegie Commission on Higher Education: *Quality and Equality: New Levels of Federal Responsibility for Higher Education,* McGraw-Hill Book Company, New York, 1968.

Carnegie Commission on Higher Education: *Quality and Equality: New Levels of Federal Responsibility for Higher Education, Revised Recommendations,* McGraw-Hill Book Company, New York, 1970.

Carnegie Commission on Higher Education: *Less Time, More Options: Education Beyond the High School,* McGraw-Hill Book Company, New York, 1971.

Cheit, Earl F.: *The New Depression in Higher Education,* McGraw-Hill Book Company, New York, 1971.

Clinical Education and the Law School of the Future, University of Chicago Law School, 1969.

Conard, Alfred: "Macrojustice: A Systematic Approach to Conflict Resolution," 5 *Georgia Law Review* 415, 1971.

Currie, Brainerd: "The Place of Law in the Liberal Arts College," 5 *Journal of Legal Education* 428, 1953.

Currie, Brainerd: "The Materials of Law Study," in Association of American Law Schools, "Training for the Public Professions of the Law: 1971," *Proceedings,* 1971 annual meeting, part one, sec. II, 1971, pp. 184–239.

Fein, Rashi, and Gerald I. Weber: *Financing Medical Education: An Analysis of Alternative Policies and Mechanisms,* McGraw-Hill Book Company, New York, 1971.

Freund, Paul A.: *On Law and Justice,* The Belknap Press, Harvard University Press, Cambridge, Mass., 1968.

Hazard, Geoffrey C. (ed.): *Law in a Changing America,* The American Assembly, Prentice-Hall, Inc., Englewood Cliffs, N.J., 1968.

Hurst, James Willard: *The Growth of American Law: The Lawmakers,* Little, Brown and Company, Boston, 1950.

Hutchins, Robert M.: "The Autobiography of an Ex-Law Student," 1 *University of Chicago Law Review* 511, 518, 1934.

Johnstone, Quintin, and Dan Hopson: *Lawyers and Their Work,* The Bobbs-Merrill Company, Inc., Indianapolis, 1967.

Keeton, Robert E., and Jeffrey O'Connell: *Basic Protection for the Traffic Victim,* Little, Brown and Company, Boston, 1966.

Levi, Edward H.: "The Political, the Professional, and the Prudent in Legal Education," 11 *Journal of Legal Education* 457, 1959.

Llewellyn, Karl: in Association of American Law Schools, "Training for the Public Professions of the Law: 1971," *Proceedings,* 1971 annual meeting, part one, sec. II, 1971.

Main, Jeremy: "Only Radical Reform Can Save the Courts," *Fortune,* August 1970.

Manning, Bayless: "American Legal Education: Evolution and Mutation — Three Models," address delivered before the Western Assembly on Law and the Changing Society, San Diego, June 12, 1969*a*.

Manning, Bayless: "Financial Anemia in Legal Education," *American Bar Association Journal,* December 1969*b*.

Packer, Herbert: "Piling Higher and Deeper," *Change,* November–December 1970.

Pincus, William: "The Clinical Component in University Education," address delivered at Ohio State University, November 3, 1970.

Prelaw Handbook, The Official Guide to Law Schools, Association of American Law Schools and the Law School Admission Test Council, 1971–72.

Reed, A. Z.: "Training for the Public Profession of the Law (1921)," in Association of American Law Schools, "Training for the Public Professions of the Law: 1971," *Proceedings,* 1971 annual meeting, part one, sec. II, 1971.

Schwartz, Murray L.: "Changing Patterns of Legal Services," in Geoffrey C. Hazard, Jr. (ed.), *Law in a Changing America,* The American Assembly, Prentice-Hall, Inc., Englewood Cliffs, N.J., 1968.

Stevens, Robert: "The Crisis in American Legal Education," unpublished paper delivered at Queen's University, Belfast, June 1969.

Stolz, Preble: "Training for the Public Profession of the Law (1921): A Contemporary Review," in Association of American Law Schools, "Training for the Public Professions of the Law: 1971," *Proceedings,* 1971 annual meeting, part one, sec. II, 1971, pp. 142–183.

"Symposium on Legal Paraprofessionals," 24 *Vanderbilt Law Review* 6, 1971.

Warkov, Seymour: *Lawyers in the Making,* National Opinion Research Center, Aldine Publishing Company, Chicago, 1965.

Woodard, Calvin: "The Limits of Legal Realism: An Historical Perspective," 54 *Virginia Law Review* 689, 1968.

Appendix A:
The Carrington Report

EDITOR'S NOTE

American legal education, like most, is a mindless growth. It has evolved by accretion, sometimes spurred by a faith in the divinity of all education, sometimes diverted by professional vanity, sometimes retarded by the excessive admiration of students, but always the product of what teachers have learned from their students. This is the way that such institutions should grow; not from a single arrogant concept, but as a flourishing of many individual wisdoms.

Those who set their hands to the preparation of such a concept should beware of the experience of David Hoffman. He prepared a grand design for legal education at the University of Maryland in the early nineteenth century; his model embraced the total sum of human knowledge and proved to be beyond his own capacities to teach. Although admired by his distinguished contemporaries, including Joseph Story, he retired from the field, tattered if not broken.

This seems, however, to be a time to look up from what we are doing and examine our results. Such an examination requires a perspective that is longer than most of us can mount quickly from the trenches in which we work. One method of gaining such a perspective is comparison. The purpose of this Report is to provide a model which will be suited to that use. The Model presents many ideas that are different from those which now prevail. No one approves all that it contains, although each idea is advanced honestly, with the conviction that it is reasonably responsive to public need. It is expected that most readers will find much to resist; as the reasons for such resistance unfold, the longer view is brought into focus.

Or so it is hoped. The shrill responses to earlier drafts indicate that the Report will be painful to some readers. One can only hope that the pains are pains of growth. It is futile to apologize for discomfort so deliberately inflicted. But perhaps one can nevertheless be heard to say that we come in peace.

We would also observe that this report commemorates the work of Alfred Z. Reed, which was published in 1921 by the Carnegie Foundation for the Advancement of Teaching. At the risk of being pretentious, the title of our report is derived from his. His work is abridged and appended to our report. An additional appendix is a review of his work prepared by Preble Stolz which describes the reaction of his contemporaries to the Reed report. A third appendix is an abridgement of the very important work of Brainerd Currie on the *Materials of Law Study,* which supplements the historical material of the other two appendices in important respects.

Professor Stolz would note that his review of the Reed book is not complete. It was written several years ago and has been widely circulated in draft form. Because much of his intended audience has read it, his interest in polishing and documenting it has declined. It is published here in its present form at the insistence of his colleagues on the committee. Stolz comments: "One thing Reed learned about lawyers and legal educators in the 1920's was that they cared not at all about the history of legal education. I fear that this attitude of splendid indifference is as prevalent today as it was fifty years ago. To myself I justify foisting this incomplete manuscript on legal educators on the theory that its publication as an appendix is an acknowledgement by my fellow committee members of the relevance of history to current decisions about legal education. That may not seem like much, but Reed, I believe, would have regarded it as important progress." It is, indeed, the hope of the committee that the appendices will not only provide readers with a better perception of the contents of the report, but also with a heightened sense of our present place in time.

Paul D. Carrington
Ann Arbor, Michigan
September 7, 1971

NOTE: This report first appeared as "Training for the Public Professions of the Law: 1971," Part One, Section II, *Proceedings,* Association of American Law Schools, 1971 Annual Meeting.

CHAPTER 1

CONCLUSIONS AND SUMMARY

The Curriculum Study Project Committee concludes that:

1. Law schools should offer education that corresponds to the varied needs of the public for legal services and to the varied goals of a wider array of students.

2. Each member school should re-examine each component of its program, and the curriculum in its entirety, to determine whether the costs in human and financial resources are justified by the benefits attained in advancing educational goals.

3. Each member school should evaluate its program to determine how well it furthers the selected goals, which may encompass:

   (a) preparing individuals to advise clients, public or private, in general law practice;

   (b) preparing individuals who seek special competence in particular fields of practice;

   (c) preparing lawyers with capacity for interdisciplinary research;

   (d) equipping individuals for careers in the delivery of legal services as members of allied professions;

   (e) providing a grounding in law for students motivated by intellectual curiosity, whether they are unsure of their career goals, or plan to follow careers in other disciplines.

4. Schools should free themselves of received dogmas, such as the conception that all graduates must be trained to omnicompetence, or that the first degree in law can be awarded only after three years of law study within the walls of a law school. Law school programs should reflect functional needs and break free of offerings and approaches that have nothing but longevity to commend them.

5. In order to encourage re-examination and to foster diversity among member schools, the Executive Committee should re-evaluate the association's accreditation standards to determine how well they advance public interests.

For the limited purpose of illuminating these conclusions and stimulating the re-examination urged, the Committee here presents a Model Curriculum. It should be emphasized that the Model is not tendered as an "Ideal Curriculum", or as uniform legislation in draft form, designed for instant enactment without change by all schools or any school. Rather, it is a set of concrete examples of how this report's concepts might find expression in a program if an institution were interested in implementing them.

The details of the Model are roughed in for the limited purpose of illuminating the larger design; details should not distract the reader from its main themes. Moreover, the Model contains a number of features which are intended for separate consideration. Separate attention will be given to these in the final portion of this report, the "Rationale for the Model", a statement of the reasons which might prompt a reasonable faculty to adopt a program such as the Model describes.

The Model, being in form addressed to prospective students of a mythical school, contains an introductory summary of its main features. It can, however, be described even more briefly. The Standard Curriculum is its core. This is a program leading to the J.D. degree and can be completed by many students with two academic years of rigorous study. It is open to students who have achieved success in three years of higher education or its equivalent. It attempts to achieve economies by abandoning the doctrinal organization which presently dominates the traditional curriculum. In doing so, it focuses more direct attention on society and on other disciplines devoted to the study of society. It seeks to allocate teaching resources more deliberately, providing for a substantial segment of "Intensive Instruction" to assure deeper penetration of professional training. This segment might be used to give place to appropriate programs of clinical education.

The Standard Curriculum in some respects anticipates further training in the Advanced Curriculum. The latter is designed to serve the needs of professionals seeking an opportunity to develop more specialized skills and insights in the university setting, including those who aspire to careers in teaching or research. It also serves students desiring to meet resident-study requirements with maximum efficiency. The Advanced Curriculum is designed to foster non-continuous law training, by helping students introduce into their law study episodes of practice work, public service, or study in law-related disciplines.

The Open Curriculum is literally open to all students in the university or in other cooperating institutions who aspire to learn about law. It not only seeks to dispel myths laymen harbor about the legal process, but also to make a direct assault on the unitary tradition of the legal profession by offering professional degrees for allied professions. As the Rationale will indicate, the latter feature is presented with some diffidence.

The Model seeks to assure continual cost-benefit analysis of all programs by charging the full operating cost, as well as one can determine it, to each program and unit of instruction. In order to prevent such added charges from inhibiting students from opting for as full an educational development as desired, payment is deferred and can be charged against professional income. Funds available for subvention are then applied to support programs identified as worthy of being offered even though they cannot pay their own way. In this way, the Model avoids using public or private support as a general subsidy to upper middle class professionals.

In short, the Model seeks to orchestrate four themes which do not always harmonize. It seeks to make legal education more functional, more individualized, more diversified, and more accessible. None of these are new goals or values. The alternatives for responses to issues such as those addressed here have not materially increased since the time Plato wrote. But the responses that fit one time and place may be less suited to another. It depends on the times. These times call upon legal educators to re-examine the basics of their calling.

CHAPTER 2

A MODEL COURSE ANNOUNCEMENT
(TO PROSPECTIVE STUDENTS)

I. THE GOALS AND COSTS OF LAW STUDY

A. Introduction

There are many reasons for studying law. Law being an intensely rational discipline, students are encouraged to begin their study with an analysis of their personal reasons for the undertaking. Those who are not familiar with professional work in law are advised to consult lawyers, attend legal proceedings, and read some of the abundant literature on lawyering, including biography, fiction, history, and social science. Beginning law students would be unwise to fix their attention on too narrow a goal, but a sense of direction will make their study more effective and enjoyable. Such a sense of direction is necessary to make best use of the options presented by the school's instructional offerings.

The school's instruction is divided into three curricula, each designed to serve students entering the school at a different level of background and training. The Standard Curriculum serves the traditional need of students for training as professional lawyers; it assumes a substantial attainment in undergraduate study prior to admission. The Advanced Curriculum serves the needs of professionals for additional university training; these needs may pertain to specialized professional competence, to pursuit of careers in teaching or research, or to compliance with resident study requirements imposed by state law. It assumes the professional standing of the students. The Open Curriculum serves students who are motivated by intellectual curiosity about law, who wish to test or demonstrate their ability to attain professional levels of competence, or who seek training sufficient to enable them to enter the allied legal professions of advocacy and counselling. This Curriculum assumes only that level of academic attainment required of almost all university students.

Students considering any of these alternatives are urged to consider the real cost of their study, both in time and money. If the period of preparation is included, at least five full academic years of demanding work is required for the attainment of the status of a fully licensed lawyer. The attainment of the goal may well be postponed by a need to prolong some portions of the exposure, or by the effect of state licensing requirements. It may prove to be desirable to renew study after a brief period of professional work in order to pursue a special level of competence. Substantially briefer periods of time may be invested to advantage in the offerings of the Open Curriculum.

Tuition costs vary, according to the nature and intensity of the instruction. Although payment may be conveniently deferred, students are generally expected to bear the full cost of all professional training which might be expected to improve their earning capacity. Cost is calculated in rough terms which are based on the premise that the cost of maintaining a single professor, including salary, fringe benefits, secretarial and administrative services and supervision, and research services is $80,000 a year. Fees are designed to produce that measure of return; instruction which makes heavy use of faculty resources is charged at a proportionately higher rate than instruction which makes light use of faculty resources. The usual assumption is that these fees will be paid out of professional income as it is earned. A discount of 10% is allowed for cash payment; interest is charged at 6%. At the same time both public and private charitable subventions are available for limited purposes. These are applied to the benefit of all students to the extent that the physical facilities are provided and maintained at no expense to students. Remaining funds are applied to support instruction and research which cannot feasibly relate to economic activity but which can be justified on grounds of public interest, and to support particularly needy or talented students.

Career choices should not be controlled by these financial considerations, but an examination of them should assist students in illuminating their non-economic goals. It is appropriate to regard the time, energy, and foregone income of the student as an investment in himself and his own future. This is so even if he does not choose to exploit his own economic value fully, or even if he should choose to devote the whole of it to a non-economic cause. With such personal considerations in mind, the prospective student is invited to appraise the several goals of the various kinds of offerings.

B.   The Standard Curriculum

This curriculum is designed to assist students in the attainment of competence as professional generalists. There is no authoritative statement of the characteristics of a professional generalist and definition is made extraordinarily difficult by the vast range of services which are provided by lawyers in their professional work. Any virtue or talent may prove useful to a lawyer. Nevertheless, it can be said that the generalist lawyer is a specialist in social conflict, its avoidance and its resolution, by means of the application of official power. There is a body of general information with which he should be familiar. There are a number of skills which he should be able to employ. These, in turn, imply some habits, traits, or values which may be of special importance to such professionals. Students aspiring to competence as professional generalists would be wise to measure themselves against the faculty's conventional conception of the model generalist. In doing so, they may gain a better comprehension of their own needs as they approach and experience the curriculum, and they may gain some insight as to what to resist, if they should, perchance, find some of the characteristics personally undesirable. It is for the purpose of facilitating such a self-measurement and the setting of individual goals, and not for the purpose of fitting all students to a common mold, that the faculty offers the following tentative description of a model generalist.

The faculty believes that the generalist should be familiar with the basic historical concepts of private law, including the basic rules of tort, contract, property, agency, trust, quasi-contract, and equity. He should be familiar with general statutory provisions governing family relations, public welfare, labor relations, commercial transactions, bankruptcy, federal taxation, and business organizations. He should be familiar with the structure of the federal, state, and local governments and have a firm understanding of the role of courts and the dynamics of the constitutional system. He should understand the rudiments of administrative procedure. He should be familiar with the principles of criminal law, and with the processes and institutions of its enforcement.

More broadly, he should be keenly aware of the importance of the interaction between legal principles and the social environment in which they operate and the process by which they are enforced. He should be mindful of the possibilities and limitations of the scientific method as a source of illumination of legal problems. He should have some familiarity with law-related disciplines; thus, he should be able to read a balance sheet and to interpret social or economic data with intelligence.

In addition to such an understanding of law and its processes, he needs skill and discipline in the practical use of that understanding. The generalist should be adept at research needed to enlarge his knowledge when enlargement is required. Not only must he be competent in working with unfamiliar materials, he should be prepared, when necessary, to make some sound hasty judgments on instinct. This requires that his sense of the purposes and values expressed in the legal system be effectively engaged in the solution of all problems. The generalist, whether serving as advocate or planner, must be skillful with language. He should possess an ingrained awareness of the frailty of words. He should also be an effective listener. In short, he should be an effective teacher. He should also be skillful in avoiding conflict by finding creative solutions to problems; this means that he should be capable of mounting a larger-than-ordinary perspective on problems and disputes.

In addition to understanding and intellective skill, the effective generalist may require certain emotional or psychological traits which are associated with the skills described. As an advocate, he should be aggressive. But his aggression should be controlled. This is especially important in negotiation or planning for the avoidance of disputes. It is important to possess a sensitivity to the consequences of stress, not only on others with whom the professional may deal, but also on himself. It is useful to under- stand the psycho-dynamics of power, especially as they operate on one's self; thus, it is important to recognize the responsibility of power over others, without being infatuated by it. The model generalist should also feature the craftsman's sense of autonomy, which enables him to withstand criticism, to express unwelcome opinions, and to cope with conflicting claims to his loyalty. He should possess a larger-than-ordinary time perspective which enables him to sacrifice present benefits for larger future ones. He should share an interest in the general welfare; the cynical lawyer is an ugly menace, not only to others, but ultimately to himself. At the same time, he should not be so committed to his personal view of what constitutes the general welfare that he is unable to reckon with the differing views of others. Even in his commitment to rigorous rationality, he should not forget that some social problems may yield more readily to poetry than to the reasoned use of power.

Plainly, very few adults could be fit to such a cast in two years (or many), even if they were completely compliant and even if the faculty were tightly disciplined and coordinated to work single-mindedly toward that result, which the faculty decidedly is not. But the Standard Curriculum is planned and taught with such goals in mind. Students seeking the opportunity to develop such understanding, skills, and traits will find it and can exploit it in a manner that seems most suitable to their needs. On the other hand, students who are highly resistant to the model, who eschew many of the traits suggested, should feel encouraged to consider other professional alternatives.

The Curriculum pursues its objective with three different forms of instruction. The program of Basic Instruction is standardized and serves to introduce the student to the profession; it requires at least a year of full-time study for completion. Intensive Instruction is offered in the second year for the purpose of developing a high level of professional skill by means of deep immersion and close supervision in the performance of professional work. Intensive Instruction is supported by an equal measure of work in the program of Extensive Instruction which is intended to broaden the student's exposure with maximum efficiency. Both the Intensive and Extensive Instruction can be completed in a single academic year, so that it is possible to attain a professional J.D. degree with two years of law study. Some students, especially those who are disadvantaged in their efforts to assimilate professional inculturation, may be encouraged to spread the Intensive and Extensive Instruction over a somewhat longer period. Preparation for this professional training program requires at least three years of higher education or its equivalent, so that those who are just entering study must plan on at least five years of preparation and law study in order to attain full professional standing. State requirements may extend this period yet another year before the final recognition of a professional license is awarded.

In addition to the time commitment required, prospective students are asked to appraise the full cost of their study. While payment can be deferred, students are generally required to bear the full operating cost of the instructional program in this curriculum, subject only to modest subventions for especially needy or talented novitiates. The program of Basic Instruction is conducted with an effective teaching ratio of about 20 to 1, with allowance being made for supporting personnel used in team teaching. The real cost of the instruction is therefore $4000 per student; this is measured at the rate of $667 for each of six courses. The program of Intensive Instruction is conducted with an effective teaching ratio of 6 to 1. The real cost of the instruction is therefore $6667; this is measured at the rate of $2222 for each of three courses. The program of Extensive Instruction is conducted with an effective teaching ratio of 40 to 1. The real cost of the instruction is therefore $1000; this is measured at the rate of $50 for each unit of credit.

Thus, the total cost of instruction in law required to assure acceptable general competence in most students should be appraised at two years plus about $12,000 in tuition cost. Against this cost should be weighed not only the benefit of the prospect of general competence, but also the benefit which may be obtained from the opportunity for still higher levels of personal development. The latter may be pursued in the Advanced Curriculum.

C. The Advanced Curriculum

This curriculum is divided into three programs, each serving different needs. Resident Instruction is offered for students who are subject to additional requirements of resident study in order to qualify for a local bar examination or for admission to the bar. It seeks to meet such requirements with the most minimal demands on student time and energy consistent with providing a suitable educational experience. Thus, it provides maximum freedom for students to make individual determinations of the extent to which additional training is required. Those who wish to devote a substantial portion of their time and energy to the pursuit of financial rewards or to service to good causes are given the maximum opportunity to do so. The primary underlying assumption is that the student's J.D. degree records the fact that he has pursued general legal education to the point of diminishing returns and that further study should be required only on the responsibility of state licensing authorities, and not on the authority of the school.

Allowance is made for students who choose to do so to pursue resident study as an interlude between the Basic Instruction and the period of more demanding study which follows as part of the Standard Curriculum. Thus, a student may choose to perform service as an assistant in a law office while acquiring credit for resident study for a period between his years of work toward the J.D. degree. The cost of resident study is small, commensurate with the portion of faculty resources which this program employs. The fee is $100 per semester, exclusive of additional fees for Special Instruction which may be included.

Special Instruction is offered to assist qualified professionals in the development of specialized competence in particular fields of practice. Small groups of professionals are provided with an opportunity to make use of the resources of the University with confined guidance by the faculty supported by practicing professionals. A Special Certificate Examination is provided as a means of guidance to study.

An effort is made to accommodate the need for reflection in study to the need of practitioners to maintain contact with their professional clients. One business day a week is always free of academic commitments. All the courses are completed within a semester or less. Some preliminary work is done by correspondence. At the same time, it is recognized that such courses cannot compete with the one-day or week-end programs of organizations devoted to continuing legal education. These courses are intended to provide both rigor, and an opportunity to assimilate learning in a relatively tranquil environment. The charge for Special Instruction is commensurate with the portion of faculty resources which the program employs, usually a little more than one full time equivalent to each group. The usual fee for a full-semester course is $2000. The fee may be reduced if the program is shorter or if a subvention is deemed appropriate; it may be larger if unusual resources are required. Payment can be deferred. Inexpensive University accommodations are generally available.

Research Instruction is designed for students aspiring to careers in law teaching or research. Students will expect to serve in careers on law faculties, as teachers in secondary and undergraduate schools, or as research specialists in public or private offices. An increasing number of centers for social research have need of persons highly skilled in law and social science research.

Although the work of each student in Research Instruction is individually designed, there is some formal instruction offered primarily for students in this program. The program is primarily intended to be interdisciplinary in its orientation. Because this kind of self-development is not generally financially rewarding, there is a substantial subvention for the cost of instruction. While the cost is reckoned at $5000 per semester, the fee is $1000 with payment deferrable. In addition, students in this program are assured of some gainful employment as law teachers in the Standard and Open Curricula. Because of these circumstances and the heavy demand which this program places on faculty resources, the number of students to be admitted must be severely restricted.

D.   The Open Curriculum

This curriculum is divided into two programs serving quite different needs. The program in Collegiate Instruction, in turn, serves several functions. It is designed for those who have a general curiosity about law. The students to be served may be undergraduates at any level who are uncertain of their career goals or who have developed law-related interests which may be advanced by an improved understanding of law and the legal process. The program may serve a "headstart" function for students whose limited cultural and academic backgrounds place them at a disadvantage in professional law study. It may also serve to provide students whose academic credentials are otherwise inadequate with an opportunity to demonstrate their ability in law study. Students attaining a high grade for a substantial body of work in this program are assured of admission to the Standard Curriculum; some course work may be transferrable for credit to that curriculum.

In contrast, the program of Instruction for Allied Professions serves students with specific career goals. It is designed to assist students in attaining professional competence in the solution of a narrower range of legal problems than that with which the generalist lawyer may be expected to cope. Training to attain that objective need not be as long or as rigorous as that required of the generalist. Students who attain the objectives of the program may be awarded a professional degree at the Master's level. With or without the degree, they may expect to enter a newer legal profession allied to the traditional bar by the common purpose of providing quality legal services to the public. The School provides training in four such professions which provide services in the fields of Compensation, Family-Welfare, Labor, and Taxation Law.

Before entering on such a program of study, students should give mature attention to the nature of the role performed by such professionals. Those who tend to be sensitive about matters of status should be especially wary. They may well be dissatisfied with their relationship to more fully trained lawyers who may sometimes command a somewhat higher price for similar services, or attain a somewhat higher status in the eyes of the public served. On the other hand, those who are more concerned and who do not respond affirmatively to long and rigorous training, may find appropriate career opportunities through this program of instruction.

In order to minimize the risk that students choosing such careers may be later frustrated by their choice, the School makes every effort to remain open to those who belatedly aspire to more rigorous training. Those who excel in the Instruction for Allied Professions are encouraged to continue their study in the Standard Curriculum. Those who excel in the practice of their profession are invited to return to participate in Special Instruction with lawyers. In this way, it should be possible for most members of such professions to acquire the academic credentials necessary for membership in the bar. Nevertheless, young and able students are cautioned against a premature limitation on their aspirations which may result from a selection of this program when the Standard Curriculum is open as an alternative. Instruction for Allied Professions is regarded as especially suited to the needs of more mature students who are dissatisfied with their first career choice, or who have completed their years of service to young children, and who wish to make a quick, efficient shift into the legal professions.

Some of the instruction in this curriculum is conducted on the premises of other institutions which cooperate with the Law School in sponsoring it. While every member of the law faculty makes a regular contribution to the instructional program, much of the instruction is not conducted by the full-time law faculty. Some of it is conducted by law students working under the supervision of individual professors. Some of it is conducted by scholars in other fields. Some of it is conducted by practicing professionals, including not only lawyers, but members of the allied professions.

Such instruction is generally less expensive than that conducted in the Standard Curriculum, not only because of the lower cost of the personnel, but because a smaller portion of research services is properly assignable to such instruction. For these reasons, the cost of a full time equivalent faculty member in this Curriculum is calculated at $55,000. Inasmuch as most of the instruction is conducted at a teaching ratio of about 20 to 1, the usual cost for instruction is $100 per unit. For non-professional students the tuition charge is the same as that generally charged for undergraduate instruction. For those who are enrolled in courses of Instruction for Allied Professions, the tuition is $100 per unit. An exception is made for the practice courses in the professional instruction program; these are taught intensively, at a ratio nearer 5 to 1, and cost $400 per unit, or $2400 for a full 6-unit course. The total cost of instruction in law for the Master's degree is about $7500. As with other programs, payment can be deferred, and subventions are available on an individual basis.

Prospective students should note that the School does not attempt to provide a full range of programs for all allied professions, just as it makes no effort to serve all fields of advanced specialization. It is not possible for one faculty to encompass the full range. Prospective students with other interests should consider other schools. Students in the school who develop other interests will be assisted in the effort to transfer, just as this school welcomes transfer students who come belatedly to programs which they might have undertaken earlier. (Casual readers not interested in details may wisely skip to the last chapter beginning on page 127.)

II. THE STANDARD CURRICULUM

A. Admission and Graduation

Students will be selected for admission to the Curriculum from among applicants who have completed 100 units of higher education or the equivalent. Students may transfer to this Curriculum from the Open Curriculum if they have completed three years of higher education or the equivalent, and if they have attained a grade nearer A than B for 30 units of law study. Open Curriculum courses in which a grade of A is received may be transferred for credit in lieu of analogous Standard Curriculum courses.

A degree of M.A. in Law will be awarded to all students who complete 36 units of work, including at least 20 units in Basic Instruction and 6 in Intensive Instruction.

A J.D. degree will be awarded to all students who meet the following requirements:

(1) completion of 30 units of required work in Basic Instruction;

(2) completion of 18 units of work in Intensive Instruction;

(3) completion of 18 units of work in Extensive Instruction.

The three types of required work are described fully below.

B. Basic Instruction

Basic Instruction consists of six standard and required courses which are generally completed in a single academic year. Each carries a value of 5 units. They are:

LAW AND SOCIAL CONTROL (S). It is the function of this course to place law and the legal process in its broader setting.

Emphasis is placed on the need to develop and use the techniques of other disciplines in the solution of legal problems. The course is taught by a team which is highly qualified in other disciplines as well as law, and assisted by graduate students who are training both in law and in related fields. This year, the course will attend to the control of three kinds of anti-social behavior: violence against strangers, drug abuse, and racial discrimination in housing and public accommodations. These problems are used to exemplify the applicability, operation, and effect of the criminal law and of the alternative means of control through civil and administrative processes. Students are expected to gain an understanding of the different limits of effectiveness of different legal sanctions, of the relation between legal doctrine and underlying social values and data, and of the utility of the scientific method in illuminating such forms of anti-social behavior. They are also expected to gain a basic familiarity with the principles of criminal law and the process by which those principles are applied in professional work.

LEGAL ADVOCACY (S). It is the function of this course to introduce the professional role of lawyers. Emphasis is placed on the need to develop and use professional skills. The course is taught by a team which includes at least one professional litigator. The team is assisted by students in more advanced programs. This year, the course will attend to the role of the lawyer presenting and resisting accident claims. The role and responsibility of the professional litigator in jury trials is studied, including the solution of problems in choosing a forum, pleading, discovering evidence, selecting jurors, examining witnesses, drafting instructions, conducting appeals, and settling disputes. Moot arguments on motions and appeals, and an experience in negotiation are included as a part of the course. Human relations training is offered in the form of an opportunity to engage in shared introspection concerning student reactions to the several roles played. Students are expected to gain not only a sense of the advocate's role and its limitations, but also a familiarity with civil procedure and with torts doctrine pertaining to liability for negligence and liability without fault. Attention is also given to a comparison of the social utility of the adversary process and the alternative methods of claims management through private or social insurance which have evolved for the compensation of some losses otherwise subject to adversary litigation.

LEGAL DOCTRINE AND METHOD I (S). It is the function of this course to develop familiarity with legal doctrine and skill in doctrinal analysis. Emphasis is placed on traditional law school teaching methods and on the historical development of common law doctrine. This year, the course will examine the law of contracts. The provisions of the Uniform Commercial Code which governs contracts for the sale of goods are compared to common law doctrine operating on employment contracts and contracts for the sale of land. Different uses of contract remedies are compared as well as doctrines pertaining to the formation, interpretation, and assignment of contracts. Students are expected to master contracts law with a suitable comprehension of its economic, social, and political underpinning, as well as its practical application.

LEGAL DECISION-MAKING (S). This course examines the social, economic, and political relationships between legal institutions engaged in making and enforcing public decisions. It builds on experience obtained in the courses in Legal Advocacy and Law and Social Control. It is taught by a team which is highly qualified in social psychology, political science, and history, as well as law. The constitutional doctrine of separation of powers is subjected to careful analysis; the relation between the Supreme Court of the United States and other organs of the federal government are examined in detail. The fact-law distinction and the concept of minimal due process, which were examined earlier, are viewed in their constitutional setting. The problems of federalism are given substantial if not exhaustive, treatment. This year, special emphasis will be placed on voting rights and the right to freedom of expression as means of assuring open access to policy-making institutions. Systems analysis is presented as a tool in the making of rational decisions. Students are expected to gain a basic familiarity with the principles of constitutional and administrative law, with the social milieu from which those principles are derived, and with the role of legal professionals in their implementation.

LEGAL PLANNING (S). This course examines the role of legal professionals in planning to avoid legal difficulties. It builds on experience obtained in the courses in Legal Advocacy and Legal Doctrine and Method I. It is taught by a team which includes at least one practitioner engaged in legal planning. Devices and disciplines used by others engaged in different, but equally difficult tasks of problem-solving, are presented as alternatives. This year, the course will center on the problems of planning simple business ventures. Students are introduced to the basic concepts of agency, partnership, and corporations, as well as to the rudimentary principles embodied in the Internal Revenue Code. Business unit liability for accidents and for anti-social conduct will be considered. In addition to an improved understanding of professional work and an increased familiarity with legal doctrine, students are expected to gain a better understanding of the utility of accounting and economics in the comprehension and solution of legal problems.

LEGAL DOCTRINE AND METHOD II (S). This course continues to pursue the goals of its prerequisite. This year, it will examine the law of property. Property concepts are compared to concepts of contracts law. Emphasis is placed on the many ways in which real property can be transferred, shared, or divided, in order to serve different social and personal needs. An extended examination is made of the law governing the relation of landlord and tenant, including the concepts embodied in housing legislation, and of the law governing the liability of occupiers of land for accidents. A substantial segment will be devoted to the principles of property law which are best understood as means of controlling anti-social land use. The roles of courts and other organs of government in the formulation and enforcement of land use controls is considered, as well as the role of legal professionals in planning to avoid the lash of such controls. Thus, the course is intended to illustrate interrelationships between all the other courses of Basic Instruction.

C. Intensive Instruction

The function of this portion of the Curriculum is to assure the attainment of high professional standards by every student. More precise goals will be stated by the instructor in each course.

Each course is elective, and can be completed in a single semester. Each carries a value of 6 units, and requires work which can be competently performed by nearly all students in not more than 250 hours of effort. The work will be professional in nature and will be closely supervised.

Most of the courses are taught by regular faculty members; a professor assigned the task of supervising as many as 18 students is regarded as fully committed and most members of the faculty will supervise a smaller number of students in addition to their other teaching assignments. Students may be assigned to the supervision of adjunct faculty members, who may include practicing professionals or students in the Advanced Curriculum; no adjunct will be responsible for more than 6 students. Insofar as possible, students are permitted to select their task and their supervisor, but no more than one course can be taken with a single supervisor.

The precise nature of the tasks available and the mode of supervision will be left to the supervising instructor and the student. Students will ordinarily be expected to repeat their efforts with successive drafts in order to improve the quality of their product and achieve professional standards. They will often be asked to edit and evaluate the work of fellow students. On some occasions, the work may include seminar meetings in groups as small as 2 or as large as 18. If it is reasonably practicable and convenient, clinical material may be used as a basis for the supervised professional work. Likewise the supervised work may include a teaching assignment, probably in the Open Curriculum. Some of the work may lead to publication in the Law Review.

For the purpose of assuring a wide range of experience, these courses are divided into three groups: Advocacy, Planning, and Research. Subject to his particular needs and interests, each student is encouraged to select one of his three courses in each of these categories. Students are cautioned not to try to specialize in this portion of the curriculum; they will be precluded from enrolling in courses which are overlapping. Broad professional competence requires broad experience.

This year, intensive courses will be offered in the following fields:

BUSINESS COMPETITION ADVOCACY

CONSTITUTIONAL ADVOCACY

CONSUMER ADVOCACY (Clinical)

CRIMINAL ADVOCACY (Clinical)

ENVIRONMENTAL ADVOCACY

FAMILY-WELFARE ADVOCACY (Clinical)

FEDERAL TAX ADVOCACY

LABOR ARBITRATION ADVOCACY

PRISONER ADVOCACY (Clinical)

PROBATE ADVOCACY

SHAREHOLDER-MANAGEMENT ADVOCACY

ADMINISTRATIVE PLANNING: BROADCASTING
REGULATION

ADMINISTRATIVE PLANNING: PUBLIC HEALTH
REGULATION

COLLECTIVE BARGAIN PLANNING

COMMERCIAL TRANSACTION PLANNING

EMPLOYEE RETIREMENT PLANNING

ESTATE PLANNING

FEDERAL REVENUE PLANNING

LAND USE PLANNING

ORGANIZATIONAL PLANNING

PATENT LICENSE PLANNING

RESEARCH IN CLAIMS LAW (Teaching)

RESEARCH IN CRIMINAL PROCEDURE

RESEARCH IN ECONOMIC DEVELOPMENT LAW

RESEARCH IN FAMILY AND WELFARE LAW (Teaching)

RESEARCH IN LABOR LAW (Teaching)

RESEARCH IN LAW AND MINERAL DEVELOPMENT

RESEARCH IN LEGAL HISTORY

RESEARCH IN LEGAL PROCESS (Teaching)

RESEARCH IN TAXATION (Teaching)

RESEARCH ON INTERNATIONAL ORGANIZATIONS

RESEARCH ON THE LEGAL PROFESSION (Teaching)

D. Extensive Instruction

The function of this portion of the curriculum is to increase the
breadth of each student's exposure to legal doctrine. It is intended
to be as efficient as possible in its demands on student time and
teaching resources. Insofar as possible, students are urged to

develop their own capacities for self-instruction in managing the material.

Each course is elective and is based on an examination, a syllabus, and a formal presentation. The examination is offered at the end of each semester and is based on the syllabus, which is available in the library at the beginning of the same term. The syllabus will include a reference to a standard teaching work, and to a carefully selected list of additional materials, including portions of texts, articles, statutes, rules, or decisions, as well as to available recordings of lectures, programs of instruction, and self-teaching games. A formal presentation will be conducted by the faculty member preparing the examination, or by other professionals who may be designated by him.

A course may be assigned 1, 2, or 3 units of credit. The length of the examination, syllabus, and formal presentation, will be adjusted accordingly. This year, each student may select his 18 units from among the following courses:

ACCOUNTING (1 unit)

BUSINESS REGULATION (3 units)

CIVIL LAW (2 units)

COMMUNIST LAW (1 unit)

CONFLICT OF LAWS (2 units)

CORPORATIONS (S) (2 units)

EVIDENCE (2 units)

FAMILY AND WELFARE LAW (2 units)

FEDERAL JURISDICTION (2 units)

FEDERAL TAXATION (S) (3 units)

INTERNATIONAL LAW (2 units)

JURISPRUDENCE (2 units)

LABOR LAW (S) (2 units)

LEGAL HISTORY (2 units)

LOCAL GOVERNMENT LAW (S) (2 units)

RESTITUTION (2 units)

TRUSTS AND ESTATES (S) (2 units)

In making selections, students are again cautioned not to attempt to specialize or concentrate their instruction, but to relate these selections to the courses in Intensive Instruction with the goal of attaining maximum breadth.

III. THE ADVANCED CURRICULUM

A. Admission and Graduation

Students will generally be selected for admission to this curriculum from among applicants who have attained a J.D. or an M.J. degree, except that students who have completed a period of Basic Instruction in the Standard Curriculum may be admitted for Residence Instruction only. No qualified student will be denied admission for the purpose of receiving Residence Instruction. Among applicants for Special Instruction, preference will be given to those with pertinent professional experience. Research students will be very limited in number.

Certificates of resident study for one semester will be awarded to students completing 12 units of Residence Instruction. Certificates will also be awarded to those who perform ably on Special Certificate Examinations. The degree of D.A. in Law will be awarded to students who

(1) attain a Special Instruction Certificate;

(2) complete the program of Research Instruction;

(3) perform graduate level work in a law-related discipline sufficient to meet course requirements for a graduate degree;

(4) demonstrate distinction as a law teacher.

The degree of Ph.D. in Law will be awarded to students who meet the first three of these requirements, demonstrate distinction as legal scholars, and meet such additional requirements as may be imposed by the Graduate School.

B. Residence Instruction

Credit in this program may be obtained by completing additional work in Extensive Instruction in the Standard Curriculum, or for work in General Instruction in the Open Curriculum, but no double credit may be obtained. 12 credits will also be awarded for satisfactory performance on a Special Certificate Examination. Or, as many as 15 credits will be awarded for graduate-level work in a law-related discipline. Other credits may be obtained in the following courses:

BAR REVIEW (9 units). A course designed to prepare students for the local bar examination.

RESIDENT CLINICAL WORK (up to 12 units). This is a course of professional work performed under professional supervision. The work may coincide with regular employment opportunities. Supervisory plans can be arranged on an ad hoc basis with the Dean's office. The supervisor will generally be expected to provide some training in office and personnel management (including the use of lay assistants) and in professional responsibility.

RESIDENT TEACHING WORK (up to 12 units). This credit may be obtained by providing instructional services. In order to obtain the maximum credit, a student must undertake a substantial teaching assignment. All work is performed under the supervision of the regular faculty.

All work in this program is conducted on a pass-fail basis.

C. Special Instruction

Programs of special instruction are generally offered to groups of twenty-five professional students. Each course may be offered in any semester in which there is sufficient demand. New courses may be announced on short notice.

Each course is the product of a small faculty committee, which designs the examination and selects the syllabus with the help of practicing specialists. Some of the preliminary work may be assigned as correspondence work. The formal presentation involved in each course will generally engage the efforts of several practicing specialists selected by the faculty committee. The formal presentation will generally be supported by student-planned seminars. Each student will be expected to assist in the conduct of Intensive Instruction in the Standard Curriculum or in the Planning or Advocacy courses of the program in Basic Instruction. The period of study for each course will be one semester or less.

The programs currently available are:

BUSINESS REGULATION (A). This course examines the subjects of micro-economic theory, mergers and competition, international trade regulation, pricing and trade practices, utility regulation, and state and local regulation of business.

CIVIL LITIGATION (A). This course examines the subjects of anatomy, torts, civil procedure and evidence, safety engineering, damages, equitable remedies, and federal jurisdiction.

CRIMINAL LAW (A). This course examines the subjects of psychiatry, anatomy, police science, corrections, criminal evidence and procedure, as well as the substantive criminal law.

INTERNATIONAL TRADE (A). This course examines the subjects of international trade, monetary theory, private international law, taxation of international trade, international organizations, and civil law.

LOCAL GOVERNMENT LAW (A). This course examines state and local regulation of business, state and local taxation, utility regulation, political theory, public employment law, land use control, and equal protection law.

OIL AND GAS LAW (A). This course examines oil and gas taxation, mineral estates, petroleum engineering, and oil and gas regulation.

TAXATION (A). This course examines state and local taxation, taxation of international trade, corporate taxation, advanced accounting, revenue economics, and estate and gift taxation.

D. Research Instruction

Each student aspiring to develop and demonstrate distinction as a legal scholar is required to design his own program of self-development. He will be assigned to a special faculty committee which will provide advice and appraise his progress. As a part of his work, he will generally be expected to involve a few junior students in his project; three or four may be so assigned to receive credit for Intensive Instruction in the Standard Curriculum. Three units of instruction are designed primarily for research students:

> RESEARCH METHODOLOGY (4 units)
>
> LEGAL PHILOSOPHY (4 units)
>
> LEGAL EDUCATION AND THE LEGAL PROFESSION (4 units)

Each is taught as a student-planned and conducted seminar, although a faculty member is assigned to serve as chairman of each group.

IV. THE OPEN CURRICULUM

A. Admission and Graduation

This curriculum is open to any student who is admitted to the

University or to any of the neighboring institutions which have established a relationship of co-sponsorship with this Law School.

Work in this curriculum may be recognized in any of the following ways:

(1) Students receiving a B.A. degree in another field of study will be awarded a minor in Law if they present 18 units of work in this Curriculum, including the course in Legal Decision-Making (O).

(2) A B.A. degree with a major in Law will be awarded to students who complete 100 units of University work, including work generally required for such a degree, if they present 30 units of work in this Curriculum, including the courses in Legal Decision-Making (O) and Law and Social Control (O).

(3) A degree of M.J. in Compensation Law, Family Welfare Law, Labor Law, or Taxation Law, will be awarded to students who present 132 units of University credit, including 66 units of work in this Curriculum, and who pass the appropriate professional examination.

(4) A certificate will be awarded to students passing a professional examination, even if they are unable to meet degree requirements.

B. Collegiate Instruction

The program of collegiate instruction consists of four types of units of instruction:

(1) Legal Process Seminars

These are topical seminars. The topics selected will depend on the interests of the available instructors and the students. Each seminar will assume no previous background in law or higher education and will seek to introduce students to legal analysis and the legal approach to the solution of current social problems. Each will be completed within a single semester and will carry 3 units of credit. This year, the following seminars will be available:

CIVIL LIBERTIES. An examination of the history and politics of recurring issues, with emphasis on wiretapping and incursions on privacy; the concepts of procedural due process will provide a central theme.

CRIME AND PUNISHMENT. An introductory exploration of criminal justice in America and of the processes and institutions involved in its formulation and administration.

LAW WITHOUT COURTS. An anthropological and sociological study of conflict resolution outside of courts, including labor and commercial arbitration and marital counseling; a comparison is made to other social orders.

POLITICAL TRIALS. A study of the intersection of politics and justice, including an intensive examination of such trials as Sacco-Vanzetti, Eichmann, The Chicago 8, Daniel and Sinavsky.

THE JURY. An exploration of the civil and criminal jury in England and America; the study will be historical, comparative, empirical, and technical.

THE LAWYERS. A study of the history, sociology, and economics of the legal profession, with emphasis on the concept of professionalism as an ideal and a practice.

WOMEN AND THE LAW. An examination of the history and philosophy of the rights of women, including a technical study of proposals for change.

(2) Courses About Law

These courses are more formal, more structured, and more rigorous than the introductory seminars, but do not assume a prior knowledge of law and seek to initiate students to an awareness of the relation between the legal system and the larger society of which the students are a part. Each is a single-semester course and carries 5 units of credit:

COMPARISON OF LEGAL INSTITUTIONS. An anthropological and historical comparison of legal institutions in medieval England, 19th century America, primitive societies, and contemporary America, Europe, and the Soviet Union.

JUSTICE. An examination of the work of legal philosophers and philosophers of justice and of psychological work bearing on the issue of individual accountability; applications of this learning will be made to such problems as civil disobedience and international organizations.

LAW AND SOCIAL CONTROL (O). This course is an analogue to Law and Social Control (S), offered in the Standard Curriculum. It presents the same or similar material, but the presentation is somewhat less rigorous. The course is required for a B.A. degree with a major in Law.

LAW IN THE AMERICAN ECONOMY. A study of the historical and contemporary role of contract and property law in economic development, including a study of legislative efforts to regulate business enterprise and industrial relations.

LEGAL DECISION-MAKING (O). This course is an analogue to Legal Decision-Making (S), offered in the Standard Curriculum. It presents the same or similar material, but the presentation is somewhat less rigorous. The course is required for a major or a minor in Law.

(3) Service Courses

Each of these courses is co-sponsored by another unit of the University. None presumes prior training in law or any other discipline, but each is designed to serve the needs and interests of a particular group of students. Because the matters under study may be of general as well as particular interest, students outside the particular constituency are invited and encouraged to enroll. Each is a single-semester course and carries 3 units of credit:

CHURCH AND STATE. An examination of the law governing the management of private religious associations, private education, the First Amendment, and other matters of interest to clerics. The course is co-sponsored by the School of Divinity.

CONSUMER PROTECTION LAW. An examination of the obligation of sellers to provide satisfactory goods and of sellers to pay the price. The course is co-sponsored by the Department of Home Economics.

CORPORATIONS (O). An examination of the law governing private business enterprise. The course is co-sponsored by the School of Business.

FAMILY LAW. An examination of the law governing family relationships. The course is co-sponsored by the School of Social Work.

HOUSING LAW. An examination of the law governing the development and occupation of housing, including a study of the rights of landlords and tenants. The course is co-sponsored by the Center for Urban Studies.

LAW AND FREE EXPRESSION. An examination of the law of defamation and the constitutional rights of freedom of expression. The course is co-sponsored by the School of Journalism.

LOCAL GOVERNMENT LAW (O). An examination of the powers of local governments and the processes by which they are exercised. The course is co-sponsored by the Center for Urban Studies.

NATURAL RESOURCES LAW. An examination of a wide range of problems bearing on resource management. The course is co-sponsored by the School of Natural Resources.

PUBLIC HEALTH LAW. An examination of the law regulating the health professions, the powers of public health officers, and other topics including the problem of air pollution control. The course is co-sponsored by the School of Public Health.

PUBLIC SCHOOL LAW. An examination of the law of public school operations. The course is co-sponsored by the School of Education.

RACE RELATIONS LAW. An examination of the role of law and lawyers as instruments for changing or improving the status or condition of Afro-Americans. Emphasis is placed on fair employment laws. The course is co-sponsored by the Institute of Afro-American Studies.

SECURITIES REGULATION LAW. An examination of state and federal law bearing on the issuance of corporate securities. This course does presume some knowledge of Corporation Finance, but no specific prerequisite is imposed. The course is co-sponsored by the School of Business.

WELFARE LAW. An examination of the law governing the right to welfare benefits. The course is co-sponsored by the School of Social Work.

(4) Senior Projects

Students majoring in law as an undergraduate study are invited to undertake theoretical or empirical studies on an independent basis. Arrangements for supervision can be made with the Director of Collegiate Instruction. As much as 6 units of credit may be obtained by this means. The Director maintains a list of opportunities to observe and participate in the work of courts, law offices, and other legal institutions which may serve as the basis for such individual projects. Such projects may be joint undertakings of several students and may be planned to relate to subsequent political action or journalism.

C. Instruction for Allied Professions

All instruction offered in this program pertains to particular professional goals which are defined by comprehensive examinations. Four allied professions are served by this Law School: Compensation Advocacy, Family-Welfare Advocacy, Labor Counselling, and Taxation Counselling. The comprehensive examination given in each field is designed by members of the law faculty in consultation with practitioners. Each is based on a series of courses of professional instruction, all of which must be completed before the examination may be taken, as follows:

(1) Compensation Advocacy

LAW IN THE AMERICAN ECONOMY (5 units). See Courses About Law, supra.

LEGAL ADVOCACY (O) (5 units). This course is an analogue to Legal Advocacy (S) offered in the Standard Curriculum. It presents the same or similar material, but the presentation is somewhat less rigorous.

LEGAL DECISION-MAKING (O) (5 units). See Courses About Law, supra.

LEGAL DOCTRINE AND METHOD IA (O) (5 units). A systematic examination of the law of torts and the alternative methods of compensating for industrial and automobile accidents, with emphasis on the development of analytical skills.

ADVANCED COMPENSATION LAW (4 units). An examination of the law governing the measurement and proof of damages for physical harm, including a study of the human anatomy and the role of the medical expert. Legal Doctrine and Method IA (O) is a prerequisite.

COMPENSATION PRACTICE (6 units). This is a practical course using clinical or simulated clinical material. It is taught intensively and is an analogue to the courses of Intensive Instruction in the Standard Curriculum.

(2) Family-Welfare Advocacy

LAW AND SOCIAL CONTROL (O) (5 units). See Courses About Law, supra.

LEGAL ADVOCACY (O) (5 units). See Compensation Advocacy, supra.

LEGAL DECISION-MAKING (O) (5 units). See Courses About Law, supra.

CONSUMER PROTECTION LAW (3 units). See Service Courses, supra.

HOUSING LAW (3 units). See Service Courses, supra.

PUBLIC SCHOOL LAW (3 units). See Service Courses, supra.

FAMILY LAW (3 units). See Service Courses, supra.

WELFARE LAW (3 units). See Service Courses, supra.

FAMILY-WELFARE PRACTICE (6 units). This is a clinical course. It is taught intensively and is an analogue to the course in Intensive Instruction in the Standard Curriculum.

(3) Labor Counselling

LAW IN THE AMERICAN ECONOMY (5 units). See Courses About Law, supra.

LEGAL ADVOCACY (5 units). See Compensation Advocacy, supra.

LEGAL DECISION-MAKING (O) (5 units). See Courses About Law, supra.

LEGAL DOCTRINE AND METHOD IB (O) (5 units). A systematic examination of the law governing the collective bargaining relationship with emphasis on the development of analytic skills.

ADVANCED LABOR LAW (4 units). An examination of the processes of public regulation of the bargaining process, with special attention to the rights of members of labor organizations and to the public's right to continuing public services.

LABOR PRACTICE (6 units). This is a practical course using clinical or simulated clinical material. It is taught intensively and is an analogue to the courses of Intensive Instruction in the Standard Curriculum.

(4) Taxation Counselling

LAW IN THE AMERICAN ECONOMY (5 units). See Courses About Law, supra.

LEGAL ADVOCACY (O) (5 units). See Compensation Advocacy, supra.

LEGAL DECISION-MAKING (O) (5 units).   See Courses About Law, supra.

CORPORATIONS (O).   See Service Courses, supra.

TAXATION I (O) (3 units).   An examination of the provisions of the Internal Revenue Code bearing on the liability of individual taxpayers.

TAXATION II (O) (3 units).   An examination of the provisions of the Internal Revenue Code bearing on the liability of business taxpayers.

TAXATION III (O) (3 units).   An examination of the provisions of the Internal Revenue Code bearing on the taxation of gifts and estates.

TRUSTS AND ESTATES (O) (3 units).   A study of the law and process governing the transmission of wealth.

TAX PRACTICE (6 units).   This is a practical course using clinical or simulated clinical material. It is taught intensively and is an analogue to the courses of Intensive Instruction offered in the Standard Curriculum.

CHAPTER 3

A RATIONALE

A faculty explaining its attraction to the Model just described might begin from the premise that a university law school should serve as a conduit between the worlds of affairs and inquiry. Through this conduit pass both ideas and people. It is a means by which the university can share its values and traditions, such as humanism and rationality, with the institutions of public decision-making. In return, the university can receive a better purchase on reality and a better sense of the limits of its insights. The law school can serve its public both by means of a penetrating academic inquiry into law and legal institutions and by helping professionals to develop the skill to apply the insights obtained in the delivery of legal services. The Model subscribes to the hope of Karl Llewellyn that, "if there be one school in a university of which it should be said that there men learn to give practical reality, practical effectiveness, to vision and to ideals, that school is the school of law."

At the same time, the Model recognizes that there is conflict in dual obligations, such as those of the law school to the worlds of inquiry and affairs. Thus, it recognizes that some kinds of training that might benefit the consumers of legal services are not well-suited to the university environment. In particular, this is true of training to perform highly standardized tasks useful in the mass-production of legal services. Effective performance of such work generally requires that the spirit of intellectual inquiry be anaesthetized. There are better means of providing such training, if it is needed, than by appending it to the university.

In the same vein, the Model also recognizes that the university law school has a special obligation derived from its unsought position astride the gates of entry to professional careers. If, in its desire to attain academic excellence, it imposes academic requirements which are not functionally justified, it inflates the cost of legal services and inhibits social mobility. Indeed, such non-functional academic requirements can be said to violate the spirit of the national policy now expressed in Title VII of the Civil Rights Act of 1964. This undesired restrictive effect occurs even if the financial cost of the non-functional requirements are borne by public funds not otherwise available, because limitations on such funds tend to discourage enlargement of the numbers participating in the public benefit. Thus, the costly, elite medical education of recent decades has had an unwelcome effect on the cost of medical services. Meanwhile, it has made no measurable contribution to the health of the burdened public. It is an excellent example of what legal education should not permit itself to become. Moreover, the need for economy and self-restraint is especially important in law, for the reason that restrictions on access tend to cause public institutions to become less sensitive to the values and concerns of those segments of the public which are less represented among the academic elite. Accordingly, the Model seeks to pursue academic and professional excellence, but not heedlessly of social, economic, and political costs.

Despite these points of tension, the law school's two relationships are importantly dependent on one another. It is possible to conduct education for lawyers which has almost no point of contact with practical affairs; such education is exemplified in many civil law systems. But such arid educational enterprise may well have even less value to the mission of inquiry than it has to the improved conduct of affairs. It is equally possible to conduct education for lawyers which has almost no point of contact with any intellectual inquiry; in some respects, such education is now exemplified in the English apprenticeships. But this kind of educational enterprise may be quite destructive of the capacity of the legal system to respond to the broader needs of the society it serves and of the profession to maintain a suitable understanding and appreciation of its role. Thus, for too long, legal education in this country aspired to a pose of splendid isolation which was thought to exalt the law as a superior discipline. That isolationism has now gone the way of America First, as Legal Realism has triumphed over doctrinal purity. What remains of law as an independent discipline is in a state of intellectual crisis; the doctrinal axioms which sustained the image of sovereignty have lost their vitality, like so many sunken battleships, leaving many of the assumptions of legal professionals all but defenseless. The Model seeks to pursue a broader, more stable intellectual framework to sustain the craft of law.

I. TRAINING TO GENERAL COMPETENCE

A. Articulation of Goals

An obstacle to the pursuit of goals by legal education has been the failure to identify them. The Model seeks to be articulate in explaining what it is about; this is for the benefit of faculty and students alike. This is done initially with the description of the model professional generalist. That description is perhaps painful reading for some. While most law teachers would assert that they are teaching much beside legal doctrine, few are eager to say precisely what. Some have been content to describe their work as teaching students "to think like lawyers", although that phrase is so circular that it is essentially meaningless. Perhaps the reluctance to be more specific is borne in part by a distaste for platitudes. Or perhaps it reflects the instinct of lawyers (shared by others who are experienced in human conflict) that it is more difficult to secure approval of goals than means. This reluctance should be overcome, partly to try to help students get a better sense of direction, but also in order to direct attention to the "hidden curriculum" which serves to transmit professional traits and values by the process of subliminal inculturation. In publicly exploring the limits of its own understanding of what a lawyer is and how he thinks, the Model brings some of the issues of the hidden curriculum into the open, and facilitates the effort of law teachers to cope with the issues of professionalism.

Perhaps more important is the Model's proposed redefinition of the courses of Basic Instruction to reflect the goals stated in the description of the model professional. The traditional titles of first year courses are seen to be obstacles to an understanding of the educational process. The doctrinal organization reinforces the usual expectation of students that their job is to master doctrine. The non-doctrinal organization permits the teacher to place the objectives of professionalization and inter-disciplinary insight in a position of prominence. The Model would liberate the teacher from the domination of the doctrinal text-writer and assure the students that work devoted to the development of professional skills and broader insights is not tangential to their law study. The Model recognizes the importance of initiating novice students to more practical and broader views of law before they become too entrenched in a narrow view of the appropriate limits of law study. This achievement is attained at the cost of eliminating the familiar first year course titles from the curriculum. This radicalism may seem threatening to many, but most law teachers would, on close examination, find their current efforts moderately close to those described in one of the courses set forth in the program of Basic Instruction. It should be emphasized that the program contemplates substantial flexibility in the designation of the legal topics used as vehicles for the pursuit of the several stated goals. It would be quite consistent with the concept of the program to substitute a course centered on the economic underpinnings of contract and property law for the offering centered on the social psychology of criminal law. The doctrinal offering could as well be torts; the advocacy course could as well be centered on consumer protection or property disputes. The most troublesome feature of this change would arise from its dependence on the coordination of the efforts of first year teachers; the total independence of teachers from their colleagues would be somewhat impaired.

B. Staffing Patterns

In articulating different goals for different units of instruction, the Model permits a more coherent use of available teaching manpower. It seeks to provide different levels of manpower to different teaching assignments which have quite different staffing needs because of differences in method. Law schools have long made some distinctions of this kind in seminar programs, but the Model enlarges on the theme by making a massive commitment of teaching manpower to the program in Intensive Instruction which is the core of the second year. A major fraction of the faculty resource is devoted to about one quarter of the student's program. This is accomplished *without any increase in the total manpower used to train generalist lawyers,* partly by reducing the number of units of instruction, and partly by reducing the commitment of resources to the other half of the second year. The latter program is identified as Extensive Instruction because it serves to extend the teaching resources as far as possible consistent with the educational goals assigned to it.

In addition to the alteration of teaching ratios, the Model would alter staffing patterns by making much heavier use of adjunct faculty, particularly in the Basic Instruction, which uses both practitioners and social scientists in team teaching relations. The assumption is made that such teaching relationships will help to break down the insularity of academic law, providing more contact with both worlds of affairs and inquiry. Few who select themselves as academic lawyers are motivated by an intense interest in the practical arts; if students are to be taught to apply their intellects to a wider range of professional tasks, it is likely to require the participation of those who have not chosen to leave the practice. Similarly, few law professors are competent scientists. Until the scientific method penetrates much more deeply into academic law, the scientific perspective will have to be supplied in part by outsiders. The Model would provide for increased use of joint appointments, at least until the Advanced Instruction in inter-disciplinary study became more widely accepted as the entry into the academic legal profession. There is, however, a price to team teaching which should not be overlooked: increased use of this technique, like the change in the first year, will impair the autonomy now enjoyed by the law professor.

C. Teaching Methods

The Model does not contemplate fundamental change in the mode of presentation for the bulk of the Basic Instruction. A third of the program is devoted primarily to traditional case analysis, and such analysis would be expected to play a large role in the balance of the program. Some methodological changes are suggested. Presumably, the team teaching practitioners and social scientists would be prone to adopt teaching methods more suitable to their special roles. For example, an introduction to systems analysis as a useful tool in understanding processes is not likely to be efficiently achieved through the use of the case method. Yet, it is assumed, an introduction to the systems analysis approach and perspective will be an aid to understanding the utility of the traditional lawyer's approach.

Other modifications of teaching methods are motivated by the Model's desire to broaden the novitiate's understanding of the profession. It seeks to introduce him to a variety of professional skills and to provide him with an opportunity to reflect on his own role in the development and exercise of those skills. Thus, the Model seeks to enlarge student perspectives by including a minor segment of "human relations training" in the program. Such training, conventionally based on "T-Group Theory," or the Laboratory Method, generally features experiences in shared introspection under the supervision of trained teachers. The goal of the teacher or leader is to assist members of the group in gaining a better sense of self and inter-personal relations. Claims for the benefits to be obtained by such instruction seem extravagant; it seems hardly likely that deep-seated traits can be fundamentally changed by such methods. On the other hand, use of such methods in moderation can offer a sharp contrast to traditional law school teaching and assist students in understanding the process by which they are socialized with professional traits, values, and insights.

The same goal is also served by the inclusion of instruction in other techniques of problem-solving. Again, the claims made on behalf of those who purport to teach "thinking" or "creativity" seem extravagant. But it is not unjust to suggest that lawyers whose training is limited to traditional case analysis and criticism may tend to be too quick to reject novelty. A very brief exposure to the loosely scientific literature and teaching which aims to develop the discipline of improving bad ideas is likely to provide some advantage to most students. Even if they are not made "more creative" in solving problems, they may gain a better sense of their limitations.

Just as Basic Instruction would depend largely on traditional methods, the program of Extensive Instruction would likewise mark only slight change. Its assumed goal of efficiency in transmitting familiarity with doctrine does imply a relatively limited role for the student with respect to the formal presentation; but this would be little different from the existing practice in third year classes. Probably the most serious consequence would be the need to edit current presentations to make them more compact.

The Model is tempted to rely more heavily than it does in the program of Extensive Instruction on the techniques of programmed instruction and computer-assisted instruction. It would be theoretically possible for much of the material to be transmitted more efficiently by such methods. Unfortunately, a heavy investment of great skill is required to develop such material, and there seems to be no effective way to provide appropriate incentives to get the job done. For this reason, Extensive Instruction is not expected to take a very different form from traditional upper class instruction.

But the program of Intensive Instruction contemplates a significant change in teaching method. The purpose of the heavy allocation of resources is to permit much closer supervision of student work than is now customary even in seminar instruction. Lectures and group discussions would be largely displaced in this segment of the curriculum by critical evaluation of written work, or other professional exercises. It is assumed that such supervision is essential to the planned development of high professional standards of craftsmanship in the exercise of a variety of professional skills. The goal would be to provide an experience for all students comparable to that customarily provided only to those who write for publication in the law review, or who become employed by the most prestigious law firms.

One must doubt whether the Model can achieve this goal, because of limitations which may be inherent in law teachers. Most would surely be quite capable of performing the intended function for some period of time; most have performed it in school. But few have exhibited a taste for this kind of work and experience tends to indicate that many individuals are unable to sustain enthusiasm for it over an extended number of years. It is at least possible that a tolerance for it is inversely related to the skills and traits of the virtuoso scholar, teacher, or lawyer. Perhaps this obstacle can be overcome if the assignments of students can relate to matters of immediate interest and concern to the faculty. This would frustrate the desires of some students, but would assure a better prospect for adequate feedback. The problem can also be helped by making good use of advanced students and adjunct faculty in this teaching role. If the number of individuals which the permanent faculty must supervise can be kept small by making this kind of teaching only a small part of their teaching load, it might achieve its goal. Otherwise, the benefits to be derived from the inadequate faculty feedback to the students would be too small to merit the cost.

Intensive Instruction could be used as a vehicle for developing a program of peer group instruction. With a high level of supervision, many law students could be put to good use in tutoring students in Basic Instruction, or in making more formal presentations in the Open Curriculum. This innovation would be intended to help the novice students by providing intensive teaching at less cost; but it would be primarily intended to help develop the capacities of the teaching students. All professional students should be encouraged to think of themselves as teachers; the law reviews have long provided this service for the intellectual elite. Guidance must be provided to prevent misinstruction, but young professionals who will soon be instructing their clients should have the opportunity to test their capacities in the less hazardous work of assisting their less experienced colleagues.

Intensive Instruction can also facilitate the use of teaching clinics. Without such a high level of supervision, the clinical experience can be counter-productive as a means of inculcating professional standards of craftsmanship. With such supervision, there can be no doubt that clinical experience can be effectively used in teaching. It is motivational for some students. It may help many to grasp more effectively the relation between thought and action, between intellectual discipline and practical affairs. It may be particularly helpful as a basis for shared introspection and other instruction designed to provide deeper understanding of the professional role and responsibility.

On the other hand, clinical education (narrowly defined as simultaneous service to clients as a part of academic training) is not assigned a major role in the Model for the reason that it cannot withstand a cost-benefit analysis as a dominant method of instruction. The problem or simulated clinical method is far more efficient as a means of transmitting most of the skills which are suitable objects of study. There is no legal clinic which compares to a hospital in the variety of experiences it can provide; such variety can be provided by simulation. Clinical work necessarily features much legal mechanics; simulation avoids the deadening routine of the standardized task. Liberated from the needs of clients, simulated clinical experiences can more easily fit academic schedules and calendars. A clinical method which introduces real clients into the teaching activity distracts both teacher and student from one another and from the learning process to the pressing needs of clients.

Perhaps some students may become more sensitive to difficult social problems by reason of work in such clinics. But it would be hard to find a correlation between such experience and concern for social justice; if the present bar is insensitive, it is not because its members are not exposed to reality. Moreover, mere exposure to social problems can be acquired by far less expensive means than teaching clinics. There is also the risk that the teaching clinic designed for these purposes can be used by students as an escape from the intellectual rigors of sound professional training if such clinics are assigned a dominant place in the curriculum.

Yet another difficulty with a larger commitment to the use of teaching clinics is the staffing problem created. The clients of the clinic need attention even when the students are unavailable. The remaining burden must fall on the faculty supervisors. As a result, the problem of recruiting and retaining faculty staff for Intensive Instruction is compounded. The teacher willing and able to give both effective personal supervision to students and effective service to clients is difficult enough to find; it is perhaps too much to expect such persons also devoted to intellectual inquiry.

The disadvantaged clients who are served by the teaching clinics might be seen to benefit substantially by a greater abundance of services. But this benefit is subject to a substantial discount because the working professionals are distracted from client service by the competing claims of the students.

Despite these limitations, it should be emphasized that the Model is not antagonistic to the clinical method; its one insistence would be on candor in disclosing the costs and benefits; if the informed consumer is willing to pay the cost, the Model would pose no obstacle to larger use of the clinical method.

D. Teacher-Student Relations

It deserves separate note that the foregoing changes from traditional law school training would bring a significant change in the relationship between law teachers and students. In this respect, the Model makes a conscious effort to alter the "hidden curriculum". The change would be expected to result from the fact that the teacher would become less an authority and more a resource, while the student would become more a captain of his own fate. To some extent, this would result from team teaching. To some extent, it would result from the articulation of goals. In part, it would result from the increased use of students as teachers, and the inclusion of teaching methods such as shared introspection, which depend on student initiative. In part, it would result from the proposed structure of the courses in Extensive Instruction, which emphasizes student self-management. Finally, it would result in part from the overall structure of the Model, which invites the student to choose among fundamentally different roles in the delivery of legal services. All of these features together suggest a different role for the law student than is now customary. He would, in short, be cast in a professional role from the beginning, bearing at all times a share of the responsibility for the quality of his own learning.

The Model might expect these features to have twin consequences. It might expect to produce students who are both more self-reliant and less authoritarian. One need not accept some of the more acerbic comments on the alleged tyranny of law professors in order to recognize the possibility that the traditional relation between law students and teachers is one which has tended to reinforce such aggressive, authoritarian, and dependent traits as may be present in those choosing careers in law. Law teachers have themselves long decried the passive and doctrinaire qualities of many second and third year students. In response to that concern, the Model seeks to depend more on student initiative and creativity in learning and to make the faculty more accountable by easing the way for students who depart from the structure of the teaching presented. This kind of accountability may be especially desirable for a faculty which professes the rational accountability of judges and other officials, as all law teachers must. It has long been somewhat paradoxical that law teachers have proclaimed democratic values from autocratic roles.

Of course, the features of the Model do not guarantee the result that faculty or students will be either more self-reliant or more humane. But, over time, in many hands, it is reasonable to hope that such a program would have some such effects.

E. A First Year Degree

The Model proposes to award an M.A. degree to all students who complete a full year of study and complete a single course of Intensive Instruction. This degree is intended to serve two purposes.

First, it invites very competent students in other disciplines to invest a single year in the Standard Curriculum as a means of establishing their interdisciplinary competence. Such students might be expected to add a dimension to the law school student body while serving their own goals.

In addition, the first year degree serves to encourage students who are so inclined to step off the professional track. This might relieve some suffering by those who remain only because there is no stopping point. But, more affirmatively, it might be expected to promote more discontinuity in study patterns. Many who step off might return after usefully maturing experiences, with some chance that the impact of legal education would be magnified. In providing this option, the Model gives additional reinforcement to its policy favoring student independence and self-management.

F. Economy of Time

An important goal of the Model is to reduce the time frame for general and professional education so that roughly five years of higher education will suffice for most students to attain professional status. Thus, the standard of admission for the Standard Curriculum allows entry after three years of undergraduate study; and the requirements for the professional degree are such that some students will be able to complete it in two academic years while most will complete it in less than three.

In the pursuit of this goal, the Model seeks to reverse a long term trend. With few exceptions, instruction in law was not a two year program until after the Civil War. Harvard offered the first three year program in 1876 and that became a standard of the American Bar Association as recently as 1921. At that time, two years of undergraduate education was the usual admission standard. Now, an undergraduate degree is widely required, so that the minimum measure of time served is usually seven years. Many educators have long questioned the wisdom of escalating requirements. Many of the decisions, such as that made by the American Bar Association in 1921, expressed economic and social policies which would not stand public inspection today. The general trend is now under attack in such reputable quarters as the Carnegie Commission on Higher Education and the American Academy. The case for reversing it with respect to legal education rests on several considerations.

Before appraising them, it may be important to emphasize that the Model does not propose to standardize or limit the length of professional training for generalist lawyers. It proposes to eliminate the time-serving requirement, but with the expectation that most professional students would ultimately receive somewhat more than two years of instruction, while many might well receive more than three. The amount of instruction assured is at least equal to that provided by the new program at Northeastern University. The Model seeks to facilitate student decision-making as to the length and intensity of instruction.

The case for this change could rest simply on the values already expressed in this Rationale, which favor the development of student freedom and responsibility. It is quite reasonable to assign the burden of justification on those who impose constraints. Indeed, such an allocation of the burden might be viewed as an obvious application of the morality of a free society.

That moral judgment can be reinforced by reference to the apparent adverse consequences of time-serving requirements. Most of these consequences derive more or less directly from the fact that longer training programs are less attractive to prospective entrants than shorter ones, other factors being equal. Thus, as the Model shortens the investment of time and foregone income required of its students, it becomes more attractive. While it is fair to say that few law schools now need a stimulus to their admissions programs, there are advantages to enlarging the range of their appeal.

The first advantage is an impact on the long-term availability of legal services. Even in a services market which is rigged by a licensing authority, there is some relation between the attractiveness of entry and the supply of service. Unless prevented from doing so, old schools enlarge and new ones open. The resulting steady increase in the supply of services maintains pressure on the price of service, and service is extended into new areas. The deterrence on price rises would be particularly effective in enlarging service to middle and lower income groups. (The Model assumes this to be an objective; it could be questioned if it is assumed that lawyers are a contentious lot who engender conflict.)

The increased appeal of law study would also operate to improve the quality of services delivered to the public. Most directly, it would enlarge and improve the pool of applicants from which the entering classes are to be filled. This factor may operate with special effect on students drawn from disadvantaged economic backgrounds, because such students are more often afflicted with a short time perspective. This is to say that the offspring of the poor tend to have a more urgent appetite for reward and are less likely to await the long-term payoff provided by extended professional training. The effect would be magnified by the fact that scholarship resources would be effectively enlarged by half. This special effect can be seen to offer additional benefits in assuring to disadvantaged groups and individuals a better chance of obtaining advocates from among their own and in assuring that power is more frequently exercised by persons sympathetic to moral values other than those of the dominant middle class.

Less directly, the reduction in the time frame might be expected to improve the quality of services by facilitating improvements in the quality of training. More students would be financially able to pay for quality instruction if they could gain access to professional income sooner. This is reflected in the Model's proposal to retrieve the full cost of most instruction in the Standard Curriculum from the prospective professionals. Also some of the time gained may be applied to more effective academic pursuits such as joint degree programs and Special Instruction.

A final objective served by the Model's reduction in time-serving is to provide leadership among the professions: all the professions need to be led away from what has become an "academic credentials race" that is increasingly costly to the public. The principle of Title VII has yet to be observed in operation among the professions and much professional employment is now over-rated with respect to academic qualifications. Somehow, the impulse to collect academic funeral beads for whole professional groups must be contained; a trend which sends prospective plumbers into the intricacies of hydraulic engineering in order to qualify to perform a change of washers has to be corrected. Who is to lead the way back to a more rational allocation of resources, if not the lawyers?

While some of the foregoing considerations are speculative, their impact gives substantial reinforcement to the earlier assertion that requirements of time-serving are subject to a continuing duty to justify themselves. Thus, law faculty who have long wondered what to do with the third year must require of themselves an answer to the more basic question, why must there be a third year for all? Few serious attempts have been made to provide such an answer.

One might try to fashion an answer on the basis of an assumed relation between time-serving and professional maturation, or basic skill development. This is a frail assumption, at best. It can be supported by no data except the observations of some faculty who feel that some students achieve maturation in the third year. To the extent that this is an accurate observation, some of the growth would surely occur if the students passed the same time engaged in some other useful activity. Some of it is attributable to leisure and the opportunity for reflection which can be acquired less expensively. And few would challenge the assertion that there is very little growth, indeed, for many third year students. In fact, data derived from their performance on law school examinations in which they compete with second year students suggests the possibility of retrogression for quite a few. To the extent that some students can be identified as needing additional socialization, the Model contemplates that they would be encouraged to extend their stay. Such counselling would be a natural outgrowth of Intensive Instruction.

A somewhat different answer might be fashioned on the basis of an assumed relation between time-serving and the transmission of important information. This might take the form of concern for the transmission of information about legal doctrine. In this form, it might reflect a notion that students should learn all the law in law school. This notion abides only in the minds of law students and some faculty with no practical experience. Those who have had experience are aware of the inevitability of memory failure; very little of the detail that is learned in law school is accurately remembered for long enough to be useful. A general familiarity with legal doctrine is vital; an over-burden of details is not. The loss of a minor fraction of the effort now invested in the elaboration of details is not likely to have significant effect on the competence of a practitioner.

Alternatively, one may fear that the portions of the transmission which would be omitted are those which have less direct economic value. All the philosophy, all the history, all the comparison, might be squeezed out of the curriculum by students dashing freely toward professional goals too clearly held in view. While we have learned the futility of compulsory culture, we ought not to encourage students to abandon the liberal pursuits. The Model is at pains to prevent this. If necessary, the "perspective requirement" which has been widely abandoned in recent years could be reimposed, at least for a transitional period until students became more relaxed about the process of compression.

Yet another variation on this theme is the concern for the quality of the formal presentation. The Model does, indeed, propose to limit the use of case analysis as a means of elaborating doctrine. Some observers suggest that this may threaten the intellectual rigor of the presentation. The Model assumes that some of what passes for rigorous analysis is more accurately viewed as a precious elaboration of details of little value to the generalist. That this appraisal is widely shared is demonstrated by the facts that few upper class students fail to find diversions from traditionally "rigorous" presentations and that few faculty expect them to do otherwise. Indeed, it should be observed that any general faculty concern that students must all experience three full years of exposure to instruction in law is belied by the growing frequency with which students are permitted to substitute marginally related non-law courses or lightly supervised clinical courses for the formal instruction. In any event, the Model assumes that Intensive Instruction, especially, will be more rigorous, not less.

A more subtle answer might relate the time-serving requirement to the functional utility of the quality of time perspective which is established by selecting only students who are willing to forego benefits during the longer period of study. As the Model concedes, there is no doubt that the quality is a useful trait. But, because it is class-related it will not do to select for it; to do so would be to impose a clog on social mobility. The quality is not one that is universally required for all, or even most of lawyers' work; those who are a little lacking in that trait should not be cut off from performing services which they may be better equipped to perform than those more endowed.

The most troublesome response to the challenge posed by the Model is to justify time-serving as a means of maintaining the level of professional income. It might perhaps be assumed that the pressure on the price of legal services projected by the Model would lower professional incomes, and thus impair the quality of services by discouraging new entrants and by creating insecurity among practitioners who would be forced to protect themselves at the expense of their clients. Complete reassurance cannot be given. It is very unlikely that the elite legal professionals would suffer any noticeable loss of income as the result of an increase in the availability of services and it would be a minor concern if there were some loss inflicted there. And econometric estimates indicate that the effect on other lawyers' income would be proportionately less than on price. The primary effect of a reduction in time serving would be to enlarge the range of services provided by lawyers; some lost income would be retrieved as a return for new services and some would be retrieved at the expense of accountants, insurance agents, and real estate brokers, all of whom are somewhat threatened by the increased availability of legal services. But even a small loss of income for the marginal lawyer is a matter for concern, at least to those who are acquainted with the threat which the financially insecure lawyer poses to all who deal with him. It may be a partial answer to suggest that there will always be some dangerous marginal lawyers at any price or income level. It may be a better answer to suggest that the solution to the problem lies in a better professional organization which features risk-sharing and specialization.

The justification for requiring a fourth year of time-serving in undergraduate institutions is even harder to make. The case would have to rest on some assumed relation between the fourth year of preparation and the capacity to study or practice law. Any requirement based on concern for the fullness of life of the students, or on the economic health of the nation, should be imposed on all students of undergraduate age, not merely those who want to study law. It would be difficult, indeed, to demonstrate that the information or skill acquired in that fourth year is related to the capacity to study or practice law, because no one can presume to identify the information or skill thus acquired. Rising teaching ratios have made it increasingly unlikely that fourth year students are engaged in supervised writing, or other activities which are rigorously supervised by undergraduate faculty. If the issue is one of maturity, an age requirement would seem to be more appropriate as an admission standard than a degree requirement. If the baccalaureate is regarded as essential to the status of the student or institution, this problem can be solved by awarding a bachelor's degree at the end of one year of law study.

These several justifications for time-serving requirements are seen by the Model as insufficient to weigh against the advantages gained by the proposed reductions. Those who are less moved by the Model's argument may be attracted to the proposal elsewhere advocated by David Cavers. His plan would achieve some of the same result by manipulation of the academic calendar. The single important difference is that his plan would save less on instructional cost. Also, for those who are compelled by the arguments, but offended by the idea of a two-year doctorate, it would be possible to change the nomenclature, or delay the award of the degree.

II. TRAINING FOR PROFESSIONALS

A. Finesse of License Requirements

Residence Instruction in the Advanced Curriculum is intended to support the judgment that time-serving requirements should be reduced. The Model discharges its full responsibility by posing the issue squarely for the licensing authorities, who must have the final say. To the extent that the licensing authority is unwilling to accept the judgment of the law school, as reflected in its award of the professional degree, it is left with the duty of defining the additional requirements to be imposed. The Model will provide the student with the means for meeting these requirements, but will impose nothing beyond the minimum. If the requirements are non-functional, the licensing authority will be obliged to face directly both the public and the individual students who are inconvenienced.

It will be observed that the program of Resident Instruction includes a bar review course. This is contrary to an existing standard of the Association of American Law Schools. The standard appears to rest, however, on the assumed importance of traditional formal study, and a sense that such presentations are beneath the dignity of an institution devoted to inquiry. The Model is less concerned with its dignity than with serving the needs of students who are otherwise exposed to exploitation by well-rewarded entrepreneurs who not infrequently employ the talents of moonlighting faculty. Given the premise on which the program of Resident Instruction is conducted, there is no reason not to include this service to students as a part of it.

It should also be observed that this program contemplates a very liberal policy with respect to transfers of credits. Because of the very minimal demands made on the resources of the institution, all of which are fully compensated, any student needing the resident credit should be admitted. Credit should also be given for work taken elsewhere if necessary. In this way, free movement is assured to students who have completed the professional degree early and accepted employment in some distant community.

B. Training for Special Competence

This feature of the Model is an effort to support the development of professional specialties in law. Such a development has been the object of debate within the organized bar for many years. Although the bar has tended to cling to the romantic tradition that all lawyers are omnicompetent, the reality is that a large number of lawyers are specialized in their practice. While there has been no licensing system, or any authoritative recognition of the development, sections of the state and American Bar have provided communities of special interests. The California Bar is now conducting an experiment in the certification of specialists in three fields. The experiment seems to have widespread support within the bar of that state; it is being watched closely by the American Bar and by other state bar groups. It seems quite possible that certified specialization will be quite widely employed within a decade.

There are several reasons why this is in the public interest. First, it seems clear that specialists can provide superior services. This assumption is supported by observation in any other field of endeavor and by the organization of the law offices which provide the best service. It can also be supported by the observation that the public is increasingly attracted to the services of non-lawyer specialists who compete with generalist lawyers. The public's evaluation is also reflected in the rise of Group Legal Services, which is a means of offering specialized service. Moreover, it seems appropriate to add that those who have attained special competence in law have probably thereby improved their basic skills and understanding.

Secondly, it seems equally clear that specialization has a favorable effect on the cost of service. While specialists may charge higher fees for their time, this is possible only because their time has achieved a higher value to the consumer of service. The specialist is more efficient and the economics of production operate in his favor; even charging his time at a much lower rate, the generalist cannot provide service of equivalent value at the same price. Indeed, there are many legal services that would require the specialist to exert a high level of effort and skill which would be beyond the competence of the generalist to perform at all within the limits of reasonable time and price.

Thirdly, specialization operates to facilitate access to needed services. If the bar is specialized, whether practicing singly or in groups, the client is far more likely to find his way to one who is competent to meet his needs. Because he will be better able to find a qualified lawyer who will give better service at a lower price, the consumer of services is more likely to develop an affirmative attitude toward the legal professions, and more likely to make use of legal services instead of competing non-legal services, or instead of suffering his misfortune passively. In this way, specialization operates to enlarge the market for legal services, and enhances both the social and economic status of the professionals.

There being no real issue as to the desirability of developing professional specialties, the only question is the proper role of the university law school in promoting the development. The specialization which has already developed has resulted from self-instruction and on-the-job training, sometimes supported by short programs of continuing education institutions which are sometimes connected to law schools. It is arguable that these means are adequate to the task that lies ahead.

Nevertheless, the Model assumes that the development can be assisted by the efforts of a university law school with benefit and no impairment to its other activities. It therefore concludes that the law school is obliged to undertake assistance to professionals seeking to establish special competence beyond that of the generalist.

The primary asset which the university law school brings to the undertaking is an environment conducive to sustained endeavor. In this respect, it is equipped to perform a role quite different from that of most institutions devoted to continuing legal education. But the university law school also has a foundation of existing graduate programs on which to build, a physical plant which could be more fully utilized, and a tradition of rigor which is needed to sustain the development of quality. By utilizing these resources, law schools could provide effective stimulation and assistance to the development of professional specialization.

In return, there may be significant benefits to the other programs of the law school. Special Instruction would provide a natural setting for the return of practitioners to the law school environment, where they might be put to service in the training of noviatiates. It also provides a natural contact between the law faculty and the practicing bar, in which they can share in a common endeavor. And it would bring the law faculty into contact with the most difficult current problems of practice without imposing on them the responsibility for the affairs of clients. As a substitute for the required third year of residency, Special Instruction would serve to stimulate a desirable discontinuity in study and would encourage transfers of students from one law school to another during the period of instruction; both of these features could be reasonably expected to magnify the impact of the educational experience.

Several characteristics seem to follow from the goals of Special Instruction. The pace of the program should be rigorous, but not so demanding that the professional students have no time for reflection, or for sharing their experience and maturity with younger students. It must also allow time for the professional to maintain some contact with his clientele; otherwise the cost of the program in foregone income would be prohibitive to many. Because the students are already professionals, they should be assumed to be quite capable of self-management; authoritative presentations which reinforce the dependence of the student on the teacher should be avoided. The role of the institution should be to assemble the professionals sharing a common goal, to provide them with a suitable environment for their common pursuit, to assure the availability of adequate learning resources, and to provide a definition of the goal in the form of a structured examination to measure their achievement. In providing resources, it would be especially appropriate to utilize the talents of practicing specialists, as well as full-time faculty in law and related disciplines.

The credentials awarded should be adequate to reinforce the awareness of professional achievement, but not so tinseled that they become yet another set of funeral beads to be won in the "credentials race". The law school need not enlarge its unsought position as a gatekeeper to professional status by an attempt to certify competence in the fashion of public licensing authority. But there is no reason why the law school specialist examination cannot co-exist with certification systems.

It is assumed that the specialty courses offered would reflect the interests of the faculty as well as the market demand. Quite possibly, the specialty courses would serve as foci of faculty interest; if many schools were so engaged, each would develop special interests of its own. The specialization of law faculties might occur spontaneously, or it could be planned by a consortium of schools. In this way, Special Instruction might serve as yet another device for breaking down the isolation of academic lawyers by bringing them closer together in shared interests.

There is room for doubt as to the existence of a market for this kind of service to professionals. Over time, such a program would be dependent on the development of sabbatical leave programs by the government offices, corporations, and large firms which employ the majority of the country's lawyers. Such a development would, however, be quite consistent with a widely recognized goal of "lifetime learning" and greater freedom of movement for mature workers.

During an initial period in which the educational market is explored, it would be acceptable to fill the Special Instruction courses with students continuing in a third year of study. This is not desirable because it frustrates some of the goals pursued by the reduction in time-serving requirements, and because instruction would be superior if discontinuity and professional experience could be presumed by the planners.

If Special Instruction could not survive in the marketplace, little would have been lost by the effort to create it. The marketplace failure would establish a solid judgment by the profession that law schools have not enough to give to the practitioner in a third year to merit the investment of time. In this respect, the program serves as insurance against error in the reduction of time-serving. Because the goals of such instruction would be clearly defined and understood by all involved, the conditions for success would seem to be near optimal. If additional training under those conditions cannot justify itself, the Model can reasonably contend that its judgment in reducing the amount of training designed to pursue more obscure goals is fully vindicated.

C.   Inter-Disciplinary Research

The program in Research Instruction is the heart of the Model's effort to establish a stronger intellectual underpinning for law. It seeks to establish new patterns of scholarship and teaching for the coming generations of teachers who will supply the new intellectual leadership of the profession. It hopes to secure the effort to supplement the intuitive, prudential values which the profession brings to official decision-making with the skeptical methodology of the best social science.

The movement toward more scientific, data-based scholarship has been marked for a half century. But those who have marked the trail have so far been unable to induce the profession to follow it. In part, this has been because of the great difficulty to be encountered by those who attempt to relate different frontiers of inquiry. Such persons are quick to find that the differences in epistemology, assumptions, values, goals, vocabulary, and techniques are such that his conclusions are exposed to a bewildering array of possible attacks. During the decade of the twenties, the Columbia law faculty demonstrated that men of the greatest competence and industry cannot achieve more than slight, incremental progress at the task of re-building the foundations of the law curriculum. Their work has moved forward at a glacial rate, while many have invested their careers to produce the smallest gains.

The lack of progress is, however, not entirely owing to the inherent difficulty of the task. In part, it has been the product of a mentality that is resistant to the use of hard data. Almost ingrained in many lawyers is the assumption that reality is the world described in judicial opinions. Teachers and students tend to reinforce one another in this belief, because it is convenient to both. If the legal discipline is to be made a better companion for others, so that what is known and knowable about our universe can be better used as a basis for public decisions, it is important to move both students and teachers to be more receptive, more willing to abide the dictates, frustrations and ambiguities of science.

Some of the changes in the first year, it will be recalled, were intended to meet this problem by encouraging students to approach law study, from the beginning, as an inter-disciplinary venture, before they began to experience the maturation process sometimes known as a "hardening of the categories". But the purpose of that change will be frustrated if those who lead the discussion tend to view the universe through the eyes of appellate courts. The program of Research Instruction is the Model's bootstraps method of providing the needed remedy, of assuring that future teachers and scholars have a clearer view of their relation to other intellectual endeavors.

The Model is skimpy in detail with respect to this program, because it is to be expected that much of it would be individually tailored. It can be assumed that most students would point their programs at the strength of the particular university and law faculty. Presumably, many schools offering such programs would tend to specialize.

It may be illustrative to suggest that one school, at least, might direct its attention to the scientific study of the legal profession and legal education. This report seeks to be as candid as possible in identifying the untested assumptions which underlie the planning of the Model. Undoubtedly, there are many more which remain unidentified. While not all of these assumptions can be tested by any known method, many could be. There is some literature which does apply the scientific method to some of them, not infrequently with unconvincing results. But there remains a great void of questions which no one has attempted to answer, concerning the nature of the lawyer's work, his relationship to it, and the consequences on both of curricular decisions.

For example, more than one career might be usefully invested in the study of the psychology of the lawyer's relation to authority. The authoritarian personality has been a subject of intense interest in social psychology for two decades. This appears to be a complex syndrome and may well relate to the openness of students to new modes of thought and perception. Students of differing orientations to authority and authority figures profit differentially from differing modes of teaching and degrees of structure in curriculum. While the dynamics of interaction between the nature of learning and the personalities of students are not yet well-understood, the pertinence of the inquiry for law school curriculum planning is obvious.

There is similar data and methodology to be harnessed in illuminating the relation between legal planning skills and future time perspective. Or the relation between learning and style of teaching: what is the applicability to legal education of data suggesting that degree of learning is a function of the degree to which the students are able to internalize as their own the goals of the instructor presenting the material? Similar inquiries might bear on the effect of different law school environments on different kinds of students; data gathered elsewhere confirms that there are measurable educational consequences which correspond to different social relationships.

These suggestions bear on only a few of the psychological aspects of legal education. An equally challenging vein of issues are presented by some of the economic assumptions which underlie the Model. It may be suggested that academic lawyers cannot proclaim themselves as qualified scientists until they begin to bring the techniques of science to bear on their own problems. There will be no cheap, easy answers; and few which are fully dispositive. But until law faculties manifest an interest in asking the questions, their claim to intellectual distinction must remain in doubt. The Model hopes that Research Instruction will arouse that kind of interest.

The Model is explicit that the program of Research Instruction should remain small. Care should be taken to prevent such expensive training from becoming a device for screening the academic elite to serve the highest bidders. This is probably a small risk, but it should be gravely regarded. The Model does propose to train more than enough teachers and scholars for its own use. It assumes that there will be some market for the skills developed in smaller law schools, in independent research organizations, and in the teaching of law in undergraduate institutions and secondary schools. In serving the latter markets, it hopes to imbue a much wider audience than its own with the understanding that law should not be comprehended in isolation.

III. TRAINING NON-LAWYERS

A. Law As A Liberal Art

In presenting a program of Courses About Law, the Model makes a vigorous effort to present legal study as an appropriate object of curiosity for those who have formed no professional goals. Of course, law teaching has long been conducted in many schools and departments outside the law school, much of it in institutions which have no law school.

Law is a desirable object of undergraduate instruction for several reasons. Many of the most troubling and fundamental intellectual problems can be visited in the setting of the legal system and process, including the pervasive tensions between stability and change, freedom and security, history and logic, ideal justice and justice in practice. There is an advantage to encountering these problems in a more worldly, practical setting because the student faces the consequences of imposing his own values and solutions on others who may be tangibly affected by their application. This is often a maturing experience. Moreover, the law offers an extraordinary abundance of data revealing the human experience in trying to solve problems by intellectual means. For such reasons, the medieval curriculum of the University of Bologna made law the core of all its training.

Aside from its value as an intellectual exercise, law training has special importance to citizens in our society. The increasing penetration of law into all social affairs and relations and the increasing democratization of our institutions are developments which increase the need of citizens to understand how official decisions are made and implemented. Citizens who have a better understanding are likely to make better use of professional legal services. This is especially true of particular professional and vocational groups who are likely to be in regular contact with the law and lawyers.

A third goal of undergraduate law training is to provide an opportunity for students to test their interest and capacity. Students who have experienced such training can gain a better sense of their own goals and a more mature confidence in their ability to cope with professional training. This last can be especially important to students whose family and class backgrounds cause them to be unfamiliar with the law or the traditions and values which it reflects. In this respect, undergraduate law study can serve the role of a senior "headstart" program.

Since 1968, the Council on Legal Education Opportunity has conducted summer institutes designed to serve this role. Not surprisingly, it is quite difficult to appraise their success in meeting a difficult problem. Minority students (a group which overlaps the disadvantaged group and is more easily identified) tend to perform less well on the Law School Admission Test. Moreover, they sometimes tend to perform below predictive expectations. These data tend to confirm that legal education itself is a highly inculturated process which places a premium on cultural experience. To some marginal degree, it may be possible to make the law curriculum less culture-bound. Some progress in that direction might be achieved as a result of the kinds of changes which the Model proposes for the first year. Traditional instruction has tended to focus primary instruction on problems and issues which are most familiar to the usual upper middle class student; the abandonment of contracts, torts, and property as course titles should encourage more variety in this regard. On the other hand, there are severe limits on the degree to which it is possible to make an acultural presentation of a legal system which inevitably reflects the dominant values of the culture.

To attempt to overcome the cultural disadvantage in a summer program is a worthy undertaking and should be continued. But undergraduate training in law which can be spread over a longer time period has a somewhat better chance of providing the needed socialization. The proposed program offers the additional advantage that it does not isolate "headstart" students from others. Thus, it avoids the pitfall of remedial programs which sometimes reinforce the debilitating self-doubts of students by identifying them as in need of special help. Those students who need and desire a third year of law study can acquire it before as well as after the standard two years.

It may also be an important function of undergraduate law study to identify students who have a special capacity for law study that may not otherwise be discovered. It is widely recognized that the usual predictors do not identify some students who would do quite well in law despite their failure to attain distinction in other fields.

There are several reasons to engage the law school in the effort to provide undergraduate law instruction. Primarily, law school involvement should improve the quality of such instruction. While the Model does not contemplate the use of full-time law faculty to conduct all of the instruction, its participation in planning courses and materials and in selecting staff should assure a broader, deeper, more coherent program. In return, the law school can gain a good opportunity to bring its faculty into contact with the rest of the university, and a good outlet for the energies of law student-teachers working under law faculty supervision in the program of Intensive Instruction. Law school involvement also substantially increases the utility of the program as a "headstart" and as a predictor of law school success. Finally, law school involvement is a means of providing leadership for undergraduate institutions in the development of three-year B.A. program. That development is one favored

by the Carnegie Commission, among others, and would serve the
same goals as the reduction of time-serving requirements associated with professional education.

There are no apparent, substantial disadvantages to law school
involvement in such a program. There is no reason for undergraduate law training to be significantly more expensive than undergraduate training in other fields. It should be entitled to the same
level of university support, and should require no reallocation of
financial resources away from existing law school programs. There
is a marginal hazard that such programs might be defeated by their
own success. Thus, if Collegiate Instruction became a very effective avenue of access to law school, it might become too attractive
to marginal or insecure students and might tend to homogenize the
undergraduate training of the student body in the Standard Curriculum. If necessary, admissions policy could be adjusted to control this risk.

B.   Training for New Professions

The boldest feature of the Model is its effort to develop new legal
professions. Such an effort can be justified on the basis of two
assumptions. One is that the demand for legal services will and
should substantially exceed the capacity of existing or projected
training programs. The other is that persons of ordinary ability
can, with a modicum of training, perform creative roles in meeting
excess demand. Both of these assumptions can be debated. In addition, there are several problems raised by their implementation.

The difficulty of appraising the elastic demand for legal services
has already been noted. If society were to undertake to provide
professional service for every possible grievance, it would surely
fulfill the prediction of the medieval Chinese Emperor, who feared
that "contests would be interminable, and the half of the Empire
would not suffice to settle the lawsuits of the other half." And, if
we are to judge wholly on the basis of the existing market for the
services of lawyers, there is no great popular outcry for a massive
distribution of more legal services.

Nevertheless, the Model assumes that a market can be created
for legal services which will be available at less expense and will
employ more ordinary talents. The concept is closely analogous
to that which gave birth to the Volkswagen. In seeking to provide a Volkswagen legal service, the Model assumes that it is desirable to maximize the opportunity of all citizens to have professional

assistance in dealing with the many major disputes and planning problems which confront every member of a highly industrialized society. If all citizens are forced to choose between deluxe service or none, many must be denied service that they desire and are willing to compensate. In substantial measure, it should again be noted, the market will provide substitute service by others, many of whom may have no legal training whatever. One aspect of the Model's program would be to provide an appropriate measure of legal training for those who serve in such already existing "allied professions." But the Model hopes as well to create some new professions to reach, even to create, markets not now served.

In seeking to provide legal careers for persons of ordinary ability, the Model again pursues the policy of Title VII of the Civil Rights Act of 1964. It assumes that the qualifications for bar admission are much higher than necessary to assure competence in the performance of much legal work. The educational premise is that more students can be trained to competence more quickly and less expensively if the goal of producing omnicompetent generalists is forsaken. This assumption is verified by the fact that much legal service is now delivered by persons of ordinary ability who have no legal training; they are permitted to do so without offense to unauthorized practice law because their roles are narrowly defined and because it is not generally economic for lawyers to compete with them. It is difficult to resist the conclusion that such persons could do better jobs, and perform a wider range of services at lower cost, if they were given some legal training.

A rational fear is that cheaper service will eliminate better service in some areas. This result will occur because the consumers will not have the information needed to recognize those occasions in which the more expensive service is worth buying. This means that the allied professional will be left with some matters which are beyond his abilities to perform adequately. Although others may appraise this risk more gravely, the Model does not assign it sufficient weight to make it deterrent. One purpose of the moderate dose of legal training provided for the allied professions would be to give them a better appreciation of the uses of lawyers, making it more likely rather than less that hard problems will find strong problem-solvers.

In embracing this feature, the Model eschews a role in the training of "para-professionals", "sub-professionals", and "lay assistants". It recognizes the force of the argument being advanced by many that lawyers can increase their incomes and deliver services more efficiently and more cheaply, if they develop the habit of using assembly line methods. This alternative approach features the standardization of much legal work so that it can be performed routinely by secretaries and others of comparable training. While a portion of the program in Residence Instruction is devoted to training lawyers to use such personnel more effectively, the Model does not deem the law school to be a suitable place to train them. The reason for this is that the performance of standardized tasks is antithetical to the enterprise of inquiry. One who is steeped in the traditions of a law school may well be harmed in his ability to perform such work. It is also possible to object to this kind of development on the ground that it is exploitative and de-humanizing. While the Model's position with respect to the paraprofessional development is not necessarily influenced by that view, it is appropriate to note that the objection cannot be made to the kinds of roles which the Model seeks to enlarge and develop. Persons practicing in the Model's new professions would be expected to provide some creativity and judgment on their own and would not, in any sense, be lashed to a lawyer's oardeck.

Once again, the question may be asked whether the law school is the proper agency to take responsibility for the development of such new professions, assuming that the development is desirable. The case for law school participation can almost be stated in terms of necessity; nothing is likely to happen unless the impulse is provided. If not by law schools, then by whom? The new professions would be far more likely to gain the necessary level of status and acceptability if they begin with a share of law school status. Especially in the early decades, the placement service of the law school could make a crucial difference in the creation of opportunity and the development of professional pride. Moreover, the planning and development of curricula are likely to require the creative talents of legal scholars. While these can be applied in settings outside the law school, it is not likely that the interest of such scholars would be widespread or easily maintained without some institutional responsibility to reinforce them. Presumably, many programs might be co-sponsored by universities without law schools and conducted on their premises; the newer state universities seem most appropriate, although there may well be a place for community college participation as well. Presumably, also, successful programs might be duplicated without law school sponsorship. A law school relationship would also facilitate the use of Standard and Advanced Curriculum students in the teaching of the Open Curriculum courses. Proximity would also improve the prospects for effective and creative counselling, and transfers of the most able and ambitious students to the Standard Curriculum. It would also facilitate the transfer of some students from the Standard Curriculum to the programs for allied professions, where that seemed to be in the best interest of the student. Finally, there is the fact that subventions are far more available for programs conducted by law schools than for those which lack law school support. For all these reasons, the Model concludes that it should assume responsibility for the task to be performed.

The Model would expect to attract mature adults who are unwilling or unable to invest longer periods of time in study. Such programs would be especially appealing to mothers who have completed their years of service to children and seek a second family income. They would also be attractive to adults who are dissatisfied with their first career choice. Experience in other fields suggests that a somewhat disproportionate number of those attracted would be minority members. Assuming that these students would be attracted out of lower job classifications, the programs would be effective instruments of social mobility, while providing a service capability within ethnic groups. The latter development may be especially important for those groups which are so disadvantaged that they now have no access to lawyers because the ethnic differences are too great to sustain the essential communication and trust.

There are three problems encountered with the Model's implementation. First, it must be expected that many of those attracted to such professional roles would become dissatisfied with them. There would be some conflict with the bar as the members of the new professions sought to enlarge their roles. An example of this kind of stress can now be seen in the relation between nursing and medicine. The Model would foresee the creation of some new "treaties" between the bar and the newer professions, similar to those which now exist. The Model also seeks to reduce the potential for bitterness by maintaining a very open stance in welcoming experienced practitioners who seek to return for more rigorous training and more elegant credentials. Finally, it accepts the fact that some irritations are inevitable if labor is to be divided among those with different levels of skill and knowledge.

An additional problem exists with respect to the ethical standards which can be expected to prevail among the allied professions. Because they have less invested, are less socialized, and are less well rewarded, the new professionals will tend to develop different ethical codes. In order to protect the bar from guilt by association, the Model is careful not to describe these new professionals as lawyers, but complete success in this effort is too much to expect. The Model also seeks to distribute the services of new professionals in areas where most will often be working in large organizations or under supervision which will control the unwelcome tendencies. This direction will be reinforced by the law of unauthorized practice which will tend to restrict the activities of new professionals in those areas in which harm would be most likely to result. In appraising the ethical risk, the Model notes that the problems created by the ethical standards of real estate brokers, claims adjustors, labor negotiators, and others are not now a grave public problem. Such problem as may exist is not likely to be worsened by providing such persons with some legal training.

Thirdly, the Model is aware of a risk which is associated with the prospective success of its enterprise. If the demand for such services and training can be established, the programs may prove attractive to youth who would otherwise aspire to the more demanding goals set by the Standard Curriculum. It is especially worrisome that the attraction might be greater for disadvantaged youth who tend to have a more urgent appetite for reward. In order to guard against this, an earlier draft of the Model limited admission to those who were 27 years or older; such a constraint might well prove necessary, although it is not now presented because it is not demonstrably needed.

None of these three problems seem to be disabling to the Model's proposal. Far more likely to prevent widespread acceptance are a series of objections which can fairly be described as irrational. The first impulses of many sensible readers of the proposal are to label it anti-professional, racist, sexist, or anti-intellectual, or perhaps all of these.

The first response is likely to come from the organized bar, as some of its members loft the flag of unauthorized practice and demonstrate against the training of "unauthorized practitioners." Some practitioners would fear the competition offered by the new professionals; to the extent that this fear is realistic, it derives from the fact that some lawyers make some of their income from charging prices for their services which are not reflective of the measure of skill invested. While there is the noted risk that some matters might be handled by professionals not fully equipped to handle them, there is the offsetting advantage that such matters are more likely to be identified by the person handling them as in need of the most talented professional attention if that person has had legal training than if he has not.

The second and third responses come from women and members of minority groups who are quick to see the proposed programs as a thinly disguised "tracking" system, which will consign blacks, Chicanos, and women to second class careers in the delivery of second class services to poor clients. Despite its great emotional appeal, this objection is ill-considered. It assumes that it is realistic to train all comers for exciting, highly rewarding careers in the delivery of deluxe legal services for all. This is not possible; the real alternatives for those who would be affected is a career outside the law (or perhaps no career at all) and a choice between no legal service or service that is beyond their means. The hostile reaction is reinforced by the romantic illusion of a unitary bar. The illusion is produced by the fact that all lawyers are now trained for the same length of time in the same way; this provides an egalitarian appearance which is false, as anyone familiar with the bar can attest. The maintenance of the illusion of equality has ill-served the public. It has prevented useful careers from developing and it has caused services to be more expensive than they need to be. Certainly, the choice to be faced is not ideal. The Model is not insensitive to the emotional discomfort of those who would perform as members of the new professions. But it recognizes that such suffering will have to be borne if the real interests of the people are to be served.

The final response comes from law school faculty who find the prospective relationship with less intellectual students distasteful. They are prone to feel that the association will be detrimental to the quality and status of their institution. Presumably, a somewhat similar reaction might be expected from Mercedes assembly line workers asked to make Volkswagens. It is true that the best law schools derive their quality and status from the excellence of their students. To accept responsibility for less able students is, in one sense, to forsake the pursuit of intellectual excellence. That is something that no right-minded academician can comfortably contemplate. As a realistic matter, it is not likely that the presence of such programs on the premises of a good law school would detract from its appeal or harm its intellectual climate; surely, there can be no such problems if the program is conducted largely on other premises. But the objection can be overcome only if the pursuit of excellence can be redefined to appraise the effects of education on the public welfare rather than the affects of peer esteem. Perhaps such a change might occur if the academic profession can assimilate recent data suggesting that the "best" undergraduate schools produce the least value-added to their students.

Perhaps this feature of the Model can be fairly described as sadistic in forcing such painful thoughts in so many directions at once. The excuse for such an aggression is that such thoughts may be the most illuminating. The issues and values to be considered are essentially the same as those to be considered in appraising the Standard Curriculum, but here they are seen in a somewhat different relation to one another. It may be helpful to suggest that the program for training new professions is, in a way, an alternative to the proposals to economize in the Standard Curriculum. As the training of conventional lawyers is made more expensive, the case for the new professions becomes more compelling. Those who resist economy, and urge larger investments of time and resources in the training of lawyers should be prepared either to support new professions or to find other options.

IV. FINANCING

A. Full-Cost Tuition

The purpose of identifying the real cost of each unit of instruction was stated in the introduction; its relationship to the main theme of the Model is now apparent. If legal education is to make a rational analysis of itself, and if it is to encourage students to make a rational analysis of their individual goals, it is essential to analyze the real cost of instruction, so that it can be kept in mind at all times.

The method of cost analysis may bear some examination. Other, more sophisticated, methods could be applied. The Model assumes that the Standard Curriculum is its essential operation; most of the research and administration costs are chargeable to it. The crude figure of $80,000 used as the cost of a single full time equivalent faculty member is based on the following calculation:

Average salary	$25,000
Fringe benefits	5,000
Reserve for sabbatical	5,000
Secretarial service, including fringes	7,000
Research assistance	2,000
Teaching assistance	10,000
Library acquisitions, $150,000/50 faculty	3,000
Library staff, $150,000/50 faculty	3,000
Administration $200,000/50 faculty	4,000
Insurance against non-collection (5%)	4,000
Return of capital (15%)	12,000
Total	$80,000

Each of these figures is debatable and depends on the level of support to be provided to the faculty. The cost of instruction in the Advanced Curriculum is calculated by the same measurement as the Standard Curriculum.

The Model recognizes that it cannot charge full-cost tuition to non-professional undergraduates, unless this is done generally with respect to other undergraduates. Otherwise, the presumed cost of a full time equivalent for the Open Curriculum is $55,000. This figure is not calculated in the same manner as the larger figure used for the other Curricula. Library and administration costs are substantially discounted, and the larger sum is further diminished to reflect the fact that a substantial portion of the instruction would be conducted by less expensive teaching staff. If this general approach is to be implemented, greater precision would be desirable.

The program of Research Instruction would clearly require a subvention. The Model would also apply a subvention to all by making no charge for physical plant. It assumes that other funds would be applied in a deliberate manner to serve specific goals and not as a general subsidy to middle class youth.

B. Deferred Tuition

Full cost tuition cannot be charged unless students are provided with a means to pay the larger sums. The Model assumes that new funds for large-scale subventions are not likely to be forthcoming. Most institutions of higher education are in such straightened circumstances that it will be a substantial achievement if they are able to maintain the customary levels of support for professional education. There is a growing awareness that public investments in professional education are regressive. This is most apparent with respect to medical education, which is very expensive to taxpayers, and financially very rewarding to the beneficiaries. Thus, generally, the most expensive schools confer the largest subsidy on the student groups with the best prospects for future income and, thus, the least need. Law students, only somewhat less than medical students, make an unappealing claim to public charity. When their pleas for subsidy are weighed against grave public needs in such fields as public education, welfare, health, transportation, housing, environmental protection, and even legal services, they cannot seem very compelling. It is not unreasonable to expect affluent professionals to bear the cost of their own training. Not only is this fairer, in the distributive sense, but it also promotes a more rational allocation of educational resources.

Needed is a means for anticipating the professional income. Professional income is now used by some lawyers to repay loans or to make annual gifts which support the educational program. But professional students have not yet learned to think of tuition payments as capital investments which yield a net credit on the balance sheet. Even those who will buy an expensive vacation on credit are reluctant to incur indebtedness to pay education costs.

The Model, nevertheless, proposes to facilitate payment by means of a massive loan program which would deter payment routinely. In order to prevent such loans from deterring students from lower economic situations, who are prone to a special reluctance to borrow, grant funds would be concentrated on such students at the time of their entry decisions.

In order to gain the needed capital for the loans, the Model contemplates a substantial borrowing by the institution which would be financed by returning 15% of tuition collected to the capital account.

This is a simpler version of the plan recently instituted by Yale University; the Yale plan is more flexible in relating tuition to income earned, so that the Yale surgeon pays part of the cost of training the Yale clergyman. The Model's plan is limited in its application to professional students and does not reach the problem of financing non-professional undergraduate education. It assumes that almost every legal professional should carry his own weight. It does plan on an uncollectable rate of 5%, which includes a factor for life insurance. Because it strives to relate tuition to real costs, the Model creates no incentives to compete for students, as the Yale plan may. In order to maintain that relationship, it would be well to be explicit that the 15% surcharge would be steadily reduced to zero, the latter point being reached when the capital account was large enough to finance current needs and provide a reserve to meet additional needs created by the time lag between announced tuition increases and increases in tuition receipts. Each tuition increase would have to include a surcharge sufficient to replace that depleted reserve.

V. CONCLUSION

The Model described would serve many goals. Its principal goal is to demonstrate that many values are inextricably involved in curricular decisions. There is no neutral curriculum; however unintentionally, any program of instruction in law serves either well or ill:

(1) the quality of legal services;

(2) the availability of legal services;

(3) the degree of access of all groups in the society to a voice in the exercise of power;

(4) social mobility;

(5) the individual freedom of students;

(6) the humane qualities of the educational environment;

(7) lawyers' understanding of the problems of other professionals and of society as it is affected by lawyers' work;

(8) the public's and other professionals' understanding of the legal process and professions;

(9) the public fisc;

(10) the congeniality of the law school to intellectual inquiry;

(11) the rigor of the rationality which has marked the American legal professions at their best.

The Model is not the only, nor necessarily the best, means of serving and reconciling all these goals. It is a device for inducing those who make curricular decisions to think about them all.

Radical as some features of the Model may seem, it is conservative in two important respects. The first is that the Model abides what it regards as the appropriate jurisdictional limits of curriculum planning. It does not presume to express any grand design of the society in which we should live, but meets the social issues only when they intersect with the educational mission of facilitating the attainment of individual goals by students and teachers. In this respect, the Model assumes that a law school is not equipped with a suitable process for identifying the ultimate goals of society. It also assumes that no institution committed to inquiry should attempt firm conclusions because to do so would impair its receptivity to other ideas. It expresses the faith that the university law school can best serve by continuing the tradition of the university as a harbor for reason, tolerance, and speculation. It expresses skepticism that a law school can be effectively used as a means of altering the goals of the larger society. In this respect, it assumes that those changes which might be accomplished through the use of the law school curriculum could be accomplished at least as effectively by other means. It should be conceded that this is a debatable conservatism. Thomas Jefferson, for example, planned his University law school as a school for Whigs, as an incubator for generations of like-minded Jeffersonians. In resisting this kind of manipulation, the Model can fairly claim to be more Jeffersonian than Jefferson.

The Model's second conservatism is that it expresses faith in the institutions of legal education and in the tradition of rigorous rationality which have been their pride. Indeed, it seeks to turn that tradition on itself. In an effort to "think like a lawyer" about the problems of legal education, the Model warmly embraces tradition; it celebrates more than it changes.

TRAINING FOR THE PUBLIC PROFESSIONS OF THE
LAW: 1971

A REPORT TO THE ASSOCIATION OF AMERICAN LAW SCHOOLS

SEPTEMBER 7, 1971

APPENDIXES

APPENDIX I

by Alfred Z. Reed (1921)

Edited by Kate Wallach

INTRODUCTION

Half a century ago, the ABA Committee on Legal Education and Admission to the Bar, motivated by a survey on the medical profession, requested the Carnegie Foundation to sponsor a study on the education of lawyers. A. Z. Reed's *Training for the Public Profession of the Law,* prepared by a non-lawyer educator, has lost none of its timeliness throughout the years. "The historical treatment makes clear the fact that the questions which divide lawyers today in regard to legal education . . . are not new, but are the same questions which have presented themselves again and again ever since the days of the earliest teaching of law." (Preface, p. xvi)

America inherited from England the tradition that practicing lawyers and judges should be responsible for legal education. In many European countries universities shared in this task. Until about the middle of the nineteenth century aspiring American lawyers served an apprenticeship in an older lawyer's office. There were few aspirants to the profession and each lawyer was limited in the number of apprentices he could train. Depending on the character and ability of the master, the apprentice received more or less education and developed the necessary legal skills by hand-copying of legal documents, serving process papers and reading the few textbooks, primarily Blackstone and later the scholarly texts prepared by university professors.

Thomas Jefferson was the first to establish a law school within a university where comprehensive knowledge could be acquired in addition to legal techniques.

As colleges and universities grew they slowly assumed their share in the legal educational process. While at first they provided a narrow technical base together with office apprenticeship, they gradually expanded the curriculum and finally replaced office training completely. In addition to the universities, private schools conducted by practitioners for future practitioners rather than for future legal scholars, and night schools for those who had to earn a living while preparing for admission to the bar, were other types of legal education which evolved over a span of about one hundred years. There is not much difference in the range of legal training between 1920 and 1970—Reed's time of observation and ours today.

Reed recognizes the difficulty inherent in the adaptation of the ancient profession of the law to modern ideals of popular self-government and points out the demands which a democratic state makes of its lawyers: They "shall be at once educated specialists and yet not too far removed from the common people; their course of preparation and conditions of admission shall be at once rigorous and yet not beyond the reach of the average man; calculated to produce broadly and thoroughly trained experts, to whom the clients can resort in full confidence that without undue delay or expense they will be honorably and competently served, and yet providing an opportunity to all elements of the community to be adequately represented in the lawyer class, privileged by law to exercise the primary governmental function of administering justice." (p. 28)

"The policy of the state, as reflected in its bar admission rules, has been greatly affected by attempts to realize the ideal of popular self-government. The problem of how to make the bar efficient has been complicated by a desire to make this branch of the public service accessible to the average citizen." (p. 4)

A.   The History of Legal Education

1.   Thomas Jefferson's University Law School

To Thomas Jefferson belongs the credit of initiating university instruction in professional law in this country. His task was the easier because the apprenticeship system was not so firmly estab-lished in Virginia as in the northern states; but his chief asset was his own daring and constructive mind, which had no respect for tradition as such and erred, if at all, on the side of too broad and too original conceptions. Believing that even private law study was preferable to office work, and cherishing a comprehensive plan, only partially realized, for the reorganization of education in Virginia, he first revolutionized, in 1779, the organization of his *alma mater,* William and Mary College. His conception of a univer-sity, in so far as it owed anything to foreign models, followed the later Continental rather than the later English type: the various faculties were thought of as coordinated, rather than as branching out of a central college of arts or philosophy. With characteristic audacity, Jefferson departed from the orthodox four faculties— Philosophy, Theology, Medicine and Law. Discarding altogether the already established theological faculty along with all classical instruction, he accepted Medicine and Law, while Philosophy he split into four parts, thus securing a symmetrical coordination of six faculties. . . . Each faculty was reduced to a single professorship, termed, in accordance with local tradition, a "school." One of these six faculty chairs included "Moral Philosophy and the Laws of Nature and of Nations." Another, filled by Jefferson's law teacher and fellow Revisor of the Virginia statutes, Chancellor George Wythe, was the school of "Law and Police." Wythe's course included not only lectures on municipal (professional) law, of which Blackstone early became the basis, and moot courts, an inheritance from the English Inns [p. 116], but also lectures on government and moot legislatures, designed to train students in parliamentary law. Practical law and practical politics, in short, already differentiated but still combined, were fully recognized as fit subjects to be pursued within academic shades, under the instruction of a practitioner. International law was pushed to one side as an appendage to the related topic of ethics [p. 117].

Jefferson's educational plans culminated in the opening of the University of Virginia in 1825. His original design, which was merely an expansion of his William and Mary scheme, called for ten distinct professorships or "schools", three of which were to cover the field of what that eminent Harvard graduate and independent member of Jefferson's "Republican" party, Mr. Justice Story of the Supreme Court of the United States, had recently described as "moral, political and juridical science." These three schools corresponded roughly with Story's analysis. Private ethics was to be combined with general grammar, rhetoric, and belles-lettres and the fine arts under a professor of "Ideology." A professor of "Government" was to give instruction in the Law of Nature and Nations, Political Economy and "History, being interwoven with politics and law." Coordinate with these and with the seven other schools, a professorship of Municipal Law was to be established. Practical exigencies reduced the three professorships concerned with the laws of human conduct to two, one of Ethics and Moral

Science and one of Law and Politics[3] [p. 118]. The latter chair
was filled in 1826, after failure to secure a more distinguished
incumbent of sound Republican views, by a practitioner, John T.
Lomax. Under him and his successors both law and politics — or,
to use the modern term, government — continued to be taught
together. As the field grew too large to be cultivated by one man,
an additional professor, specializing in Constitutional Law, was
appointed in 1851. . . . International law, under the Blackstonian
influence, likewise continued to be offered by the law department
rather than by the college. Political economy and history were
crowded out of the law course, being given in other schools when
given at all. For many years a law student was encouraged, though
not required, to register in more than one school of the university
[p. 119].

2. Harvard Before Story

In 1816 Chief Justice Isaac Parker was appointed as the first
Royall Professor of Law at Harvard. He conceived the Law School
as a *professional* school, devoted to the training of lawyers, in the
spirit of Litchfield; it was not to cater to civilians and lawyers at
the same time, in the compromise spirit of Blackstone and Kent.
It was to cover only *part* of the professional training of the lawyer,
leaving practice to be acquired in the office; although, in language
resembling Jefferson's, the inadequacy of office training is set
forth, Parker is quite clear that "the practical knowledge of business
may always be better learnt in the office of a distinguished counsellor." It was to be a *local* school, tending "greatly to improve the
character of the Bar of our State;" the advantage to the Union as a
whole of a "national law school" was not yet perceived by Harvard.
Finally, it was to be a *graduate* school. . . ; the precedent of theology rather than of medicine was to be followed; the college was not
to build up a law school competing with itself, but to superimpose
one upon a college basis [p. 138].

Only one feature of Parker's suggestions was followed: the
creation of a professional school intended primarily for the future
practitioner. Harvard had at last taken this decisive step. A degree

NOTE: 3, pp. 118–119: In the School of Law shall be taught the common
and statute law, that of the Chancery, the laws Feudal, Civil, Mercatorial,
Maritime, and of Nature and Nations; and also the principles of Government
and Political Economy.

was given to those who remained at least eighteen months. In 1823 a total period of three years of study was expected. No sequence between resident and office was insisted upon [p. 139].

Admission was thrown open to applicants from any state, . . . If Harvard has more recently taken the lead in replacing legal education upon a graduate basis, it is only fair to recall that it was Harvard that gave the signal for encouraging a merely nominal connection between the college and the bar. She lent the prestige of her name to the doctrine that calling a practitioner a university professor is equivalent to making his proprietary law class a university school; and that an academic law degree may properly be conferred upon students entirely destitute of academic training [p. 140].

3. Litchfield

Connecticut, immediately after the Revolution, had proportionally a much greater population, as compared with other states, than she has today. She was geographically accessible to students from other states. Her rules for admission to the bar, by prescribing a definite term of office clerkship, protected the practitioners in the educational monopoly [p. 128] which they enjoyed as a class; by not limiting the number of students in any office, they permitted free competition inside of the profession. Every lawyer received all the students he could get. The only limitations upon the size of his class were his own organizing and business-getting ability, and the leisure that was left to him from more important occupations.

The Litchfield school was the creation of Tapping Reeve, a Princeton graduate, who, in addition to his other qualifications for this work, had married into the influential Burr and Edwards families. Admitted to the bar in 1772, after studying under Jesse Root, he settled in a town which, although small, was convenient of access, being an important postroad junction. Deprived of opportunities of practice by the war, and yet protected by his location from its actual depredations, he devoted himself to teaching law, and at the close of the war found himself at the head of a fully developed law school.[3] A successful theological school, conducted by Dr. Bellamy in the neighboring town of Bethlehem, perhaps suggested to Reeve the possibility of developing a similar

---

NOTE: 3, p. 129:   1784 is the date usually assigned as the foundation. Its catalogue claims 1782. Doubtless it was never born — it simply grew.

institution for law students. Several causes contributed to his success. The publication in 1789 of the first volume of American Law Reports by a fellow townsman, Ephraim Kirby, attracted attention of lawyers to Litchfield. A successful girls' boarding school, started in 1792, was a great help on the social side; Mrs. Reeve informed young Augustus [p. 129] Hand, when he entered the school, that "the young ladies all marry law students." Finally, the influence of Mrs. Reeve's father, the president of Princeton, and of her brother, Aaron Burr, future Vice-President of the United States, and himself a student under Reeve, was undoubtedly exerted in his behalf. His school acquired a national reputation, numbering among its graduates young men from every state.

James Gould, a Yale graduate and tutor in the college, came to Reeve in 1795. Three years later he became his partner. Up to this time the total number of graduates is said to have been 210, or an annual average, since the war, of some ten or fifteen. Gould was a man with teaching experience and inaugurated a more regular system of records. Although during the next ten years the school did not show any great growth, it at least maintained itself, with an attendance sometimes as high as twenty-one, sometimes as low as nine students. In 1809, the attendance suddenly rose to thirty-three students, and in 1813, the year of its greatest prosperity, to fifty-five—a figure which for over twenty years stood as a record for American law schools.[1] The school continued in operation for twenty years longer, and with a good attendance as late as 1826. Thereafter, it rapidly declined. Its decay may be attributed in part to the rise of rival institutions commanding greater resources and headed by younger men; in part to the general sagging of educational standards throughout the country, incident to the democratic movement, which made the path of any law school hard; and in part to the fact that Gould, like Reeve, allowed himself to be tempted from his sheltered retreat into the glare of public life, and thus not merely neglected his school work, but exposed himself to the disrepute that eventually attached to Federalist judges. Politics, ambition and advancing years had undermined the school even before the advent of Judge Story to Harvard contributed the finishing touch. By 1833 it had sent out over a thousand graduates [p. 130].

NOTE: 1, p. 130: A new record was first established by the University of Virginia Law School in 1835, with 67 students, followed by Harvard in 1838 with 78.

The distinguishing characteristics of the school were its systematic course of lectures, delivered daily, and the fact that these were never published. Later college law school instructors, like Tucker, Kent and Story, having worked up lecture courses, were quick to publish their systematized results for the benefit of the profession at large. The inevitable effect of such publication upon students is to diminish the interest and importance of the lectures and to bring textbooks into prominence. This was the more natural in the study of law, for the reason that under the original apprenticeship system textbooks had always been the source to which students had been referred for the theory of the law. The preceptor's function had been to systematize the readings and to add practical training. Reeve and Gould preserved their system of lectures as a jealously guarded asset of their school. As delivered by Reeve alone in 1794, the course consisted of 139 lectures, covering, under a different arrangement, the same ground as Blackstone, except that the latter's discussion of governmental agencies and of criminal law were omitted. Later, the Law of Sheriffs and Gaolers and Criminal Law were added, and the complete course comprised a daily lecture, lasting from an hour and a quarter to an hour and a half, during a period of fourteen months. This included two vacations of four weeks each; for out-of-state students who would not take Connecticut Practice, it is clear that not more than a single year's residence was contemplated.[2] Students were required to write up their notes carefully, to do collateral reading, and to stand a strict examination every Saturday upon the work of the week. . . . Doubtless from the beginning, and certainly during the later years of the school, optional moot courts and debating societies were in operation. The school offered a good narrow course in which the common [p. 131] law was taught as a "system of connected rational principles" rather than as a "code of arbitrary, but authoritative, rules and dogmas." Concerned with law as a "science," in the brief time at its disposal it did not undertake to do for a student everything of a practical nature that needed to be done. Under the rules for admission to the bar prevailing in the several states, attendance at this school, if allowed to count at all, would count for only part of the prescribed period of study [p. 132].

NOTE: 2, p. 131:   Gould wrote in 1822 that by lecturing a full hour and a half every day except Sunday, and in giving a supernumerary lecture one evening a week on Criminal Law, he had once succeeded in covering the entire course in about a year.

In the absence of endowment, and before the discovery that an independent law school might attract students by conferring the university degree of LL.B., a school of this type was entirely dependent for its success upon the personal force of its proprietor. When he died, or aged, or secured something better to do, there remained no definite asset upon which a successor might build. The significance of this group of schools in our educational development is that they served temporarily to bridge the gap between the students who wished systematized instruction in law and the colleges that were not yet prepared to give it [p. 133].

4. Early Private Law Schools

The early private law school was essentially a specialized and elaborated law office. It originated in New England, where the apprenticeship system was most firmly established, spread from there into other states, and was eventually not so much destroyed as absorbed by the college or university law school, whose character it largely determined. As a fully developed, self-conscious institution, announcing itself as such, it appeared slightly later than the early southern college law school. Unlike this artificial creation, however, it developed by imperceptible steps out of a practitioner's class and represents a more primitive type of educational organ. The two conditions requisite for its appearance were, first, a reasonably large and accessible supply of prospective law students, among whom it could market its educational wares; and, second, an attitude in the profession favorable to specialization in legal education. Certain states continued at first the tradition (English statutes) that it was unethical on the part of a single practitioner either to attempt to corner the profitable educational market for his private gain, or to teach law so extensively as to flood the profession. . . . It was not until after Harvard had made its first unsuccessful incursion into the field of legal education that professional vigilance in Massachusetts relaxed and that this state fell into line with the general movement [p. 128].

5. Law in the Colonial Colleges

The following tradition had been established in regard to the proper relationship between a university and legal education. First, it was generally felt that, for those who aspired to reach the higher ranks of the profession, a university education was desirable. Secondly, the advantages to be derived from this education were primarily social and cultural; it was by no means contemplated that the university should undertake the technical training which the practitioner already provided under the apprenticeship system. Thirdly, the law had recently come to be regarded as a fit subject for academic treatment; one to which the university might well devote greater attention than it had been in the habit of doing, both in the general interest of all its students and in the particular interest of those who might subsequently undertake professional law studies. This tradition we had to apply and to adjust to our own cruder facilities of higher education as best we might. We had no university embracing, like those of Oxford and Cambridge, separate colleges united by a common bond. Nine meagerly endowed colleges, having no organic connection with one another, and separated by wide distances, were all that the new-born country had to offer. The expansion of these units into complete institutions—the later binding together of these local institutions into national associations working together for a common end—all this was still far in the future.

That a college education, irrespective of its content, is desirable, was expressed in the bar admission rules of two colonies: New York as early as 1756 required college graduates to study three years under a counsellor, seven years for other applicants. In Massachusetts the Suffolk County rules of 1771 required all applicants [p. 112] to have a college education, or a liberal education equivalent thereto, before entering upon the period of office study.

The second element, that strictly professional training was the business of the profession itself, was assumed without question everywhere. Even in Virginia, without requirement of a definite period of study, aspirants for the upper branch of the law who had not been to the English Inns of Court studied law, as did Jefferson under George Wythe, in the office of a lawyer.

The third traditional idea—that colleges should have something to say concerning rules governing the relations between men—may be seen as early as 1642 when Harvard announced second-year lectures upon "Ethics and Politicks at convenient distances of time." Under prevailing theological influences, Ethics, either under this name or under the labels of "Moral Philosophy" or of "Natural Law," easily established itself as an orthodox college subject everywhere. . . . Subsequently logic and metaphysics were added, and these chairs gradually [p. 113] developed into modern philosophical departments. "Politicks" either disappeared entirely, as at Harvard, or gradually cut loose both from morality and from philosophy and developed along lines of its own. The first curriculum of King's College (1755) listed "Chief Principles of Law and Government, together with History, Sacred and Profane" and this with the ethics group ("Metaphysics, Logic and Moral Philosophy, with something of Criticism") constituted the entire fourth-year curriculum. College of Philadelphia seniors in 1756 had a somewhat more detailed plan of study. Civil law was specifically mentioned in the politics group. The object of these studies was stated to provide "a knowledge and practical sense of the student's position as a man and a citizen." . . . Systematic instruction in law, as a subdivision of politics, now distinguished from ethics, was at least an idea familiar to academic thought when the doors of the colonial colleges were closed by the Revolution [p. 114].

What, then, was to be the line of development after the Revolution? Was English tradition to be preserved? Was an academic education (including political studies or not) desirable but not essential for all good citizens—lawyers among the rest—but that actual professional instruction may best be left to practitioners? Or, following the precedent in medicine and theology, may some or all of technical training be given under academic auspices, and a new complex institution arise—a university? What relation should then obtain between the old college and the new professional work? Should college be merely an optional preliminary to professional work, as in medicine? Or should the university's professional work be strictly postgraduate, as in theology? And finally, to the extent that the university might properly displace the practitioner in the field of professional education in law, what should be the policy of the state in its bar admission requirements? Should it merely place the university, in its competition for students, on an equal footing with the practitioner, giving it an opportunity to prove its claim as to the superior efficacy of its methods? Or should university law preparation be encouraged as inherently superior to office work, and if so, to what extent and how?

Even today the public, the profession and the universities are far from having reached an agreement in regard to more than one of these problems. It is now universally admitted that at least a part of the process of preparing applicants for the bar is a task that the university may properly assume. The following chapters will show how difficult it was to establish even this proposition against the conservative forces of tradition [p. 115].

6. General Similarity of Early Law Schools

At the beginning Virginia and Harvard sacrificed their colleges in different ways, and in pursuit of different ideals. Jefferson deliberately planned to abolish the college in favor of his more comprehensive university scheme, under which academic and professional chairs or "Schools" were to be coordinated on equal terms in a free democracy of learning. Harvard preserved its college organization intact, but set up beside it rival schools of medicine and law. Jefferson's scheme was the more idealistic and symmetrical. Its defect was that it ignored the fundamental distinction between cultural and professional education, and therefore could not be made to work, even badly, as did the Harvard system. The Virginia academic "Schools" continued in fraternal union with one another. The professional "Schools" expanded, through the creation of additional chairs, into professional departments, demanding [p. 154] the full time of their students, and standing apart from the rest of the university, which thus again became a virtually independent college in fact, if not in name. This development occurred in medicine as early as 1837; in law in 1851. After this date there was no real distinction between the Virginia and the Harvard type of university.

Similarly, as regards the curriculum of the law department, the Virginia ideal was much broader at the start. "Politics" for legislators as well as law proper for practitioners was in the beginning taught in this state and in the Kentucky school. When, in 1851, the rapid growth of American law threatened to crowd out politics, and statutes, and international law, the University of Virginia appointed a second professor, in order that justice might be done to all these topics. For the moment this was decidedly in contrast with the Harvard ideal. We have seen how narrow was the practitioners' course introduced by Stearns, and how Judge Story's efforts to broaden it culminated merely in the addition of his own important studies in the federal constitution. The field that a professional law school can profitably cultivate was defined, in short, quite differently in New England and in the South. Harvard, though it had a larger teaching force, cultivated a much smaller area. Here again events proved that, with the resources at their command, Harvard was right and Virginia was wrong. The volume of judicial decisions grew faster than did the capacity of the Virginia school to expand its teaching force. The charge of superficiality could be avoided only by dropping some of the subjects. Thus all schools have been forced to devote their main energies to the common law; and while the question of what they do with the rest of their time will eventually become of great interest (see p. 273 ff.) the total thus diverted does not bulk large in the final result. "Politics" even in the South has been relegated almost entirely to the colleges, where it has been developed in departments usually bearing the name of "Political Science" or "Government." In the University of Virginia itself, government courses are now given by the academic School (department) of Economics, though Parliamentary Law, as a direct inheritance from the original William [p. 155] and Mary curriculum (see p. 117) was offered until recently as a law school elective. Another minor consequence of Jefferson's broad ideas is the tendency, among universities influenced by Virginia, to place such borderland subjects as international law in the law school rather than in the college.[2] But on the whole, with whatever aspirations the schools started, in the end there was no substantial distinction between northern and southern courses of study.

. . . The two New England schools were alike in seeking to train only the practicing lawyer, and not the politician and legislator as well. Where they differed was in their estimate of the kind of training that the practitioner required. Harvard was slow to assume entire responsibility for this task, as a substitute for the system of office training. Its original conception of its mission was to leave to the office what the school cannot do so well. Yale from the start frankly attempted neither more nor less than an ordinary practitioner's course, annexing to itself what was essentially a systematized law office. Traces of this early conflict of ideals may at all periods of our history be found between school and school, or in the same school at different periods: now a somewhat greater emphasis upon a scholarly treatment of the broader aspects of the common law; now a greater attention to the minutiae of practice, to the drafting of written instruments, to the purely local law of the jurisdiction. Early law schools cannot be satisfactorily classified from this point of view. As the pressure to secure students,

NOTE: 2, p. 156: It is significant of the extent to which the divorce between law and government work has been carried in most universities that at Harvard, as the result of a recent attempt on the part of the law school to broaden its curriculum, independent courses in International Law, Roman Law, and the history of English law were in 1916–17 offered both by the law school and by the college Department of Government.

and therefore [p. 156] to give students what they demanded, has made itself felt under a competitive regime, few schools have pursued a consistent policy in this respect. The variations spring partly from the calibre or temperment of the instructors—the relative importance they attach to thorough grounding in fundamental principles, as against an education that will be of immediate use—and partly from the nature of the clientele to which the school most naturally appeals—whether to a national or to a local student body. The main significance of the shifting policy and general uncertainty as to precisely what subjects shall be taught is the evidence which this affords that the community demands more than a single type of legal education. In the attempt to be all things to all men, a standardized curriculum has been sought. Failure after all these years to agree as to the content of such a curriculum is a pretty fair indication that the task is impossible.

Everywhere, accordingly, university students and their instructors tended to become divided into independent and more or less competing groups: on the one side, college students who were taught only by the college faculty; on the other side, undergraduate students who were registered only under the professional faculties of law or medicine. The lines of division were sometimes blurred, it is true, because it was not unusual for students to carry academic and law work at the same time. This blurring occurred somewhat differently in the two sections of the country. In the South it was the result of the Jeffersonian tradition, which encouraged college students to elect professional work. Students registering both in the academic and in the law "Schools" appear in the University of Virginia catalogues until a late date. The notion survived even where the northern type of university organization was definitely introduced. . . . In the North, on the other hand, the rigorously prescribed college curriculum, the more intensive character of the law work, and—in the cities—the physical location of the law school near the courts instead of at the university, operated to exclude college students from the practitioners' classes. Here the pressure to break down artificial barriers was exerted in the opposite direction. The tendency was for law students occasionally to take a little academic work, rather than for college [p. 157] students to take law courses. At Harvard, although outside of Ticknor's modern language courses no effective instruction in academic subjects was open to law students, the privilege of attending the "public lectures" of the college faculty was for many years highly prized.

Furthermore, in an effort to counteract the excessive narrowness of the northern curriculum, a partial blending of the college and law school faculties sometimes occurred. During the first period of the Harvard Law School, for instance, the Royall Professor continued in theory to be primarily engaged in lecturing to college students. His lectures were merely "open," on the same principle as other public lectures, to Stearn's law students, who by this means secured their contact with nonprofessional law. It was only with Judge Story's arrival that this chair became technically part of the law school, that the work of its incumbent became avowedly professional law, and that instruction in government for the time being disappeared from the college. A generation later, a somewhat similar development occurred at Columbia. As part of an abortive plan to develop graduate studies in 1857, Francis Lieber was brought from South Carolina to occupy a chair of History and Political Science in the college. Just as the establishment of the Royall professorship at Harvard led at once to the opening of a practitioners' law school, so at Columbia the introduction of Lieber's work in government was followed the next year by Theodore W. Dwight's narrow professional course. Lieber continued to give [p. 158] undergraduate instruction in the college, and since Dwight's students could not conveniently leave their downtown location to attend his classes, it was arranged in 1860 that he should go down to give a special course in public law to them. Five years later, the college connection was broken and Lieber, like the Royall Professor at Harvard, became attached exclusively to the law school. Instead of working into the technical curriculum, Lieber continued to give lectures in his own nonprofessional field — optional, and rarely attended by more than four students. The ultimate results of the tradition thus started at Columbia have proved to be of some importance. It is obvious that so far as their immediate influence upon legal education was concerned, none of these devices bridged in any satisfactory way the widening gap between the academic college and the professional school. Northern and Southern schools became surprisingly alike in this as in all other respects, considering how different were their origins [p. 159].

7. Reorganization of Harvard Under Story

Whether this early Harvard school, turning out large numbers of young men into the profession and serving, because of its success, as a model to colleges in other states, exercised an equally beneficial influence upon legal education is a question more difficult to answer. Taking the brighter side first, Dane's original and primary purpose was the development not so much of lawyers as of law. He expressly stipulated that Story should be allowed time to publish as well as to teach. Another proviso he made, suggested both by the character of his personal labors and by his opposition, as an old school Federalist, to the doctrine of states rights then being agitated by Calhoun. Story was to confine himself to law "equally in force in all branches of our Federal Republic," supplemented . . . by "state laws useful in more states than one, law clearly distinguished from that state law which is in force, and of use, in a single state only." This is the origin of the Harvard tradition of scholarly publication as one of the main objects of its school, and of the [p. 143] "national law" as opposed to the "Law of the jurisdiction" as the main object of its study.

Criticism   A college education may properly be required by a university of its own law students, as a portion of a completely rounded education for the higher ranks of the bar, even if it may not properly be demanded by a democratic state as a qualification for the entire profession. Such was the English tradition, and such would seem to be the logical position for a college that is sure of its own worth. This was not the conception of university education held [p. 144] by Jefferson, who was constitutionally opposed to requirements of any sort. But Harvard, although just beginning to be influenced by Jefferson's liberalizing views, was far from accepting his radical reconstruction of the whole scheme of higher education. . . . Harvard has tenaciously clung to her college as the essential kernel of her entire university system. In spite of this fact she went even farther than Jefferson in discouraging law school students from acquiring a liberal education. In the University of Virginia the "schools" were so correlated that it was easy for the law student to take liberal studies at the same time. But at Harvard, although law students were admitted to the "public lectures" of the college, it was only in modern language courses that actual instruction might be secured, and then only by paying an additional fee. Except for this possibility, the law school was then, as now, maintained as a virtually separate institution. Its students were freed even from the college requirement or residence in Cambridge. Liberal studies must be pursued, if at all, before the law was begun. And yet the school did not demand any preliminary education in its students. So far from requiring them

to be college graduates, it did not even require them to have enough
education to be admitted to college [p. 145].

That under these circumstances a considerable proportion of
Harvard law school students should have continued to be college-
bred men is a tribute to the tenacity of the college tradition among
applicants for the bar. . . . Story's failure while professing to believe in the value of such studies (general Philosophy, Rhetoric,
History, Oratory) for lawyers, to find any place for them in the
curriculum of his school is of interest chiefly as destroying a possible defense for his failure to insist upon college study [p. 146].
State government and also statutory law were eliminated. A valid
defense exists: Harvard has endeavored to cover part of the broad
field of legal education thoroughly, instead of dissipating its energies. . . . Whether by deliberate choice, or through necessity, or
through apathy and neglect, thoroughness rather than breadth has
remained Harvard's dominating ideal [p. 147].

The particular portion of "Ethicks and Politicks," of "moral,
political and juridical science", on which the Harvard Law School
has concentrated its energies from the start, was just that portion
which the practitioners most wanted. A wise adjustment of educational supply to public and professional demand is of course
always in order. . . . It is impossible to avoid the suspicion that
. . . Story was pursuing the line of least resistance. The university
was following, not leading, the profession. Furthermore, as regards
one highly important feature of the narrowed curriculum — its recognition of the needs only of the practitioner and judge and its apparent ignoring of the service that a university law school might perform in training legislators. Story concentrated on common law and
judicial decisions. He thought that government ought to be studied
in the elementary schools along with ethics, natural law and theology. Under the lead of this most successful [p. 148] of American
law schools the orthodox province of law school teaching was now
defined. Politics and law were no longer to be joined as in Jefferson's two Virginia institutions. Politics, as a subject of university
study, was eventually to be developed by the college in its departments of government or political science; the particular function
of the law school, from now on, was to cope with the increasing
flood of judicial decisions.

From some points of view this record is not inspiring. Educational standards were subordinated to the ambition of building up
attendance. More students mean more money and more fame. Fame

means still more students and hence more money. . . . However, Harvard made solid contributions to legal scholarship during these years and devoted the law school receipts to the benefit of the school [p. 149]. The law library grew. From accumulated surplus future buildings could be built. . . . The ideal of conducting the best possible school for contemporary lawyers was sacrificed, perhaps justifiably, to the development of American law and to the ultimate strengthening of legal education.

8. Spread of Standardized Type of Law School

The leading colleges and universities of the day having finally agreed upon a general policy in regard to legal education, there followed a long period of formal imitation. Virginia and New England — Thomas Jefferson and Harvard — representing though they did opposing influences in American life, had combined to establish the principle that instruction in technical or vocational law should be provided for students who had taken none of the work offered by the traditional Anglo-American college. This decision, following the similar step that had already been taken in connection with medicine, gave us the American university in its original and still prevailing form — the form that it universally bore prior to the introduction of graduate study. Professional schools conducted by and for practitioners were to be loosely coordinated with the original college rather than worked into an integrated educational scheme. Under Harvard's influence no premium was placed upon college work as a desirable element in a fully rounded education for the bar. Prospective lawyers might, as always, go through the college before they began their law studies, or they might not. So long as they could be persuaded to enter the university law school on any terms, the university authorities were glad to take them in. Even the state did more to encourage academic training than this. Several states permitted college graduates to complete their strictly professional training in a shorter period than was normally required. . . . If it was desirable that two grades of practitioners should be trained — the liberally educated leaders of the profession and the mere technical craftsmen — and that the university should train both, all such distinctions were ignored in the school itself, which placed students of both types on an identical basis in the classroom. The interests both of the college and of the profession were subordinated to the widespread desire to secure professional students in medicine and in law in order thereby to expand old-fashioned colleges into up-to-date universities [p. 151].

This development of a regular degree course of a definite and gradually increasing length may be summed up as follows: the colleges were still under the influence of what may be termed the quantitative theory of education—the notion that the entire field of any science can be mastered within a definite period of years. They had not yet reached the conception of the boundlessness of human knowledge that underlies both the elective system and graduate research study. Had the colleges been in control of legal education, they would doubtless have devised a curriculum, occupying some period assumed to be adequate for the purpose in view—in all probability three years. They would have fortified this curriculum by requirements of admission at the start, and by the award of a degree at the end. American legal education [p. 178] would have been cut and dried, more effective, less plastic, less of a tax upon the powers of one who attempts to describe it. The colleges were not in control of legal education, however. On the contrary, they were only humble aspirants, seeking to gain a foothold. Prospective practitioners did not see the necessity of devoting much time to law study, in states where no period of preparation was prescribed; they were far from being certain that theoretical school studies were necessarily preferable to practical office work, even in states where they were obliged to take a definite amount of one or the other. The colleges might, by judicious use of their power to confer academic degrees, enhance the apparent value of their instruction to some extent; these degrees possessed at first only sentimental value, and, because of their novelty, not much even of this; bait of this sort was therefore not remarkably effective. Moreover, the colleges did not command sufficient financial resources to warrant them in offering instruction that few or no students would take. They were obliged to organize their law schools in such manner as to appeal to the greatest possible number. In the first place, they had to meet the wishes of those who would not come to the school if required to do more than the irreducible minimum of work demanded by the state. No vexatious obstacles must be thrown in the path of possible students. Entrance requirements were accordingly scrupulously avoided. In the second place, it was impracticable to offer these students more technical work than a considerable number could reasonably be expected to take, whether influenced by the desire of knowledge for its own sake, or by other considerations. The schools could offer a little more, but not much more, than the states required. The promise of a degree was utilized for the purpose of making this extra work attractive.

Prior to the Civil War, two years of honest work was or was thought to be, a little more than the traffic could bear. . . . Some schools made no pretense of giving more than a single year's course. Some gave a two years' course only in name. Some granted concessions to particular types of applicants, or made small demands upon the time and energies of any student. Harvard came to two full years of work, but did not raise its briefer degree requirement to correspond [p. 179].

The creation and permanent establishment of university law schools has been the most important forward step taken by American legal education prior to the Civil War, and one which went far to offset the demoralization of the bar produced by lowered state requirements. Primitive as were these ante-bellum schools, they represented a type of educational organization capable of infinitely greater development than the apprenticeship system of legal training that they replaced. The period as a whole was one of educational advance.

From a political point of view, more can be said today in defense of the policy pursued by the states. Today we can devote our energies to the task of making democracy operate more efficiently, for the reason that the democratic principle itself is secure. Before 1870, democracy was fighting its way into its own. It took the Civil War to prove that government could be strong and yet that the right of every man to participate in it could endure. . . . Every feature of governmental administration that was not affirmatively democratic came under suspicion. Of this sort were bar admission rules that tended not merely to qualify but also to exclude — whose apparent effect, if not whose deliberate intent, was to make law practice a social monopoly. The right of every man to participate in the making of his own laws is indeed a hollow mockery, if only strangers may participate in the administration and enforcement of these laws. Undemocratic restrictions had to be abolished before extra-democratic regulations could be devised — regulations calculated not to [p. 203] undermine popular self-government, but to make this type of political organization, in its own interest, more efficient. So, here, as in the civil service, the gates of privilege, when they would not open, were battered down, and the way was paved for future progress [p. 204].

9. Efforts to Broaden Legal Education, 1865–90

The overwhelming majority of students, then as now, frequented law schools, and came up for bar examinations, with the intention of actually practicing law in some particular jurisdiction. A few cherished the intention of becoming teachers or scholars, or studied law as an elegant accomplishment, or as an aid in administering their private fortune, or as an introduction to a political career, or as an anchor to windward in case no better opportunity of earning a livelihood presented itself. . . . The [p. 276] main purpose for which all law schools existed was to train practitioners of private law. They were successful in securing and holding students only in so far as they could show that the training represented by their degree was of value for this purpose. . . .

There are three component parts of an ideally complete preparation: practical training, theoretical knowledge of the law, and general education.

 a. Object of training must be to develop skill or discipline, as distinguished from information or knowledge.

 b. It must give the student such a mastery of theoretical legal knowledge as may ultimately assist him to attain the object in view. Law itself must not be narrowly defined. Borderland and allied [p. 277] studies, such as jurisprudence and government, must be included.

 c. It must include such additional sciences or arts helpful to the prospective lawyer. Medicine for use in personal injury cases, science for use in patent cases, any study that promotes accuracy of reasoning and effectiveness of expression that are so essential in the practice of law. Studies that have no practical application to a lawyer's professional work and yet may contribute to make him a better citizen and a happier individual belong here also [p. 278].

Probably from the idealistic point of view and certainly in our existing scheme of educational organization, practical training, technical knowledge and general education each has its different subordinate aim. All have their place in a fully developed curriculum, designed to prepare for an elaborate art or profession [p. 279].

Centres in legal education are, first, the law office, or such other centres of active professional work as may arise. If practical training in the law is to be conducted under conditions resembling actual practice, it must be through cooperation between the schools and these outside agencies. A second centre is the law school itself. Whatever may be attempted in the way of providing practical training under academic conditions, the special function of a law school is to provide, if not adequate theoretical knowledge of the law, then at least the training which will enable students subsequently to acquire this knowledge for themselves. Incidental to the discharge of this function, the school must decide which portions of the law may best be taught by methods appropriate to it, and which may better be left to the practitioners' centres. The third centre is the mechanism of lower schools and colleges, upon which the responsibility for general education is properly thrown. . . . The final stage in educational development is attained when the three centres learn to cooperate instead of to compete. A single larger organization, the several parts of which are mutually supporting in a spirit of subordination to the common whole, is the goal toward which American legal education is moving [p. 280].

However shallow may be the theoretical knowledge imparted by the weakest night school it at least constitutes a better preparation for practice than the haphazard empiricism of an office [Note 1, p. 282].

One difficulty in practical training is that of securing objects upon which the students may practice, authentic clients. Until quite recently the legal profession has conspicuously failed to support charitable institutions in which a varied assortment of patients may be secured. Legal aid has just begun to develop. . . . [p. 282]. In the judgment of the writer, the movement is too promising a one to be disregarded in any comprehensive view of the subject. They might ultimately be able to play that part in the legal educational process for which the private law office is no longer fitted [p. 286].

The importance of bringing theoretically educated students into contact with genuine practice is such that, as a matter of principle, this general requirement might well be insisted upon and its admitted inadequacy be made a ground, not for opposing it, but for trying to make it better [p. 287].

The sound argument in support of a national law school is based on a frank recognition of the fact that a school of this type is designed to serve a different purpose from that of a local school. Its primary interest is not with the law as it is, but with the law as it may become. It recognizes the lack of uniformity in the law of the several states as a fact, but as a regrettable one, and conceives its mission to be to do all in its power to remedy this evil, both on the personal and on the scholarly side. It sends into practice, into the legislature, onto the bench, men who, understanding the ideal as distinguished from the actual law, recognize their responsibility as parts of a general law-making machine and are animated with the ambition not merely to utilize the law as it is, but also to convert it into a more efficient instrument of justice. It [p. 291] produces textbooks and periodical articles with the same end in view. It is not daunted by the sneering comment sometimes made that it encourages its youngest graduates to think that they know more law than the courts. . . .

This was the tradition of Dane and Story—the conception of institutions of learning which should slowly dominate the law, fusing into a coherent homogeneous body the scattered and frequently contradictory principles that are ground forth by overburdened courts or adventurous legislatures. The difficulty with carrying this conception into effect is that pending the time when the law becomes what it ought [p. 292] to be, practitioners have to make their living out of the law as it is. There is an insistent pressure upon the national schools to supplement their particular function of teaching ideal or generalized law, by courses which shall not leave their students suspended in this rarefied scholarly air [p. 293].

Schools that exist primarily to satisfy a public demand, which in a democratic community is bound to be reckoned with, will be stronger at the hither end of the instruction, where immediate utility is most manifest. Schools that exist primarily to exercise that leadership which a democratic community requires will be stronger at the farther end, in studies whose utility is perhaps even greater for being more remote. When each type of school learns to respect the other's especial field, and the state devises a bar admission system capable of doing justice to both, the problem will be in a fair way of being solved. It is probable that in our final educational scheme, the two types will be found cooperating with one another [p. 295].

This restriction of the law school curriculum to technical law was bad for the lawyer, and perhaps even worse for the politician. For in spite of the fact that legal education was not keyed to his special needs, the inherent connection between law and politics has made the law school the nearest thing to a training ground for the profession of politics that we possess [p. 296].

The trouble with our lawyer leaders is not alone that they have never been given an opportunity to make a careful study of the political mechanism that has been confided to them to operate and to perfect. In addition, they carry over into public life the particularist as opposed to the social point of view. Their primary interest, as private practitioners, having necessarily been to serve their clients, they continue, often in good faith, to serve primarily their constituents in public life — corporations or labor unions, as the case may be. They are predisposed to identify the interests of the community with those of some special party or part, rather than to subordinate special interests to the common welfare [p. 297].

Although a considerable measure of specialization has begun to appear in the practice of the law, none is recognized by the bar admission rules of the states. A practitioner may confine himself in his practice to admiralty or patent laws, to defending criminals . . . but to do any of these things he has to be a general lawyer first. In this, as in other questions of policy, the schools must conform to the traditional organization of the profession. . . . Confronted as they now are with the triple responsibility of teaching law that is increasing daily in bulk, and of teaching law by modern and more thorough methods, they show signs of giving way under the strain. Technical law threatens not merely to crowd everything else out of the curriculum, but to be itself too heavy a burden for any single school to carry as a whole. Some have lessened the burden by eliminating local law. . . . As there seems to be no practicable means of reducing the volume of the law in the near future, and nobody wants the law to be less thoroughly taught, the only available remedy is in the direction of specialized schools leading into specialized branches of the profession. This development will probably not occur very soon [p. 298]. It will probably not occur as soon as it ought. Sooner or later, as the existing unitary organization of legal education, and of the profession itself, proves inadequate to meet the requirements of actual practice, the organization will be changed to correspond. Even then it will not meet these requirements perfectly, for conditions change more quickly than mechanical improvements can be made. But the capacity of the system will be less hopelessly overtaxed than it is at present [p. 299].

General education If, in concession to democratic feeling, entrance to the profession was not to be absolutely restricted to college graduates, at least it seemed reasonable that students not liberally educated should devote additional time to mastering technicalities [p. 312].

Harvard, and following its lead, all other colleges, let everybody into its law school indiscriminately, and put them all through the same course of study, whether college graduates or not. The two types of prospective practitioners (the one animated by professional, the other more by commercial ideals) were completely merged, in other words, in the technical portion of their training. The distinction became merely that after leaving the lower schools some students continued to go to college before beginning specialized professional work, while other students short-circuited the college. Legal education, inevitably became defined in terms of the element common to both types of students — the technical training afforded by law school or office. The four-year college course came to be regarded as something that might or might not be interpolated between this and the lower schools, and that was more closely allied with lower schools than with law school work. It was justified not as part of a student's preparation for admission to the bar, but as an extension of his preparation for admission to law school. No state and no school has ever dared to require this much preliminary education of all its entrants. Many have encouraged it, but weakly [p. 313].

It is very difficult to show that any definite type or definite amount of preliminary education is peculiarly adapted to preparing students to undertake with profit law school or office work to the preliminary education actually possessed by the students. This was the policy universally followed by law schools prior to the Civil War. All could argue that their students might profitably pursue the studies of the school, because all adapted the studies to the students. There was inherent in the system a tendency to sag on both sides of the line. The general educational attainments of the profession were lowered, because little general education was needed to do justice to the law school work. The technical attainments of the profession were lowered, because the law school work was conducted on a plane suitable for students with little general education.

The prescribed age of twenty-one years, made by many states, maintained something like a general standard of maturity, and was the practical substitute for entrance requirements in [p. 314] legal education before the Civil War.

The recovery from this shocking degradation of legal education has been very slow. The law schools have been handicapped by the policy pursued by the states. The state policy has been largely determined by lawyers who have picked up, as students or practitioners, legal technique, and little else. Narrowly expert themselves, they have not realized how much American law has suffered from losing contact with education as a whole. They have brought the entire profession into disrepute by cultivating an exclusive class consciousness, blind to its own defects, contemptuous of the suggestion that a phase of education that they themselves have lacked could be of any real benefit to a lawyer. Reference to State Bar Association Proceedings will reveal how much easier it is to persuade the bar that the period of technical training should be lengthened, or that the examining machinery should be strengthened, than it is to secure sympathetic consideration for a proposal to require general or "academic" education. The entire blame cannot be laid on the shoulders of this ignorant vested interest. Part of it must be borne by advocates of general education, who have not stated the argument for it as effectively as they might. If the only purpose of entrance requirements were to prepare students to wrestle with the complexities of technical law, then—let us be honest about it—no fixed amount of preliminary education need be insisted upon. The habit of doing mental rather than manual work is of course necessary. This habit may be acquired in so many ways, outside of schools and colleges—and the extent to which the habit is inculcated even by schools and colleges is so much a matter of dispute—that there is much to be said in favor of the proposition that [p. 315] the best way of discovering whether an applicant is prepared to study law is to let him try. A bright high school graduate or a zealous self-educated clerk will often play around a college graduate in law school courses organized as they are today.

Prospective practitioners of different vocations must receive part of their education in common, for reasons of economy: the community cannot afford to establish specialized machinery for more than the final stage of the training. They must do so for what is technically known as "orientation": when they start their education, they do not know what they will eventually do, and it is against public policy that they should be forced to make a too early decision. They must do so in order to establish an equipoise to [p. 316] the narrowing tendencies of training for one particular end: the late war has fortified in this country the English tradition that education which conduces in no way, that human calculation can foresee, to the efficient discharge of our particular duties, whether as citizens or as individuals, may nevertheless have a value of its own, by widening our sympathies, teaching us toleration of another's point of view, freeing us from the temptation to subordinate humanitarian impulses to the demands of ruthless logic. The organization of American education as a whole along lines that shall give due weight to the frequently conflicting demands of economy, efficiency and idealism, is a colossal task, in which historical reasons prevent rapid progress from being made. The worker in any particular field is compelled to accept the general system as it is, and fit in his specialty as best he can. This predetermined general system consists, so far as law schools are concerned, in the first place of the lower schools, both elementary and "high"; and in the second place of the colleges [p. 317].

There was for a time a marked contrast between the position of northern and southern colleges in legal education, due ultimately to the fact that the northern colleges did not pay serious attention to the needs of lawyers until after private law schools had been organized, while in the South the academicians preceded the practitioners. Whereas in the North, the college acted principally as the foster mother of the law schools, in the South it was in many cases a true parent. We cannot do justice to peculiarities of southern law schools if we do not realize that they were much less definitely professional annexes to the college than were those of the North; that their position was for a long time that of specialized departments not completely separated. In Alabama students were urged to take college courses in English language and literature and in ancient and modern languages, simultaneously with their regular work. Combination courses of different lengths prevailed in other southern schools [p. 324].

The general principle that underlay the varying southern provisions was to preserve, so far as possible, the academic element in legal education, though not positively to insist upon it, if a student wished to hurry through. If he were willing to devote as much as four years to his education, he seems commonly to have been able to secure an A.B. and an LL.B. simultaneously.

This was one method whereby a minority of lawyers were enabled to secure the broadening advantages of higher academic education in addition to the prevailingly technical instruction offered to all lawyers in the law school itself. It represented a survival of English traditions of university organization, as originally exemplified in this country in William and Mary College [p. 166].

Its distinguishing characteristic was that students were encouraged to do two quite different types of work at the same time. Its special merit was that law students were continuously exposed to the academic virus, so to speak. They might at any time take up this additional work. If they did not do so themselves, they were in constant personal contact with those who did. Had the mastery of technical American law remained the relatively simple task that it was when legal education was started in the South, the educational relationship of the college to the law school might have developed permanently along these lines. The lower ranks of the profession would have taken, after leaving the lower schools, a brief technical course. The higher ranks would have taken, either in the same schools or in separate schools intended for them alone, a longer course, containing parallel strains of general and of technical training [p. 324].

Technical American law has become so difficult to master that those who have had to teach it have been jealous of any division of their students' time. They have felt that the educational system just described encourages diffusion of effort when intensive study is required, and that it often leads also to an overcrowded curriculum. In this attitude they have certainly been right. The impulse back of [p. 325] optional parallel college work is a good one, but the actual operation of an educational system thus organized is bad. To the extent that traces of it linger in a few institutions even to the present day, these institutions may fairly be said not to have faced conditions as they are. They are still under the influence of primitive ideals, originating in a college professor's atmosphere, and perpetuated by influences out of touch with the outside world.

The successful American law school is not an organic outgrowth of the American college. Although greatly helped by its association with the college, it found its true starting point when its practitioner teachers insisted that during that portion of the student's education which was entrusted to their care technical law should be his sole pursuit. Even the borderland subjects, as to whose practical utility judgments may vary, were less commonly offered by northern than by southern law schools, more commonly offered by northern than by southern colleges. As for "culture," that was emphatically relegated to the preliminary college years. Efficiency, with all its limitations, was erected as the appropriate ideal of the law school itself, and a proper division of functions between the generalized and the specialized parts of our educational machinery was thus encouraged.

There was no general revolt in these better organized law schools against the college as a factor in legal education. South and North agreed in the main points of their educational program: (1) that there was much training of value to the lawyer that could not be given either by the lower schools or by the law school itself; (2) that more or less adequate opportunities to secure this training were provided by the colleges; (3) that this college work must, under democratic conditions, be regarded as auxiliary training to be taken voluntarily by the few, rather than as essential training to be required of everybody. Where southern and northern practice differed was simply as to the stage of the student's career when this optional supplementary training might be taken. The northern schools were the first to realize that the latter years of a student's education must be focused upon the more narrowly vocational aspects of his work, that the distinctively broadening portions of his training must come, if at all, in the years before he enters law school [p. 326].

This much of the problem has been solved on rational grounds, logically justifiable and generally accepted today. For while there are not wanting extremists on the one side who believe that no one who has not taken a full college course should be permitted to study law, and extremists on the other side who argue that all college work is a waste of time or worse, the definitely established practice lies between. Those who have no temperamental sympathy with democracy still think it unfortunate that any one who has not received the best possible legal education should be permitted to practice law. Fanatical democrats still regard college education as a device whereby a favored class secures benefits denied to the masses. Meanwhile, some students continue to gain these benefits and some do not, and those who believe that the mission of the favored minority is not to dominate, but is to lead, regard this division of practitioners along educational lines as not merely inevitable, but sound. So far as concerns the broad underlying principle involved, the present system seems, at least to the writer, entirely satisfactory.

Historical reasons, far more than conscious adaptation of means to ends, explain the precise position that the college occupies in legal education today. A four-year college had taken an alien two or three-year professional school under its wing. Two quite different points of view thus became represented in the university faculty, with the advantage of numbers for a long while on the side of the college. The merging of these two points of view into a single "university" policy, that should enable the college to do for legal education all that the college ought to do, has necessarily been an extremely slow process. Among the most unfortunate results of the divergence of purpose and of fundamental aim has been that, until quite recently, no university has been willing to concentrate its energies upon the task of training the minority of broadly educated lawyers that the community needs, and to abandon to institutions with less ambitious aims the preparation of other types of practitioners. Throughout the period under review students were everywhere encouraged to take college work first, and to follow this up with a law school course. But if a student wished to omit the college and to proceed directly from the lower schools to the study of technical law, the authorities preferred that he should secure his preparation [p. 327] in their own law school rather than in some "inferior institution". Undoubtedly, the universities honestly thought that they were in this way serving the community. They simply failed to realize that this policy tended both to keep these other institutions inferior, and to prevent their own schools from realizing their possibilities to the fullest extent. Obsessed by the theory of a unitary profession and of a uniform preparation and tests for admission to the bar, they tried to develop a single type of law school, open to students whose preliminary training had been most diverse. The problem of properly adapting the technical work to the capacity of the student has thereby been greatly complicated. It is cruel, after having enticed a student into a school, to keep the work on a level to which, through no fault of his own, he cannot rise. On the other hand, it is unfair to the better prepared and more mature man, and against the interests of the community at large, to bring the general level of instruction down to the relatively juvenile plane suitable for many students. So long as the doors are kept wide open for students of diverse capacities, there is no way of avoiding the one without running into the other of these evils.

This ideal of being all things to all men was the ideal in accordance with which all law schools operated, until Harvard placed its school upon a college graduate basis in 1896 [p. 328].

Under Langdell Harvard made various changes in its institutional methods and devoted itself to law reform [p. 344]. The improvements were calculated not so much to produce a permanently satisfactory method of training lawyers as to supply the particular sort of training that the immediate situation demanded most. They took the form of testing the student's proficiency by a system of formal examinations: increasing the amount of instruction and altering its distribution among the students and the teaching force; substituting finally, for older methods of classroom work, the now famous "case method" [p. 345].

[So much has been written about the case method that those interested in Reed's observations and criticism may simply be referred to pp. 369–388.]

[Reed regrets that the attempt to construct a comprehensive classification of the law had to be abandoned.] Textbook writers, in the schools and out of them, defined each for himself his field of study, and thus crystallized the law into units which subsequent text writers and subsequent law schools were compelled to recognize. There resulted not merely a confused, but also an incomplete, covering of the field. The task of keeping pace with the volume of decisions proved so enormous as to leave time for little else. [Reed points out to the] opponents of technical law-reform that the community at large is not satisfied with the present condition of American law. [He realizes though that] steps taken toward remedying its confusion are not likely to be attended with such immediate success as to place a strait-jacket upon the body politic. The danger is rather that unless some action is taken to clarify and simplify the hodgepodge of moss-grown precedent and popular petulance which courts and legislatures have fastened upon us, the people will destroy this existing law entirely, with all its evil and with all its good, not distinguishing between its repellently mysterious shell and the core of justice and of truth that lies deeply concealed within it [p. 349]. This necessity for a technical reshaping of the law is entirely distinct from the question of what substantial changes are or are not also needed in order to bring it into harmony with the conditions under which we live today. This latter is a question of policy, as to which men will always disagree. . . . Discussion of new law cannot intelligently proceed, so long as existing law is virtually unintelligible.

Whether Harvard could have done more than she actually did to introduce order into chaos (during the period 1865–1890) cannot be definitely answered. She accomplished so much and established herself so definitely as the leader of other schools in a thorough going analysis of the law, that her actual achievements far out-weighed her probably inevitable omissions. What she failed to do was to display any interest in a future synthesis of the scattered titles of the law. The nearest she came to it was Langdell's attempt to build up a prescribed honor "curriculum", consisting of compara-tively few titles, later abandoned. Harvard deserves credit, not because she has done anything directly to further a comprehensive reclassification of the law but because she undertook a type of work that first had to be done before a subsequent synthesis could be profitably attempted [p. 350].

The law to be analyzed and classified was no longer regarded as a flat field, to be studied as it exists today. Time was recognized as an element that must be considered in gauging the authority of decisions of other days. The field of law became a body of three dimensions. This thoroughgoing working over of the material resulted in changes in the courses or subjects taught. . . . The working classification of some twenty courses was accepted, and it was only within these compartments that [p. 351] the principles were reformulated and recombined.

. . . The condition of American law combined with the traditional manner in which the law was parceled out among the professors to perpetuate the patchwork character of the curriculum as a whole. Formed by a rough piecing together of rather large-sized scraps, it resembled nothing so much as a crazy quilt, that most inadequately covered the body of the law. Sometimes the patches would overlap in several thicknesses. Sometimes an ugly gap would be left. More important even than this, statutory law and government were largely ignored. While the torso of the legal anatomy was covered more or less, its most rapidly growing portions stuck out [p. 352] in ungainly fashion. All this the schools did nothing and could do nothing to change. What they did was to substitute for threadbare material more modern and less sleazy stuff. The garment was basted together much as before, but the individual pieces were infinitely better woven. For this invaluable preliminary reconstruction of the law Harvard deserves the princi-pal credit, on three counts: First, because she inaugurated the movement. Second, because more clearly than her rivals she appre-ciated the difficulty of the task, and devoted to it an amount of effort commensurate with its importance. Third, because she saw that the best way to improve American law is to improve American lawyers, by whom, as private practitioners, as judges and as legislators, American law is made. Avoiding ineffectual "graduate years"—sacrificing even scholarly publication to the exigencies of a laborious pedagogical routine—she turned out not books, but men: men who were not merely themselves trained to a new understanding of the law, but could fight to make their interpretation accepted generally as the true one [p. 353].

Since the advent of Story, Harvard has always provided her law students with a greater amount of instruction than she has obliged them to take in order to secure her degree. . . . Perhaps eighteen year-hours, representing less than 600 actual hours, were offered when Langdell came to the school. During the next twenty years this total was just about doubled. . . . This increase in the time devoted to instruction must all be charged up to the account of thoroughness or depth of treatment [p. 354].

Until Langdell's time, Harvard had no regular examinations, only recitations as part of the lecture work. Since attendance at lectures was voluntary, the proficiency of the students was not tested at all, which was justified on the ground that the student had to take a bar examination in his own state, and that the LL.B. was "honorary" [p. 356].

Langdell introduced an examination system far more rigorous than that in force in any other school. His innovation consisted not in instituting final degree-examinations—those existed in other schools. It consisted in making the examinations written, in accordance with the practice prevailing in the college. And in replacing the single final examination, covering the work of the entire curriculum, by annual examinations, covering the work of each year separately, with the student's promotion to second-year work dependent upon his success in passing first-year examinations. In the technical language of pedagogy, Harvard became for the first time a "graded school," with promotion and graduation determined by written examinations. This system went into full effect at Harvard in the academic year 1871–72. It now exists in every law school and the feature of written examinations has become part also of our orthodox bar admission machinery [p. 357].

Langdell found it impossible to reduce the law to a body of principles that could be mastered in three years. The extension of the elective system after 1886 [p. 309] was equivalent to a formal recognition of this fact, and forced the case-method missionaries to justify it on more limited grounds. They made no claim to be accomplishing what heretofore had been assumed to be the function of every institution of learning—namely, to put its students into possession of some definite field of knowledge, however small. The case-method school no longer professed to give its students a present mastery of judge-made law. It prepared them merely to master judge-made law in the future.

This was and is the most important service that, under existing conditions, any school can render. It is pertinent to recall how much of the curriculum had already been left out: no practical training in advising clients or in conducting litigation, but only for acquisition of theoretical knowledge; no insistence upon a cultural college foundation, but only upon work done in the professional school itself; no attention to government or borderland subjects, but only to technical private law; no interest in statutory enactments of legislatures, but only in decisions that judges had made [p. 379]. The omitted portions were relegated to after life [p. 380].

While it is true that the textbook lawyer will still constitute in a sense, as he does now, an inferior grade, to whom the highest professional honors will not be paid, this is the inevitable and proper result of the smaller sacrifice of time and intellectual effort that he has devoted to his preparation [in night school which cannot use case method effectively]. It is by no means certain that as a money-maker he will not excel his more thoroughly and more liberally trained colleague; and because he stands nearer the people, he is more likely to desire and to secure the honors of political preferment. If he resents the subordinate position that to a certain extent he will occupy in the private practice of law, he may make himself in the legislature the master to whom the expert law drafter is subservient. These schools may look forward, therefore, to occupying a respected and self-respecting position in American legal education.

The reason why today textbook schools do not, as a whole, occupy the position that they should is because there are at present so few satisfactory legal textbooks. Built, as these schools are, upon the products of legal scholarship, instead of upon personal contact with scholarly men, first rate legal textbooks are as indispensable for them as first rate legal scholars and teachers are for case-method law schools. Books which are mere compilations of all previously decided cases, attempts at rational re-arrangement of an inherently irrational body of precedents, produce lawyers who are not only steeped in an old-fashioned theory of what constitutes contemporary American law, but who are inadequately trained to put even this theory into practice. . . . [p. 385].

The theory of law that lies at the bottom of Langdell's reform must in time dominate, but the preparation for its practice must be conducted by institutions of two radically different types: those that teach law as a science, gradually assuming form out of the inchoate mass of judicial decisions and statutes in which it at present lies; and those that teach the same law, to the extent that it is already formed, as the basis of a thoroughly practical vocation. The scientifically grounded lawyer can in time, if he has the ability, overtake the other. There is no danger that he will be crowded out of the profession. . . . Young men qualified to conduct the routine business of the lawyer are imperatively required. They can be best supplied by institutions which accept the labors of legal scholars as authoritative, and utilize them in that portion of their fuller curriculum which deals with the general principles of national judge-made law [p. 386].

The method of Langdell needs to be more consciously combined with the original ideal of Story. To a certain extent it is already so combined. Numerous exponents of the case method, beginning with Langdell himself, have as a matter of fact published texts. Articles contributed to legal periodicals, conducted by many law schools, since the establishment of the Harvard Law Review in 1887, are a step in the same direction [p. 387].

The greatest service that case-method schools can render is consciously to endeavor to express American law in such a form that inordinate effort on the part of both students and teachers will no longer be required in order to produce the unsatisfactory results yielded today even by our best law schools [p. 388].

The most important independent action taken by any law school during [p. 392] the period after 1890 was Harvard's revival, in 1896, of Chief Justice Parker's original idea of restricting admission to college graduates.

The effect of this movement to increase entrance requirements has been not to increase the amount of college education obtained by law students as a whole, but to introduce a new and important distinction between different types of educational preparation characteristics of different types of schools. The framers of our bar admission rules, however, have continued to impose uniform examination tests upon all applicants, however prepared. They have been blind to all distinctions of type, whether of this sort, or whether arising from differences in method of instruction, or in the kind of law, local or national, emphasized in different schools. Simultaneously, a great increase in the number of evening law schools has brought to the front a distinction between two general types of applicants that is even more obvious, and that has been equally ignored [p. 393].

10. Part-time Students

In law schools situated in small towns, such as Cambridge, instruction was naturally offered from the beginning during the regular working hours of the day, as in other departments of the university. Students had no access to a sufficient supply of law offices. Subject to the usual undergraduate distractions, they gave their full time to their law school work. The requirement of a certain period of study in the school, for the purpose of obtaining the degree, signified that this much time was supposed to be entirely devoted to the study of law. Whether it actually was all thus devoted depended of course upon the standards maintained at the particular institution. If any law office training was secured, this occurred before or after the student had entered the school. Under the original Harvard rule, college graduates were obliged to supplement a period of eighteen months in the law school by an additional period of eighteen months' office work. This yielded a total of three year pretty full law work in school and office combined.

In the larger cities, there was an equally natural tendency for instruction to be given at irregular hours, for the convenience primarily of the instructors who, as judges or practitioners, had other things to do [p. 394]. While the arrangement was primarily to suit the convenience of instructors, it also fitted in well with the tradition of law office study. The bulk of the students were clerks in law offices, who supplemented their practical routine by systematic work in the school. This division of labor grew up naturally. . . . The crash in bar admission standards affected all schools adversely, proving especially disastrous to the early type of city school. For if the country school was left unsupported by state requirements of a long period of law study and unsupplemented by subsequent office work, at least the tradition of full pressure work in the school itself was preserved. . . . The three-year law school course of today has claimed for [p. 395] its own all the ground lost when the supplementary training was abandoned.

Quite different is the situation into which the city schools drifted

Theirs was the tradition of much less strenuous work, so far as the school itself was concerned. . . . To the extent that the student continued voluntarily to attend the law office, he continued to absorb as much law as before, partly from the school and partly from the office. Gradually, as the state relaxed its requirement, the tradition of law office work, as an essential element in the training, also faded away. Students who were not in law offices—students who were supporting themselves in occupations entirely disconnected with the law—tended to take advantage of the convenient hours and to press for admission to these schools. The schools themselves found it convenient to continue their instruction on the old low pressure plan, and to confine their demands to what could be satisfied by the new type of student as readily as by the old. They did not take the step either of restricting admission to law office clerks or of intensifying the work to such a pitch as to require morning preparation from all their students. Insensibly, and we may say innocently, there thus arose "part-time" education in law . . . in the sense that students give only part of their time to any sort of legal training [p. 396].

Now, let there be no misunderstanding as to the significance of this development. Broadly considered, with reference to what can ultimately be made out of these part-time schools, the phenomenon is a healthy and a desirable one. Humanitarian and political considerations unite in leading us to approve of efforts to widen the circle of those who are able to study law. The organization of educational machinery especially designed to abolish economic handicaps—intended to place the poor boy, so far as possible, on an equal footing with the rich constitutes one of America's fundamental ideals. It is particularly important that the opportunity to exercise an essentially governmental function should be open to the mass of our citizens. Undoubtedly, there are many ways of attempting to realize this ideal, and some of these ways are bad ways, that defeat their own end. Inherently, the night school movement in legal education is sound. It provides a necessary corrective to the monopolistic tendencies that are likely to appear in every professional class—tendencies that in some professions may be ignored, but that in a profession connected with politics constitute a genuine element of [p. 398] danger. A decidedly intolerant attitude toward any sort of night law school training is sometimes displayed by those who have received their education in other ways. When this attitude does not reflect merely a failure to grasp the necessary implications of a democratic form of government it is itself an indication of how badly these schools are needed.

. . . As instruments for training competent servants for the democracy they are far from having realized their latent possibilities. On the contrary, it is not too much to say that up to the present time they have done more harm than good to legal education.

The evil that has been wrought has been of two kinds, the one negative and incidental, the other positive and direct. The incidental effect of letting city schools be overrun by young men who are employed elsewhere than in law offices has been that what may be termed the English type of legal education has expired in this country without being given a fair chance. Only by actual test could it be determined whether the continuous correlation of theoretical instruction in a law school with practical work in a law office is suited to modern conditions in this country or not [p. 399].

The idea that theoretical instruction shall be correlated with some sort of practical activity pursued outside of the school is absolutely in line with modern theories of educational organization in other fields (engineering, military training). Its revival in legal education was an attempt to remedy the weakness, on the side of practical expertness, that is generally conceded to characterize young law school graduates today [p. 400].

B. The Bar and Admission Requirements

1. Influence of Political Philosophy Upon Organization of the Legal Profession

The institution of a self-perpetuating class enjoying special governmental privileges, was entirely repugnant to American efforts to build up unitary democratic states possessing paramount authority over what may be loosely described as feudalistic survivals. . . . The attempted development of a virtually independent bar, under cover of judicial control, was contrary to the spirit of our developing institutions. The general tendency of our people has been in the opposite direction of taking steps to prevent the judges themselves from becoming too independent, in their exercise of their admitting power as in other matters. Even so, the system of independent bar control might have lasted in New England longer than it did, had the bars [p. 37] exercised their control in a broader spirit. The requirements they exacted for admission to their privileges were in some cases so severe as to justify the suspicion that they were more interested in fostering their own monopoly than in serving the state. The reaction against Federalist politicians was a factor inducing the legislatures to sweep away the entire system.

Since then the power of admitting lawyers to practice has been universally regarded in this country as a function of the bench rather than of the bar. . . .

Democratic desire to keep the privilege of practicing law within the reach of the average man accordingly reinforced the natural tendency of a unitary state to help governmental functions under its own control, and so prevented one feature of the traditional English system—that of a self-determining bar—from securing permanent lodgment in this country. The same democratic impulse combined with the exigencies of a newly settled country to prevent the English distinction between attorneys and counsellors from taking root; and combined later with the natural force of inertia to prevent official recognition of any other distinction between different types of practitioners [p. 38]. Several of the colonies introduced distinction between lower-court and upper-court practitioners. . . .

All these distinctions naturally flourished most in states where the democratic impulse had not begun to operate. As this made itself felt, they were identified as devices intended to help make the bar inaccessible, and were either formally abolished or reduced to empty forms. There is no inherent conflict between throwing widely open the official privilege of practicing law professionally in the courts and official recognition of different types of practitioners, each enjoying its special privileges in this respect. The democratic wave, however, sweeping away the internal barriers that protected particular sections of the profession, converted it as a whole into an officially undifferentiated and . . . flattened-out profession. Since then we have become so accustomed to thinking in terms of a unitary bar that we are prone to forget that this unity has long since become only a legal fiction, not related to the facts of legal education and of legal [p. 39] practice. We have not even tried to introduce among our lawyers official distinctions corresponding to the wide differences that actually exist in their preparation and subsequent professional activities. . . .

Broadly speaking . . . the general tendency up to the Civil War was to make admission to the bar more and more easy.

2. Relation of the Public Profession of the Law to Governmental Organization

By an unbroken tradition, handed down from the first establishment of English courts, our lawyers have always been recognized as constituting a branch of the government to be treated as such; not a private but a public profession.

. . . A generation that was interested primarily in throwing open public offices by denying the quasi-vested rights of functionaries, by abolishing property qualifications, by shortening terms of official tenure, was not ready to attack the problem of making its public servants competent. Rather, it was inclined to view with suspicion any regulations that tended to place obstacles in the path of those who aspired to enter the public service. In the case of lawyers, it identified requirements of fixed periods of preparation, followed by rigorous examinations, as part of the general restrictive rubbish which it was trying to clear away. Thus somewhat ruthlessly the bar, like the civil service, was popularized at the cost of efficiency. Similarly, after the Civil War, when this task had been pretty thoroughly accomplished, it was natural that attention should be given to the task of restoring such educational requirements for the public service as are compatible with the ideal of not making it too difficult of access for the average man. In the general history of our political development, the agitation for the improvement of our bar examination system is thus seen to constitute a movement parallel to that of civil service reform. . . .

Even those who do not sympathize with this ideal must recognize its importance as a practical factor in determining standards for admission to the bar. Its tenacity cannot be appreciated unless its nature is clearly understood. It is not the expression of an easygoing social [p. 42] philosophy that denies to the state the right to regulate, in the interests of all, the conditions under which individuals may in general earn their livelihood. It is grounded in a militant political philosophy that sees in the administration of justice a primary function of the state, and demands that those who earn their livelihood in this particular way shall be regarded, not as private citizens, but as public servants of a democracy. From this point of view, adequate preparation for the discharge of their responsibilities is as requisite for lawyers as for those engaged in private professions; but something else is necessary as well: namely, that the opportunity to share in these responsibilities shall not be unduly restricted. . . .

The proper organization of the legal profession is not, like that of the medical profession, primarily an educational problem that might be solved under any form of government in much the same way. It is primarily a part of the general problem of political organization, the solution of which in a democracy presents peculiar difficulties . . . [p. 43].

3. Effect of Weakened Bar Admission Requirements Upon the Development of Law Schools

In [Virginia], for a combination of reasons—the relative unimportance of manufacturing and trading interests, the contempt felt by the Colonial aristocracy for native attorneys and the libertarian policy of Jefferson himself—the requirements for admission to the bar were already so weak that William and Mary's law department had no difficulty in securing its start at once. Subject to the vicissitudes caused by the Revolutionary conflict, it was in operation from 1779 until the Civil War. Its later and more successful rival, the University of Virginia law school, owed its origin to the same combination of personal and social influences, and, except in a strictly organic sense, is really a continuation of this, the first American law school.

In the middle states, on the other hand, the requirements for bar admission were for many years too severe to make possible the successful inauguration of institutional instruction in vocational law. After the Revolution, and again during the first quarter century after the War of 1812, several colleges attempted to expand elementary legal instruction, intended merely as part of liberal education, into general professional schools, but all failed. Finally, in New England, in addition to the obstacles imposed by the early bar admission requirements, the colleges themselves, prior to the War of 1812, were less ready to broaden their activities beyond their traditional scope of non-vocational education [p. 44]. Harvard and Yale lagged behind the University of Pennsylvania and Columbia in attempting to establish professional schools, either in law or in medicine.

The special obstacle in the northern states, during these early years, was still the prevailing requirement of a period of clerkship. Even more important was the fact that attempts to limit the number of clerks who might study under one attorney were soon abandoned. This paved the way for the thoroughly natural development of a private attorney's law office into a private class or school.

This [Litchfield] was not the first law school in America, but it was the first law school of national reputation that taught students from all parts of the country.

The success of this institution led not merely to the founding of similar private law schools in other states. Coupled with the earlier development of independent medical schools conducted by practitioners, it also proved to be influential in determining the manner in which university professional work would eventually be organized throughout the country—more so than Jefferson's two Virginia institutions. These had attempted to introduce the European idea of professional facilities strictly coordinate with faculties offering instruction in the liberal arts. When Harvard and Yale entered the field of professional education . . . they each preserved their old college unchanged. They merely attached more or less loosely to it professional departments controlled by practitioners. They thus exemplified a compound type of university organization which, although recently somewhat modified in individual instances, furnished the model to which American institutions of higher learning still pretty generally conform: at the core, a college of liberal arts; around this, a circle of vocational schools in varying stages of administrative dependence. In both cases legal education was undertaken later than medical education —at Harvard in 1817, and at Yale in 1824. The Harvard law school had no success until it called in the acting head of a private law school of the Litchfield type to take charge of its routine work. The [p. 45] Yale law school was for many years an independent institution only loosely affiliated with the university.

Expansion by one or the other of these two methods—by the new establishment of a law department conducted by practitioners or by taking some already established school under the college wing—became the typical process by which American colleges succeeded in securing a foothold in legal education. With the progressive weakening of bar admission rules, this step in the conversion of a "college" into the greater dignity of a "university" was possible everywhere, and was very commonly taken. The few institutions that had embarked upon the study of law under the slightly earlier Jeffersonian influence were eventually obliged to conform to this prevailing model. Law degrees were established and for a time the tradition continued that such degrees could properly be conferred only by a university. This contributed to the replacement of technically independent schools by more or less spurious unions. Although the general tendency has been for these unions, once established, to become more intimate, in some cases development in this direction has been arrested by peculiar contracts or types of university organization. Later it was discovered that by appeal to the legislature, or under general incorporation acts, any incorporated medical or law school might obtain the privilege of conferring degrees. A second crop of independent law schools then arose. Still later, other organizations entered the field, notably the Young Men's Christian Association, as an incident to its general educational development.

At present, therefore, in addition to law departments that are attached to colleges or that form parts of more or less genuine universities, there is offered an abundance of institutional work leading to a law degree. Opportunity to engage in legal education has been extended to the colleges, but it has by no means been confined to them. Over-rigorous apprenticeship requirements stunted the development of legal education in England; the decaying remains of these requirements produced in this country a soil favorable to a rank growth of law schools [p. 46].

4. Points of Dissimilarity Among American Law Schools

Under a superficial similarity wide and even widening differences exist between the schools. The fact that no corresponding distinction has been made in the position accorded to them in our system of preparation for the bar must be ascribed primarily to the fact that they were originally interlopers in the field of legal education, and had slowly to fight their way to recognition against the prejudice of men trained by earlier methods. To these older men in actual control of the details of bar examination systems, distinctions between school and school seemed at first slight compared with the distinction between office training and law school education in general. Owing to this, and to the general laxity of professional control, little inquiry was made as to details. The schools reached their present position as an undivided group. When later the differences between them became still more marked, and control of the bar examinations passed into the hands of [p. 50] men better qualified to appreciate how important these differences were, the tradition of a uniform system of admission into a unitary bar was too firmly established to make possible a varying treatment of recognized law schools.

In facing the problem created by the existence of widely different institutions, all purporting to do the same thing, recent effort has taken the direction, not of according varied privileges to schools of different types, but of denying any recognition to schools not possessing certain qualifications. Among the more important variations of which no cognizance is taken are differences in kind of law taught—local and concrete, as against national and generalized—and in the method of instruction employed—textbook or dogmatic, as against a critical examination of cases or original sources. Even the amount of time devoted by the student to his education is generally ignored. The amount of general education required for the law degree has been left to the schools themselves. There is a distinction of utmost importance between schools intended for students who during their years of residence devote all their time to their studies, and schools designed for those who can set apart for this purpose only part of their working hours. Under our present system of bar admissions both types of schools stand on an even footing [p. 51].

Those who appreciate the force of the democratic contention that the bar must be kept accessible will feel that the question at issue is rather whether superior general education should be a requirement enforced as in France, not for legal practitioners in general, but for an upper professional branch still to be established. The question runs into the broader problem of whether a formal differentiation of the technical bar can be and should be secured. If it is neither practicable nor desirable to accord varied privileges to schools of different types, then there is much to be said in favor of continuing the English custom of relatively low formal requirements by admitting authorities, and of leaving individual law schools free to decide for themselves [p. 53] whether they prefer to restrict their own activities to the preparation of that element in the profession which is willing and able to preface its technical studies with college work, or whether they would rather prepare a larger number of less well educated students [p. 54].

5. Evil Effects of Combining Radically Different Types of Preparation with Theory of a Unitary Bar

If law school graduates enjoyed different privileges in the practice of law, corresponding to the differences in educational effort between full-time and part-time work, the two types instead of rivaling would supplement one another. . . .

The evil of the present situation, as a result of which all part-time legal education now rests under a justified cloud, lies in the perpetuation of the theory of a unitary bar, whose attainments are to be tested by uniform examinations. This formula, once adequate to the needs of sparsely settled communities, has been carried over into a period when it is no longer workable. Under the notion that there is such a thing as "a" standard lawyer, radically different educational ideals are brought into conflict with one another, to their mutual injury; this in face of the fact that they actually produce radically different types of practitioners. To begin with, the night schools are damaged by the obligation placed upon them to cover the same curriculum as the day schools. Since they can do this only in a relatively superficial way, the best teachers, and to a considerable extent also the best institutions, often hesitate to enter into what, from a scholarly point of view, is low-grade work. This throws the field open to more or less well-equipped promoters who operate proprietary schools—[p. 57] a necessary preliminary phase in the development of our educational system, but a phase that is being rapidly outgrown among full-time schools because it exposes school standards to obvious dangers. Competition, fear of losing students, these make schools thus hesitant to raise their own entrance requirements to the level that they really believe in [p. 58].

A great opportunity is open to the [bar] associations to make more explicit the identity [p. 60] that already to a considerable extent exists between their own membership and that element in the legal profession that has graduated from colleges and from full-time law schools. A combination of the three forces that make for the highest type of lawyer—a liberal education, an intensive course of technical training superimposed upon this, and the maintenance of bar association standards of professional ethics—would be practicable today if it were confined to the younger men, and did not exclude from bar association membership those whose professional record alone would give them a valid claim for admission. This union of the best scholastic and the best professional elements would be an important first step toward introducing some sort of order into the present chaos of the legal profession. There would then stand out among the mass of technically identical, but actually most dissimilar, practitioners, such as different methods of preparation are certain to produce, a well-defined, powerful, and respected inner bar.

It could be left to the future to determine what further steps might prove necessary to prevent less soundly trained practitioners from abusing the privileges that democratic philosophy demands shall be theirs—whether these privileges must be restricted by law, to correspond to the type of training such lawyers receive, or whether popular and professional reputation, accompanied perhaps by a corresponding development of their own professional associations, will provide a sufficient sanction to accomplish this purpose [p. 61].

The bar examination system has collapsed under the strain. Students who could not secure the degree even of a poor law school are admitted to the bar with the same privileges as are acquired by honor graduates of the best schools.

It is emphasized that a bar that includes elements so diverse is a unitary profession only in theory. In actual practice its members cannot work together in a professional spirit. Differences in training and in social standing are recognized, and we have actually a differentiated profession. Membership in selective bar associations produces an organic line of division, that is already to a considerable extent determined by considerations of this sort. The explicit recognition of educational standards as the basis of admission into these associations would constitute an important step toward the rational organization of the profession [p. 64].

6. Early Bar Admission Systems: A Graded Profession Based on Long Periods of Preparation

Whether responsibility for ensuring proper educational attainments among those admitted to the bar is assumed by legislatures, by courts, or by the bar itself, the same choice of means is open. Either prescription of a definite period of training under competent instruction, or a final examination, or a combination of the two must be relied upon. The order in which these means were preferred was a natural result of the traditional method of training lawyers as attorneys' clerks. For more than a hundred years after the Revolution, no adequate examination machinery existed in any state. During this time, owing to differences in emphasis produced by our political philosophy, the bar admission system passed through three stages: (1) long periods of training, especially in connection with a graded profession; (2) until the Civil War reduction or abolition of time requirements, coupled in some cases with doing away even of rudimentary final examination; (3) restore or lengthen prescribed period of training; (4) improve examining machinery [p. 79].

A graded profession The divided or graded profession must not be confused with mere technical classification of practitioners, according to different privileges they enjoyed. Following English tradition, early admission rules distinguished between barristers or counsellors and attorneys, and between solicitors or equity practitioners and those practicing in the courts of common law.

In England a definite line of division has always been drawn between the bar proper and lower practitioners. The same individual cannot enjoy both sets of privileges. This division of the profession was quickly abandoned.

The reason why this division was originally impracticable is clearly that there was not, in the beginning, enough law business to support specialized groups of practitioners. The general practice of the law was not a field so broad that the older practitioners wished to lose the [p. 80] privilege of cultivating it in its full extent. For the same reason they were not anxious to have too many competitors in it. One method of combining a more or less conscious monopolistic tendency with an effort to insure adequate educational attainments in the profession was to prescribe long periods of training before admission to lower courts and additional periods of practice there before additional privileges could be secured. These considerations led to the establishment of a graded profession, as a perfectly natural outgrowth and strengthening of the traditional English idea of apprenticeship training for the law. The same causes that militated against a permanent division of the profession fostered the introduction of successive grades, of which only the highest enjoyed the privilege of general practice.

Only in northern states was this idea elaborated. It was a southern custom to send young men across the sea to be educated in the Inns of Court. These practitioners had constituted a natural upper bar. In the northern colonies, distinctions among native-trained practitioners had greater vitality. While in the South, the Revolution, by closing the Inns of Court to Americans, virtually destroyed the upper bar, in the North it produced no such effect. The indigenous institution of a graded profession, which had already arisen in Massachusetts, [p. 81] developed and spread throughout New England, in the congenial atmosphere of the county bar system of admissions, and was extended from here to New York and the Northwest Territory.

Association with a practitioner is the natural method of acquiring the rudiments of any art. In simpler occupations the relationship does not need to be hedged about by any rules. It continues merely until its object has been attained. As the complexity of the task increases, and as a guild spirit arises among those who are already masters of the art, we pass into the apprenticeship stage of educational development, in which the relationship must continue during a definite period. A still later stage is that in which specialists arise to teach and train, whether as individuals conducting classes or instructors in organized schools, colleges or universities.

During the eighteenth century education of English attorneys and solicitors was in the pure apprenticeship stage. A uniform five-year service as articled clerk was prescribed by Parliament. Some courts prescribed periods, and in some colonies or states there was no uniform period; in many states, also, the length of the period was reduced below the English standard. Virginia is the only one of the thirteen original states that prescribed no period of training at any date until quite modern times [p. 82].

On the eve of the democratic upheaval, Massachusetts required a course of training and practice that aggregated eleven years if it included a college education, or nine if it did not; New York required ten years. Instances such as these help to explain the popular reaction against the prescription of any definite period of preparation [p. 83]. [For a list of states and periods required see pp. 83-84.]

7. Educational Requirements for Admission and Bar Examinations

The essentially governmental privilege of practicing law was thrown more widely open for the same reason that qualifications for governmental office were reduced. The movement was grounded in the political philosophy of an insurgent democracy, which was fighting its way into [p. 85] control of our governmental machinery, and was less concerned with making sure that privileges bestowed by the state should be well bestowed than with guarding against their again becoming a monopoly of a favored class in the community.

The tendency to lower educational standards was widespread [for detailed figures, see p. 86].

Coupled with this tendency to do away with requirement altogether was reduction of its length and a weakening of admission regulations needed for its enforcement.

In Massachusetts applicants with or without previous training might take their chances with the courts. If they were of good moral character and had studied law for three years in an attorney's office, the courts were obliged to admit them. A few years later, the democratic movement reached its culmination in four states which abolished all educational requirements whatsoever [p. 87].

This legislation did not destroy the traditional conception of a bar, as a governmental order or public profession, distinguished from the general body of citizens. The precise privilege that was widened was that of admission into the profession, not the immediate privilege of practicing law. Admitting courts remained, with power to pass upon non-educational qualifications of applicants [p. 88].

The bar was not made into a mere private money-making occupation. It is fortunate that into whatever excesses our law makers were led, in their revolt against high educational requirements for admission into the profession, at least they did not take this final step. So long as the conception of a professional bar was retained, it remained possible to encourage educational standards even in states where they could not be required by law [p. 89].

Professional ostracism was directed against those who insisted upon entering under the [democratic extremist] statute; thus a "regular" or inner bar came into existence. Another device was that of forcing an applicant to prove his character before a jury, in case he should refuse to waive his constitutional right to be examined only as to his moral character.

These devices are of special interest as indicating the possibility of dividing the profession on educational lines, when the state itself provides a unitary bar and demands little or nothing in the way of educational qualifications.

Reaction set in and after the Civil War corruption of judges and politicians brought about strengthening of bar requirements as part of an orthodox programme of reform [p. 90].

It is clear that the transfer of control from the profession to the state, while justifiable on political grounds, had results which, from the purely educational point of view, were unfortunate in the extreme. The democratic movement tended to destroy systematic training, the only foundation upon which an effective educational system can be safely built, and to leave in its place the unworkable scheme of an unsupported examination [p. 96].

Examinations conducted by judges are still examinations conducted by lawyers. An important distinction is that the examining machinery is organized and controlled by the state. The profession is no longer an *imperium in imperio* entrusted as a whole with important functions closely connected with our political life, and permitted to determine its own membership. Government acts now on the individual lawyer. His personal relationship to the state is emphasized. The official obligation of judges, of examing committees, and of the ordinary practitioner, supersedes, in all cases of conflict, the professional bond. The individual lawyer has ceased to be responsible solely to his professional brethren while the profession itself is responsible to the state. The middle element of corporate responsibility and control has been short-circuited. It is a general tendency of governmental development to cut out what in a broad sense may be termed feudalistic remains, and to get down to the individual. If we were to become a democratic community in fact as well as in name, it was necessary for us to take the action we did with regard to lawyers. There is no reason why the state, having destroyed professional responsibility, should not build up educational standards of its own. Prior to the Civil War these were democracy's primary concern. This was the area of broadening suffrage, removal of property qualifications for office, rotation in office, destruction of privilege in many forms. Hence both the willingness to regard an unsupported bar examination as sufficient protection for the community, and the failure to provide adequate machinery even for this. Constructive work was to come later [p. 100].

8. Legal Profession After the Civil War

The impulse behind the new organization of the profession was primarily ethical. The corruption in national, state and local politics after the Civil War was almost beyond belief. That lawyers and judges contributed their full share to the low tone of public life was early recognized. The lead in reforming lawyers was assumed by lawyers themselves. To regain their lost leadership in public life, selected groups came together "to maintain the honor and dignity of the profession" as their primary object. Educational reform demanded attention. The greater practical difficulties that confront the [p. 206] organizers of state as compared with city associations led to a less rigorous scrutiny of qualifications for membership in the state association, especially in the West (1873–78). The selective principle was applied to future admissions in provisions requiring assent of members already enrolled.

Thus arose the modern system of a self-constituted, self-perpetuating legal profession organized within the body of lawyers as a whole. The quasi-corporate control once possessed by the lawyers over admission to the entire bar had passed away. In its place arose control over admission to bar associations. It was an act of considerable daring to take a step which, outwardly, was not in harmony with democratic doctrines as correctly understood. The New York City association was on the defensive in this respect from the beginning [p. 207].

To non-members, the animating spirit of a membership committee has sometimes seemed to be one of narrow exclusiveness, based upon considerations of caste or wealth or age or race; while doubtless some associations have really allowed such considerations to influence their policy. Like many colleges and law schools, others have let their entrance barriers down. They have organized campaigns to drag in all new members they can find. Like the college and the law schools, they have honestly thought it "democratic" to prefer quantity to quality. While the mechanism of formal election to membership has been retained, the actual standard of admission has been debased to little more than willingness to pay the dues of the association [p. 217].

The leaders of the early legal profession in the majority of instances were not themselves schoolmen. Although since then law school education, as preparation for practice, has become usual, it still is far from possessing the sanction that the medical school enjoys, in the way of either popular, or legal, or professional recognition. The public regards the LL.B. as only an empty academic distinction. No state requires law school training for admission to its legally privileged bar. No bar association imposes any such qualification upon those admitted to its own inner professional circle. . . . The legal profession, as organized in bar associations, has not yet come to the point of insisting that training in any sort of law school must be secured.

In so far as prevailing opinion as to the distinction between good and bad education may be said to exist, practitioners naturally tend to emphasize the importance of practical training. They are predisposed to stigmatize as theorists those law teachers who are not in active practice, or who do not attempt to conduct ambitious "practice" work; or if they recognize that adequate practical training cannot be given within academic walls, they are apt to feel that the education that can be given there should be supplemented by adequate training elsewhere. They come thus into conflict with a group of scholars who feel that in the law, as it is actually administered by present-day practitioners and judges, technique counts for vastly more than it should. Such men have made it their mission not to perpetuate this evil by increasing the ranks of the mere technicians, but to remedy it by sending out graduates with a broader conception of the [p. 219] law. They are jealous of any attempt to pre-empt the student's time with matters that they deem of subordinate importance. Discussion between this group of teachers and general practitioners, as to the precise objects for which additional time is needed, prevents the student from devoting sufficient time to any part of his education.

It may be that each party underestimates the merit of the other's position. It may be that neither sees with sufficient clearness the necessity of diversification of crops in the law school field — of cultivating, by methods appropriate to each, both wheat and oats, rather than simply grain in general. Each may too hastily have taken it for granted that there must be a substantial identity of purpose and of structure among all law schools worthy of the name. Evidence of superiority or of inferiority is seen in what may be the marks of generic difference only. Considerations such as these are particularly applicable to the vexed question of night law schools.

The establishment of organized bodies of practitioners, independent of the already existing organization of law teachers in their several schools, has brought it about that legal education must now reckon with two types of institutional forces whose points of view inevitably diverge. . . . Individual schools and bar associations, bar examiners, courts, legislatures, and the public at large, all hesitate to act, for lack of a centralized organization competent to thresh out the many disputable points involved in the formulation of a consistent programme [p. 220].

If it is [the bar associations'] ambition to play a leading part in a democracy organized for effective action, they will have to avoid two quite different evils. On the one hand, in the interest of their own capacity to initiate, there must be no hesitation in fearlessly applying the selective principle. They must not be a heterogeneous collection of individuals incapable of uniting on a definite forward policy. On the other hand, if they hope to win popular support, they must not appear to represent a class or clique, and so discredit in advance any policy upon which they do unite. The ruling populace is suspicious of elements that are not in touch with itself. In political life proper, the competition for leadership between two party organizations, each possessing a consecrated and, as it were, a common-law right to try to lead, tends to keep both of them fairly responsive to the wishes of the unorganized mass of voters outside. Yet even here it has been thought necessary to try experiments designed to diminish the power of rings and bosses.

The weakness of the profession, as at present organized, is clearly in part attributable to both these causes. Some bar associations exhibit the one defect, some the other . . . [p. 227].

That blend of qualities which enter into the Anglo-Saxon concept of a "gentleman" is a very precious heritage for an individual to possess; but anything that looks like a claim on the part of the well-bred to constitute a separate interest in the state provokes violent opposition from a still sensitive democracy. It is not here asserted that any city bar association is being run on the lines of a social club. It is asserted that some city bar associations appear to be so run. If they are content with being only dignified, the suspicion may be ignored; but if they aspire to be permanently influential, care should be taken not to arouse the bitterness of an excluded class. No American citizen of sound professional training and good repute should be given even an excuse for asserting, on however insufficient grounds, that neither he, nor his son, nor his son's son can ever hope to be one of the inner circle of lawyers.

In avoiding this second evil, we must be careful not to fall into the first. The solution of the membership problem does not lie in ignoring distinctions which, whether we like it or not, divide practitioners into different types, and are far stronger than the bond of being a "lawyer". It consists rather in discriminating even more carefully than at present between these different types, but discriminating between them on grounds that can be avowed as distinguishing not the good lawyer from the bad, but the true professional from the practical craftsman. Between the product of a strong university law school, resting upon a certain amount of liberal education, and a young man who has secured just enough training to be admitted to the bar, there is a gulf, which their subsequent experience in practice is more likely to widen than to bridge. To expect individuals so different from one another to be able to cooperate, on an equal footing, in a professional way is to expect what, except in the rarest instances, never can be and never ought to be, so long as we look to education to mould character. The comparatively untrained man may be equally worthy, and in his own line of work equally competent. But if the one who has enjoyed the greater opportunities has not in many ways grown apart from the other, and if, in particular, he is not the better qualified, to discharge professional responsibilities in the spirit of *noblesse oblige,* then American higher education is indeed a failure. The truly democratic attitude for the bar association to adopt would be to recognize that the community needs a greater variety of legal practitioners than can be made [p. 228] to cohere into a single professional class; and the truly democratic method of selecting the members of such a class out of the wider practitioner group would be for the association to require stiff educational qualifications for admission into their own membership.

When these associations were first organized out of lawyers of all ages and all sorts, moral qualifications only were sought. . . . In proportion, as the educational tangle may become unsnarled, to that extent it may become possible to advance the new profession from a vague moral basis to a definite educational one. If an association should think it desirable to demand for admission to its membership, in the case of younger practitioners, attainments decidedly higher, as respects both general and technical education, than those required by the state for admission to the general bar, and should admit virtually as of right young men so qualified, the system would operate more as an incentive and less as a barrier. Those law schools and those practitioners that cherish genuine professional ideals could fortify one another in this way. The door of opportunity would still open with greater ease to some young men than to others, but to none would it be definitely closed. An irregular education would not, of course, preclude the admission of older practitioners, on the basis of distinguished careers at the bar; membership secured on these grounds would constitute a real professional tribute to their ability. A profession, the bulk of whose membership was thus united by a background of similar educational experience, would be far more cohesive, far more [p. 229] able to act as a vigorous unit than it is today. And if in the process of passing through the colleges and the law schools a student, of whatever origin, did not absorb, in addition to his formal education, the essential characteristics of an American gentleman as well, . . . a grievance committee, with a reputation for holding its fellow members to higher standards of conduct than would be permissible outside, would constitute a sufficient correc tive and would provide a highly appropriate means of maintaining the "honor and dignity of the profession" [p. 230].

The net result has been that an increasingly important group of schools has come to be more and more out of touch with the organized body of practitioners. Neither supports the other as it might, and the influence of both is weakened at the bar of public opinion.

The solution of this problem that commends itself to the writer has already been indicated. The suggested requirement by the bar associations of high educational requirements for admission to their own membership would enable the minority of law schools and the minority of practitioners that cherish the highest professional ideals to fortify one another. Freed from the influence of the craft school and its product, they should be able to reach a common understanding as to the proportion of theory and practice that would justify alike the school in awarding its degree to a young man, and the profession in admitting him to its privileges and responsibilities. Two at present inchoate groups of professional organizations, the one standing primarily for sound ethics, the other for sound education, would thereby be fused into one, to their mutual benefit. For although in the preceding discussion the bar associations have been considered as the only organized exponents of professional ideals among practitioners, this is a slight overstatement of their position. Law school alumni associations, first formed by Harvard in 1880, represent the extension of school-men's lines of institutional division out of the academic into the practitioners' field, and suggest that if the group of bar associations refuses to accord proper weight to sound institutional training, it may some day find itself faced by a rival professional organization based entirely upon such considerations. On the other hand, it is far from certain that the mixed membership of existing bar associations would look with favor upon the step proposed. Time only will show whether factional divisions in the profession will be harmonized by a method of treaty and [p. 236] alliance between the relatively conservative practitioners and the progressive schools; or whether, through a federation of alumni associations, these schools will be able to dispense with the cooperation of orthodox bar associations in securing action from the legislatures, similar to that which occurred in the medical profession, schools that possess sufficient financial resources to realize their aims will gradually, through their graduates, obtain control of the American Bar Association, and thus be in a position to force its unqualified endorsement of their entire programme.[1]

One point of fundamental importance must be reiterated. In whatever way a united profession is finally formed, the selective principle must be kept to the fore. The state determines the minimum conditions under which young men may be authorized to practice law. Although these conditions need to be made and will in time become less liberal than they now everywhere are, political considerations will prevent them from ever being brought up to the standard properly insisted upon by a minority of law schools. Lawyers constitute our governing class, not merely because a large proportion of public officials and representative law-makers are chosen from their ranks, but, more fundamentally because even in private practice they play a supremely important part in the administration of the law. Even under an ideal system of government they would continue to occupy this position. It is equally important for the preservation of our democratic ideals that this class shall not be made inaccessible to young men of moderate means, and that attainments more extensive than the minimum required for admission to the bar shall be utilized for the benefit of the community. Our legislators can be trusted to keep the minimum sufficiently low, and even to overdo their caution in this respect [p. 237].

It remains for a selected minority to render the public service, in the improvement of our law, that can be accomplished only by those whose training has been both broad and thorough. The mission of a certain type of law school is to provide this training. To accomplish the end in view, much more than the work of scholars and teachers is required. Practitioners of standing must apply their professional experience and their professional influence to the same task. They must cultivate and develop into a living growth the seeds implanted in their student days. They must not be content with futile recommendations of some idealistic scheme,

---

[1] NOTE: 1, p. 237: Discussion of relations between the American Bar Association and the Association of American Law Schools—one of the sore points of current controversy—is purposely excluded. . . . It is the writer's belief that the establishment of educational standards for admission into bar associations is a necessary preliminary step, before cooperation between these two organizations can be secured. Meanwhile the law teachers' association—for this is what the AALS really is—has as its special province the solution of a large number of educational problems, not directly connected with the organization of the profession.

but must labor zealously to secure the actual adoption of concrete measures.

This is today the particular responsibility of bar associations. It is a responsibility that they cannot discharge if they endeavor to make of themselves inclusive associations of all reputable practitioners. The state will always admit to its general bar practitioners of types too diverse to be capable of uniting into a single forward-moving profession. We need one group of lawyers who have enough in common with one another to be able to reach an agreement upon something definite—enough at stake to stimulate them into conducting a vigorous campaign in its behalf—enough breadth of view to realize that democracy will always insist upon retaining ultimate control, and will never unreservedly commit either the making or the administration of the law into the hands of any self-constituted body, however deserving. This group should include the lawyers of superior attainments, of broader vision, of greater ability to identify themselves with a larger whole than is possible for relatively untrained minds. The highly trained type of lawyer is most interested, as well as best qualified, to undertake the task of making the law of the community better. We need also, outside of this strictly professional group, less highly trained lawyers to administer, in behalf of the people, the law as it is— lawyers who command their confidence more than the inhumanly expert—lawyers whose own training should be carried at least so far that they can intelligently appraise the activities of the expert group, deferring to them where they so deserve, opposing them when opposition seems needful—a class in the community that may help to bridge the chasm of mutual misunderstanding and distrust that is always likely to appear between those who know too little and those who know too much about a subject. We do not want a heterogeneous organization which, in the vain effort to do two things at once, endeavors to ingratiate [p. 238] itself with public opinion by letting discordant elements in, and ends as a flabby body incapable of coordinated action. No demagogic talk about "exclusiveness" should keep the professional group from excluding those who do not measure up to standards that, independently of state action, itself defines. That these standards should be educational, is the suggestion advanced here. But better even that professional exclusiveness should be of the wrong sort than that members should not be united by ties of mutual sympathy and understanding [p. 239].

9. General Relation of the Law School to the Profession and the State

Political considerations have always urged that the creation and the administration of law, insofar as it affects the well-being of the average citizen, cannot be safely entrusted to a separate class, but must be kept within the reach of the great bulk of the population. Prior to the rise of law schools, the obvious solution was to distinguish between two types of lawyers. The precise English distinction between barristers and solicitors was not suited to the simple organization of American society. English attorneys were originally distinguished according to the courts in which they were privileged to appear (bars of lower and upper courts) [p. 403]. From the upper bar it was hoped that judges be chosen. Jefferson, quite as strongly as any New England Federalist, cherished this ideal.

The principle on which the division was made was unsound, even if those in charge of the system had been animated by broader views. Too much attention was paid to guarding the sacred portals of the bar. Too little assistance was rendered to forces that sought to liberalize our political and juristic structure. In sharp contrast with the inefficient idealism that characterized the more democratic states, the northeastern states developed a bar which though divided in theory was unified in fact, a bar permeated with noble professional traditions, the loss of which we [p. 404] still regret.

The political argument triumphed over educational considerations even when these latter were backed by a socially and politically influential professional class. The professional bar was destroyed with all the good and all the bad in it — its insistence upon thorough training and its selfish exclusiveness, its high ethical standards and its narrow political vision. . . . Broadly speaking, everywhere, north or south, the legal profession was replaced by the individual lawyer, serving in private practice his clients, in public life his constituents. A nominal bar examination was a mere historic relic inherited from the time when there had been a genuine bar. Formerly either the profession itself or the state had undertaken to ensure that those who enjoyed a lawyer's privileges were trained to discharge his responsibilities. Under the new dispensation the easily gained privilege meant little, and the surviving fiction of professional or public responsibility meant less. Structure of the bar by function was followed by a later, still less successful effort to build up a unitary profession. We came to assume without discussion that there is or can be a standardized lawyer — an object to be treated with scrupulous uniformity by the state, whatever be the precise form of treatment.

All this was not so wholly regrettable as it may at first appear. It should never be forgotten that the England from which we inherited our institutions was in no sense a democracy. It is a pity that the old bar should have let itself become identified in the public mind chiefly with the idea of privilege, and so have put itself in the way of being destroyed more completely than it need have been. Yet [p. 405] this destruction was by no means an unmixed evil. The old tradition of a professional "bar"—a literal barrier intervening between the professional order of lawyers and the public outside—had to be weakened, before it could be replaced by the modern ideal of public servants proceeding from and responsible to the people at large. And it was necessary to rid ourselves of an antiquated and unworkable distinction between lower-court and upper-court lawyers—it was necessary, perhaps, even to forget that lawyers can be distinguished from one another at all—in order to pave the way for more intelligently conceived lines of division, based not on paper rules but on popularly respected institutions.

Such an institution existed in the American college. Those who had enjoyed the educational benefits of a college course tended to carry off the higher rewards in both private practice and public life. When the colleges began to lend support to law schools proper, the germ of another possible distinction appeared—between education under a practitioner and education in an institution. The value of office training everywhere diminished because of the general degradation of the bar. The school was doing the work formerly done by the law office and doing it more efficiently than the law office could [p. 406].

The schools were capable of exercising a political leverage through their graduates and through the friends of the university at large, while the practitioners were disorganized and weak. Hence the ease with which changes in bar admission rules were secured from the legislature or the courts—changes which either put the schools on an equality with other methods of training, or even gave them a positive advantage. The theoretically indefensible exemption of law school graduates from the regular state bar examinations thus became rooted in many states.

So long as no educational standards existed other than those that the schools themselves imposed, it was natural and proper that they should be given all they asked for. They were the torch bearers of legal education throughout the land. The immediate result of the democratic onslaught had been to deprive the greater number of practitioners and judges of all sense of professional responsibility. The bar had ceased to exist except in a purely fictitious sense. In the absence of external sanctions each lawyer and each judge became the arbiter of his own conduct, and was checked only by such negative restrictions of decency as his individual conscience bade him maintain. The notion that he ought to step outside the narrow path of fidelity to his client or to his official task, for the purpose of rendering service to his profession or to the state, was entirely foreign to prevailing habits of thought. Corruption, immediately following the Civil War, was properly ascribed, in part, to the absence of a genuine legal profession. The establishment of selective bar associations meant that it was then for the first time recognized that among the responsibilities which the democratized body of lawyers had proved incapable of discharging was responsibility for education of its recruits. Care for this devolves at least as appropriately upon the existing members of a profession, when such an institution exists, as it does upon a university that is concerned with all branches of human knowledge. It is only through cooperation between a school which intelligently devises the means, and a profession which properly defines the ends, that sound professional training can be established. Prior to the Civil War, legal education was at a low [p. 407] ebb because, of these two necessary institutions, only the law school existed. Bearing thus the entire burden, it did the best it could. It received and it deserved every encouragement.

When there arose a new profession, organized in selective bar associations, it was properly critical of the schools on general grounds, holding that they were superficial and perfunctory, that they did not thoroughly teach their students law. The profession initiated steps to make the schools better and the entire system of preparation for the bar, better. They sought to regain control of legal education by abolishing diploma privilege and substituting stringent bar examinations conducted by [active practitioners] themselves. Questions that arose: Should credit be given for law school work in a school outside of the state? Should supplementary office work be required? What should characterize examination questions? Should applicants be appraised on the basis of information or reasoning power? What kind of law and of lawyers were to be tested by state examinations? Prevailingly the preference of the profession has been for local law, with emphasis upon information and practical expertness rather than upon reasoning power. Schools had different ideas. The result has been a continuing controversy between certain leading law schools and the bulk of the profession with its satellite schools, over the proper method of devising and administering rules of bar admission [p. 408].

Outwardly there is no great difference between the curricula of the several types of law schools. Basing superficial tests upon this standardized curriculum, ignoring the vital differences which actually exist among the schools, and operating under the fetish of a uniform examination leading into a unitary bar, the present system of professional control serves only to encourage the same sort of law school education, in some amount, as against pure office training. Except for a more general insistence upon three years of law study and upon some general education, the relation between the schools and the state examining authorities is virtually the same today as it was prior to the Civil War when there really was no great difference between the schools, and the encouragement of law school training in general was all that was needed.

With the rapid multiplication of law schools, this once [p. 409] vaguely apprehended division of the profession into the two groups of school-trained and office-trained men is rapidly ceasing to have any substantial importance. In states with large urban populations, suited to the development of law schools, younger members of the bar will no longer have office training. A difference now emerging but ignored is that between lawyers with or without college education. It is the basis of genuine differentiation among lawyers which, in defiance of legal theory, now exists, and makes of American legal practitioners, not a united bar, but a heterogeneous body.

Some schools cover borderland subjects — moot court, legal aid. Under present conditions, no law school can, in its regular professional course, devote great attention to such matters. The path indicated by Harvard rather than by the early Virginia institutions, has been followed by all the schools. Their main activities are devoted to instruction in the relatively narrow, though exceedingly important and difficult field of the judge-made technical law. Some offer richer curricula than others [p. 410].

A minimum standard of four years of high school and three years of law school is now the minimum standard, a service performed by the bar associations in their undiscriminating attitude toward schools of every type.

The important lines of division originate in departures from the traditional practitioner's conception of legal education: the local law of the jurisdiction (including its practical application) was to be taught by means of textbooks, to students who devoted their entire time to law, and who might or might not be college graduates.

The first innovation, made by Harvard, was to substitute national for local or severely practical law. Prior to the Civil War, it was the only departure. Harvard textbooks were used in other schools. Proclaiming of a national ideal was a highly significant fact [p. 411].

The next two innovations were the case method as a substitute for textbooks, and establishment of late night and evening classes avowedly intended for students engaged in other occupations. Immediately after the Civil War, these originated at Harvard and Washington, D.C., and later (1890) in New York City.

After 1890, under Harvard's lead, only those students were received who possessed a certain amount of preliminary college training [p. 412].

The disposition of the generation that came into power about 1890 has been to accept too easily the ancient formulas without questioning their applicability to present conditions. The most clearly indefensible of these formulas has been the assumption that all lawyers do, and ought to, constitute a single homogeneous body—in common parlance, a "bar". The development of different types of legal education has established in legal practice groups of lawyers of different types, each of which has been properly interested in perpetuating its kind. Under the influences of an inherited prepossession, each has thought it necessary, not only to do this, but also to impose upon the totality of practitioners its own special conception of legal education. Each has thus come into conflict with the other when their views did not happen to coincide. Each has seen clearly that if all American lawyers were educated in accord with the other's plans, we should be in a bad way. Each has tried, when most intolerant, to defeat the other's plans outright. Each has tried, when most conciliatory, to concoct some device whereby the training of the unitary bar should include the best features of all suggested systems. If one-tenth of the thought that has been given to this vain effort had been expended upon the problem of dividing the bar along lines that can be justified on both political and educational grounds, by this time we might or we might not have attained a solution entirely satisfactory from both points of view [p. 417].

Once it is recognized that a unitary bar not only cannot be made to work satisfactorily, but cannot even be made to exist, then the development of our present differentiated system into one that shall produce better results will be a slow process. . . . The amount of time that students can reasonably be expected to devote to their education, both preliminary and professional, determines the curriculum and methods of each type of school; and these in turn determine the character of the subsequent bar admission test. Only insofar as bar examinations are adjusted to the training that is practicable for the particular type will they be of service in ensuring high standards of proficiency among those admitted to the bar. Only in this way can completely incompetent individuals be prevented from securing the privilege of practicing law. Only in this way can each school be aided to develop its own training up to the limits of its possible development [p. 418].

The task of preparing students to engage in the general practice of law has now become a very difficult one. The more scholarly institutions may in time be glad to lighten their own burden by throwing upon schools of other types responsibility for certain portions of this broad field. Conveyancing, probate practice, criminal law and trial work are examples of topics that seem particularly appropriate for the relatively superficial schools. . . . It is not certain that a rigorous functional division of the bar will even develop. The dividing line between the different types of lawyers may be determined by the economic status of the client rather than by the nature of the professional service rendered. The general principle of a differentiated profession is something that we already have, and could not abolish if we would. The particular principle of a functionally divided bar is something that we may or may not be able eventually to introduce as one means for making the general principle work better. All that can positively be asserted is that if a specialization of lawyers according to their functions does come, it will rest in the immediate future upon social and professional sanctions rather than upon provisions of law. Concerted action by bar associations to make these sanctions as powerful as possible will produce more beneficial results, a generation from now, than immediate attempts to secure, from legislatures and courts, an ideally perfect system of bar admissions. The legalistic tradition of a general practitioner of law has been too long established in this country to be lightly overturned, peculiarly inappropriate though this tradition is to a community that combines an exceedingly complex system of law with determined faith in popular self-government. Even under the handicap of this tradition something can be done at once to tone up statutes and rules of court, both for assisting conscientious law teachers in the better schools of each type, and for introducing into the training of lawyers valuable elements that the schools themselves cannot provide. And [p. 419] if there is truth in the theory that law is but the laggard expression of community ideals, then assuredly in time that portion of our law which controls the making of lawyers, and thus affects our system of government at its very core, will be brought into harmony with popular needs and aspirations [p. 420].

APPENDIX II

by Preble Stolz*

Those who would reform legal education today would do well I think to read this book even though it is now nearly 50 years old. Like Biblical texts and maxims of construction, the lessons of history have a way of cutting both ways at once. It might help if we shared not only a sense of malaise but also some perception of the history of legal education in this country. There is no better way of learning about the period up to the depression than by reading A. Z. Reed's, *Training for the Public Profession of the Law.*

Nearly all of Reed's book looks backwards from 1921. Only the last relatively brief section contains his suggestions for the future of legal education and the profession. His history has been definitive, except for some authorized chronicles of particular law schools no one has or probably ever will re-examine the data Reed collected. He did an extraordinary job and, although his prose perhaps is somewhat overblown for today's taste, it is still highly readable. It is not my purpose here to summarize what Reed reported—he did that himself in the first 64 pages of his book—but rather to use his findings and some history that came afterwards to try and understand how it is that legal education has come to its present state.

The Civil War marks the beginning of modern legal education in this country. Jacksonian egalitarianism had succeeded by then in eliminating all but the formality of admission to the bar. We abolished any requirement that a number of years be spent in training for the bar, either as an apprentice in a law office with supervision by a highly organized bar as in England or in Universities as on the Continent. There was no organized bar. What little training lawyers got, they were most apt to get studying in a lawyer's office. There were, of course, good lawyers then, men who were broadly educated and widely read professionals. And there were lots of bad lawyers. Law Schools started as a supplement to and then as a substitute for law office training. They were strictly voca-

*See Editor's Note, page 96.

tional in orientation with no admission requirements and with a course of study that lasted less than two years. Students would come and stay for as long as they thought it useful to do so. Without much difficulty a student could arrange to be admitted to practice wherever he wished.

On this kind of *tabula rasa* about 100 years ago legal education as we know it begins. Reed's vantage point was roughly halfway between then and now. What is startling today is how much took place before he wrote and how little it seems has happened since then. This is especially true if we look at the "best" schools then and now. By 1920 the best law schools were all connected to a University, their students got a degree after three years of study, the curriculum was much like today's with the principal difference being that we have added third-year courses in subjects that were scarcely known in the '20's. Most schools required some college education (typically two years) as a condition of admission; a very few required an undergraduate degree. The case-method of instruction by 1920 was used in all the better schools. Even the criticisms are the same. Fifty years ago law professors were saying that the case-method was unsatisfactory, especially in the second and third years when students seemed less interested. Legislation and administrative law instructors were complaining that their subjects were not given sufficient attention, there was talk about the need for "practical" instruction. Legal aid offices were being used for "clinical" exposure. Articles could be lifted out of the Law School News of 1915 and passed off today as tolerably fresh ideas in the Journal of Legal Education.

That first impression of historical rigidity is not fully accurate. Though it is true that Harvard today is much like Harvard of 50 years ago, it is not true that the bulk of legal education is the same. The best schools then were educating only 25 to 30% of the law students, the remainder were coming to the bar from a multitude of schools that for the most part have no parallels today. The world of legal education then was almost completely open, there were no legal or even social constraints on how a man qualified himself to pass the bar and become a lawyer. That meant, of course, that a lot of bad education was going on, it also meant that the best schools had to sell themselves. Langdell at Harvard and Dwight at Columbia developed contemporaneously two quite different ways of training lawyers—both very successful in attracting students. Their graduates, presumably in part because of what happened to them while they were in school, turned out to be very good lawyers. Langdell and Ames were better at acquiring disciples, and their system was more flexible so that by Reed's time Harvard had become the dominant model in the better schools.

The free market analogy can doubtless be pressed too far, but its operation is nicely illustrated by the gradual shift of legal education towards graduate education. Langdell at Harvard started the process in 1886 when he required law students to be college graduates or to be eligible for admission as seniors at Harvard. Enrollment promptly dropped, but it picked up soon and by 1900 Harvard was requiring all students to have a college degree. Plainly, or so it was thought, it was easier to teach law to a homogeneous student body all of whom had some college experience. They also thought, probably rightly, that students with a college background were likely to learn more. The idea was attractive to legal educators and spread, but slowly. When Reed wrote only three law schools required a college degree as a condition of admission. A number of schools were trying various schemes that combined college and law school, usually by telescoping the senior year of college and the first year of law school. And, of course, even in schools that did not require a degree, many students were choosing to finish college before starting law school.

That kind of flexibility, both institutional and individual, is very hard to find in legal education today. In very large part all of legal education has adopted most of the characteristics of Harvard in 1920. Law students now must have a college degree, they must go to law school for three years, the better ones should edit a law review, all take substantially the same courses, after they graduate they take a cram course and pass a bar examination. And Harvard, and all of its followers, have stayed pretty much in the same place. Why is it that legal education is so monolithic, so uniform today when it was so loose and open 50 years ago? I had always supposed that it was just one of those things that happened, and perhaps it was inevitable. Nonetheless, Reed's book should give fatalists some pause. Reed argued very ably that legal education ought not to try to mold itself into the image of Harvard. His advice was consciously and deliberately rejected by a relatively small group of very able legal educators. We are now living out the result of that decision. If, as many seem to believe, it is likely that structural changes are shortly to come in the profession, it might be well to look back and see how successful legal educators were the last time they thought they were doing something towards self-conscious reformation of the profession. Reed's book was central both because it was a remarkably conscientious attempt to understand how legal education had gotten to where it was, and because his book was thought to have a potential role in changing the shape of legal education. It was an "historic" book in both senses—it attempted to report history and it was itself influential (if in unexpected and unintentional ways) on the course of history.

There was a precise precedent for Reed's book: Abraham Flexner's report on medical education. To understand what was going on in legal education in the 20's it is necessary first to know what had happened to medical education in the previous two decades because that was the model lawyers were trying to emulate.

In the last half of the 19th century medicine in this country fell well behind European medicine and was coming to be dominated by charlatans who had minimal medical education and little if any clinical exposure. In 1901 the American Medical Association reorganized itself as a kind of federated union of all local and state medical societies and promptly began considering ways of improving medical education as well as stiffening or establishing state licensing authorities. In 1904 a Council on Medical Education was formed which met informally with President Henry S. Pritchett and Mr. Abraham Flexner of the Carnegie Foundation. The minutes of that meeting include the following:

> Dr. Pritchett had already expressed, by correspondence, the willingness of the Foundation to cooperate with the Council in investigating the medical schools. He now explained that the Foundation was to investigate all the professions, law, medicine and theology. He had found no efforts being made by law to better the conditions in legal education and had met with some slight opposition in the efforts he was making. He had then received the letters from the Council on Medical Education and expressed himself as most agreeably surprised not only at the efforts being made to correct conditions surrounding medical education but at the enormous amount of important data collected.
>
> He agreed with the opinion previously expressed by the members of the Council that while the Foundation would be guided very largely by the Council's investigations, to avoid the usual claims of partiality no more mention should be made in the report of the Council than any other source of information. The report would therefore be, and have the weight of an independent report of a disinterested body, which

would then be published far and wide. It would do much to develop public opinion. . . .

Flexner made his survey and the Carnegie Foundation published the results in 1910. It had a dramatic impact as suggested by the following table:

LEGAL
EDUCATION
TABLE 2
*Number of law
and of medical
schools, and
of their
students, 1890
to 1936**

Year	Law†		Medicine	
	Schools	Students	Schools	Students
1889–1890	61	4,486	133	15,404
1899–1900	102	12,408	160	25,171
1909–1910	124	19,498	131	21,526
1919–1920	146	24,503	85	13,798
1928–1929	173	48,942		
1929–1930	180	46,751	76	21,597
1931–1932	182	42,165	76	21,135
1932 (Fall)	185	38,260		
1932–1933	185	41,153	77	22,466
1933 (Fall)	190	38,771		
1933–1934			77	22,799
1934–1935			77	22,888
1935 (Fall)	195	41,920		
1935–1936			77	22,564
1936 (Fall)	190	40,218		

* Figures for number of law schools and students have been taken from reports of the Annual Review of Legal Education. For sources of information concerning medical schools and students, see Physicians and Medical Care, by Luther Lucile Brown p. 29.

† Figures for law schools are for degree-conferring schools until 1935, for 1935 and 1936 they are for law schools as defined by the Section on Legal Education of the American Bar Association. For some recent years two sets of enrollment figures are available, those for the full year being somewhat larger only than those for the fall quarter.

In short, what happened was that a lot of bad medical schools were driven out of business, partly by publicity, partly by state licensure restrictions and partly by being absorbed into other schools, with the end result that nearly all medical schools were tied into Universities. Whether as a result of reducing the number of places in medical schools or otherwise, admission standards for medical schools also moved up; in 1914 a high school diploma was required, in 1916 a year of college, in 1918 two years of college including prescribed pre-medical courses in the basic sciences. Standards calling for some full time faculty and substantial clinical training were also imposed.

On February 7, 1913, the following not altogether spontaneous letter was addressed to President Pritchett of the Carnegie Foundation:

> This communication is addressed to you by the American Bar Association Committee on Legal Education and Admissions to the Bar, and has attached to it the signature of each member of the Committee.
>
> The Committee was greatly impressed by the investigation, made a few years ago under your direction by the Carnegie Foundation, into the conditions under which medical education is carried on in the United States. That the medical profession and the entire country was placed under lasting obligation to your organization because of the service that was then rendered is acknowledged by all who know the facts.
>
> The Committee of the Bar Association is most anxious to have a similar investigation made by the Carnegie Foundation into the conditions under which the work of legal education is carried on in this country. There is an imperative need for such an investigation, equally searching and far-reaching with the other, and one equally frank and fearless in its statement of the facts which the investigation may reveal.
>
> It is to be hoped that, if your organization decides to adopt the suggestion the Committee makes, your investigation will not be confined to the law schools, but may be extended to the matter of admission to the bar in the various states of the United States, with a view of making known to the entire country the facts relating to this important subject.
>
> This Committee has not at its disposal either the funds or the time needed for the comprehensive investigation that is so much to be desired, and it appeals to you, therefore, to undertake the task and assures you of its readiness to co-operate with you so far as possible should you conclude to comply with this request.
>
> Yours sincerely,
>
> [Signed]   Henry Wade Rogers
>   Lawrence Maxwell
>   Selden P. Spencer
>   Roscoe Pound
>   W. Draper Lewis

Pritchett accepted the offer and Alfred Z. Reed, not a lawyer, was appointed to head up the investigation. The signers of that letter were the members of the American Bar Association's Committee on Legal Education and Admission to the Bar. Unfortunately, to understand what happened later, it is necessary to reconstruct some of the Byzantine complexity of A.B.A. politics around the turn of the century.

The American Bar Association was quite different from the American Medical Association. The A.M.A., from the beginning, was a body whose policy making functions were performed by delegates from state and local medical associations. Nearly all doctors were members of some such group. The A.B.A., which began in 1878, was and remains in large part an organization of individual lawyers. In 1900, the A.B.A. had only 1.3 per cent of the nation's lawyers as members. By 1920 this had grown to over 9 per cent, but it still had only 12,000 members, and critical decisions were left often to general meetings of the membership and, of course, only some of the members would be at any given meeting of the association.

A Committee on Legal Education was one of the A.B.A.'s first subgroups. This Committee was always more or less in the hands of what Reed called "the schoolmen", i.e., those who were connected with or believed in legal education in law schools rather than in law offices. In 1880 the Committee recommended a resolution for the general meeting that study in law schools be an essential prerequisite to admission to practice as well as passage of a bar examination. The Association rejected that declaration and several like it in later years despite frequent dilution. In 1893, presumably as a way of focusing attention on the problem (and of building a more congenial constituency) a Section on Legal Education and Admissions to the Bar was formed, the first Section, as a matter of fact, created by the A.B.A. Legal education meant law school education and the focus was on ways of improving law schools. The Section, open to anyone interested, had only some difficulty in passing resolutions favoring lengthening the period of law study to three years in law school in 1895; the A.B.A. resolved similarly in '97, but left out the words "in law school".

Still searching for compatible constituency, the Section in 1899 issued a call for an organization of law schools and in 1900 the American Association of Law Schools was started. At the start

A.A.L.S. imposed standards as a condition of membership, but they were not very onerous: students should have a high school diploma, they should have access to a library and the program of study should last for at least two academic years of 30 weeks each. In 1905 the years of study were increased to three, but two-year schools were not denied membership until 1907.

Meanwhile the Section undertook a larger project on admission to the bar. A seven man committee was appointed in 1906, a questionnaire sent out and lengthy (at least for that time) reports filed that were extensively debated and widely circulated. The project envisioned more or less standardized rules for the administration of the bar examination and flirted with requiring attendance at law school as a condition to taking the bar examination. This last was sometimes in and sometimes out of the proposed rules. It was in the proposed rules suggested by both the Section and the Committee in 1916 and '17, but managed to avoid being voted on at the A.B.A. convention. The Committee's proposal was renewed in 1918 and finally voted on; the critical Rule 8, however, was withdrawn by the chairman of the Committee, Harry Wade Rogers of Yale, as being "revolutionary" and never voted on. It called for: "Every applicant should be required to have successfully completed the prescribed course of instruction and passed the examination of a law school approved by the board, which requires for the completion of its course not less than three years of resident attendance during the daytime, or not less than four years of resident attendance if a substantial part or all of the exercises of the school are in the evening."

What was "revolutionary" about that Rule? The idea that prospective lawyers should attend law school for three years was certainly not new. Nor by 1918 was it very important. The typewriter had won the war against law office training of lawyers because there was no longer a need for clerk-copyists learning the law. By then there were law schools all over the country and education in a law school was available and generally regarded as more efficient and better. To be sure, relatively few states required law school study as a condition of licensing, but very few who had not gone to law school were in fact qualifying for the bar examination, much less passing it and practicing.

What was new in the Rule was the implicit suggestion that someone would go into the business of classifying law schools, approving some and not others. That idea was also not new — it was derived from the experience of the medical schools—but it had never even come close to presentation to the A.B.A. and doubtless was not presented in 1918 because it would have lost had it been voted on. Furthermore, and probably more important, the "schoolmen" in 1918 thought they were well on the way to approval and disapproval of law schools by another route.

In 1915, on the occasion of the 15th anniversary of the founding of the A.A.L.S., Dean Richards of Wisconsin took advantage of the occasion to review in his presidential address the history of the A.A.L.S. and to make some sort of tentative assessment of its accomplishments. He was struck, not surprisingly, with the contrast with medical education. The vigorous campaign to eliminate the inadequate medical school was by then well on the way to success, whereas the growth in legal education had principally been in law schools not even meeting the very low standards of the A.A.L.S., and even more in commercial correspondence law schools. Although the A.A.L.S. had lifted its standards somewhat, two years of college education was only recommended as a condition of entry and the bar in general seemed hostile to steps to be more rigorous. Dean Richards was also puzzled over the relationship between the A.A.L.S. and A.B.A. For several years the A.A.L.S. had been meeting during the Christmas recess in Chicago rather than at the same time and place as the A.B.A.: that had improved attendance at the A.A.L.S. meetings, but had left the Section on Legal Education much more open to manipulation by "non-schoolmen" whose inclinations were not necessarily compatible with the best in the law school world. Dean Richards suggested that perhaps abolition of the Section and the substitution of the A.A.L.S. might be advisable.

The next President of the A.A.L.S. was Walter Wheeler Cook, then of Yale, and his Presidential Address carried forward the ideas of his predecessor with some programmatic content. It was an age that could stand long speeches, and Professor Cook took what must have been several hours to put before his fellow law teachers the history of what had been done for medical education, contrasting it with the feeble efforts to raise the standards of admission to the bar and the quality of law schools. He saw as central to medicine's success the creation of a small Council on Medical Education whose task it was to classify schools, establish standards and see that they were complied with. He urged, among other things, that the A.B.A. be invited to appoint such a Council for Legal Education. The A.A.L.S. followed his suggestion with an appropriate resolution. There will be occasion to refer to other matters in Cook's speech later. For the moment it is sufficient to note that his colleague at Yale, Henry Wade Rogers, was then Chairman of the A.B.A.'s Committee on Legal Education charged to report to the next meeting of the A.B.A. in 1917 on the recommendations of the Section concerning admission to the Bar.

The Committee made a lengthy report to the A.B.A. accepting much, but not all, of the Section's suggestions. Chairman Rogers apparently persuaded his fellow committeemen to include as part of their report a recommendation that the President of the A.B.A. appoint a Council on Legal Education along the lines proposed by Professor Cook. The course of history was, at this point, thrown off balance by a strike somewhere between Baltimore, where the report was printed, and Saratoga, where the convention was held. Because of the strike, the Committee's report was not available to the convention until the night before. When the matter first came to the floor, Rogers agreed to put the matter off to a later session at the same convention so that the members could have a chance to read the report. At the later session, Rogers had but five minutes and put before the body only the recommendation for the creation of a Council on Legal Education. That passed in the flurry, but some accompanying legislation abolishing the Committee on Legal Education was never considered.

A Council on Legal Education was promptly appointed composed of Rogers as Chairman and the deans of Harvard (Roscoe Pound), Columbia (Harlan Stone), Northwestern (John Wigmore) and Minnesota (W. R. Vance). Rogers as Chairman of both the Committee on Legal Education and the Council made the report to the A.B.A. convention previously discussed and, at the same time presented, but not for a vote, a proposal by the Council to abolish the Section on Legal Education and replace it with the A.A.L.S. and a conference of bar examiners. Reading all this, it seems perfectly clear that the "schoolmen" forces thought they were riding high and were in control of what the A.B.A. was likely to do with respect to legal education.

The next year, 1919, saw a sharp reversal of fortune. The Council was dependent for financial support on the Executive Committee of the A.B.A., and substantial support if it was to do its job of classifying schools. The Council staggered through 1918 on less than it needed, but aware of the competing needs of the Association during the War. They spent 1918 planning what they would do in the next years. But in 1919 the Executive Committee of the A.B.A. refused them any support whatsoever for reasons that are not clear and, in a general reorganization of the Association, abolished the Council, or rather, made it subject to the control of the Section. In other words, to those who would raise the standards, all that seemed promising in 1918 was in 1919 threatened with destruction.

The Council fought as best it could. It wrote a lengthy report including a communication from the Deans of twenty-odd schools (the best, all members of A.A.L.S.) urging the membership of the A.B.A. at its annual meeting to preserve the Council; a resolution for the preservation of the Council was pushed through the A.A.L.S., and the matter was vigorously debated on the floor of the A.B.A. meeting. The forces of good lost, 63 to 123.

Harlan Stone was the President of the A.A.L.S. in 1919 and his Presidential address given in December of that year reflected a profound disenchantment with the A.B.A. He reported with sorrow the demise of the Council and urged the group to consolidate its position and to hold fast to its belief that legal education could best be done during the day time, and that some collegiate training was important to success in law school. What he was saying in essence was that law schools were not in a strong position in the A.B.A., and that it was important that they speak clearly if they could not speak loudly and, therefore, the Association should limit its membership to those who shared his, or the better, views on legal education. The A.A.L.S. later that year raised its membership standards to exclude effectively all night schools. Stone professed confidence in the long range picture, but he doubted any immediate improvement through the A.B.A. comparable to that achieved by medicine. His speech was an eloquent call for the membership to unite and propagandize those in the bar who might be sympathetic.

It was then the custom to discuss the President's address at the A.A.L.S. meetings. Amidst the gloom and general despair—voiced loudest by Beale of Harvard—W. Draper Lewis of Pennsylvania, who had been on the Committee which signed the letter to the Carnegie Foundation, laid out an aggressive affirmative program. He saw what others had not, that the A.B.A. general meetings could be manipulated if the right kind of people made the presentation; that the indifference of the bar to legal education could be an asset as well as a liability. If men of real stature could be persuaded to support simple straightforward resolutions, almost anything could be passed on the floor of the convention. The problem was to get resolutions to the floor. Under the new constitution of the A.B.A. this could be done only through the Section on Legal Education, and as Lewis recognized, once the Section was reorganized and got rolling, it would be difficult to get resolutions lifting standards through the Section because it was "composed not only of representatives of law schools who feed on the fact and grow on the fact that the legal standards in this country are low." (L. Sch. Rev. 509)

Lewis proposed that a Resolution be offered in the next meeting of the Section calling for the appointment of a Special Committee to study legal education; that members of the A.A.L.S. make it their business to attend the next meeting of the Section to that end and so that they could sponsor for chairman of the section a candidate so eminent that his election could not be denied. Less politely, they should pack the meeting and rig a Committee. The Committee could then report to Section in 1921 and thence to the floor of the A.B.A. He thought well considered and highly sponsored resolutions could be passed. Resolutions were passed calling, in substance, for a special meeting of the A.A.L.S. at the same time as the summer meeting of the A.B.A., that a Committee be appointed "to create interest in and secure a large attendance at the summer meeting," and that schools be requested to pay the expenses of delegates to the summer meeting.

The key to the Lewis strategy was eminent men and the ideal candidate was Elihu Root, then in his 70's. Root had been active in the bar, past president of the A.B.A. and had spoken then of the importance of sound legal training. He agreed to be chairman of the Section of Legal Education for 1920 and Lewis proposed and got the section to pass the following innocuous sounding resolution:

"The Chairman for the ensuing year [i.e., Root] and six other members of the Association appointed by him shall be a Special Committee. The Committee shall report to the next meeting of the Section their recommendations in respect to what, if any action can be taken by this Section and by the Association to create conditions which will tend to strengthen the character and improve the efficiency of those admitted to the practice of law." Root went to work immediately and circulated a comprehensive questionnaire to Bar examiners, law schools and others asking their views on legal education. He avoided the mistake of the Council on Legal Education and appointed non-law schoolmen to his committee (with one exception, W. Draper Lewis). The Committee met first in March and then again in May when it heard from a number of people including, of course, the Deans of Harvard, Yale and Columbia, as well as some prominent state Bar examiners, and a representative of night law schools. A. Z. Reed also spoke to the Committee.

Root and his Committee engineered a compromise. The school men got two things they wanted badly: (1) a declaration that only in law school could one get an adequate legal education and (2) a statement that two years of college education should be required before admission to law school. The opposition got night law schools legitimated—law schools that catered to those who devoted only part of their time to legal education were satisfactory provided that the course of study was longer so that "equivalent" hours were given to law study. The Bar examiners got an endorsement of publicly-administered bar examinations and disapproval of the diploma privilege. Finally, a revived Council on Legal Education was directed to publish the names of those law schools complying with the standards and instructed to urge adoption of the A.B.A. standards as minimum legal qualifications for admission to the bar.

This compromise went through the Section of Legal Education in August of 1921. Elihu Root made the motion for its adoption and Chief Justice Taft a suitable seconding speech reflecting rather more regard for Mr. Root than familiarity with the details of the Committee's report. Two brave souls resisted, suggesting that Reed's first book had just been published and it might be well to see to what extent his views were consistent with those proposed by the Committee. Root answered that argument with the bland statement that the Report had been available to the Committee (which was true), and that "the recommendations of the committee were based upon their study of the report". The inference that the Committee and Reed were in full accord would not be accurate. But the report was endorsed and sent on to the floor of the A.B.A. The move to delay on the floor also lost and with even less debate the A.B.A. was finally on record as endorsing the following resolution:

Resolved, (1) The American Bar Association is of the opinion that every candidate for admission to the bar shall give evidence of graduation from a law school complying with the following standards:

(a) It shall require as a condition of admission at least two years of study in a college.

(b) It shall require its students to pursue a course of three years' duration if they devote substantially all of their working time to their studies, and a longer course, equivalent in the number of working hours, if they devote only part of their working time to their studies.

(c) It shall provide an adequate library available for the use of the students.

(d) It shall have among its teachers a sufficient number giving their entire time to the school to insure actual personal acquaintance and influence with the whole student body.

(2) The American Bar Association is of the opinion that graduation from a law school should not confer the right of admission to the bar, and that every candidate should be subjected to an examination by public authority to determine his fitness.

(3) The Council on Legal Education and Admissions to the Bar is directed to publish from time to time the names of those law schools which comply with the above standards and of those which do not, and to make such publications available, so far as possible, to intending law students.

(4) The President of the Association and the Council on Legal Education and Admissions to the Bar are directed to co-operate with the state and local bar associations to urge upon the duly constituted authorities of the several states the adoption of the above requirements for admission to the bar.

(5) The Council on Legal Education and Admissions to the Bar is directed to call a conference on legal education in the name of the American Bar Association, to which the state and local associations shall be invited to send delegates, for the purpose of uniting the bodies represented in an effort to create conditions favorable to the adoption of the principles above set forth.

The final recommendation of the Root Committee for a Conference on Legal Education composed of delegates from state and local bar associations to consider the A.B.A.'s resolution was essentially a publicity device which, it was hoped, would serve to energize the local bars and thus state governments to incorporate in law the A.B.A.'s minimum standards. The Conference was held in the spring of 1922. It was a two-day session with a long agenda of speeches mostly from prominent men whose position could easily be anticipated. Ultimately the delegates resolved to endorse the A.B.A. resolution weakening it only slightly by suggesting that educational experience other than that obtained in a college might be treated as the equivalent of two years of college and that in some states, where there were not adequate law school facilities, the bar could properly give first priority to encouraging the development of such schools. Root delivered a dramatic speech at the end of the session just before the delegates were to vote on some weakening amendments. The speech does not read very powerfully today, but apparently it had a considerable effect. In any event, the delegates turned down the amendments and went home confident they had done something important.

They had. They had passed a resolution that in one particular went well beyond what Henry Wade Rogers three years earlier had thought too revolutionary to put before an A.B.A. convention. Rogers thought requiring graduation from an approved three-year law school (or four if it was a night school) too much to ask; now the A.B.A. went even further and specified that to be approved a law school must have as a requirement for admission at least two years of college education. If that conception had been translated into law in the 1920's, it seems reasonably plain that most of the night or part time law schools would have died, just as their medical school analogues perished a decade earlier. It is almost certain that that expectation was what led Harlan Stone and others like him to accept the Root compromise which, contrary to the A.A.L.S. position, said that part time legal education could be the equivalent of full time study. The A.A.L.S., to be sure, the next year did open its membership to night schools, but it is plain that the leadership did so solely in the interests of unity with the A.B.A. and without a strong sense of conviction.

Reed warned those who would listen that legal sanction for requiring two years of college before entry into law school was not going to come quickly. He was right. The A.B.A. resolution, of course, had no immediate legal effect; admission to the bar was solely in the hands of government and for most purposes state government. Although there was agitation and change in bar admission standards, the two-year requirement was very slowly adopted. Six years after the A.B.A. resolved, only six states required any college education. It took about 15 years, and a good depression, to get the ball moving. In 1935 30 states required two years of college, 19 required no college at all. By the outbreak of the Second World War, all but a few states required two years. It is clear that in general the legal requirement followed rather than led the growth of college education. Thus contrary to the hopes if not the expectation of the A.A.L.S. leadership, there was no significant reduction in the number of law schools, or of law students, nor was there any very rapid change in the quality of education most law students were receiving after 1921.

The other provisions of the A.B.A. resolution were far less important. Favoring the training of lawyers in law schools rather than in law offices was of little significance because few were coming to the bar that way anyway. Requiring three years of law study (or its equivalent for part time schools) was the practice of all but a few schools in 1921; the worst of the most commercial night schools had no difficulty in accepting that standard. The requirement of an "adequate" library and a "sufficient" faculty provided a rich source of argumentation. The Council was cautious in the business of classifying schools. It came out with a list of Class A and Class B schools in 1923, both being approved, Class B so to speak provisionally. In 1925 it abandoned the B classification and listed only those that were approved. It never published a list of disapproved schools. One consequence of the Root compromise was that membership in the A.A.L.S. tended to be the same as the A.B.A. approved list, although membership in the A.A.L.S. has gradually come to be somewhat more selective than the A.B.A.

W. Draper Lewis was a sound political strategist. The program he laid out in 1919 worked. It is not so clear that his program was statesman-like, however, because the clear implication of his tactic was that whatever the A.B.A. did in 1921 it would not be able to undo or even change in significant part for many years. Lewis saw that the Section on Legal Education would tend to be in the control of marginal schools and bar examiners (who fed on each other to a substantial extent) and that the Section would be in a position to obstruct and prevent change. His strategy called for a fast takeover of the newly reorganized Section, aiming towards a one-shot chance on the floor of the A.B.A. Big names like Root and Taft could be had for that kind of enterprise, they could not be held for sustained operations. Lewis obviously was not responsible for the succeeding fifty years of inactivity, but in evaluating what was done in 1921 it is fair to note that he should have seen, if he did not, that what was done then was going to be the position of the A.B.A. for some time and that dramatic changes of direction were not going to come easily. There has never been a dramatic change of direction. There have been gradual movements from two years of pre-law college study to three; regulations defining equivalence and "adequate" library and "sufficient" faculty have been stiffened or, in the earlier years, relaxed, but no sweeping reevaluation.

So much for what happened on the surface. It is now time to go back and examine what A. Z. Reed contributed to the process and how much what he had to say influenced what was done.

Reed was clear, as few others were, that the problems of legal education were markedly different from those of medical education, and he early cautioned that the example of the Flexner report was a very dubious model. The largest difference which he identified was wrapped up in the title he gave his first book: *Training for the Public Profession of the Law*. The important word was *Public*. He believed that lawyers were an integral part of the process of government; that the creation and enforcement of the law—public and private—required the active involvement of lawyers. That being so, the profession must be open and accessible to people of all classes and kinds else the promise of democracy would fail. As he looked backwards from 1920, he found ample historical justification for this position. In colonial times the bar had a kind of shadowy elite status derivative from the English experience; this quickly evaporated under the egalitarian pressures of Jacksonian democracy. It was not until after the Civil War that efforts began to be made to impose some sort of educational or examination standards for entry into the bar. Although their objective was protection of the public from the unqualified, these standards could easily be converted into monopolistic restriction for the economic benefit of the bar and, they were, accordingly, viewed with suspicion if not hostility by the public.

Reed also saw that legal education in the country was a new kind of beast without clear analogue in Continental or English experience. Although some early attempts were made to include law as one of the subjects a cultivated man should know something about, legal education in this country was predominantly an outgrowth of schools that purported to do no more than a better job of training than could be obtained as an apprentice in a law office. We thus lacked influential law faculties at Universities comparable to those on the Continent. The early American law schools were rather more supplements to law office training than substitutes for it. They were thus, from the outset, vocationally oriented and, unlike the English Inns of Court, quite independent of any organized bar. Modern legal education begins in this country in the period following the Civil War. The paradigm school was Harvard—at least until Reed wrote Harvard was usually somewhat ahead of the rest of the law school world. It was the first economically successful marriage of a University with vocational legal education. The University connection added breadth to the purely professional training. Ames was the first to start his career as a law teacher rather than as a practitioner. The Langdell case method of instruction was believed to teach law as a science. By the time Reed wrote there were, of course, many law schools following the Harvard model; what Reed saw very clearly, but others did not, was that the law schools were ranged along a continuum with Harvard and its kind at one end and the others spread out to schools that attempted no more than to qualify their people to pass the bar examination. Reed thought that the history and future of legal education were inextricably connected first to the American University and second to the organized bar. The first was by 1920 reasonably clear; the better law schools were, as with medicine, University schools. The bar's connection to legal education was by no means well defined in 1921.

The bar was substantially unorganized when Reed wrote. There was only a voluntary national bar—the A.B.A.—which claimed only 10 per cent of the lawyers as members, and a multitude of voluntary state and local bars whose functions were often as much social as anything else. There was a tradition of a qualification examination for admission to practice, but in 1920 bar exams were just starting to be more than formalities. Reed saw a distinct parallel between the bar examination process and the growth of civil service. He thought the egalitarian pressure for free access to public position—the extreme of Jacksonian democracy—was beginning to yield to a need for efficient government which in turn called for some test of competence both for public servants and lawyers. He thought there was yet a chance for the bar to develop in a way that would facilitate measures of competence. As he phrased it, the issue was whether legal education and the profession would strive towards a "unitary" as opposed to a "differentiated" bar.

The concept of a unitary bar Reed saw was much more of a theoretical concept than a living reality. Once admitted to the bar all lawyers were in law equal, presumptively equally trained for their professional role and equally competent to perform any legal task. Assuming that a man's competence was related to his training (an assumption no law professor can comfortably deny), the eyes of the law were blind to reality because there was a vast difference in the quality of education offered in law schools, and in his book Reed described a wide range of kinds of legal education then common in this country. The poles were Harvard at one end requiring substantial pre-legal education (a college degree), a curriculum that was national (or general, or scientific) in orientation, instruction by the case method with a faculty dedicated in significant part to the production of works of scholarship, and at the other extreme, the night school where the admission requirements were at best a high school education, a curriculum confined to a single jurisdiction, instruction largely by lecture and drill by a faculty of practitioners. The issue as Reed saw it was whether to try to force everyone into the image of the Harvard graduate or build a differentiated bar with some trained to do some things (he suggested that conveyancing, probate and trial practice might be possible), and others more broadly trained to be more widely competent.

Reed thought an effort to force all legal education in the mold of Harvard unlikely to succeed. He relied primarily on his conviction that the lawmakers in charge of the admission process would never tolerate a system that cut off access to the bar for the poor and underprivileged (and in the 1920's that meant children of the foreign born, not racial minorities). In other words, as he viewed it, the "public" nature of the profession required part time legal education for those financially unable to attend college and full time law school. That being his prediction, it seemed to Reed more likely to be productive to work on redirecting the goals of part-time legal education. Classify the bar, either functionally or otherwise, with the part-time schools graduating men competent to perform the relatively routine tasks within the confines of a single jurisdiction, well-trained to do that and with pretentions to no more and presumably bar examinations that tested no more. The "public" functions of a lawyer—which must be open to all classes—would thus be served and such a division would permit a sharp lifting of the requirements for admission to the inner bar open only to those more broadly trained and, perhaps, more widely experienced.

Although I am not aware that he ever gave credit, Reed must have seen and been aware of Walter Wheeler Cook's presidential address given before the A.A.L.S. in 1916. In that talk Cook, speaking of the problem of admission to the bar, saw essentially four alternatives open to the profession. The first three were: (1) continuing the present scheme of loose bar admissions which resulted in licensing many incompetents; (2) abandoning any test and admitting all (worse than the first, but not much); (3) creating a very rigorous test that would prevent the incompetent from passing. Like Reed some years later, Cook doubted the political feasibility of a rigorous test although he thought that such was the policy implicitly favored within the A.A.L.S. That led him to the following:

> With the permission of the Carnegie Foundation, I venture to call your attention to the proposal of a fourth plan, contained in an unpublished report to the Foundation, made some time ago by my colleague upon the Yale faculty, Mr. Hohfeld. After discussing the three plans I have mentioned, Mr. Hohfeld suggests as a possible solution that two grades of practitioners be recognized. The first or highest would be called attorneys and counselors, as at present, and would be required to satisfy tests sufficiently exacting so that there would be every reason to believe that as a class they would be able to handle efficiently the legal affairs of their clients. The second or lower class would have to pass lower tests, designed to weed out the least competent of the applicants, but not high enough to guarantee competency on the part of those satisfying the tests. This second class of practitioners would be permitted, equally with the attorneys, to engage in the general practice of the law, but would not be permitted to call themselves attorneys until they had passed the highest test laid down for the latter. The advantages of such a plan would be obvious. The

"poor boy", of whom we hear so much, if unable to satisfy the ideal requirements in the way of a legal education, would not be debarred from practicing law, and might ultimately succeed in entering the higher class. Practitioners of this lower class might perhaps — to revive a good old common-law term — be known as "Apprentices at Law."

A plan of this kind would have the following advantages: (1) It would prevent the absolutely incompetent from practicing; (2) it would not mislead the public; (3) it would enable the public to choose between competent and incompetent lawyers if they so chose; (4) it would leave the way still open for those of small means to enter the profession, with the chance of ultimately reaching the higher rank. I recommend this plan to the careful consideration of all those who are interested in raising the standards for admission to the bar, in the belief that, under the circumstances existing in particular states, it may in many cases prove to be the best solution of this very difficult problem. It would more especially meet the needs of those parts of the country just referred to, in which for any reason the educational conditions or the attitude of the public render it impossible to adopt immediately a standard that insures efficiency on the part of all members of the bar. Once in force, it would, I am sure, pave the way for the higher standard which should ultimately be adopted everywhere.

Unfortunately, the timing of events rendered it unnecessary for Reed to develop his ideas at length. The Root Committee was given copies of Reed's book before it was available generally, and in their report in support of the 1921 resolution they dispatched the idea of a differentiated bar with the following:

Turning first, then, to a consideration of what a lawyer's training should be, we meet the suggestion that there must be different kinds of training to produce different kinds of lawyers.

With this position we do not agree. In spite of the diversity of human relations with respect to which the work of lawyers is done, the intellectual requisites are in all cases substantially the same. From the first interview with his client to the last step in litigation the lawyer must be trained to apprehend and to state the pertinent facts in logical sequence, to perceive clearly the questions of law presented, and to extract from statutes and decisions the principles of law applicable. And in every case, whatever its nature, he must be able to apply the fundamental principles of the common law.

If an admiralty lawyer's work were fundamentally different in kind

from a probate lawyer's work, a different training would be required
for each and a consequent classification of the bar would follow as a
matter of course. In our opinion, however, there is no such difference
between kinds of legal work. All require high moral character and
substantially the same intellectual preparation.

Nor can there be tolerated a recognized distinction between good
and poor legal education. There should be no distinction in training
which does not find its complement in a distinction in practice. Because we cannot favor the continuation of a class of incompetent
practitioners, we cannot favor the continuation of a system of training
which fails to reach the highest practicable standard.

Assuming, therefore, that all who intend to practice law should
receive a training in accordance with certain prescribed and uniform
standards, it becomes necessary to inquire what those standards
should be.

The same response to Reed's idea came from other quarters very
quickly. In the American Bar Journal, Harlan Stone, in a rather
ill-tempered review, said:

> For every one who has had any extensive experience in practice is
> well aware that there is no functional cleavage of the bar between the
> superficially trained and those who are thoroughly trained. It is well
> that it is so, for it is impossible to segregate into any one class the
> professional business who does not on occasion require all of the
> skill of the well trained lawyer and with respect to which the con-
> sequences of superficial training may be fatal alike to the interests
> of the client and to the proper development of the bar. 7 A.B.A.J.
> 643.

And in the same Journal, in a much more balanced effort to assess
the differences between Reed and Root Committee, W. Draper
Lewis observed:

> But the position of the committee is that the intellectual processes
> necessary for efficient work in all branches of professional activity
> are so essentially similar that all members of the bar should have
> as a foundation a like cultural and technical training. 8 A.B.A.J. 41.

Professor Corbin, President of the A.A.L.S. in 1921, devoted
most of his address to refuting the suggestion of a differentiated
bar without adding very much. As Reed himself observed in 1922,
the idea of a differentiated bar "is the one feature of the Bulletin

that has been almost contemptuously dismissed. The indivisibility of the legal profession is as much a fetish of the existing generation of lawyers as it was forty years ago." With that wry comment, Reed more or less dropped his proposal. For the next decade or so he contented himself with watching the very slow process of democratization of higher education which would permit the bulk of legal education to adapt itself to the Harvard model. That process, which is still incomplete especially for racial minorities, has only come close to fruition since the G.I. Bill. But now, nearly 50 years after the A.B.A. resolved, we are on the threshold of achieving a unitary bar at least to the extent that nearly all practitioners approach the bar with the benefit of a college education and with substantially equivalent training in law schools that are very much alike.

The rejection of the idea of a differentiated bar, explicit in the Root Committee report and implicit in the 1921 resolution of the A.B.A., seems to me the most important action the A.B.A. has ever taken with respect to legal education. The resolution certainly did not create a unitary bar, nor did it affirmatively contribute much towards achieving that goal. What it did do was negative; it cut short any efforts that might have been made anywhere to build a differentiated bar. It is possible that such efforts would never have been made; by 1920 we were a nation with a national bar despite the fact that admission to practice was controlled at the state level and it would have been difficult for any state to depart from the traditional norm of a theoretically unitary bar. But somebody somewhere might have tried it. It is at least possible that if the night law schools had not been embraced by the A.A.L.S. some might have tried to develop a different kind of training towards a distinctive narrow competence as Reed hoped. The enormous weight of the A.B.A. resolution, however, crushed any such kind of experimental mutation. The consequences of attempting to build a unitary bar are pervasive and perhaps it is worthwhile to work out some of the effects for legal education explicitly.

1. Bar Examinations

The bar examination was, of course, an indispensable part of the conception of a unitary bar. The 1920's had a faith in the process of examination that seems now startling, almost naive. Reed may well have been right in suggesting that confidence in the bar examination was only part of the more general belief in civil service for public employment generally. But there are, of course, some important differences. Any objective test, no matter how inadequate it may be as a measure of competence, has some advantages over the spoils system. Fairly administered it will at least eliminate some of the grosser forms of corruption. That is no part of the problem for the bar examination. Furthermore, the civil service examination is designed to select the most competent; the bar examination to cut out the incompetent. The significance of this difference comes forward with the cram course problem. It is one thing to run a cram course designed to get people selected from among a pool that is constantly replenished by reasonably able candidates—that is the problem of the person running a cram course for civil service examinations—it is quite another to run a course designed to qualify people to meet some minimum standard—that is much easier, especially if candidates can take the examination repeatedly. That, of course, has been the history of the bar examination which has never been able to escape passing the ill-trained, repeating graduate of cram courses. Despite constant tinkering and improvement, the bar examination is still impaled on the dilemma Langdell identified nearly 100 years ago: "It is impossible that such examinations should be at once rigorous and just. They must admit the undeserving or reject the deserving; and in the long run they will be sure to do the former."

Men in the 1920's were not blind to some shortcomings of the bar examination process. They recognized that no test can probe effectively a man's moral standards and that inevitably some would pass the bar who would not comply with ethical standards. They hoped that a college education might help, an idea that almost certainly was derivative of prejudice against the foreign born. The A.A.L.S. schools were also bothered by the mechanical rules and rote learning that the bar examinations then commonly called for. They wanted tests that would measure analytical ability as well as knowledge of "fundamental principles". What they did not see, or at least discuss, was that any kind of bar examination would tend to some extent to make legal education conform to the examiner's model of what a lawyer ought to know. A school might disregard that model if its graduates had the diploma privilege (but the Root Committee came out against that) or if there were available an adequate cram course, but, much more important the bar examination carried with it inevitably the conception that anyone who passed the examination was a fully qualified lawyer, as competent as the next to handle any legal problem. That is what the bar examination tells the public, and, unless other examinations or certifications are added on (as Walter Wheeler Cook suggested) no amount of public education will alter that misconception.

2. Legal Services for the Poor

One of the major arguments put forward in support of lifting the standards for admission to the bar was the concern repeatedly expressed that the poor were being cheated by incompetent lawyers mishandling their affairs. The solution to this problem, as Root and others saw it, was to raise the standards of the bar. But raising the standards of the bar to a single highly qualified standard creates other pressures not necessarily consistent with the best interests of those least able to afford legal services.

The discussion here must necessarily become somewhat detached from reality. We should, however, begin with one hard truth: the best way to provide adequate legal services for the poor is to make the service cheap enough so that the poor, or at least those above an indigency standard, can afford it. Anything which tends to increase the cost of legal services is going to make the problem worse, not better.

Training all lawyers to be competent to handle the most complex of legal affairs will necessarily increase the cost of their services. Not only will lawyers have spent more time getting qualified, but presumably they will be able to offer their services to a wider range of clientele and thus be in greater demand. Of course, it was not true that all lawyers were fully competent to handle anything in the '20's any more than it is today, but the rhetoric of a unitary bar permitted the creation of a legal monopoly that gave lawyers something close to the economic consequences of that result. The argument is simple: only lawyers can adequately perform certain tasks and the public must be protected against untrained persons attempting to do so, hence the strictures against the unauthorized practice of law; well-trained lawyers cannot afford to perform this service unless they are permitted to charge a reasonable fee, wherefore the minimum fee is set at a level adequate to attract or at least not discourage a lawyer who has broad competitive demands for his services; finally — with an assist from the conception that it cheapens the profession to advertise — charging less than the minimum fee is itself made unlawful. Thus whether we assume that omnicompetence is a realistic or a false goal, the end result is in either instance to raise the cost of legal services to the inevitable detriment of the poor.

Another argument, less frequently made directly but firmly believed by many in the '20's, was that the bar was desperately overcrowded and that much of the inferior service being given to the poor was necessitated by the inability of many practitioners to resist the temptation to engage in unethical conduct, including charging less than the minimum fee. The way to meet this problem they thought was to reduce the supply of lawyers by increasing the training required to become a lawyer. On its face this was a device that could only increase the cost of legal services. A sharp reduction in the supply of lawyers, of course, did not materialize although it may be that some potential law students were discouraged.

Reed never made the argument that a differentiated bar might serve to lower the cost of legal services and thus benefit the less affluent. Walter Wheeler Cook suggested it but no more, and the argument has not really been made until recently. Training people to relatively narrow competences will take less time and will restrict the demand for their services. The combination should ultimately result in a lowering of the charge. The process is clearly possible in law. Insurance companies use adjusters, not lawyers, to do things for their employers that plaintiffs' lawyers do for their clients. The reason is that an adjuster costs less. The conception of a unitary bar gives the plaintiff the alternative of representing himself or using a presumptively omnicompetent lawyer. He is not allowed the choice of an adjuster.

The impact of this on legal education is less direct than the bar examination. Some people are being overtrained, they are learning more than they need to know. Harlan Stone, of course, asserted the opposite. "It is impossible," he said, "to segregate into any one class the professional business which does not on occasion require all of the skill of the well-trained lawyer and with respect to which the consequences of superficial training may be fatal alike to the interests of the client and to the proper development of the bar." It is true that legal problems frequently involve subtle ramifications that are not immediately apparent and it is possible that making all lawyers fully competent might bring to the surface matters that less trained men would not see or be able to handle. It does not follow, however, that these fine points, if seen, will be exhaustively explored. They will be if the client can afford it, they will not be if he cannot. For the most part those who can afford to have the subtleties in their legal problems worked through will get adequate service no matter how the legal profession is organized, those who cannot afford more than the standard charge will get standard service whether their legal problem is complex or not.

3. Super Qualification

Reed's charge from the Carnegie Foundation was to examine the world of legal education and bar admissions. He was not asked to consider the effectiveness of legal education as a method of training people to do what lawyers do. Accordingly, he made no effort to find out what lawyers in fact did or to evaluate how well legal education related to the practice. He was thus spared consideration of the reverse of the problem just discussed—super training for legal operations that are particularly complex, what is today usually described as specialization (probably because medical specialists are super-qualified).

We know appallingly little about what lawyers do in fact today, and of course even less about what they were doing fifty years ago. Undoubtedly, there were some lawyers then who concentrated their practice on certain kinds of problems. A very rough measure is provided by the growth of large law firms which just started in the biggest cities in the first decades of this century. A large law office will contain specialists capable of handling legal problems beyond the competence of an inexperienced general practitioner, at least without the investment of an inordinate amount of time. What was known in 1920 has been growing steadily since then, stimulated both by the urbanization of the bar and the increasing complexity of modern life. The increase in specialization in the sense of super-qualification has undoubtedly accelerated rapidly since the Second World War. We should not fault Reed and Root for failing to identify the pressure towards specialization as an almost inevitable development of the future, but they did miss it. They focused their attention on training the "typical" or "average" lawyer of their time, then likely as not to be located in a rural or semi-urban context with the bulk of his practice revolving more or less directly around the courthouse. That model lawyer was less typical in 1920 than it was 20 years earlier, but it still probably was a tolerably accurate reflection of the world around him.

It was a bad prediction of what was to come. Some degree of specialization seems now to be the dominant characteristic of lawyers. A recent survey indicates that roughly two-thirds of the California bar regard themselves as specialists. Many of these lawyers are, of course, over-trained rather than super-qualified specialists (they are nurses, not surgeons), but the figure does suggest how wide of the mark Reed and Root were in thinking about the typical lawyer of the future.

The conception of a unitary bar is, of course, inconsistent with recognition of specialists. This is not the place to explore the reasons for and against public certification of specialty competences — that has been done elsewhere — but nonrecognition has carried with it important implications for legal education. The Root Committee asserted that an admiralty lawyer's work was not fundamentally different from a probate lawyer's and that both required substantially the same intellectual preparation. With respect to what a law school should teach, the Root Committee said:

> In such a school we believe that there should be no attempt to give a complete knowledge of the substantive law. The complexity and bulk of American law today would make such an attempt hopeless. Specific knowledge in certain fields and a knowledge of fundamental principles are of course necessary. But the most important duty of the school is to teach the ability to find the sources of the law and to use those sources intelligently.

The clear implication of this statement is that the law schools have nothing to contribute to the process of educating specialists. Experience alone was the route by which a lawyer acquired specialized competence to handle particularly complex kinds of legal problems. The law school's contribution was to train men so that they could benefit from their experience, but it had no direct input to make towards achieving that goal. The idea of a unitary bar thus has led to nonrecognition of specialty competences which, in turn, has positively discouraged law school involvement in developing training materials which would help a lawyer become qualified to handle especially difficult kinds of problems. The only way he can do it is by practicing on a client.

The law schools, of course, have for years offered courses in subject matters that can only be described as specialties — admiralty and probate to use Root's examples, are old-timers, Labor

Law and Land Use Planning are relative newcomers and there are many, many others. These courses do help the budding specialist principally by providing texts and articles. But there is no very clear relationship between taking a specialized course in law school and developing a practice in that field. Furthermore, the courses tend to be survey courses of an area with in-depth exploration, perhaps, of a few isolated issues. Student and instructor both conceive the purpose of such offerings not as qualifying the student as a specialist, but as an intellectual exercise to expose the student to a different way of looking at legal problems.

4. Training in the "Fundamental Principles"

The idea of a unitary bar presumes that there is a body of knowledge central to the functioning of a lawyer that all good lawyers must know. Without such a central core a unitary bar would be impossible. Root, of course, assumed that it existed. The phrase "fundamental principles" is several times repeated although never defined in the Root Committee report: "And in every case, whatever its nature, he must be able to apply the *fundamental principles* of the common law. . . . Specific knowledge in certain fields and a knowledge of *fundamental principles* are of course necessary. . . . Legal education should produce a real knowledge of *fundamental principles* and a mind which thinks in terms of the common law."

A careful reading of Reed's book should have given Root's Committee pause on this point. Reed reported a generally recognized flaw in the reasoning of Langdell on the case method of instruction. Langdell thought there were relatively few essential principles of law and that close study of carefully selected cases would permit the student to discover the "true rule" on analogy to the scientific study of empirical data. The true rule is much the same if not identical to fundamental principles. As early as Ames, legal educators began to doubt Langdell's rationale for the case method. They learned that it was a sublimely effective pedagogical device but not a particularly effective way of discovering truth. That there was a truth to be discovered was not generally questioned, certainly Reed never doubted it, but the ideas behind legal realism were about and someone should have been worried whether the bar was not committing itself to an educational system that was at least open to doubt on its primary assumptions.

Another danger signal that might have alerted someone was Reed's criticism of the elective system. Early in Langdell's administration the curriculum was entirely prescribed. When the years of study expanded from two to three, some optional offerings were included and, as the faculty grew, the number of electives increased. By the time Reed wrote that pattern was overwhelmingly dominant in any law school with a faculty large enough to afford it. Reed could not understand that; it seemed to him self-evident that experienced law teachers should know better than law students what were appropriate subjects for study. This is because Reed thought there was a body of knowledge every lawyer ought to have, and, on that assumption, he was clearly right. To Reed's mind the need for direction was increasing because the law was becoming increasingly complicated and difficult to master. Many prominent legal educators were talking about adding another year to law school so that essential subjects could be covered. The more essentials there are to be covered, the more important it obviously becomes to control the material students are exposed to. But it was clear to Reed, and it should have been to the Root Committee, that the trend was towards expanding electives. That trend has continued so that in most schools today the third year is mainly electives and in many schools the same is true of the second year as well. Leaving aside the first year, only two inferences are possible: either legal education cannot agree upon what principles are fundamental or they do not exist. Reed assumed the former. The legal realists have persuaded most that the latter is more accurate.

There is still the common curriculum of the first year which has remained the same since Langdell's day—Contracts, Property, Torts, Procedure and Criminal Law. It might be supposed that such "fundamental principles" as exist are covered during that year. That is a debatable proposition, first because although the nomenclature has been constant, the content of those courses has changed greatly and second because at least today the first year, far more than either the second or third, is devoted to teaching skills rather than substantive content. The vocabulary of law, the framework of its institutions and understanding the literature of appellate opinions are the real subject matter of the first year, not concepts such as offer and acceptance, or negligence or the estates in land.

The difficulty of isolating fundamental principles is also reflected in the search for a suitable pre-law required curriculum on analogy to the scientific courses medical schools require as a condition of admission. Most of this has taken place since Reed's book was published, but an enormous amount of energy has been spent trying to develop an "ideal" pre-law curriculum. By 1952 the A.A.L.S. officially gave up any attempt to prescribe any undergraduate background for law, limiting its advice to the single negative proposition that "[s]o called 'law' courses in undergraduate instruction should be avoided. Generally, they are not intended as education for lawyers but for other purposes." If there were a central core of principles essential to lawyering, the chances are law teachers could agree upon a few subject matters that law students should know something about before they come to law school. Reed, for example, supposed that the political history of our legal institutions could usefully be known by all law students. Today, probably, many law teachers would not choose that over a solid understanding of the scientific method; they have different but equally significant relevance to law study.

To summarize all this, the A.B.A. in 1921 deliberately put its full weight behind the conception of a unitary bar. The gain was the very slow elimination of some very bad legal education whose eventual death was probably at least as attributable to the growth of higher education generally as to anything else. The price has been commitment to the fiction of a unitary bar, one of the law's least constructive flights into fantasy. It was founded on a false premise, that law was like medicine, and it failed of its immediate objective, the prompt destruction of the part time law school. By discouraging the development of what are now called paraprofessionals and divorcing the training of specialists from the law schools, it has significantly interfered with what might be thought the natural evolution of an educational system that catered to the needs of a profession. The image of omnicompetence has vastly inflated the role of the bar examination which, in turn, has led law schools to concentrate on teaching those things that readily admit of testing and held course content to traditional issues.

The next issue is what is to be done, assuming that rational argumentation can lead to changes. As noted earlier, in my view the great asset of legal education before 1921 was its freedom. Ideas about how to train lawyers could be tried and had a chance to work themselves out in the market place of the profession. The point can be illustrated by contrasting law schools today with large law firms. The modern, large metropolitan law firm as a common way of organizing law practice is barely a generation old. Its antecedents can, of course, be found in New York and Chicago in the '20's, but the phenomenon has spread, much the way the model of the Harvard Law School was copied throughout the country before the first World War. But the large law firms have continued to respond to new demands from their clients. They are constantly testing the efficiency of their methods, looking around to see what the competition is doing and adopting successful ideas of others. A simple illustration is the recent development of summer clerkships. Ten years ago a law student between his second and third year could get a job in a law firm only if the managing partner was his uncle. What started as a wild idea of a few progressive firms has now become a commonplace. The large law firm demonstrates that there is nothing inherent in the law that makes its institutions inflexible and unresponsive. But legal education is not, and the problem is to restore some measure of receptiveness to innovation.

One plan has been put forward recently that seems to me to have considerable potential: reducing the required years of law study from three to two. This would require some adjustment in the curriculum of law schools today, presumably more courses would be required and some would be shortened. Some students, perhaps most, would leave law school after two years. Some would stay on for a third year immediately after the first two. A larger number would come back to law school after some time in practice. Perhaps the third year would have to come in the form of summer courses or evening classes to accommodate the convenience of lawyer-students. The charm of the proposal is that it puts law schools back in the business of selling themselves. Schools will have to design course offerings that lawyers will think it worth their while to take. That kind of competition should stimulate the kind of creative energy characteristic of the best of legal education in the '20's. We can also anticipate a considerable diversity in the sort of programs offered by various schools responsive both to local conditions and

Total number of law schools classified according to the minimum number of years of law work required to secure the degree	1800–1809	1809–1900	1900–1910	1910–1920	1920–1921
One or one and a half years	9	8	3	1	1
Two years	45	47	37	18	14
Three years or over	7	47	84	127	135
Total number of schools	61	102	124	146	150

the strengths of their faculties. Before examining the merits of this proposal in greater details, however, two preliminary matters should be discussed.

1. What was the original rationale for requiring three years, and

2. How much of a change over what was contemplated in 1921 does a two year program involve?

Unfortunately, no very good explanation can be given for the third year requirement because it was a totally noncontroversial aspect of the Root resolution. It was noncontroversial because what the A.B.A. decreed in 1921 simply reflected what was then the practice of all but a few law schools. It had not, however, been standard for very long, as shown in the table below.

Harvard in 1878 was the first school to require three years of legal education for a degree although before then a number of schools had flirted with various kinds of postgraduate courses designed, unsuccessfully, to persuade students to stay for more than two years. Why did Langdell think three years was right? So far as I know, he never explained. Presumably he thought more law could be learned in three years than in two, and that he and his faculty had enough to say to warrant holding students for an additional year. In the '80's and '90's Harvard probably could have gone on and demanded four years but, if it had, the effect would have been to discourage prospective law students from finishing, or perhaps even starting, college. I'm guessing, but it seems likely that because of the potential adverse effect on the College, the Law School chose instead to concentrate on requiring a complete college education before entering law school rather than on lengthening the

1921–1922	1922–1923	1923–1924	1924–1925	1925–1926	1926–1927	1927–1928
1	2	2	2	2	2	2
8	7	6	8	7	8	8
141	144	147	152	159	164	166
150	153	155	162	168	174	176

period of law study. And so, at the turn of the century, Harvard and those who would copy Harvard, were offering a three year law degree program.

During the '20's a number of schools considered the possibility of a four year law curriculum. Much of this, however, was in truth a form of advancing the required pre-law training rather than an expansion of the amount of law study. A few legal educators, however, did seriously argue for a fourth year of law school primarily because they thought the law was getting more complex and more time was needed for its mastery. That idea was revived briefly following the Second World War, but now seems quiescent. The law has not gotten any simpler since 1921; perhaps because it is now indisputably impossible to learn it all no one now argues that law schools should attempt to teach its content.

The sum of the matter is that there never was a well-articulated basis for requiring three years of law school; perhaps the most persuasive reason is that English custom requires a prospective barrister to dine at an Inn of Court for three years before he can be called to the bar. The Root Committee departed from its task of stating *minimum* standards when it required three years of law school. At the time the Root Committee spoke, three years had been standard for no more than a decade and it is hard to believe that there were not other combinations of more college and less law school that they would have regarded as minimally satisfactory. For example, four years of college and two years of law school is as likely to produce an adequate lawyer as two years of college and three years of law school. Root and Reed had no occasion to consider that combination because the pressure at the time was against requiring any college education, and the most commercial of law schools had no objection to requiring three or four years of law school rather than two. It is, of course, that precise combination of four years of college and two years of law school that is now being proposed. No one can say for certain, but in all probability the Root Committee would have regarded that as minimally satisfactory if somewhat visionary.

The 1921 resolution called for three years of study in a law school. The Root Committee made no attempt to prescribe what should be done during those three years, presumably thinking that a subject best left to the discretion of the individual schools in the future. Reed, as noted earlier, was deeply skeptical about the wisdom of the elective system; he was particularly hard on Columbia for permitting students to fill out some part of their studies with what he called "borderland" topics such as Roman Law, International Law and Jurisprudence. On this point the Root Committee and Reed probably would have been in agreement; there was too much hard, technical law of a fundamental nature to be learned to allow for any substantial consideration of frills. If so, the trend has been all in Columbia's direction. Law schools are now offering many courses inconceivable even to Columbia that expose students to social science materials and other matters involving law only indirectly. To the extent that non-law subjects are permitted to fill out the law school program, there is a de facto reduction in what Reed and Root would have regarded as the required years of law study.

A similar cheapening of law study is currently popular in the form of clinical courses. In these courses the student is confronted with legal problems in the context of a law office rather than law school, most often a legal aid office. There are all sorts of good reasons for such programs, but Reed and Root would have had no difficulty saying that such courses were not law study in law school. That, as a matter of fact, was a problem of the '20's and, indeed, later: how much credit, if any, should be given for "study" in a law office towards the three year requirement. To the extent that legal education is done outside of the law school, or is concerned with non-legal materials, the number of years of law study has been reduced. In some schools (in general, the better schools) it is now possible for a law student to cumulate nearly a year's worth of what Reed and Root would have said was not law study. Put in that context, reducing the required years of law study —assuming we went back to a largely prescribed law curriculum—would not be a very large step measured against what Reed and Root imagined was being required.

If the goal is an educational system that responds to the needs of the profession —and thus to society generally —we ought to know much more than we do about what lawyers do. Hard information is very skimpy and inadequate for these purposes. We know, or think we do, that about one quarter of the lawyers work for a single client, either the government or as house counsel. Another quarter earn most of their living from commercial clients. The remaining half serve the needs of individuals principally from the middle and lower classes. The world of lawyers can be divided up in other ways that are not much more informative. Over half of the bar practices in large cities over 200,000; in California the urban concentration is even greater. In the nation as whole about 40 per cent are solo practitioners; in California about 40 per cent are in partnership with at least one other lawyer, an additional 20 per cent are associates, only 20 per cent are solo practitioners. In California about 12 per cent of the lawyers are in firms of more than 20. It seems fairly clear that the California data suggests what will happen nationally in the future. The bar has been getting steadily more urbanized and the number of individual practitioners has been declining.

There is a correlation between specialization and firm size, but it is by no means a perfect relationship. Similarly, large firms are more likely to be in large cities than otherwise, but again the connection is only partial. Both of those relationships might have been guessed without data, and the data does not improve much on common sense. The California survey on specialization suggests what some lawyers do in fact. Roughly two-thirds of California lawyers think of themselves as specialists in that they concentrate their practice in one of a few fields of law. The most common primary specialties are indicated in the following table:

Field	Percent primary specialty
Negligence	11.1
Probate and trusts	8.8
Business and corporation	7.8
Criminal law	7.4
Real property	5.3
Tax (federal and state)	4.3
Estate planning	4.1
Workmen's compensation	3.3
Patent	2.9
Local government	2.7
Administrative law	2.2
Divorce	2.1

None of this advances us very far as to what lawyers do in the sense of what they sell. Lacking real facts it is possible to work from models. For example, a distinction can be drawn between lawyers who write and lawyers who talk. All lawyers, of course, occasionally do both, but many if not most concentrate on one or the other. For example, the subject matter specialist in the large law firm has as his primary stock in trade his capacity to handle legal materials. He spends most of his time working with books (or supervising those who do) and writing. This is not to say that he has not benefited from his years of experience, but he could probably write down and communicate to others most of the things he has learned from experience. The talking lawyer, on the other hand, is selling primarily his experience in handling facts and bureaucrats. Legal knowledge is not irrelevant to his skill, but most transactions pass through his office without anyone referring to law books except possibly in the most superficial manner. Large law firms have many such men in them, but a typical talking lawyer is one who does a high volume of criminal trial work either as a prosecutor or defender.

This distinction between the talking and the writing lawyer is not the same as the traditional differentiation between the courtroom and the office lawyer. There are some high-powered trial lawyers who spend most of their time with books and conversely many office lawyers who devote themselves primarily to working out deals, negotiating settlements and the like. Nor is this distinction the same as that between the general practitioner and the specialist. The negligence specialist or the lawyer who concentrates in criminal defense work think of themselves as specialists, but they spend nearly all of their time dealing with facts and people, not manipulating legal abstractions. The significance of the distinction, of course, is that law schools should be able to do quite a lot towards training the lawyer who writes, the man who deals with books and ideas; there is much less that a law school can do for the talking lawyer whose role is primarily to talk to people through bureaucracies. As presently organized, however, law schools do not do a very good job on what they ought to be able to do best.

I earlier indicated that one consequence of the unitary bar conception has been the divorce of legal education from training the highly qualified specialist, using that word not in the sense of a lawyer who concentrates his practice, but rather on whose practice is built on a base of broad knowledge of some field of law, e.g., taxation. Perhaps the best reason why law schools have not done a good job is because the timing is wrong. In the third year of law school a student has only a hazy notion of what he will be doing in practice, and can only guess what he will want to know 10 years later. Students are not interested in concentrating their studies in one area and law schools discourage it. Students do not want to learn detailed content since without constant reinforcement from practical need details will be forgotten almost as rapidly as they are learned, and, in any event, details change over time. As a result, training for super-qualification is done after admission to practice and, as practical matter, almost entirely in large firms or in the government. The process is both fortuitous and clumsy. Large law firms will support men while they are learning and provide some guidance some of the time, but the process is apt to be unduly prolonged because the availability of training turns on the needs of clients. A young lawyer's interest in tax may be postponed or totally frustrated if there is no need for an addition to the tax department of his firm.

Learning a specialized competence in practice is also apt to be undemocratic because access to large law firms and government employment is primarily through a relatively limited number of law schools which are themselves highly selective. Thus a lawyer who has not gone to one of the better law schools, despite inclination and ability, is largely cut off from any opportunity to gain a highly specialized subject matter competence because there is no place he can go to get it. The logical place to gain that kind of competence is in law school and the opportunity to provide this kind of training would be one of the larger virtues of a shift from a three to two year law school.

Super qualification training would be something different from what law schools have traditionally done. They have always been somewhat ambivalent about teaching content, especially in advanced courses. To probe any issue deeply it is necessary to know at least the framework, but the minutia of content is rarely worth learning except as an exercise unless the student is going immediately into that particular line of practice. But a man who has returned to law school after some years and wants to acquire some sort of specialty competence can quite properly be asked to learn and remember content. For law professors this is a new pedagogical problem; they ought to be able to design materials that communicate more efficiently than any practice experience can subject matter competence. Furthermore, that should be a salable product.

With few exceptions the law schools have not sought to supply this kind of education. The exceptions are worth noting, because they are just what one might expect. New York University and the University of Southern California are running successful graduate programs in Tax Law—the most obvious subject matter specialty in the largest cities where there is, of course, the greatest concentration of lawyers. Southern California also has a shorter program in Entertainment Law, and Southern Methodist an even shorter program in Oil and Gas Law. Some of these courses parallel the regular law school, others are given at night or in the summer. These shade into the Continuing Education of the Bar programs run mainly by bar associations. Some C.E.B. programs involve a series of lectures given at week-ends or in the evenings; the less ambitious programs involve a day or two. California's C.E.B. program, undoubtedly the most successful, publishes books that typically contain forms, checklists and other how-to-do-it type aids and, in general, tend to serve the needs of the talking lawyer rather than the writing lawyer.

All these programs share one characteristic: they must be totally self-supporting. This is in sharp contrast to the regular law school program which is heavily subsidized. There was a period when a law school was likely to be a money-maker for any university with which it was associated. That is no longer true. The demands of a library and faculty are such that even though the law school is relatively cheap graduate education, it is still a substantial drain on an institutional budget. There is surely something wrong-headed about subsidizing substantially the first three years of law school and forcing post-graduate education to be self-sufficient. The N.Y.U. and U.S.C. tax programs are apparently fairly substantial sources of revenue for their instituions; the California C.E.B. program has also been a prosperous operation supporting in part the University Extension system generally as well as experimental C.E.B. programs that have at best only a promise of financial success. This experience suggests that graduate subject matter courses offered in less populated areas, or concerned with subject matter that would appeal to fewer lawyers could probably be made to go only with financial assistance. It is also possible that some degree of institutional specialization could be useful. The demand would probably not be sufficient to support a full dress tax program in every law school, but there is no obvious reason why every school should strive to offer complete subject matter coverage in their "third" year offerings.

APPENDIX III

THE MATERIALS OF LAW STUDY
Brainerd Currie (1951, 1955)*

Edited by Alan D. Cullison

I. Introduction

In the history of American legal education there have been certain veritably epochal events. Thomas Jefferson created a professorship of law at William and Mary College in 1779, which marked the beginning of professional legal education in American universities. The Litchfield school, started in 1784, offered the first substantial challenge to the system of training by apprenticeship. Joseph Story's reorganization of Harvard in 1829 provided a definition of the scope of legal education which went almost unchallenged for a century and is still generally accepted in practice. Langdell's case method of 1870 still sets the pattern for instruction in almost every course. Since the founding of the *Harvard Law Review* in 1887, the unique institution of professional journals edited by students has not only stimulated scholarship and enriched the literature of the law, but has afforded to the few who participate the best training that law schools have to offer. With the founding of the AALS in 1900 the requirement of a modicum of general education as a preparation for university law study became general, and the law schools entered upon a period of organized self-criticism and mutual assistance.

In the intervening years since the most recent of these events, profound changes have taken place in the conditions of human life, in the role of law in society, and in thinking about the nature and purposes of law. Unless legal education has ceased to grow, or indeed to develop in any direction irrespective of progress, one would expect, making all due allowance for developments of a more gradual and less spectacular kind, to be able to extend the series, to find in the recent history of legal education some similarly striking evidence of vitality and adaptability. Has there been, since the beginning of the twentieth century, any development of comparable significance?

*3 J. LEG. ED. 331 and 8 J. LEG. ED. 1.

Only one development which might possibly be so characterized comes to mind—the movement which has been calling for reorganization of the law curriculum along "functional" lines and for the broadening of law school studies to include non-legal materials, drawn principally from the social sciences. In much the same way that earlier broad trends have been traced to specific origins, this movement may be said to have begun in the studies in legal education undertaken in 1926–28 by the Faculty of Law of Columbia University. These studies constituted the most comprehensive and searching investigation of law school objectives and methods ever undertaken. Leon C. Marshall, Professor of Political Economy at the University of Chicago, was chosen, because of his experience in the organization of business education, as general director of the studies. The faculty resolved itself into a seminar in legal education and met in "extended weekly sessions". There were frequent consultations with other departments of the University. Individuals and committees prepared for discussion at the faculty conferences approximately one hundred reports, covering eight hundred mimeographed pages, on various aspects of legal education. The fundamental thesis which emerged was this: Since law is a means of social control, it ought to be studied as such. Solutions to the problems of a changing social order are not implicit in the rules and principles which are formally elaborated on the basis of past decisions, to be evoked by merely formal logical processes; and effective legal education cannot proceed in disregard of this fact. If men are to be trained for intelligent and effective participation in legal processes, and if law schools are to perform their function of contributing through research to the improvement of law administration, the formalism which confines the understanding and criticism of law within limits fixed by history and authority must be abandoned, and every available resource of knowledge and judgment must be brought to the task. A drastic retooling would be required to convert the facilities of legal education to such an effort.

The philosophy underlying the fundamental thesis was not new. It was simply the sociological jurisprudence which Dean Pound's eloquent interpretation had made familiar. What was new and startling was the proposal to apply the teachings of sociological jurisprudence to the practical business of legal education. For a law teacher to be intellectually persuaded of the soundness of the new jurisprudence, for him to adopt its vocabulary for the adornment of his speech and writing, was one thing; it was quite another for him to give up the familiar courses in which he had achieved a feeling of security and competence, to surrender his beloved casebooks, to uproot his established methodology, to undertake the mastery of new fields of knowledge and method, and to introduce even into his classes a whole new apparatus of evaluation and criticism. The impact on the teaching profession of the Columbia studies, with their rigorous insistence on consistent development of the implications of the new jurisprudence for legal education and their Spartan determination to face up to the consequences without flinching, was therefore unsettling. Whatever else they accomplished, the Columbia studies loosed a turbulent flood of discussion which has not yet subsided. The proposed program could be denounced, ridiculed, viewed with misgivings, or enthusiastically supported; it could not be ignored.

There was opposition not only from those who rejected the philosophical premises, but also from those who, accepting those premises, nevertheless denied their significance for legal education. There were influential defections from the cause. Many others grew "weary of well-wishing" and returned to their familiar routines. Expeditions which had set out to explore the beckoning fields of social science returned with discouraging reports that these had, after all, nothing to contribute to the science of law. Moreover, the progress of the movement was impeded by the enthusiastic embraces of some who misinterpreted its philosophy and purpose, and unwittingly added their distracting advocacy to the obstacles it must overcome. But above all, the movement faltered under the staggering weight of the problems of execution it entailed. These have been sufficiently formidable that not only the movement's supporters but its opponents as well could take refuge in them.

Even the most enthusiastic supporters of the movement would concede that the Columbia studies are not—at least, not yet—to be classed as epoch-making. A turning-point there was, but the new era has not arrived. Legal education has been in no great hurry to leave its low-vaulted past; the more stately mansions promised by the program have been slow to build. Within a few years the pace of reform moderated at Columbia, and while other schools have attempted to put similar programs into operation, the course of development has been decidedly irregular. The main stream of legal education flows on much as before. The typical casebook, although its banner now reads "Cases and Materials," is essentially like its predecessors. There are still courses in Contracts, Torts,

Property, and Trusts, retaining their old names and shapes; and even in those courses which have been revamped and renamed the appellate decision is the focus of study still. Law and the social sciences remain unintegrated. Yet, it is too soon by far to pronounce the movement dead and the experiments a failure. Among a new generation of teachers, exposed to at least the attitudes of sociological jurisprudence in their formative years, there is probably more general acceptance of the principle of integrating law and social science in legal training than there has ever been before. Notwithstanding the disappointments of the past, there are those who persist in experimentation. The work goes on, and slowly the materials for a more fruitful study of law accumulate.

This is a study of the movement sketched here, and especially that phase of it which calls for the enrichment of the law school curriculum by the infusion of materials other than the traditional cases, statutes, and texts. The demand for nonlegal materials so frequently heard in recent years is often undiscriminating; it is a congeries of specifications and purposes, some of which would have been unintelligible to the men who formulated the Columbia program. A restatement of the reasoning that went into that program should, therefore, contribute to that understanding of the meaning and purpose of the movement which is the first objective of this study. A second aid to understanding is the perspective which comes from viewing this movement in the light of the historical relation between general education and the study of law. A third is identification and review of the ideas about law which provided the original motive force of the movement. A review of these three factors should give definition to the movement, facilitate appraisal of its viability, and enable us to recognize and distinguish some of the parasitic clamor for "nonlegal materials" which has attached itself to the movement's fringes. The final object is to determine what the practical significance of the movement is for the law teacher of today, and what the prospects are for its continued development. This study, then, is an essay in interpretation.

II. The Relation Between General Education and the Study of Law: Historical Background

A. In Europe

At least since the close of the Middle Ages a strong tradition has affirmed the importance of general university education for lawyers, but it speaks ambiguously of the values attributed to such education for professional purposes. Until the rise of the modern American law school, law training was conceived predominantly as training for the practice of an art. The materials of the art were contained in books, often in languages other than the vernacular; hence such education as would yield a reasonable proficiency in the use of language was a mere necessity. Beyond this, it is difficult to find convincing evidence of any ancient and sustained belief that general education is an essential part of the lawyer's equipment.

Even on the European continent, where a university degree (representing approximately two years of general studies in addition to the theoretical study of law) has long been a prerequisite to admission to the bar, the distinctively professional training has been furnished by an elaborate system of apprenticeship. The theoretical study of law in the university, although a necessary step toward a professional career, is regarded as nonprofessional; the law degree is widely sought for the prestige it carries as evidence of fitness for positions in commerce, banking, and industry, and the course is not shaped to the requirements of the fraction of the students who contemplate careers in law. Moreover, the requirement of a university degree as a condition to professional training does not appear to have resulted from any deep conviction of the relevance of university education to the work of the lawyer. Membership in the legal profession carried high privileges and opportunities of political advancement; the requirement of educational attainments must be regarded frankly as being, at least in origin, a device for limiting access to those privileges and opportunities.

In England prior to the separation of the American colonies there was no such requirement, presumably because the education of lawyers had developed as a function of the bar instead of being controlled by the universities; yet the tradition was continued, since practically all barristers in fact possessed university training. Here again, however, one looks in vain for solid indications that the tradition signified appreciation of any functional relationship between general education and the study or practice of law. The circumstance that barristers were as a rule educated men was rather fortuitous: "The same social and economic standing that made it possible to enter the Inns made possible a university career as well, and thus brought into the bar men of broad general education." For the barrister the benefits of general culture were as much desired as for other gentlemen of station. The social position and the professional achievements of barristers so trained, and the brilliant careers of English judges who, doubtless, owed much to the breadth of their training, must have served to buttress the tradition. Only rarely was there an explicit suggestion that general learning might have a direct bearing on professional competence.

B. In America From The Revolution to the Jacksonian Period

In this country also legal education was regarded generally as training in an art, to be acquired by apprenticeship—a conception which is unfriendly to the thesis that higher learning is essential. But, in general, university education came to be associated with the practice of law in our early history through the operation of the same factors that had brought about that association in Europe. Educational requirements were not generally established: there had been none in England; our few colleges were not conveniently accessible; we had no publicly supported systems of secondary schools. But long periods of clerkship were commonly prescribed, and substantial fees were paid for the privilege of serving the apprenticeship under lawyers of established reputation. Membership in the bar carried with it a prestige which made careers in law attractive to men who not only appreciated the cultural values of a broad education but could afford a college education here or in England. Such conditions were favorable for the preservation of the tradition of a learned profession.

There were isolated early instances of specific educational requirements—in New York City (1764), Boston (1771), and New Hampshire (1805). The context of the New York and Boston requirements makes it clear, however, that these were transparent and egregious efforts by the existing members of the profession to buttress their personal monopoly.

A majority of the states in the early part of the nineteenth century permitted substantial reductions in the required period of clerkship as a credit for college education. It has been suggested that this practice was attributable to the influence of the colleges, which, confronted with competition from undergraduate law schools, fought to keep alive the tradition that a liberal education is a desirable end in itself for lawyers, and to establish the proposition that the ideal legal education consists of a liberal education followed by a period of practical professional training. The explanation presents difficulties: There were no law schools to compete with the colleges; and it is difficult to believe that academic interests could have exercised so effective an influence on so important a professional prerogative as the standards for admission to the bar. One has the suspicion that a college education was simply accepted as being in terms of its limiting effect a satisfactory substitute for a portion of the period of clerkship.

The relationship which tradition had established between general education and the practice of law, as of the early part of the nineteenth century, may be summarized somewhat as follows:

1. The practice of law was a bookish art; adequate professional training was to be found in reading and practical exercises under the guidance of a member of the bar; no educational attainments beyond the necessary degree of literacy were essential.

2. Devices for limiting the enjoyment of professional privileges had operated, directly and indirectly, to produce a well-educated bar.

3. The position of lawyers in society was such that a liberal education was prized for its social and cultural values, apart from any implications it might have for professional competence.

4. There were the beginnings, at least, of a realization, not very clearly worked out, that a general education could make a positive contribution to professional effectiveness at least in the higher levels of legal work. This idea was seldom made explicit on theoretical grounds; it was revealed only dimly in official requirements. Its strongest support was undoubtedly furnished by the successful careers of educated lawyers and judges.

C. Blackstone And The Early American Professorships

But this is not the complete story. Up to this point we have been considering the place of general education in professional law training; the position of law in general education developed somewhat differently, with significant effects on legal education itself. On the continent it had been firmly established that the theoretical study of law as a science was an appropriate element of general university education. For this purpose the study of law was intimately associated with—indeed, was not clearly differentiated from—the study of politics, ethics, and philosophy, which is to say the whole body of knowledge concerning social affairs. In England, from the fifteenth to the seventeenth century, the Inns of Court appear to have functioned as a university to such an extent that the study of English law formed part of a liberal education; but when they ceased to attract nonprofessional students the common law dropped out of general education. Oxford and Cambridge continued to give instruction in civil and canon law, but in the eighteenth century these studies had become as decadent as professional education in the common law. It was not until Blackstone instituted his lectures on English law at Oxford in 1753 that the tradition of university-taught law acquired real significance for modern legal education. It is true that this development had little effect on the professional training of English lawyers; but its significance for legal education in America is such that it cannot be dismissed simply as a step toward "the broadening of the college curriculum" in the continental tradition.

It was on the basis of a double justification that the common law won a place in English universities. The advertisement of Blackstone's pre-Vinerian course of lectures announced:

This Course is calculated not only for the Use of such Gentlemen of the University, as are more immediately designed for the Profession of the Common Law; but of such other also, as are desirous to be in some Degree acquainted with the Constitution and Polity of their own Country.

Of these two purposes, only the first, relating to professional education, was mentioned in Viner's will. But in his inaugural lecture as Vinerian Professor, Blackstone returned to the dual-purpose theme. If it were necessary to choose between the two justifications, there would be little question that the purpose closest to Blackstone's heart was that of contributing to the improvement of professional education.

But the fact of greatest importance for the purpose now at hand is that Blackstone proceeded to affirm on its merits the value of a general university education in the professional training of lawyers, coupling this argument with his defense of the scientific study of law in the university. He deplored the pernicious practice of dropping all liberal education in favor of the illiberal influences of apprenticeship, and suggested the consequences of having the interpretation and enforcement of the laws fall into the hands of "obscure or illiterate men." Blackstone had little reason to be concerned about the "overcrowding" of the bar; as we have seen, the English system in his time effectually took care of that problem without the aid of educational requirements. His proposal, therefore, that "academical education" be made "a previous step to the profession of the common law" is largely free of the ambiguity which is introduced into the continental requirement by the probability that it was intended merely as a limiting device. Moreover, Blackstone was specific in enumerating the professional values to be expected from a university education; the education which is required for exclusionary purposes is normally one of unspecified content. But the conclusion that a vital conception of the relation between general education and preparation for law practice had at last come to the fore does not rest alone on such negative evidence. For the first time in English history, a philosophy of law had been applied to legal education. The conception "Of the Nature of Laws in General" which Blackstone explicitly professed, drawn (somewhat confusedly, it is true) from Grotius, Pufendorf, Locke, and Montesquieu, was that of the natural law of the Enlightenment, which identified law with ethics and appealed to human reason as the instrument for its making, interpretation, and criticism. In such a view the study of law is closely allied with all other studies dealing with human conduct, and history, philosophy, and politics assume a positive relevance.

In summary, this was Blackstone's conception of the function of the university in relation to the study of law:

1. The common law is an appropriate part of the university curriculum because (a) a knowledge of its fundamental principles is part of the equipment of the liberally educated layman and (b) because the scientific study of law is a necessary preparation for the practical training which precedes admission to the profession.

2. Either prior to or concurrently with the scientific study of law, the prospective barrister should acquire a general university education, embracing a knowledge of the classics, logic, philosophy, ethics, and Roman law; such education is important to the intelligent study of law and ultimately to the soundness of law administration.

In the last quarter of the eighteenth century four university professorships in law were established in this country, and three others were projected. In 1779 Thomas Jefferson established a professorship of "Law and Police" at William and Mary College, with George Wythe as the first incumbent. In 1790 James Wilson was appointed professor of law at the College of Philadelphia. In 1793 James Kent was appointed professor of law at Columbia. Finally, in 1799, Transylvania University appointed George Nicholas, a graduate of William and Mary, "Professor of Law and Politics."

It has sometimes been assumed that these professorships, as a group, were inspired by the example of Blackstone's Vinerian professorship. In one way or another, traces of Blackstone's influence can be found in most of the early American professorships; thus the *Commentaries* almost from the beginning formed the basis of instruction at William and Mary. But the *Commentaries* had an influence of their own, quite distinct from and even counter to that of the institution of a university professorship in the common law and Blackstone's arguments in its justification. Of all the innovators of this period, it was Thomas Jefferson whose plans, as applied at William and Mary and later developed at the University of Virginia, had the most lasting significance in the establishment of a connection between the study of law and university education; and no one can say that Jefferson owed his ideas about legal education to Blackstone's influence. In Jefferson's view, Blackstone and his patron, Mansfield, represented all that was anathema in politics, law, and legal training. They were enemies of the American Revolution; Blackstone's "wily sophistries" and "honied Mansfieldism" were making Tories of young American lawyers; the *Commentaries* were a superficial text, and "Blackstone lawyers" were "ephemeral insects of the law." The creative genius which is the foundation of Mansfield's fame was to Jefferson, who had no use for judicial legislation, a manifestation of absolutism so insidious that Jefferson would have forbidden the citation in American courts of any English decision since Mansfield's accession to the bench.

It is abundantly clear, therefore, that Jefferson did not share the view which has been attributed to Blackstone concerning the function of non-legal learning in the judicial administration of law. The Jeffersonian relation between legal and general education has two aspects: (1) law is treated as a branch of government, and the course of legal study embraces constitutional law, political economy, and legislation; (2) the curriculum is so organized that the study of law can be pursued, as the field of special interest, concurrently with other university studies. There is here no suggestion whatever of any concern with the traditional exclusionary function of university education. Jefferson was too completely committed to the democratic ideal to have any sympathy with prescribed periods of preparation or their equivalents in rules for admission to the bar. For this reason, unlike Blackstone, he had no wish to make the acquisition of a general education prerequisite to the privilege of practicing law. But he regarded law office study as tending more to the exploitation of the student than to his education, and believed that even unsupervised reading was preferable. It was therefore natural that his plans for higher instruction in Virginia should include instruction in law. The encouragement which was given to parallel professional and liberal studies may be due in part to the example of continental universities, but is perhaps sufficiently explained by the fact that Jefferson himself had taken all learning to be his province, and wished to make it possible for succeeding generations of Virginians to work toward the same ideal. The close relationship which was established between law and politics was clearly the result of his conception that the basic function of the university is public service—training for the duties of citizenship and self-government.

It is sometimes said of the eighteenth-century law professorships, that they were not intended to furnish professional training, but only to supply that elementary acquaintance with law which had come to be regarded as an appropriate part of liberal education. There is some support for such a view in contemporary statements of purpose. But in appraising the evidence on this point and its conflicting interpretations there are certain considerations which may usefully be borne in mind: First, the founders of the early American professorships were confronted with the same necessity which Blackstone had experienced, of justifying to a hostile academic world the inclusion of law in the college curriculum; second, a polite struggle still goes on over the right to claim the first American university law school. It is not surprising that our early apologists for university legal education talked, like Blackstone, of a dual purpose, nor that modern law schools of later origin should emphasize the expressions of nonprofessional intent. A third consideration is, perhaps, of even greater importance: characterizing the early professorships as nonprofessional tends to explain away, as having "cultural" value only, the elements of broad, nontechnical treatment which characterized the first university law courses, and thus indirectly to justify the absence of those elements from the modern law curriculum. A fair estimate which applies to all four of the chairs actually established is that of Dean Ames: "It seems probable that these professorships were created with the hope that they would soon expand into university schools of law. Such an inference derives support from the high character of the first incumbents." So far as William and Mary is concerned, at any rate, it seems quite clear not only that the purpose was to supplant law office study, but also that, because admission to the bar of Virginia was conditioned only upon passing an examination, and not upon prescribed periods of clerkship, the school could and did furnish the whole of professional training for many of its students.

Merely to describe these early professorships is, perhaps, to give them disproportionate emphasis. In the country at large, office study remained the normal method of preparation for law practice. In Connecticut the highly successful Litchfield School had been operating since 1784 on the narrow basis of an extension of the idea of practitioner training, quite without the benefit of academic connections. Wilson's course lasted not quite two years; Kent resigned his chair in 1798. It may be assumed that these academic developments did not greatly modify the prevailing estimate of the value of general education to the lawyer. But wherever the influence of these professorships reached — and it reached forward in time — a new principle had been advanced: the training of the lawyer should be broad; it should include university training; and positive professional values were attached to nontechnical elements of university training.

When, after the War of 1812, other institutions began to display an interest in university law training, there was a distinct tendency to preserve the breadth of treatment which had characterized the early professorships. The tendency was most evident at the University of Virginia, which was organized in accordance with the Jeffersonian plan that had already been applied at William and Mary. In 1817, having been appointed professor of law at the University of Maryland, David Hoffman published an elaborately comprehensive — and completely impracticable — *Course of Legal Study* embracing Moral and Political Philosophy, International Law, Roman Law, and Political Economy. (At the beginning of the third year of his lectures he had not covered the third of the thirteen titles of his original outline.) In 1815 Harvard finally established the professorship of law which Isaac Royall had endowed in 1781 with Chief Justice Isaac Parker of Massachusetts as the first incumbent. His inaugural address is strongly reminiscent of Blackstone's—with the difference that Parker quite clearly did not propose to attempt professional instruction. However, it was he who was responsible for the founding, in 1817, of a separate school of law with distinctly professional objectives. In accordance with Parker's design, this professional instruction was intended primarily—though not exclusively—for college graduates. And, while the course of instruction (by Asahel Stearns) was almost entirely technical, the law students were entitled to attend other lectures in the College, including those of Judge Parker, and the privilege seems to have been regarded as a valuable one. Thus there was for a time at Harvard something of the parallelism between professional and liberal education which characterized the Virginia system.

D. Story And The Reorganization of The Harvard Law School

In the meantime, however, forces had been accumulating which were to disrupt the traditional association between law and general education, and to crush out these nascent attempts to teach law broadly in its philosophical and political contexts. The fundamental one of these forces was the strong tide of extreme democratic feeling which swept the nation, demanding the abolition of all political and even intellectual inequalities. One of the strongest props of the learned tradition had been the restrictive conditions for admission to the bar, which had tended to exclude all except the representatives of a favored economic class from the participation in government and the avenue to political preferment which the legal profession afforded. These, along with property qualifications for voting, were natural targets of the democratic movement. The barriers which had been erected by rules requiring long periods of preparation were beginning to crumble; in the course of a few years they were to be drastically modified, and in some states swept away entirely. In the wake of the conflict with England the country had suffered a severe economic crisis. There was a swelling demand for universal, publicly supported education, and popular insistence on vocationalism made itself felt throughout the educational structure. Finally, and ironically, another side of Blackstone's influence had come to the fore. The *Commentaries* were phenomenally popular in America; Henry St. George Tucker had published a republicanized edition which made them tolerably palatable even to Jefferson; the impression was widespread that the law was contained not only in books but in one book in particular, and that self-education for the bar on the basis of that book was perfectly feasible. The work of the pioneer who had labored to establish the scientific study of law on the highest university level had become a powerful factor in dissociating preparation for the bar from any formal training at all.

Against these forces the new law school at Harvard fought a losing battle. Tuition and expenses were high; competition from law offices, private schools, and colleges in other parts of the country kept the number of students small; and Professor Stearns's compensation was entirely dependent on fees. It was a time for eliminating frills. In 1825 the catalogue announced that "Persons qualified by the rules of the courts in any of the United States to become students of law may be received in the Law School;" by request, Parker resigned the Royall professorship in 1827. But still the situation grew increasingly desperate. In the fall of 1828–29 there were only four students; in the spring there was just one. Stearns resigned in failure, laying a heavy share of the blame for the ruinous dearth of students on competition from law offices and other law schools—particularly the University of Virginia. But Virginia was holding students only by an equally deliberate sacrifice of all except the narrowly vocational elements of legal education. The students demanded that their studies "be devoted to such instruction as shall practically fit them for their profession," so the "municipal law" studies were collected in the regular course and the broader ones were relegated to an optional year.

In 1828 Andrew Jackson, apostle of the new democracy, was elected president of the United States. In 1829 Joseph Story, retaining his seat on the United States Supreme Court, accepted the new professorship of law which Nathan Dane had endowed under circumstances which strikingly paralleled the establishment of the Vinerian chair at Oxford. The question of the value to be attached to general university studies in the professional training of a lawyer had now been divided into two parts, the first concerning the need for such studies as a preliminary to the study of law, the second relating to the place of such studies in the professional curriculum itself. In both cases Story pronounced judgment. The spectacular success of his reorganization of the Harvard Law School meant that his answers to these questions would have wide influence. When that influence was added to the other forces which were breaking down the relation between general education and the study of law, the results were that for the next fifty years the necessity of university education as preparation for law study was to be denied, and the scope of the university law curriculum was given a narrowly professional definition which was to be controlling for more than a century.

That this should be so is one of the paradoxes of the history of legal education. Story has been identified as one of those who carried over what was best in eighteenth-century juristic thought into the nineteenth century's period of legal development. His enthusiasm for Mansfield, and thus for the constructive employment of informed judicial discretion, resembles that of the modern sociological and realist movements, which have supplied the intellectual force behind the current demand for breadth in legal education, and contrasts sharply with the views of Jefferson. He did not undertake to justify on theoretical grounds the divorce of convenience which he effected, for law school purposes, between "moral and political science" and "juridical science," although the seeds of the analytical and historical philosophies which were later to furnish the theoretical basis for such a separation were already at hand. There was, simply, a yielding to pressures; what was done was done as a matter of educational expediency.

In the matter of admission requirements, the Law School catalogue announced flatly in Story's first year that "No previous examination is necessary for admission to the school." This meant not only that college education was unnecessary, but that the beginning law student need not even be qualified for admission to college. In fact, a large proportion of the law students continued to be college-trained—a majority, until 1869–70; but the necessity of such training had been denied.

It seems clear, also, that opportunities for parallel study in the college were limited, and that the distractions of such study were discouraged. Immediately after Story's appointment, the Royall professorship, vacant since Parker's resignation, was filled by a young lawyer who had been associated with a practitioner school in Northampton—a school which Stearns had named as one of the sources of the competition which led to his failure; and this chair was subjoined to the Dane professorship, the two constituting the law school or department. Thus there was removed from the college curriculum the instruction which would most pointedly have related other fields of knowledge to the study of law.

As for the professional curriculum itself, Story specified that there were to be five branches of the law—the law of nature, the law of nations, maritime and commercial law, equity law, and the constitutional law of the United States. He characterized the law of nature as the philosophy of morals, and as embracing the whole study of man as a member of society. He combined political emphasis of Jefferson with the idealism of Blackstone to produce the broadest conception of the relation between law and other fields of knowledge that had ever been formulated in connection with legal education. But at the same time he banished the philosophical and institutional considerations from the professional school because "in the course of the academical instruction in this University, already provided for, the subjects of ethics, natural law, and theology, are assigned to other professors."

Even if the professional course were to be confined severely to the body of positive law, the law school seemed to be confronted with a Sisyphean task. The quantity of authoritative materials, and semi-authoritative commentaries upon them, was rapidly multiplying—a fact on which Story more than once commented. At a time when the published reports of American cases were contained in one hundred and fifty volumes, he spoke apprehensively of "the fearful calamity, which threatens us, of being buried alive, not in the catacombs, but in the labyrinths of the law." As a partial safeguard against such a fate, he relied on "habits of generalization" which would be cultivated by a deeper study of special pleading, the doctrines of equity, the civil law, and the law of nations; but the only adequate defense, in his opinion, was the construction of a digest, modeled on the Pandects of Justinian, which would reduce the welter of "jarring and discordant opinions" to a systematic statement of principles. In the solution of the problem, learning had no vital part to play. The task of the instructor was to cope as best he could with the oppressively expanding mass of legal materials, meanwhile devoting his scholarship to the building of an internally consistent synthesis of the rules of law.

The immediate practical success of the educational enterprise which Story conducted on this strictly professional basis is unchallengeable; so also is the dignity with which he clothed that enterprise by the remarkable productivity of his scholarship. The very establishment of a full-fledged professional school in connection with the university at Cambridge was infectious. The traditional attitudes of American law schools toward local law, legislation, and criminal law can all be traced to decisions made in the course of Story's reorganization. In the years that have passed since that period, the leadership of Harvard has been strengthened; yet not even Langdell's case method, the best known of all Harvard influences, has had a more pervasive and significant effect on legal education. Story's judgment was not seriously challenged until the 1920's, when the modern movement toward integration of law with other social studies began.

Once it had been decreed that the theoretical study of law could be undertaken without benefit of previous university training, strong forces were set in operation tending to preserve this arrangement with its resultant conditions. The interests of law schools as competitors of the colleges became vested. Lawyers were apathetic toward, if not resentful of, suggestions that the system under which they had attained their own positions was seriously deficient. In addition, facilities for general education grew only slowly out of the stage at which it would have been a serious violation of the democratic principle to have set up general educational requirements for admission to the bar. The state of bar admission requirements continued to have a limiting effect upon law school aspirations. In consequence, it was nearly fifty years before any law school established any educational prerequisite to admission.

E. The Establishment of Educational Requirements for Admission To Law School

After the Civil War, however, other forces began to operate. It has been suggested that the war itself exerted an influence in reviving general interest in educational standards—that it "taught us the meaning and the value of efficiency in public life, and the need of democracy for the expert," and that "its aftermath of corruption made certain political reforms indispensable, and thus brought reform as a whole into fashion." The strengthening of bar admission requirements became part of the orthodox programme of reform; the more readily, because it was not difficult to trace a connection between the existing low standards of admission to the bar and the existing corruption of judges and politicians.

It was in the decade 1870–1880 that the modern campaign to reestablish some relation between legal and general education took form. It precipitated the problem of "prelegal" requirements with which educators and bar associations have struggled for more than two generations. It did not reopen the question, settled by Story upon grounds of expediency and educational policy, as to the content of the law curriculum itself. Indeed, this movement was preceded by Langdell's promulgation of the case method of instruction, a pedagogical device which was destined to furnish further occasion and justification for confining the scope of the law course to authoritative legal materials. In 1874 Columbia announced a system of entrance examinations requiring of the student substantially such academic education as was required for admission to college. A number of schools shortly did likewise, and by 1890 eighteen of the sixty-three law schools in the country had roughly similar requirements. In 1893 Harvard took a commanding lead by announcing that all candidates for its degree must, upon admission to the law school, either hold a college degree or be qualified to enter the senior class of Harvard College. The Association of American Law Schools, formed in 1900, required that its members admit as regular students only those who possessed a high school education or its equivalent. In 1950 the American Bar Association, followed by the Association of American Law Schools, established standards which approved schools to require three years of prelegal education. In seventy-five years American legal education progressed from a condition in which no law school required any preliminary education whatever, to such a point that the standard requirement for admission was three years of college.

There was evidently little appreciation of any vital interrelation between law and the studies which the students were required to pursue before admission to the law school. During the continuation of the drive when emphasis had shifted to the requirement of some college work, the leadership of the movement was furnished principally by the bar, and educational theory played no great part. Throughout the fifty years of the movement the effective motivating purposes of its supporters were, on the educational side, to provide a homogeneous and literate body of law students, and on the side of the profession and the public interest, to prevent such an over-crowding of the bar as had led to unprofessional practices and to a lowering of the reputation and dignity of the bar. To a very considerable extent the educational requirements established were erected as obstacles set in the path of the less mature and persistent, and resembled closely the requirements, common in the period of no educational qualifications, that applicants for admission to the law schools or to the bar should have attained a fixed age.

Additional evidence in support of this criticism is furnished by the fact that there never was, and indeed there is not yet, any agreement as to what the nature and content of the prelegal education should be. Surely, if the improvement in educational standards had been achieved through a general conviction of the integral connection between law and any of the fields of study which had been excluded from the scope of the law school curriculum, there would have been some consensus as to the identity of these studies, and a general disposition to specify them. Yet such was not the case. The view which has dominated legal education since the time of Story is that the law is an autonomous system which can be mastered without the benefit of enlightenment from without; a liberal education is desirable for cultural reasons, but has little to do with the study of law, or with any of the "technical" aspects of the lawyer's work. Such a view is closely related to the concept of the value of general education which prevailed in the eighteenth century, outside the sphere of influence of the early law professorships.

F. The "Southern Tradition"

There remains to be considered the somewhat different concept of the relation between law and other university studies which was developed particularly in the South. The recognition of an "academic tradition," characteristic of the southern schools, whereby the study of law was more closely correlated with liberal studies than it was in other sections, rests on two bases: first, on the questionable conclusion that in the South, more commonly than in the North, the university law schools were expansions of university departments rather than independent practitioner schools which had been annexed; second, on the fact that the organization of the University of Virginia and of other southern schools was such as to encourage the parallel study of other subjects by law students. The vigor and distinctiveness of this tradition are probably exaggerated. And whatever difference this tradition may have produced in the character of the law school curriculum itself was short-lived. As we have seen, pressure from vocationally minded students and from the growing mass of strictly legal materials had begun to crowd related subjects out of the Virginia law curriculum when Story went to Harvard; by 1851 the process of elimination was substantially complete, and such subjects as history and political economy had been definitely committed to the nonprofessional departments of the University. Nevertheless, while the typical practice in the country at large was to require that the necessary general education be acquired before admission to the law school, a number of schools followed the Virginia plan to encouraging parallel work in other departments of the university during the professional course. Such measures as these, since they did not set up general education as a necessary qualification of the entering law student, were clearly inspired by a theory of the relation between law and other university work different from the disciplinary theory which motivated the drive for prelegal requirements. Since the courses to be taken were either unspecified or were required for the purpose of reinforcing linguistic skills, the theory was also different from that which was responsible for the broad scope of the early Virginia law schools. The theory was "to preserve, so far as possible, the academic element in legal education, though not positively to insist upon it, if a student wished to hurry through."

G. NonLegal Materials In The Law Schools: Two Anomalous Developments

Finally, in the last quarter of the nineteenth century there were at Columbia and Yale extremely interesting developments in the scope of the law curriculum which cannot readily be identified with any of the broader trends in the relationship between legal and general education. They have been largely forgotten by the law school world, and the scantiness of available information about them makes them difficult to classify. The events at Columbia show a marked resemblance to Jeffersonian ideas, though it would be difficult to establish a direct connection; and there is no reason at all to suppose that the curriculum developed at Yale was influenced by the southern tradition. We must, it appears, accept the simple, anomalous fact that, at a time when appreciation of the relationship between law and other social disciplines was at its lowest ebb, Columbia restored the identification of law and politics which had characterized the early Virginia establishments, and Yale anticipated the functional course construction and the reliance on social studies which characterize the modern integration movement.

Francis Lieber, a German immigrant, became Professor of History and Political Science at Columbia College in 1857. In the following year, professional instruction in law, which had been absent from the Columbia scheme since the retirement of Kent in 1826, was revived under Theodore Dwight. Almost from the beginning, Lieber gave instruction in history and political science in the Law School. In 1865, for reasons that are not entirely clear, President Barnard asked the Board of Trustees to remove him from his professorship; and Lieber's friends, unable to forestall some such action, succeeded in having him transferred to the Law School, where he devoted his full time to teaching constitutional history and public law. The evidence is conflicting as to his success as a teacher, and especially as to the reception which was given his lectures. Although Dwight, in later years, spoke graciously of Lieber's contribution, the importance which he attached to the scholarly lectures is indicated by the fact that they were optional, and by his attitude toward the work of Lieber's successor.

In the realm of political theory, Lieber was no Jeffersonian. Nevertheless he had his own convictions, very similar to Jefferson's, on the indivisibility of history, political science, and public law. Perhaps his greatest claim to remembrance lies in the fact that he pioneered in the application of empirical method to the social sciences, and thus constitutes a connecting link between the eighteenth century and the twentieth.

Lieber died in 1872. In 1876 the vacancy created by his death was filled by the appointment of John W. Burgess, a young man from Tennessee, educated in Germany, who had been teaching political science at Amherst. He was to divide his time between the law school and the college, the plan being to "reintroduce those branches of jurisprudence lost by the death of Lieber." To the intrinsic difficulties of the undertaking there was added the opposition of Dwight, who feared that any expansion of the courses in political science and public law would jeopardize the efficiency of the school in the training of practical lawyers. Finally, in 1880, in order to find for the development of his plans the opportunity which he could not get either in the law school or in the college, Burgess succeeded, by a "masterpiece of diplomacy," in persuading the Trustees to organize a separate School of Political Science. All concerned seem to have been well satisfied with this denouement—particularly Dwight. Thus the scope of the university law school was once more narrowly defined, and thus ended an experiment which, if it had been successful, might have profoundly affected the course of legal education and the development of legal institutions in this country.

At about the same time, Northwestern and Michigan were also making "a genuine effort to restore government to the place from which the growth of technical law had dislodged it." But the most striking evidence that there was in this period a vital conception of the relationship between law and the problems of the social order is furnished by the Yale Law School in the administration of Dean Francis Wayland. Wayland, a Harvard Law School graduate and an elected judge of probate, was a man of wide interests; he was active in politics and in the prison reform movement, and was for several years president of the American Social Science Association. The two years of work prescribed for the degree of Bachelor of Laws were devoted principally to the usual technical subjects, although lectures were included on such subjects as English Constitutional Law, International Law, Nature and History of American Law, Jurisprudence, and Roman Law. But in addition to this course, two full years of graduate instruction were scheduled, leading to the degrees of Master of Laws and Doctor of Civil Laws. The graduate program included courses in Political History and Science and Political and Social Science; Railroad Law; Railway Management and the Economics of Transportation; and at one time Public Finance, supplementing a course in Taxation. This program was inaugurated in 1876, and in 1889 was regarded as one of the most notable accomplishments of Wayland's administration.

There is, unfortunately, no *Summary of Studies* to reveal in detail the philosophy of the faculty that constructed such a curriculum; but the meager information that does exist indicates a remarkable anticipation of the kind of thinking which motivated the Columbia faculty fifty years later. If the Yale faculty's preoccupation with the perplexities which transcontinental steam transportation had but a short time previously introduced into American culture suggests a worldly consciousness of the importance of the railroad lawyer in those times, the program was none the less a remarkable instance of breadth and flexibility in a law curriculum. In its underlying conceptions, in its functional course arrangements, and in its enlistment of the nonlegal scholarship of the University — in everything, in short, except its equivocal estimate of the practical value of the graduate courses — the program strongly resembled those which were to be projected in the 1920's. And there are indications that even the distinction drawn between the practical undergraduate curriculum and the "ideal" course of study was the product of considerations of expediency rather than of a conviction that the graduate course was lacking in practical values. The feeling seems to have been that the first two years could, in view of the competitive situation, be made to provide the minimum training necessary for the average student, but that the broader training of the graduate years would provide valuable preparation for the "higher grades of practice."

There is no evidence that these early attempts to revitalize the law curriculum influenced the Columbia studies in any way; on the contrary, the indications are that the faculty was unaware of them. No comprehensive study of the history of legal education in the United States and elsewhere was attempted, and perhaps because of this omission that the faculty assumed that a program of fusing the work of the college with that of the law school had "never been tried anywhere." A less complacent attitude toward history would have revealed the reformers as something less than the radical innovators they supposed themselves to be; at the same time they might have gained assurance, and the case for reform might have gained in persuasiveness, had they realized that the eighteenth century's appreciation of the relationship between law and other social and humanistic studies had never been completely crushed, but retained sufficient vitality to manifest itself dramatically in the programs of at least two law schools in the darkest period of the law's isolation.

III.   Nonlegal Materials in the Law School: Beginnings of the Modern Integration Movement

A.   Antecedent Events at Columbia

At the close of World War I, the curriculum of the Columbia Law School was, on the whole, conventional. There was an emphasis on constitutional law which was uncommon among law schools at that time and which may have reflected the close relationship established with the political science department in the time of Lieber and Burgess. There were, and had been for some time, courses in Roman law, modern civil law, and legal history, and the "better class" of students were urged to take some of these. There was a course in historical and comparative jurisprudence. Apart from these features, and predominantly, the curriculum was devoted to the doctrinal categories of equity and the common law which had long since become standard in American law schools.

In the course of the next five years, however, some unorthodox tendencies emerged. Even while bringing out a second edition of the basically doctrinal casebook on bills and notes of which he was co-editor, Professor Underhill Moore was at work on a book designed to present the subject in terms of the business function of commercial paper. In 1922–23, two novel courses appeared in the third-year program: Industrial Relations, taught by Professor Noel T. Dowling, and Illegal Combinations (which in the following year became Trade Regulation), taught by Professor Herman Oliphant. At the same time, a course in legal economics by Professor Robert L. Hale, was introduced into the list of "special courses." To students looking forward to careers in government, the law faculty was commending courses under the Faculty of Political Science, with the objective of supplementing the instruction in "private municipal law" offered by the Law School. The attention of graduate students was being drawn to courses in the School of Political Science, the School of Business, and the Department of Philosophy by way of indicating the availability of instruction in "matters more or less intimately connected with the study of law."

It was the development of the courses in industrial relations and trade regulation, with their challenge to the accepted taxonomy of the law and their disturbing impact on the unity and the proportions of the curriculum, which was directly responsible for the extensive studies which the faculty undertook four years later. Nowadays the phrases "functional approach" and "integration of nonlegal materials" are, to a number of law teachers, trite symbols of frustration. It is enlightening to recall that the essence of these symbols is embodied in two such familiar and thoroughly established components of the law curriculum. The realization that modern legal education has profited, at least in some of its departments, from the movement toward functionalism and integration gives focus to the problem of understanding that movement: After so durable a beginning, why did the development bog down?

Considering the sharpness of the break they made with tradition, the new courses evoked surprisingly little criticism when they were announced. They filled a need which was recognized among a wide circle of teachers and lawyers, and there was no necessity for an elaborate theoretical justification of the development. The importance of labor problems and of government control of business had become apparent; equally apparent was the fact that inadequate preparation for a lawyer's dealing with such problems was afforded by the standard courses through which the relevant materials were scattered. Opinion was well prepared for such a development. Indeed, neither course originated in Columbia's hotbed of discontent: both had previously been offered at Harvard. Reviewers almost with one voice welcomed the casebooks which accompanied the new courses—Sayre's *Cases on Labor Law* and Oliphant's *Cases on Trade Regulation*—though most of them were somewhat perturbed on account of the problems of curricular adjustment which were foreshadowed. The new casebooks borrowed materials from various basic courses, and the question arose: Was there to be duplication, or were these materials to be withdrawn from the basic courses where the doctrinal context afforded the optimum setting for study?

The new courses differed in three ways from the traditional pattern. The first difference, of course, consisted in the organization of materials in terms of social and economic problems rather than of legal doctrine. Secondly, both courses proceeded on the assumption that certain nonlegal materials were directly and pointedly relevant. In his brief in *Muller v. Oregon,* fourteen years earlier, Brandeis had demonstrated how economic and sociological materials could be used to win a lawsuit; the significance of that development for the training of lawyers was beginning to be appreciated. Thirdly, both courses utilized statutory materials to an extent which was unusual. The attention given to legislative measures emphasized the role of creative reason, as opposed to deduction from *a priori* principles, in the solution of social and legal problems.

The record does not show precisely the course of developments at Columbia during the next four years leading to the decision to re-examine the whole field of legal education; but the general outline can be reconstructed with some confidence. The probability is that the problems of curricular adjustment proved unexpectedly troublesome in practice. Granting that the new courses filled a need, had the Law School adequately met that need simply by adding them to a curriculum which already had more content than could be covered in three years? The student who elected one of these specialties did so at the cost of forgoing some traditional subject; the consequent loss in terms of information and of doctrinal training was bound to cause concern. The problem must have assumed alarming proportions as the prospect of additional new courses, similarly constructed, began to open. Numerous institutions and problems suggested themselves as susceptible of similar treatment: the family, the business organization, the marketing process, crime. By 1926, the graduate curriculum was devoted almost entirely to seminars of the institutional type and was clearly serving as a proving ground for ideas which were clamoring for inclusion in the undergraduate course. At the same time, the list of "other officers giving instruction in the Law School" was expanded to include professors of political economy, philosophy, social legislation, business administration, finance, transportation, economics, government, and marketing. The problem of what was to happen to the curriculum had become acute.

At some point early in this four-year period, the idea was developed that the solution to the problem was to reorganize the *entire course of study* along functional lines. This provides the central theme for the studies the faculty undertook; it accounts for the paradox that inclusion of nonlegal materials in the course of study was actually advocated as a simplification device—as part of a scheme for enabling the Law School to keep pace with the sky-rocketing demands of an increasingly complex legal system; and it provides, also, one possible key to understanding the fate which overtook the movement. In its simplest form, the argument went somewhat like this: The difficulty grows out of the attempt to engraft specialty courses of the functional type on a course of study that is fundamentally doctrinal. As long as the law school clings to the doctrinal classifications as the basis of instruction, duplication is inevitable; but duplication can be eliminated if functional classifications are consistently substituted throughout the curriculum.

Dean of the Law School during the formative years of this movement was Harlan Fiske Stone, surely no visionary pedagogical theorist. It would be inaccurate to refer to him as the leader of the movement; clearly, the driving force was supplied by Oliphant. Nevertheless, Stone appreciated the implications of sociological jurisprudence and, as the spirit of innovation began to spread through the curriculum and to suggest an institutional policy, he became its official spokesman. Stone's report as dean for the year 1923 was the first comprehensive exposition of the ideas involved in the agitation for reorganization of the Columbia curriculum. The preceding fifty years, he said, had witnessed an enormous expansion in the coverage and content of the law; the response of the law schools had been to add more and more courses.

Instead of dissipating our energies in the vain attempt to master in the brief period of three years the vast and growing mass of technical learning of our profession as an independent and detached system, we must seek a simplification of educational methods by coming closer to those energizing forces which are producing the technical doctrine of the law. We may hope to do this by reaching a clearer and more accurate understanding of the relation of law to those social functions which it endeavors to control and by studying its rules and doctrines as tools or devices created and placed in the hands of the lawyer as means of effecting that control.

In the execution of this policy, two subsidiary problems would be involved. The first was "so rearranging and organizing the subjects of law school study as to make more apparent the relationship of the various technical devices of the law to the particular social or economic function with which they are concerned. . . . " Such a functional classification had, of course, been basic to the concept of the courses in trade regulation and industrial relations. By way of illustrating how the idea could be applied elsewhere in the curriculum, Stone advocated the development of two other courses which have likewise become familiar—Creditors' Rights (which would assemble materials from courses on procedure, equity, practice, trusts, and bankruptcy) and Security (which would draw together all security devices, regardless of their disparate origins and conceptual classifications). But no reclassification, merely as such, could rise above the level of a mechanical solution. The particular virtue of the functional classification was that it would reveal the relationship of law to social functions; it would make clear the relevance and facilitate the application of other stores of knowledge and understanding about those functions. Reclassification and the resort to extralegal insights into social processes were inseparable parts of the simplification scheme. The second problem of execution, therefore, had to do with the training of law students in the social sciences. Stone put the problem solely in terms of prelegal education.

Dean Stone's report affirmed a relationship between law and other social studies which was so vital that, according to this thesis, effective legal education was *dependent* on other social studies. What was to be done if it should develop that no satisfactory arrangements could be worked out to insure adequate prelegal training in the social sciences? In that event, unless Stone's thesis was to be abandoned, its logic required that the necessary social science training be provided in the law school itself. This was precisely the line along which the thinking at Columbia developed. When, three years after Dean Stone's report, the faculty, under Dean Jervey, turned its organized energies to the task of putting the program into execution, it was confronted almost at once with the realization that to require a competence in the necessary social studies as a condition of admission to the Law School would be impracticable. A more significant objection was also voiced by Oliphant: "Such training though good will always remain a background. Only the heat of contemporary study can adequately fuse the two bodies of knowledge." Accordingly, the faculty found itself faced with the question whether it was under "a minimum duty of partly meeting the problem by *fusing* (not scrambling and not making available in parallel courses) certain social science material with legal material." It came to answer the question in the affirmative, with enthusiasm, as the potentialities of such a program began to unfold. When the deliberations reached this stage, the modern movement toward integration of nonlegal materials with the law school curriculum had been defined.

B. The Historical Context

This definition, it has been suggested, was, at least potentially, an epoch-making event in American legal education. When Dean Stone wrote his report in 1923, there lay behind him three well-marked periods in terms of attitudes toward the place and function of nontechnical studies in the university training of the lawyer. The first was the period of the "academical" professorships, beginning in 1779 with George Wythe at William and Mary. The university study of law was closely linked with philosophy, political economy, and ethics — that is, with the whole body of knowledge concerning social problems. The second period began when the law schools at Virginia and Harvard eliminated educational requirements for admission and adopted a narrowly technical definition of the scope of legal education. This they did reluctantly, under the multiple pressures exerted by extreme democratic doctrine, competition from inferior institutions for law study, and the expanding mass and complexity of technical materials. Almost at once, however, enduring justification for the isolated position thus assumed was forthcoming in the analytical jurisprudence of John Austin — a declaration of the independence of legal science from philosophy and morals. The third period was that of the restoration of educational requirements for admission to law school. This change of attitude did not reflect a renewed appreciation of any vital relationship between law and other disciplines. Its purpose was to make the law school population reasonably homogeneous and as literate as possible, and to help close the "easy-swinging doors" of the profession against "the idle, the lazy, and the unprepared." Dean Stone wrote his report for 1923 just at the close of this period, and the valuation he placed on nontechnical studies draws significance from what had gone before.

It is instructive to compare the developments at Columbia in the 1920's with those at Harvard in the 1820's. Like Story, Stone was a leader in legal education as the head of a national law school in a time of change; like Story, he was to become, in addition, one of the great justices of the Supreme Court of the United States. Each of the two men had profound faith in the common law; each of them was apprehensive on account of its enormous and uncontrolled growth through the multiplication of *ad hoc* determinations. Facing this problem as jurist and educator, each expressed his distrust of codification as a remedy and placed his faith instead in a systematic restatement of legal principles. Here, however, the similarity ends, and a striking contrast appears. For simplification and mastery of the growing mass of legal materials, Story relied on "habits of generalization," to be cultivated by the study of special pleading, of equity, of foreign maritime law, of the civil law, and of the law of nations. The problem was that of applying logical, historical, and comparative methods to the mass of legal materials. Accordingly, Story acquiesced in the exclusion from legal studies of the nontechnical branches of learning with which the university study of law had formerly been associated. To Stone, on the other hand, the common law should be restated not only systematically but *"in the light of those social and economic functions for the guidance and control of which law itself exists. . . ."* Accordingly, he called for a return to those studies which would give the student "a thorough-going knowledge of the social functions with which law deals."

Although the Columbia faculty thought of themselves as innovators, this was essentially a return to the eighteenth-century conception of the relevance to law of all human knowledge relating to social affairs. In educational terms, it was a return to the principle of the professorships of the late eighteenth and early nineteenth centuries; to the ideas embodied in the curricula of Yale and Columbia in the last quarter of the nineteenth century; and to what had been a favorite theme for Mr. Justice Holmes. Stone's conception of the relevance of nontechnical studies to the training of lawyers differed sharply, however, from that which had dominated legal education for half a century. According to the dominant view, a liberal education was desirable for its own sake, as a cultural and humanizing experience; but it had little or nothing to do with the lawyer's professional training.

C. Results of The Studies

The Columbia faculty had some difficulty in reaching that level of discussion which is concerned with specific course content and materials. In the beginning, there was a great deal of discussion of law school objectives and "methodology" in the broad sense. In addition, the studies ranged over a wide variety of subjects. There were studies of the junior college movement, the development of collegiate schools of business, the values of the case method, the development of the social sciences, and of existing law school programs. There was discussion of devices for easing the transition to the new curriculum, and the structure and content of the new program were conceived in broad terms. But committees were quickly established to deal concretely with specific divisions of the subject matter; and, sooner than might be supposed, they were coming to grips with specific problems. The list of committees indicates both the general nature of the functional classification and its incompleteness: Labor (Dowling, Hale); Finance and Credit (Llewellyn, Moore); Marketing (Oliphant, Llewellyn); Form of Business Unit (Moore, Shanks, Douglas); Risk and Risk-bearing (Patterson, Smith, Oliphant); Law Administration (Magill, Smith, Medina); Criminal Law (Kidd, Moley); Family and Familial Property (Powell, Moe, Johnson); Legislation (Parkinson, Chamberlain, Dowling); and Historical and Comparative Jurisprudence (Yntema, Goebel). The chief value of the records which have been preserved lies in the light they throw on the solution of practical problems of course construction and on factors affecting the success or failure of the reorganization program and its constituent parts. The procedure to be followed in this review of the records will be to consider the work done in the subject-matter categories in turn (tracing the subsequent development, where that is possible) with the objectives of determining what measures were considered desirable and practical, and of gathering clues as to the reasons for success or failure.

1. Business units   The first committee to report was that on the form of the business unit. A seminar in the law of business organization was already being offered; and the report was entitled: "Business Associations: Devices for Organizing for Management, for Limiting Risk, and for Assembling Capital." This is one of the functional classifications which survived to become a familiar component of the law curriculum, which was designed to treat problems traditionally covered in Agency, Partnership, Corporations, Mortgages, and Bankruptcy, and in various courses in the School of Business. The implications with respect to staff and library suggest, not surprisingly, that financial problems may be a major obstacle in the way of such comprehensive reorganizations.

The committee's original report advocated interdisciplinary business-law research. A specific suggestion that research be done on the shift of control from ownership to managers was "molded into concrete form" by Professor Edwin F. Gay of Harvard; in 1928, the study was begun, financed by the Social Science Research Council of America and directed by the Columbia University Institute for Research in the Social Sciences. In 1932, it resulted in the publication of the well-known work by A. A. Berle, Jr. and Gardiner C. Means, *The Modern Corporation and Private Property.* The problems of interdisciplinary research were thus described by Professor Berle:

Difficulty in such cooperation is extreme; for technicians in different fields must first agree on a common language; then endeavor to apply their respective methods of approach, keeping in mind the shortcomings and advantages of the different methods; and finally work out conclusions to which both are prepared to subscribe. Since a lawyer is primarily concerned with the justice of the individual case and can never ignore the problem of what ought to be done; and since an economist is primarily descriptive and analytic, the chasm is not easy to bridge.

In the year following the intensive faculty studies (*i.e.,* in 1927–28), two new courses in business associations were added, and a third was planned for the following year. A course designed to "consider the advantages and disadvantages of different types of business associations as devices for allocating risk" was given in the first year. Another, "approaching business associations as finance devices," was offered to second-and third-year students. In the latter, the use of economic data was emphasized. The third course, planned but not offered in 1927–28, was to deal with problems of business management. The course in corporation finance was given with mimeographed materials, which were published in 1930. Although the book was greeted as being, both in the arrangement and in the selection of materials, "a challenge to traditional methods of legal classification," the extent to which it utilized nonlegal materials was not notable. About 75 per cent of its bulk was devoted to cases. The "materials" took the form of introductory notes indicating the business problems involved and summarizing the technical uses of particular devices, of corporate forms, and of incidental background material.

One thing is clear: the ideal of simplification of the curriculum through functional reorganization was not being achieved. With substantial unanimity, the reviewers noted that the old, unitary course on corporations must now become three courses—as, indeed, it had become at Columbia. Functionalism had split the study of corporations into three phases—risk, finance, and management—and enough legal and nonlegal materials had been found to stretch it throughout the three years of the curriculum.

A tentative "source book" for the course on business organization, prepared by Professor Magill, was first printed in 1930–31 and was followed by the publication, in 1933 and 1935, of Magill and Hamilton's *Cases on Business Organization.* The original division of the law of business units into the three phases was abandoned. Corporation finance was temporarily established as a separate course, but risk and management problems were to be combined in the course on business organization. If use was made of nonlegal materials, they elude the scrutiny which can be given to the book for purposes of this paper by one who is not a specialist in the field. In 1948, Professors Berle and Warren published their *Cases and Materials on the Law of Business Organizations (Corporations).* This event marked the demise not only of the "functional" combination of corporations with other devices for business organization, but also of the separate course in corporation finance—and so, finally, of the triumvirate of risk, management, and finance. On the surface, at least, the Columbia Law School had come full circle. Prior to 1927–28, it had offered a course in corporations; now it offered one in corporations—in parentheses.

It would be naive, however, to assume lightly that these two decades of experiment were without significant effect on the teaching of corporation law. Even to one having no particular familiarity with the subject, it is apparent that the course in corporations had come a long way; but the differences were not manifested in any very tangible way in terms of either "functional approach" or nonlegal materials. Some of Berle's nonlegal materials were preserved, although perhaps with less emphasis and more modesty: the objective was to supply business background rather than social science. The chief difference between this book and its "classical" predecessors consisted in its more faithful reflection of the problems actually encountered in modern corporate practice, its sensitiveness to social implications, and its receptiveness to enlightenment from sources outside the formal materials of the law.

2. The family and familial property The committee on the family and familial property undertook a brief survey of the nonlegal literature on the family, indicating that its members had canvassed and classified a remarkably large body of sociological, anthropological, historical, and economic material. It found that little was known about the nature and organization of the modern family and concluded that "the approach to familial law is at least two or three decades behind the present state of wisdom as to business law." It, nevertheless, proposed a program based upon the assumption "that familial organization and law have interacted and are now interacting with resultant modifications of each."

In planning an outline for the curricular offering, the committee proposed that "the body of law now functioning be examined and the parts thereof are selected out (1) which look as if they are attributable in part or in whole to familial factors, or (2) which seem likely to account for existing phenomena in the familial organization, or (3) which help to define the existing familial organization, and the material thus selected is arranged, for teaching." The course plan thus suggested was frankly a transitional effort; its hypotheses were to be continually tested by concurrent research. A detailed course outline was constructed. The range of this outline, owing to the diversity of the laws which may affect the family, was formidable. Substantial parts of what had been "Real Property" were so far included as to receive adequate treatment, but many phases of land law and its special techniques were left out. At this stage, however, that circumstance did not yet lead the committee to the old doubts about duplication and loss

.of doctrinal training which the first functional courses had aroused among their critics; in the committee's judgment, this merely means that other foci or typical fact situations must be thought out, about which these other essential materials may be grouped. A note of caution was sounded, however, against carrying too far the functional grouping of all laws that may bear, even significantly, on the family.

Thus, the scheme of functional classification of the law was found to have difficulties of its own, fundamental enough, as it turned out, to amount to real trouble for the reorganization program as a whole. In addition, the committee was confronted with formidable problems of finance, personnel, and execution in connection with the research program which was to be an indispensable supplement to the course. And eventually this committee likewise saw the goal of simplification receding: Not only would the course in domestic relations be enlarged, but also, since only minor segments would be taken out of other courses, there would be no compensating reduction in other offerings.

In at least some respects, the committee's confidence that the necessary research could go forward was quickly vindicated. A research proposal was drafted, and a grant of $25,000 was obtained to support the project for one year. A staff was organized, and a comprehensive report was published in 1930. As a basis for research, and especially for drawing together the diverse laws affecting family relationships, the staff followed a suggestion contained in the committee report and constructed a "fact situation outline." For purposes of teaching, a quite different outline was developed after considerable wrestling with problems of classification; the staff finally settled upon a plan of organization which it regarded as a compromise "by no means entirely satisfactory." At this point, the goal of simplification was receding even more rapidly, for each of the five main headings of the curricular outline was referred to as a *course* — although two of them were thought suitable for seminar treatment, and one might be made into a book for collateral reading. Not surprisingly, the most intractable problem was the disposal of the law of property. The temporary solution was to abandon the treatment of those areas of property law which interact with other institutions as well as the family, while retaining those which are peculiarly family law and which could be treated functionally; even so, this left in the plan much of the law of future interests and of wills, on the theory that, though it could not be treated functionally, it clearly affected and was affected by the family institution.

The resulting coursebook was published in 1933. The plan of organization was a chronological arrangement of some of the elements which had been included in the research staff's curricular outline. The cases were liberally interlarded with sociological materials, and the editor (Jacobs) regretted that more could not be included. The second edition, published in 1939, was little different in outward appearances. The same subject matter was covered, although the chronological arrangement was abandoned. The treatment of confidential communications was relinquished to the course on evidence. The emphasis on nonlegal materials was quietly diminished.

In 1952, a third edition was published, with Professor Goebel as co-editor. The basic organization was unchanged. The bibliography of nonlegal materials was considerably modernized. Nonlegal materials were still used, but their presence was not very evident. The reaction of the law teachers who reviewed this edition was startling. Dean Kingsley discussed the problems of bringing social science materials into law school courses, but that was because he was reviewing, at the same time, a new book by Professor Fowler Harper in which the social sciences (and sex as well) were rediscovered and placed prominently on display. Concluding that such materials were not adapted to the teaching methods of "conservatives" like himself, he affirmed his confidence in *Jacobs and Goebel*—that "reasonably traditional law book." And Professor Paul Sayre complained that the treatment of family relations was too detached from life, suggesting that the editors appeared to think of the law of domestic relations as "a purely verbalistic and logical system of rules put together under (preferably) Aristotelian influence."

3. Property In the Columbia faculty's organization for attack on the problems of the curriculum, no provision was made for a committee on property. The assumption, presumably, was that, when the process of organizing law studies around significant "type-fact situations" had been completed, the elements of property law would find their appropriate places. However, one member of the committee on the family submitted a memorandum in which the difficulties of classification had been made to appear in some detail. Noting that, after the distribution of substantial parts of property law to the courses on the family and on security, much of the field would remain unaffected. As a further functional classification—or, at least, a classification which would facilitate the integration of real property law with the study of economic and social phenomena relating to land—he proposed a course in land utilization. Still, a residuum comprising "a large body" of the property law in the existing curriculum would remain to be disposed of. "This is due . . . to the fact that the problem of teaching real property law is one primarily of a professional method or technique which cuts across the facts of land utilization. Whether a man buys land for a house, factory, or farm, the conveyance will be the same. . . . If this is true, we must frankly recognize the need for certain technical courses in real property which will give to the student some knowledge of the peculiarities of English real property law. All we can hope to do with such courses is to make them as realistic as possible, to give them a content and approach them from other than a purely legalistic point of view and refuse to let them be set up as an end in themselves." No less than three such courses would be required: Interests in Land, Conveyancing (or Vendor and Purchaser), and Future Interests, and, in addition, some historical matter ought to be included in an introductory course.

Meanwhile, Professor Powell (then teaching Future Interests with his own conventional casebook), began to think of the process of wealth distribution, of the social phenomena and policies involved, and of a course which would draw all of these together. Such a course, if not functionally organized in the sense of the grouping of materials around a "type-fact situation", would at least be so in the sense of focusing on a "clusterspot" and would encourage the study of law in the context of realistic social considerations. Such a course was inaugurated in the spring of 1928 (though it was modestly called only Future Interests and Noncommercial Trusts), and Professor Powell found himself confronted with a task of "immediate and appalling urgency"—exploration of the relevant nonlegal data.

In 1928, an assistant assembled a bibliography of nonlegal materials, so it was possible to include in the materials being prepared for the part of the course dealing with trusts an introductory chapter of fifteen pages and very occasional sidelights on the problems subsequently treated. But by the end of 1928–29, little or nothing had been done on correlating the nonlegal material nor on welding into an integrated, coherent whole the materials of

Future Interests, Wills, and Trusts. In 1929–30, the search for the nonlegal material was pressed with one full-time and two part-time assistants. This, however, was only one phase of the problem; another was to find out more about the problems arising in actual life and to bring the course into closer relation to them. Two assistants were assigned to gather data as to (1) the distribution of wealth; (2) the percentage of dying persons who leave assets administered in probate courts; (3) the prevalence of testate disposition; (4) the extent to which wills are declared invalid; (5) the types of assets constituting estate; and (6) the shrinkage in estates between the death of the owner and the final distribution. The researches, confined to the Surrogates' Courts in New York, Kings, and Bronx counties, resulted in the publication of a law-review article which has since become well known. Further research was done on current practices in testamentary disposition, on the possibilities of corporate organization in estate management, and on accounting practices affecting the relative interests of life tenants or beneficiaries and holders of subsequent interests.

In 1932–33, Professor Powell published his casebook on trusts and estates for the course. The critics questioned whether any significant integration of the three superseded courses had been accomplished, and they regretted the omission, or compressed treatment, of some subjects, notably those which would have illustrated the versatility of the trust. Although the nonlegal research which had been done was reflected in a chapter entitled "Some Material Facts and Trends in Current American Life," the nonlegal content was not sufficiently obtrusive to excite much comment.

In 1937, Professor Powell published a second edition of his casebook on future interests, although that subject matter had been included in the volumes on trusts and estates; and this was followed, in 1940, by a separate casebook on trusts. The idea of the integrated course had not taken hold at other schools, and the new books were designed primarily for them. At Columbia, the course in trusts and estates was continued until 1943–44, when it was divided into Trusts and Estates I, given with the 1937 casebook on future interests, and Trusts and Estates II, given with the 1940 casebook on trusts. In 1948–49, however, the course in trusts and estates was reinstated.

4. Crime and criminology Crime was not, in itself, a ready-made functional category. Some crimes were to be comprehended in the materials organized about type-fact situations—the family, marketing, and labor. The residue posed for the committee formidable problems of internal classification. On one point, there was early agreement: it was desirable to continue the separation between criminal procedure and the substantive treatment, treating procedure as a method of state control. The problem of how to treat the substantive content was more troublesome. The committee considered a classification which would entail the cataloging and separate treatment of particular crimes, and one which would "view the totality from the point of view of the person committing the act and the social conditions under which he committed it." But the literature on the causes of crime was in an unsatisfactory state. The committee turned its attention to a research program, proposing projects to determine the effects of certain legal rules, to inquire into the actual administration of prosecutions and trials, to study methods of detection and apprehension, and to be concerned with various sociological questions and problems of the treatment of criminals. The committee proposed the establishment of a school of criminology.

With matters in this somewhat inconclusive state, an arresting development occurred. At the request and with the financial support of the Bureau of Social Hygiene, the Law School extended its auspices to a survey for the purpose of determining whether or not it was desirable to establish an institute of criminology and of criminal justice in the United States, and of planning such an institute if it should prove to be desirable. The survey report, "written as if with a battle-ax," flung down a formidable challenge to the suppositions underlying the entire scheme of reorganization. In the view of the authors, their pivotal theme was the relation of law to the social sciences in general; and it was laid down that "[t]he relation of criminology to the criminal law can . . . be taken as typical of the relation, for instance, of economics and psychology to the law of contracts, and, generally, of the relation of social science to law." After a devastating examination of the literature of criminology, they announced these conclusions:

1.   There is no scientific knowledge in the field of criminology.

2.   Empirical scientific research in criminology cannot be undertaken at the present time.

They did go on to recommend the establishment of an institute, in the belief that it was possible to develop an empirical science of criminology, but only on condition that such an institute would forswear the "raw empiricism" of previous research and devote itself, with radical changes in existing methodology, to the development of theory and analysis in psychology and sociology, on which criminology was dependent. In addition, the institute should endeavor to construct a "rational science" of the criminal law, based upon the principles of the "sciences" of ethics and politics. The business of the survey was to inquire into the desirability of a research institute, not into the problems of undergraduate professional education; but the implications of the report for the pending reorganization of the curriculum were obvious and were sometimes made explicit.

Had these findings been as conclusive as the tone of the authors, there would presumably have been a sudden end of the attempt to reorganize the curriculum on functional lines and to relate it to the social sciences. This, however, was not quite the case. In a spirited counter-attack, Professor Karl Llewellyn summarized his reaction: "Altogether: as stimulating, irritating, vitally wise and hopelessly absurd a book as I have read." Acknowledging that the authors had "with utter cogency" demonstrated the weaknesses of crude empiricism, he charged them with a tendency toward crude rationalism. The "Himalayan" standards which they had erected for empirical science had led them to reject the substantial progress made by criminological research in discovering some causes of crime and controlling some criminal behavior. Much of the knowledge dismissed by the authors as mere common sense was "not the stock of knowledge common to the people, but that common rather to the skilled in a given line."

The survey report had its effect. No new casebook on criminal law grew immediately out of the faculty's organized attempt to revise the curriculum. Until 1929–30, Beale's casebook was used, as before; thereafter, through 1934–35, the casebook was "to be announced"; not until 1935–36 was it announced as Michael and Wechsler's *Cases and Materials on Criminal Law and Its Administration,* in mimeographed form. And it is reasonable to surmise that it may have had a generally moderating effect, injecting an element of skepticism into the quest for answers from the social sciences and a note of caution into the process of scrapping classifications which had utility for the rational study of law.

5. Marketing   The whole area of "business relations" was conceived of as falling into four or more divisions: Marketing, Business

Organizations, Finance and Credit, Labor Relations, and possibly Risk and/or Production. There were three basic documents on marketing. Confronted with fact situations of extreme complexity, the committee decided to "attack the division of this field primarily on the fact side, leaving, for the moment, untouched, the question of integrating the fact material with the law." After examining the literature of marketing, the committee considered three possible bases of classification. The first was that of the processes involved in marketing; the second was that of the classes of commodities involved; and the third was that of the agencies found active in the processes of marketing. The preliminary preference seems to have been for the organization based on processes, or functions, as best facilitating the integration of legal and nonlegal materials. Later, however, opinion seems to have shifted to the view that "[s]o far as we have developed in our society well differentiated specialized marketing agencies or functionaries, and so far as a sufficient number of important legal problems cluster about them, such agencies should be treated in special courses." Examples were to be found in transportation, storage, and risk-bearing. Only the residue left after this type of allocation would be organized in terms of basic marketing processes.

But the curriculum was little affected by such labors in this field. Trade Regulation, which of course concerns the marketing process, was already a well established course; indeed, the committee appears to have regarded it almost as one of the traditional courses which would raise problems if the broader functional classification were adopted. The only course outline offered by the committee was one on Competitive Practices. No new casebook in that segment of the field was published by a member of the Columbia faculty until 1937. Although it made significant use of "secular" material, it was not regarded as unconventional.

Llewellyn's *Cases and Materials on Sales,* published in 1930, was a radical departure from precedent. It focused on the business transaction rather than on traditional legal categories, but it was a far cry from the functionalism of the faculty seminar. It can hardly be said to have utilized social science materials directly, however rich it was in the flavor of the market and however keen its Mansfieldian sensitiveness to mercantile usage. Three reviewers complained of the secular content. In general, however, the business background materials were accepted with enthusiasm, perhaps, in part, because they were offered simply as such, with a minimum of the trappings of social science.

6. Finance and credit The basic memorandum on this, the third of the broad divisions of the field of business relations, treated the topic as divisible into three parts: commercial bank credit, security devices, and corporate finance. The third of these was promptly relinquished to the business organization group. So complex were the problems of internal organization that they led the committee to include in its report one of the most searching analyses of the general problem of curricular organization to be found in the records. Primary emphasis was given to the first of the three internal divisions: "The Medium of Exchange: Commercial Bank Credit." In 1927–28, a course on commercial bank credit was substituted for the old course on bills and notes; but in 1929, Underhill Moore went to Yale, and thereafter the place of Bills and Notes in the Columbia curriculum remained unchallenged.

Security, the somewhat slighted twin of commercial bank credit, was another matter. The committee's preliminary conception had been of a category called commercial credit—chiefly, credit as between buyer and seller. But a modification of the strictly functional or institutional approach was thought to be necessary because of the complexity and the technical character of legal security devices. In this field, legal concepts were so important and intricate a part of the fact situation that special attention had to be given to a plan of organization which would bring them clearly into focus. Accordingly, the category was redefined as "*legal* security devices, with special reference to commercial credit." A course on security was offered for the first time in 1927–28 by Professors Llewellyn and Douglas, and was continued by Professor Hanna, who, in 1932, published his *Cases and Other Materials on Security.* The book treated, in addition to suretyship and real estate mortgages, pledges, letters of credit, trust receipts, chattel mortgages, and conditional sales. "Much effort," the editor said, had been expended "to explain the contemporary business background, partly by cases containing exposition of business practice, partly by current business forms, and partly by notes on nonlegal topics." The reviewers were unanimously enthusiastic, welcoming both the plan of organization and the background materials. The second edition, published in 1940, was similarly received, although by that time a reviewer could refer to its arrangement as "orthodox." In short, the book achieved, if not an elegantly functional treatment, (1) a material saving of time by compressing into one course the materials of suretyship and mortgages and more besides (although no attempt was made to "merge" the various devices); and (2) a framework in which the available legal devices could be viewed comparatively in the light of their commercial utility.

Nowhere is there reference to the problem of the unsecured creditor and the insolvent debtor, although that problem would seem to be relevant to the general area of finance and credit. Dean Stone, however, had suggested a course on creditors' rights; such a course was offered in 1929–30; and in 1931, Professor Hanna published his *Cases and Materials on the Law of Creditors' Rights.* The book was designed to facilitate the "comparative study of the various ways of protecting an unsecured creditor" and covered enforcement of judgment, fraudulent conveyances, general assignments, creditors' agreements, and receivership in addition to bankruptcy. "In the nature of things the materials are largely legal, in contrast to the book on Security in which there seems a legitimate occasion for the inclusion of a generous amount of nonlegal discussions." One reviewer called the book "epoch-making," and all were enthusiastic. Here is an instance, it seems to me, in which a tough-minded lawyer, dealing with essentially procedural materials, succeeded in being more functional than the faculty planners, and succeeded very well indeed.

7. Labor Since Industrial Relations was a firmly established component of the curriculum, the task of the committee assigned to this fourth division of the field of business relations was not to innovate but to suggest methods and directions for further progress. Typically, further progress in such a venture means broadening scope and searching for additional nonlegal material of relevance, in the face of multiplying legal materials, and is not easily attained. The committee suggested a marshalling of the University's personnel assets, in all departments, for a cooperative attack on the problems of research and course organization. Its comprehensive outline and discussion of the economic aspects of labor problems was intended as a basis for continuing research rather than for immediate course construction. It was not until 1944 that a member of the Columbia faculty published a new casebook on labor law.

8. Risk and risk-bearing In 1924, Professor Edwin W. Patterson published an article entitled, "The Apportionment of Business Risks Through Legal Devices." Accepting risk as a pervasive and significant phenomenon in economic activity, he set out to trace, in a tentative and experimental way, the manner in which the courts, by applying or purporting to apply certain legal norms, were consciously or unconsciously determining the apportionment of risks. The approach was modest and skeptical, and the legal concepts examined were limited to four associated with contract and other consensual relations, each of which was regarded as a doctrinal device for risk apportionment. It was suggested that the problems involved might advantageously be stated as problems of risk-bearing rather than as "problems in the application of legal concepts which are based upon an abstraction of purely physical or other adventitious factors in the business relation in question." Whether the results reached by the courts were socially and economically expedient could be judged only by the standards of the armchair philosopher.

Here was insight that could enrich the study of law: insight into the operation of law as a means of dealing with the fundamental hazards of life and business. Here was a framework for criticism; but, typically, and necessarily, it stopped short of supplying standards for criticism. Those the law could not supply, and they were hard to find. There the matter rested until the faculty's mobilization for attack upon the problems of reorganization of the curriculum summoned all such resources to the firing line. If risk was a pervasive and significant problem of economic life, and if rules of law could be fruitfully treated as devices for risk apportionment, why not group the rules about the problem for study? Such a classification had its counterpart in the business schools, and one might hope that parallel statement of the problems and parallel study would bring to light economic theory and factual information which would supply standards of criticism. The committee's report pursued this possibility with enthusiasm. Its forty-page outline of "a course or courses on risk and risk-bearing" set forth an overwhelming diversity of subject matter relating to risks.

Risk was a pervasive phenomenon indeed; around it could be clustered a startling miscellany of legal topics, and there would result encroachment not only on traditional courses but on newly defined groupings as well. Moreover, while large segments of the existing curriculum were included, they were not provided for in their entirety; and this was notably true of torts. It is not surprising that the adoption of such a conception as a basis for course organization was "much debated," nor that, after the fervor of the concerted faculty exploration had abated, and he was confronted with the preparation of materials for the use of law students, Professor Patterson limited himself to recognition of the fact that the course in insurance was already a functional organization of materials bearing on the important core of vocational risk-bearers. His casebook on insurance was "designed to present current problems of insurance law in their relations to insurance institutions and business practices without sacrificing either the historical development or the technical analysis of legal doctrines." The organization featured the principal aspects of the insurance business: the carrier in its legal and financial structure and its relation to the state; the interests of those insured; the selection and control of risks; the marketing of insurance protection; and the settlement of claims. Nonlegal materials were interspersed with the cases and collected in an appendix. The basic features were retained and supplemented in the later editions.

9. Miscellaneous matters The group of courses dealing with procedural subjects presented a different problem from that presented by the courses in substantive law. As we have seen, some procedural law was caught up in the ultimate organization of courses on security and on criminal law and its administration. Leaving these aside, there appears to have been no discussion of resort to nonlegal materials in the procedure field. There were problems of organization of this material, however, and because they tend to throw some light on the issues raised by the reorganization effort in general, they must be briefly noted.

The report of the committee discussed three possible plans of organization: (1) one based on the point of view of the lawyer in practice; (2) one which would distribute the materials among other courses, to relate them to the functions of substantive rules; and (3) one based on the social viewpoint, treating procedural matters as a means of effectuating the purpose of law to control human behavior. The second was considered only to be rejected. The tension was between the first, supported by Professors Michael and Smith, and the third, advocated by Professor Oliphant. For Oliphant, the logic underlying the reorganization of the substantive parts of the curriculum extended equally to the procedural parts. "Granted we know from a study of substantive law how we want people to behave, what is the totality of devices, whether direct or indirect, calculated to cause them so to act?" This kind of treatment would comprehend under law administration not only pleading, practice, procedure, and evidence, but also administrative procedure, legislation, and the constitutional limitations on legislative action. It would go even farther. Oliphant had come to be impressed by the important role played in the control of social behavior by indirect sanctions, such as taxation and the denial of civil remedies. Professors Michael and Smith argued that the treatment of procedural matters from a systematic standpoint was quite consistent with the general objectives. "Law administration is itself an activity and the legal material in the field is already organized functionally." A reorganization of the materials was desirable, but primarily in order to focus attention on the purpose of the rules and so avoid the tendency to concentrate on the rules themselves and on logically perfect systems of rules. For purposes of the curriculum, these members of the committee proposed to exclude from the category legislation, administration by nongovernmental agencies, and also administration by nonjudicial agencies or devices. Their purpose was to integrate the various procedure courses as much as possible, to present judicial and quasi-judicial administration of law as a continuous process, to make that process more vivid and realistic, and to bring out more clearly the relationship between devices for law administration and the substantive law. The main body of the report was an exercise in diplomacy, designed to compose these divergent viewpoints—a feat which was accomplished by omitting such matters as indirect sanctions from the proposed course outline and relegating them to a schedule of matters to be investigated by the faculty.

In 1927–28, in cooperation with a research group at the Yale Law School headed by Dean Hutchins, Professor Michael and Professor Adler (of the Department of Psychology) participated in a study of the logical and psychological foundations of the rules of evidence. This activity resulted in the publication of a series of articles which were thus characterized by the principal author, Robert M. Hutchins, a few years later:

> What we actually discovered was that psychology had dealt with very few of the points raised by the law of evidence; and that the basic psychological problem of the law of evidence, what will affect juries, and in what way, was one psychology had never touched at all. Thus psychologists could teach you that the rule on spontaneous exclamations was based on false notions about the truth-compelling qualities of a blow on the head. They could not say that the evidence should be excluded for that reason. They did not know enough about juries to tell you that; nor could they suggest any method of finding out enough about juries to give you an answer to the question.

Hutchins concluded that the proper approach to the study of law was through analysis of its basic concepts and principles, which are derived from the rational sciences of ethics and politics. Similar conclusions were apparently reached by the Columbia participants.

Finally, the faculty gave attention to the construction of a general introductory course and to the study of historical and comparative jurisprudence. Jurisprudence was broadly conceived as comprehending not only legal philosophy, but ancient law, legal history, and comparative law. The committee, sensing a threat to such studies implicit in the particularistic approach to curricular organization, made a bold plea for an elaborate research organization and for attention in the undergraduate curriculum to such matters as logic, Roman law, and the history of the common law. It affirmed that the study of jurisprudence could and should be "directed along functional or sociological lines, *i.e.*, it should concern itself not with legal institutions as such but with legal institutions in their social and economic milieu"; and it suggested that one of the major features of work in jurisprudence would be to correlate work in the social sciences with the study of law.

D. The Aftermath

It was in the spring of 1927, in the deanship of Huger W. Jervey, that the faculty did its most intensive work on revision of the curriculum. Because of Dean Jervey's illness, there were no reports of the dean in the years 1926 and 1927. Accordingly, Dean Smith, in his report for 1928, set forth a full account of the faculty studies and the events leading to them. The account was a sympathetic exposition of the dominant objectives, and, in general, the tone was one of quiet pride in what had been accomplished and of confidence that further progress was forthcoming. Nevertheless, even this early, troublespots were visible. Plainly evident was the fear that the result of the radical revision of the curriculum, and even the purpose of some of its more ardent supporters, might be to impair the professional training afforded by the school and turn Columbia into a mere research institute for the "scientific" study of law as an aspect of social organization. There were grounds for such a fear. While some members of the faculty adhered to the view that the major objective should remain that of providing an adequate scientific preparation for public service in law, others asserted that it should be to build a "community of scholars" for the study of law as an aspect of social organization. Moreover, the latter held that no single university could effectively pursue both objectives. Dean Smith discussed fully the merits of the two views on objectives and stated firmly that, in the opinion of the faculty, it was both feasible and desirable for the School to pursue both. Few things could have been more calculated to hamper acceptance of the basic educational policy, at Columbia and elsewhere, than such a conflict. The movement was not confronted merely with uninformed opposition on the part of people who misinterpreted its objectives; some of its most ardent supporters were expressly proclaiming its nonprofessional purpose. Among those who recalled how narrowly the professional character of the school under Dwight had escaped dissipation (supposedly) at the hands of Lieber and Burgess, consternation must have been substantial. Yet any suggestion that the professional purpose of the school should be abandoned or made secondary was a needless deviation from the basic theme. No such suggestion was even remotely in the mind of Dean Stone; the changes he proposed were designed to strengthen and improve education for the practice of law. Dean Smith, in reporting the faculty's rejection of the suggestion, might have made clearer than he did the fact that the changes in the undergraduate curriculum were calculated to strengthen rather than to undermine professional training.

In the same year, two supporters of the basic educational philosophy—Professors Yntema and Douglas—resigned from the faculty; and Professor Kidd returned to the University of California. Problems of finance came to the fore: the new program would require substantial additions to the library's collection and staff, and manpower was needed for research.

In 1929, Dean Smith again discussed fully the plan of reorganization, this time taking care to emphasize the objective of improving training for law practice. Problems of personnel and of cost were again pressing. In this year, two of the principal architects of the reorganization, Professors Moore and Oliphant, resigned from the faculty.

In 1930, a new tone dominated the report—one of disillusionment and even annoyance. After recapitulating his earlier accounts of the faculty's experiments, Dean Smith said: "If we are to accomplish the aims which have inspired the developments which are taking place, the hypotheses upon which we are proceeding must be constantly tested against actual results. There must be the same zeal to recognize and admit error as there is to proclaim success. A new hypothesis is usually assumed to be better than the one which it supplants, but its truth is not established by turning it into a dogma." No academician will fail to identify this as smoke betraying the fire of personal conflict below the horizon. It is no secret that there was conflict. How could it be otherwise, given the strong personalities and the strong convictions involved? There is, of course, no record of the details, and that is just as well, since to explore them would serve no useful purpose. The sheer magnitude of the task had become oppressive.

The contribution of the social sciences had proved disappointing. Access to such assistance as the social sciences might be able to offer was impeded by formidable barriers. Finally, much of the research undertaken had produced findings without significant value.

In 1931, Dean Smith returned with renewed confidence to the theme that legal education should be improved by broad training in the social sciences. His emphasis was on the effects of specialization in knowledge and in labor, and on the need for coordination of specialized fields of knowledge. The lawyer, formerly the foremost coordinator in the field of social science, had been transformed by increasing specialization "from a social philosopher into a legal technician." The task of the law school was now conceived as that of developing a coordinating agent in the fields of law and government—a task to be accomplished only by improving the law student's "knowledge of the social sciences as a whole." In 1932, Dean Smith spoke only briefly of the integration program. Setting it against the history of legal education, he seemed to suggest that the new outlook was common to good, modern, full-time law schools, although he also seemed to suggest that it was manifested principally in the research activity of faculty members; and he was careful to add that the study of legal history and the analysis of legal concepts had not been abandoned. In 1933, he was able to point to developments under the New Deal as demonstrating "the interdependence of law and of government, and the importance of relating more closely the study of law and of its application, to the study of those social, economic and political ends but for which there would be no rational basis for the existence of law." It was in this year that he reported the establishment of a board of visitors, "consisting of representative alumni and other members of the bench and bar selected from year to year to visit the School, to study and appraise its work, to report on its condition and needs, and to make recommendations to the Faculty and to the Trustees of the

University." Clearly, the doubts which had been raised (with what justification we have seen) concerning the quality of professional education at Columbia had not been allayed, and the alumni mounted guard.

In 1934, for the first time, the Dean's Report contained no discussion of the program of curriculum revision; it was devoted to other problems of legal education. There was reference to research work in progress, but the only relevant development in the curriculum was the inauguration of Professor Hale's course on Legal Factors in Economic Society. By 1935, a new theme of curriculum revision was engaging the faculty's attention: increased emphasis on public law and on the public implications of private law. In 1936, the absorbing problem was overcrowding of the bar. Finally, in 1937, in his tenth annual report, Dean Smith summed up the developments of the decade. On the extent to which the curriculum had been functionally organized and on the incorporation of non-legal materials, he did not dwell; but he could point to the fact that, of the forty courses offered in the school, thirty-six were taught with collections of materials prepared by members of the Columbia faculty within the past ten years—twenty-six of them in the form of published casebooks, many of which had been widely adopted by other schools. In the same period, members of the faculty had published twenty-eight treatises and 356 articles in legal periodicals and other scientific journals. Not all of this product, by any means, represented progress in the integration of law and the social sciences; but much of it was stimulated by the climate engendered by the faculty's determined attack on that problem. A concrete idea of the cost of the program was afforded by the fact that some $440,000 in grants had been obtained during the ten-year period for research on law as a social institution and for the compilation of integrated teaching materials.

It seems clearly unfortunate that the new movement was so ambitious and so highly organized, and that it took the form of an attempt to reorganize and revamp the entire curriculum. Such an attempt would have encountered major difficulties in a far less complex situation. The only justification for this concerted and urgent attack on the problem—the ideal of simplifying the curriculum and avoiding duplication—turned out to be an illusion. Some areas of the law could be functionally organized with spectacular success; others were not susceptible at all of functional treatment; and any thorough-going functional organization would have

threatened duplication on a scale far beyond anything suggested
by the superimposition of a few special courses on the traditional
curriculum. One reason for this was that "functional" did not
have, and perhaps could not have, a fixed meaning. Sometimes it
had an institutional connotation, as in the case of the family; but
the course on security was functional in a different sense, and
"wealth distribution" in still another, and "risk and risk-bearing"
was so in a sense different from any of these. Nor did successful
functional classifications often result, as they were expected to,
in the saving of time sufficient to accommodate the new material
in the curriculum. On the contrary, like so much of the fruitful
work that is done, the successful efforts tended to expose the
overgeneralization of law and the need for more detailed, discriminating, and selective treatment. The functional concept of the
business organization did not fuse Agency and Partnership with
Corporations; it did threaten to make Corporations into three
separate courses. When compression was achieved, as in the course
on future interests and trusts, it was the product of legal scholarship which, while it was stimulated by the functional approach,
was by no means dependent on it. Some of this had been foreseen
from the beginning; when the truth became increasingly evident,
and the prospect of even ultimate simplification seemed increasingly remote, the faculty was undismayed. The rather abrupt moderation of the movement which had started so pretentiously probably
brought relief to conservative law teachers; but the abandonment,
when its justification failed, of a plan of action which had at best
been questionable was neither failure nor surrender.

A related difficulty was the excessive emphasis on business as
the dominant concern and justification of law. This was attributable not to any hypothetical orientation of the Columbia Law
School toward Wall Street, but to the undoubted orientation of
Marshall and Oliphant toward the University of Chicago School
of Business. It showed itself in the *Summary of Studies,* where
seven chapters were devoted to the main components of the curriculum, five of which were devoted to business categories. The
sixth dismissed such matters as jurisprudence, legal history, and
comparative law with the remark that they were important only
in so far as they contributed to the teleological criticism of law—
largely in terms, it must be presumed, of commercial and economic
ends. In the seventh, Professor Oliphant gathered together, under
the ampersand heading, "Communal Standards and Political

Relations," some odds and ends not otherwise provided for, such as the family, crime, real property, public law, and taxation. It showed itself most plainly in the proposal to treat the law of torts almost entirely from the standpoint of the risks of business enterprise. This was understandable, given the prevailing enthusiasm for the business-school curriculum as the model of functional elegance; but even in Wall Street, law is concerned not only with business, but with ordinary human relations and—as the faculty was reminded by the advent of the New Deal—with government and politics.

The greatest of the manifold difficulties associated with the assimilation of nonlegal materials seems to me to have been the lack of any sharp conception of the purpose to be served by such materials and, more particularly, the frustrations and defections which resulted when the more ambitious conceptions of the goal were disappointed. Sometimes the felt need was simply for a descriptive account of the business background against which legal doctrine operated; sometimes it was for a detailed account of the behavior of business executives or housewives; sometimes it was for the accumulation in one place of all knowledge concerning an institution, such as the family, so that all possible interactions could be observed and appreciated; and, too often, it was for ultimate verity concerning such problems as the causes of crime and the efficacy of law as a corrective. The tendency to ask the wrong questions of other disciplines and to expect too much of the replies is persistent.

The frustrations and defections stemming from the failure of the social sciences to yield promptly the solutions which were desired created an impression far out of proportion to their importance. Indeed, it is not easy to determine whether the most influential defection (by Robert M. Hutchins) was due to a philosophical rejection of the empirical method, to financial obstacles, or simply to faulty logic.

The prospects for further progress in the interrelation of law and the social sciences, so far as the law school curriculum is concerned, rest primarily on the enterprise of individual teachers. It is no longer necessary, if it ever was, to classify the curriculum functionally in order to call attention to the relevance of knowledge developed in other disciplines or to remind us that law is a means to an end. The individual teacher, preparing the materials for whatever course may be assigned to him, will seek insights and syntheses where he can find them. He will frequently question the validity of his assumptions; he will be curious about business practices, about family customs, about testamentary dispositions, and about the effects and the justification of legal rules. Since he will not often be able to obtain or evaluate the information he needs without the aid of experts in other fields, there must be adequate research facilities at his disposal. If he is thus able to compile a set of materials which significantly brings nonlegal learning to bear on some classification of the problems with which law deals, room will be found for his course in the curriculum, and his book will sell. If he does not do so, someone else will. Oliphant compiled a pioneering casebook which required the addition to the curriculum of a new course, based on a novel grouping of materials; the novel course is now standard in almost every law school. If he had devoted his energies to the improvement of that book and to the construction of others, instead of to building fires in the camps of his colleagues, he might have been remembered, like Langdell, as the founder of a new era in legal education rather than as the leader of a movement which foundered. Langdell did not originate the idea of the case method; he compiled the first successful casebooks.

Not only must research facilities be available to individual teachers to be used as the need arises, but there must, of course, be organized and systematic research in law and the social sciences directed toward the discovery of new knowledge without reference to the law school curriculum. The product will inevitably be reflected in the training of undergraduate law students, as it is incorporated by the compilers of teaching materials; but there is no necessity to revise the curriculum in anticipation of the fruits of research to come.

APPENDIX IV

THE MATERIALS OF LAW STUDY: 1971

by Lester J. Mazor

Twenty years ago Brainerd Currie looked back upon legal education in the first half of the twentieth century and concluded that the most significant development of that period was the movement "calling for reorganization of the law curriculum along 'functional' lines and for the broadening of law school studies to include nonlegal materials, drawn principally from the social sciences." Although there have been other developments in legal education since the time Currie wrote which may yet come to overshadow it, the movement to broaden the materials of law study continues to have many adherents. Recognition of the respectability of the movement by the legal education establishment was demonstrated in the selection of the theme "Social Research and the Law" for the December, 1969 annual meeting of the Association of American Law Schools. At the meeting, many speakers preached the gospel of the importance of social science to both lawyers and law teachers. In the words of Maurice Rosenberg, "to function as they should, lawyers need both to understand the ways in which social scientists gather data and the ways in which they analyze and interpret their findings." Carl Auerbach warned that "the time will come when no law teacher will be regarded as competent who does not possess competence in some field of social science." (How many of the prospective law teachers in attendance took the hint?) Since the meeting was specifically addressed to the relevance of social research, it is not clear to what extent the participants would make the same claims for the importance of interdisciplinary activity between law and sciences other than the social, not to mention the non-sciences. But elsewhere the call has been put more generally as a need for the law school to establish closer relationships with the rest of the intellectual world.

Set against this picture of the felt importance of an interdisciplinary approach to law study is the way in which the law schools appear to an observer of the American educational scene or, for that matter, to some law students. To David Riesman, it seems that "in most universities the law schools have remained autarchic, sharing only the most nominal connections with undergraduate and graduate education in the arts and sciences." In their 1967 study, the Yale Law Students Association found the promise of interdisciplinary activity at Yale largely unfulfilled. The autarchy of the law schools is consistent with the traditional character of American legal education as defined in the concept of the professional school, differing from the earlier English model in that it is university related and from the continental model in that its faculty is composed of lawyers and its student body of those who aspire to practice law. There have always been a few deviants, but by and large until recently both faculty and students have had contact with other disciplines principally through formal education prior to law school and by continued research and reading during and after law school based on the foundation acquired earlier. The law school has treasured its autonomy and independence. It has not offered to provide any great teaching or research service to the rest of the university, but neither has it asked for much.

We are not yet in a position to assay the significance of the apparent contradiction between the statement of the need for interdisciplinary activity in the law schools and the seeming shortage of it. To make such an appraisal we would need to know much more than we do about how lawyers function, how their education affects their mode of functioning, and what steps may be taken in legal education to support the desired result. This would be an ambitious research undertaking. At this point, we cannot even claim to have accomplished the much smaller task of describing the present state of interdisciplinary activity in the law schools.

The published literature about legal education contains numerous calls for the establishment of interdisciplinary activity but few reports of activities which are taking place. The only aspect of interdisciplinary activity to which we have ready access is that which results in published research. The 1969 annual meeting was devoted to an appraisal of the state of this type of research, and there have been thoughtful comments on it elsewhere. We lack similar access to information about other types of interdisciplinary relationships. The *Journal of Legal Education* seems to have failed us in this respect in that in seeking to emulate the format of the Law Review it has not become much of a forum for the exchange of information about educational activity at the various law schools. Although occasional reports of teaching and research activity appear, most law teachers are reluctant to put into print a description of the work that they are doing if they cannot surround it with the trappings of scholarly importance, and many seem to believe that the safest course is to rely entirely on informal methods of communication. As the size of the law teaching enterprise has grown, the informal communications network has become less and less adequate to transmit information about new possibilities in legal education.

A large task of data gathering stands between our present situation and a greater understanding of the nature and consequence of interdisciplinary activity in law schools. Currie stated his undertaking as the study of the movement for the integration of Law and Social Science, but working as he was with the historian's traditional techniques, he found it necessary to narrow his study to developments at Columbia and then again to those which manifested themselves in changes in the curriculum or in the materials used in the teaching of courses. His material was the record of the documents coming out of faculty meetings and published works of the Columbia faculty. The impact of all this on the students of the time, the effect on relationships between law faculty and the other faculty on the campus, the effect of the movement on thinking about the selection of new faculty—questions like these were beyond the scope of his resources. Yet a series of detailed case studies of developments at particular law schools, combined with material gathered by other means, would be a major contribution to our understanding of interdisciplinary work that seems sufficiently strong to warrant the undertaking of such studies.

The official catalogs and bulletins of the law schools are another source of information about the state of interdisciplinary activity. Given the way in which law school catalogs are constructed, and their immediate purpose of informing the prospective law student about the character of the school, we can be certain that they do not reflect all of the developments in which we might be interested. Many types of interdisciplinary activity would not be considered to have the formal consequences that require publication in the catalog.

Law school catalogs are not adequate to determine the number of courses being taught on an interdisciplinary basis. Course descriptions often are drafted in a way that fails to reveal the nature of the materials used in the course, and in many cases outdated course descriptions are retained in the catalog long after the subject matter or the method of instruction has been changed.

Similarly, although some schools list collaborating faculty from other departments, the practice is by no means sufficiently uniform to permit law school catalog listings to be the measure of the number of courses being taught jointly with other faculty. Some courses by their very title—Law and Medicine, Law and Psychiatry, Social Science and the Law—indicate an interdisciplinary character, but even for these there is so little that can be gleaned from the catalog alone that no effort was made in this inquiry to take a census of such courses.

Law school catalogs are generally reliable, however, as an index of the existence of certain formal interdisciplinary relationships. With a view to beginning by determining the present state of these formal programs, the first part of this investigation consisted of an examination of 119 law school catalogs. Almost all of these were published in 1970 or early 1971. They revealed some twenty-four law schools which claimed at this point to have some type of joint degree program. A few stated that programs were in development, and many of the established programs seem to have been recently created. By far the most popular combination is of a JD with an MBA; about fifteen schools now offer this option. The others are widely scattered, but there are several schools which offer programs jointly in law and city planning or law and economics. A few of the schools offer more than one joint degree program and there are some which suggest a general opportunity to engage in the pursuit of two degrees simultaneously. At some point the experience under these programs should be sufficient to warrant examination of their operation. Perhaps some of the schools involved have already undertaken an evaluation of their programs. At this point we do not have information available showing the number of students who have become involved, much less an appraisal of the effect of the programs upon the participants and their classmates and on the relationship of the faculties involved in them.

Another index of interdisciplinary activity in the teaching program of the law schools is the flow of students between the law school and the rest of the university for the purpose of formal instruction. The traditional defensive position which formerly appeared in many catalogs prohibiting students in a law school from taking courses elsewhere is now disappearing. In its stead, many catalogs now contain statements endorsing the taking of courses outside the law school by law students, though usually under specified limits of the maximum number of credits which may be applied toward the law degree and usually with a requirement of permission in each case from the dean or a faculty committee. Most schools require a showing that the outside course is related to some special research interest or field of law study, and some require approval from a member of the faculty working in the area to which relation is claimed. These restrictions indicate the belief of law faculties that they should continue to largely monopolize the attention of their students. Permission to take courses outside the law school apparently represents a hard-won victory for those seeking to break the complete enforced isolation of the law student. With respect to traffic in the other direction, only a few law schools make any mention of their accessibility to students from outside the law school. Apparently this type of activity is still at the stage where a student from another discipline who makes aggressive inquiry may find an opportunity to take a law course, but the law school is not interested in advertising that possibility.

Because we have no established tradition of the study of legal education—that is, we cannot point to any extensive programs of research in legal education nor can we with ease name any law teachers whose field of specialty we would state as being legal education—none of these phenomena have yet received any substantial study. In the face of the lack of existing studies of interdisciplinary activity in the law schools, with the assistance of Professor Robert von der Lippe, Sociologist on the faculty of Hampshire College, a questionnaire was prepared and mailed to a sample of 250 law teachers randomly selected from the list in the 1969–70 Law Teachers directory. One hundred three questionnaires were returned with sufficient data to permit them to be analyzed. The questionnaire was a rough instrument, designed as a preliminary inquiry, and it would be folly to construct an elaborate analysis upon the small amount of data which these questionnaires furnished, especially in view of the broad nature of the questions. However, some patterns appear which suggest directions for subsequent inquiry, and the absence of other patterns may justify abandoning certain lines of investigation.

One of the most striking aspects of the returns to the questionnaire is the strong favorable response to the question whether any of seventeen disciplines should be represented on the respondent's law faculty by a full-time or joint appointment to a person with advanced training in the discipline. The 103 respondents checked a total of 258 items on this question. This high number was not the product of a sharp polarization between a few law faculty who want a highly interdisciplinary faculty and those who want none. More than seventy per cent of the respondents made at least one affirmative response to this question. Just less than half of the respondents wanted at least one but not more than four such interdisciplinary appointments on their faculty. Twenty-nine respondents wanted none; only three wanted more than eight. It is impossible to say with any precision how much this represents a departure from what presently exists on the faculty of each respondent or how far it differs from the general situation prevailing in the law schools. The questionnaire did not ask the respondents specifically to reveal whether their own school had made any such appointments; law school catalogs are an inadequate basis for judging their presence because of the widely varying practice both in the listing of those who teach in the school and in the description of their credentials. About three per cent of those listed in the Directory of Law Teachers hold the Ph.D.; about ten per cent have a Master's degree other than the LL.M. The Directory fails to reveal some who are holding joint appointments and do not complete the annual information questionnaire for listing in it. There is little indication in the available material that at present many law schools have two or more faculty with advanced training in any of the disciplines listed, have joint appointments to two or more representatives of other disciplines or have any combination of the two which would reach a figure as high as that expressed as desirable by a large proportion of the respondents to the questionnaire. It could be, of course, that the question was interpreted very broadly, so that "advanced training" meant something much less than the doctorate to the respondents. Another possibility is that the inclusion of the option of a joint appointment meant to the respondents that in endorsing the presence on their faculty of a person with advanced training in such a field they were not facing the prospect of foreclosing appointments to people with more conventional legal backgrounds. At least, the data indicates a need to determine the intensity with which the view is held that other disciplinarians are needed on law faculties. We need to determine what are the conditions that translate desire into commitment of funds and positions. There has been perhaps more attention already paid to the question of the success in integrating other disciplinarians into the life of the law faculty once they join it and the extent to which they find themselves alienated from their disciplinary colleagues and hampered in their work as a result, but here too the investigation needs to be broadened and deepened. The random distribution of this questionnaire did not give this set of persons the attention they would deserve in a more thorough study.

There were at least four questions on the questionnaire which allow some tentative conclusions about which diciplines law teachers most strongly identify as relevant to their work. In addition to the question asking about representation on the law faculty, there were questions about the disciplines from which the law teacher assigns material to students, in which the law teacher encourages students to take courses while they are studying law, from which the law teacher regularly discusses matters of professional concern with a faculty member, and in which the law teacher is or plans to engage in a joint research effort with a faculty member. Overall, there is a high degree of consistency in the ranking of disciplines. Economics tops the list in all cases and is followed by sociology in four of the five. On the question of representation on the law faculty, psychiatry, psychology, philosophy, political science, accounting, and history are closely bunched behind the leaders. In assigning materials to students, history breaks ahead of the four p's. On encouraging students to take courses elsewhere while in law school, accounting becomes number three and psychology drops to seventh place. When regular discussion of matters of professional concern is the question, political science narrowly edges out sociology. Only on the subject of joint research endeavors is there any stranger to the top of the list; engineering holds down the sixth spot, ahead of philosophy. The natural sciences, mathematics, languages, literature, religion, and speech and journalism evoke little response on any of these five questions. Of the social sciences only anthropology receives a generally light response.

Of these five types of interdisciplinary activity the heaviest positive response, as might be expected, was to the question on assigning material to students. But this response (306) is, surprisingly, not far greater than that to the question on representation on the law faculty (258). Substantially fewer of the respondents claim to engage in regular discussions of professional matters with other disciplinarians (161) and only half again as many (80) said that they are engaged in or plan to engage in collaborative research. The gross response is more deceptive on the question of regular discussion with other disciplinarians than it is on some of the other questions, however, because the distribution of responses was skewed by six respondents who accounted for forty-five positive responses on this item.

Some validation of the responses to these questions, which appeared on the first page of a two page questionnaire in the form of a chart in which check marks could be made in the appropriate columns under each of the seventeen disciplines listed, appears in the fact that in a later question two-thirds of the respondents stated that they or their students had participated in some interdisciplinary activities. Responses to a question about their appraisal of these activities were sporadic, which was to be expected since this part of the questionnaire required more effort of those who were answering. Numerically, the answers indicate general enthusiasm for these efforts. There were twenty-five respondents who thought that the cross disciplinary activities had been successful and should be continued; no one indicated that there were grounds for discontinuing the activities. However, it is highly likely that many of those who are hostile to interdisciplinary activities did not respond to the questionnaire at all—a consideration which must be taken into account in appraising all of the results described above—and that the structure of the questionnaire was such that someone who was hostile to these activities was not as likely to respond to the question on evaluation as someone who was friendly to them.

An important part of any inquiry into law school interdisciplinary activity would be to try to determine the conditions which foster or hinder such activity. The questionnaire results show that both interdisciplinary activity and interest are low in law schools which are not affiliated with a university. They do not, however, reveal any sharp differentiations between those law schools which are physically situated on the same campus with the rest of the university and those which are separately located. However, the sample may have been too small in the latter category to expose the difference. One of the questions sought to elicit from the respondents their own view of the factors contributing to their interest in other disciplines. Of five factors suggested to the respondents for consideration, the strongest positive response was to nature of the subject matter (87), followed by previous educational experience (70), personal friendship (59), proximity to the other department (41), and existence of a formal cross disciplinary program (37). Currie saw the development at Columbia as the handiwork of a few strong leaders within the faculty. We need other case studies of the process by which a strong commitment to interdisciplinary activity has been made at the few law schools which have made it. The movement should also be explored in terms of intellectual contagion. We could examine the impact of faculty with strong interdisciplinary interests as they migrated from school to school and also seek to determine the role which has been played by the graduates of schools with strong interdisciplinary programs as they have moved into law teaching elsewhere.

As has been frequently pointed out, although the stratification of the law school world is not formally recognized, there are in fact substantial differences in the nature of the legal careers for which different law schools prepare their students. At present, that spectrum of career orientation has a parallel in the spectrum of degree of interest in interdisciplinary studies. Yet it is not at all clear that the judgment that interdisciplinary studies are more suitable to the one class of careers rather than the other is a sound one. This is part of the larger question of the value of interdisciplinary studies for the growth of the lawyer. One method of inquiry would be a longitudinal study of the careers of lawyers with differing types of training in this regard. At a time when a number of schools are expanding interdisciplinary activity and beginning to change the character of their faculties, it is appropriate to establish control groups and begin such studies.

Despite these developments, many lawyers and law teachers remain highly skeptical of the importance of interdisciplinary activity in the life of the law school. It has been depicted as a prime cause of "The Decline and Fall of the Institute." At the 1969 annual meeting, Jerome Carlin, himself holder of both a law degree and a Ph.D. in sociology, argued that social science has neither met its promise of an alternative to the growing sense of sterility in the conventional approach to teaching law and legal doctrine. Since he defined the greatest problem of the legal system as the inadequate supply of persons trained to provide legal services, he concurred with those who look upon interdisciplinary activity as a needless expense and prolongation of legal education. Similar sentiments were expressed by a few questionnaire respondents who accepted its invitation to append some general remarks about their interdisciplinary experience and their attitudes towards it. Others seem to have formed at some point a strong belief in the value of interdisciplinary work. There is little indication that either view is founded in something more than personal impressions, drawn from a few experiences. While those who disclaim strong interest in interdisciplinary activity may be able to take the position that the burden of proof lies elsewhere, those with a commitment to the value of interdisciplinary effort should be willing to include in their commitment a more scientific study of its value.

Appendix B: The Limits of Legal Realism: An Historical Perspective

by Calvin Woodard

THE LIMITS OF LEGAL REALISM: AN HISTORICAL PERSPECTIVE

Calvin Woodard*

An historian participating in a symposium on legal education is naturally reticent. After all, the purpose of such a project is to elicit forward looking proposals, while history is (as Coleridge long ago remarked) little more than "a lantern on the stern of a ship which illuminates only the waves that are behind us." With all the "interaction" currently taking place between law and the more progressive sciences there is little excuse indeed for an historian participating at all.

The only justification, if justification it be, is that notwithstanding the new and exciting projects and experiments now taking place there is still a mood of uneasy restlessness among many students and faculty members. Apparently, all the insights and knowledge produced by modern innovations and experiments have served only to raise, rather than to resolve, the most fundamental issues of legal education: What should we teach? How? To what end? With all our new knowledge, we are, as André Breton once observed, "lost in a forest of signposts."[1]

History, if it has any practical and current value beyond that of pure scholarship, should be able to provide some meaningful insights under the present circumstances, not because it can provide better alternatives than other disciplines, and certainly not because it can portend in any deterministic way the course of the future, but simply because it provides another, rather dif-

---

*Professor of Law, University of Virginia. B.A., 1950, University of North Carolina; LL.B., 1953, Yale University; Ph.D., 1960, Cambridge University.

[1] In many ways our present plight is that of the Roman Empire at the time of Justinian. Speaking of the circumstances that led to the preparation of the Digest, Gibbon wrote:

> When Justinian ascended the throne, the reformation of the Roman jurisprudence was an arduous but indispensable task. In the space of ten centuries the infinite variety of laws and legal opinion had filled many thousand volumes, which no fortune could purchase and no capacity could digest . . . [T]he judges, poor in the midst of riches, were reduced to the exercise of their illiterate discretion.

[2] THE DECLINE AND FALL OF THE ROMAN EMPIRE 687 (Mod. Lib. ed. 1947). This article first appeared in *Virginia Law Review,* vol. 54, no. 4, May 1968, pp. 689–739.

ferent, point of view. And lest one fear that history's point of view, derived as it is from the study of the past, can lead to only a documented defense of the status quo, one may be assured that it will, at least in this instance, lead to conclusions even less tolerant of the currently prevailing system of legal education than those proposed by the social scientists laboring on the frontiers of learning. Even though the vantage point of history may be "backward looking," it encompasses in its view more than a single problem or a single age. In a word, it embraces the whole as well as the parts. Such is perhaps the prime value, and the greatest promise, of the historical point of view.

In this Article I shall be concerned about legal education as a whole, and more particularly, about the effect of the "secularization" of law on the aims, content and methods of legal education. I have chosen this theme, and regard it as particularly apposite to this Symposium because, in my opinion, the celebrated article by Professors Lasswell and MacDougal[2] marked a formidable step in the secularization of both law and legal education.

The Process of Secularization

The notion of "secularization" has become increasingly popular in twentieth century discourse. Indeed, in some ways it threatens to captivate the modern intellect just as "evolution" did that of an earlier age.[3] Nevertheless secularization is a suggestive idea that strikes a responsive chord in denizens of the modern world precisely because it describes, in a single word, a process that we all sense is in fact going on around us. Yet despite the widespread recognition, and an abundance of learned discussion of this phenomenon, surprisingly little effort has been made to consider its impact on law. By failing to study this impact we may be over-

---

[2] Lasswell & McDougal, *Legal Education and Public Policy—Professional Training in the Public Interest,* 52 Yale L.J. 203 (1943).

[3] Some of the most interesting research in what A. O. Lovejoy christened "the history of ideas" has been centered on "evolution." His own Great Chain of Being (1936), though not concerned with science or with nature, is still among the best. Other works more directly concerned with the theory of evolution are R. Hofstadter, Social Darwinism in American Thought (1944); C. Gillespie, Genesis and Geology (1951).

Perhaps the best discussion of the impact of the theory of evolution on law and legal philosophy is R. Pound, Interpretation of Legal History (1923).

looking a valuable insight into some of the current controversy regarding legal education.

"Secularization" is a vague term that can be used either to denote a *cause* of historical change or, alternatively, simply to describe a given *effect* produced by other causes. I shall be concerned in this Article with secularization as an effect only, leaving open the immensely more complex (and, to the historian, more interesting) issue of causation.[4] Specifically, I mean by the term a cluster of three interrelated propensities which, together, have become increasingly characteristic of western thought during the past four hundred years. The first factor is a tendency to nurture a distinctive way of perceiving the environment in which man lives ("rationalism"). The second is a propensity to stimulate the development of systematic procedures and a scholarly regime capable of exploiting the rationalistic perception of law so as to produce new knowledge about the world (the "scientific method"). The third characteristic is a penchant to excite the further development of techniques and skills by which scientific knowledge can be readily adapted to the practical needs of man and society ("technology" and "applied science").

Each of these three propensities—the growth of rationalism, the development of a scientific outlook, and the invention of new technology—will be seen to have influenced the history of Anglo-American law during the past four centuries, the over-all effect being neatly summarized by the title of a well-known article by the late Felix Cohen: secularization has replaced "transcendental nonsense" with a "functional approach" to the law.[5]

I shall consider briefly how each of these three tendencies of secularization has contributed to this centuries-long, civilization-wide development; for each tendency has been inspired by and built upon the earlier collections which took the minds of men, including lawyers, ever closer to the present state of secularization.

The influence of rationalism

The spread of rationalism has brought law down from the clouds and dispelled the aura of mystery that surrounded it for centuries.

---

[4] I have considered "industrialism" as one of the basic causes of this development in Woodard, *Reality and Social Reform—The Transition from Laissez Faire to the Welfare State,* 72 YALE L.J. 286 (1962).

[5] Cohen, *Transcendental Nonsense and the Functional Approach,* 35 COLUM. L. REV. 809 (1935).

The extent to which this is true may be measured by recalling that in earlier times the law was almost as mystical, and certainly as ritualistic, as the Church itself. Not only was there pomp (Fortescue tells that the creation of a serjeant-at-law was the occasion for a seven-day feast, "such as are held at the coronation of a king"[6]); there was also ceremonial garb (besides gorgeous gowns and tippets, serjeants wore a coif that was never doffed, not even in the presence of the king),[7] and above all, the practice of law was itself a sacrament carried out in a form closely resembling the quodlibetical disputations of the Schoolmen. "The right word," Maitland noted, "must be said without slip or trip, the due ceremonial acts must be punctiliously performed, or the whole transaction will be nought."[8] And, we might add, this close connection between law and religion which continued to influence indirectly the English law down through the nineteenth century[9] survived the trans-Atlantic transplant of English law. It was brought to this country by the God-fearing but form-hating Puritans, who not surprisingly stressed substance rather than form. The first law book published in this country consisted of a code drawn up by a Massachusetts clergyman specifically providing that in all cases not explicitly covered the courts would be guided by "the word of God."[10] And as late as 1833, Joseph Story pointed out and affirmed

[6] J. FORTESCUE, DE LANDIBUS LEGUM ANGLIE 123 (Chrimes ed. 1949). Fortescue states that the office of serjeant-at-law not only confers a degree but an estate no less eminent than Doctor of Divinity. The mandatory ceremony attendant to the creation included not only the feast, but also a presentation of rings to a nobleman, princes of the Church and judges.

[7] *Id.* at 125. See also S. PULLING, THE ORDER OF THE COIF (1884) for a discussion of this privilege, and many other illustrations of the ritualistic practices of the early Inns of Court.

[8] F. MAITLAND, SOCIAL ENGLAND 171.

[9] Even Lord Coke, the uncompromising champion of the common law, is credited with saying that "the Temporal Law and the Ecclesiastical Law are so coupled together, that the one cannot subsist without the other." And Lord Hardwick, a scarcely less distinguished chancellor, asserted "the Christian religion . . . is part of the law of the land." De Costa v. DePaz, 2 Swans. 532, 36 E.R. 715, 716 (Ch. 1743).
A modern Church historian, speaking of the close connection between ecclesiastical and common law, tells us that "only in the early nineteenth century did the parliament, which alone had the power to tackle such a task, set about the untying of this old and crusted knot." G. BEST, TEMPORAL PILLARS 39 (1964).

[10] The book referred to is N. WARD, THE BODY OF LIBERTIES (1905). Charles Warren, who said it "is entitled to be the first American law book," concluded

in his inaugural lecture as Dane Professor at Harvard that "[o]ne of the beautiful boasts of our municipal jurisprudence is that Christianity is a part of the common law, from which it seeks the sanction of its rights, and by which it endeavors to regulate its doctrines."[11]

All will now agree, I trust, that the relationship between law and religion has materially changed during the past four hundred years, and even since Story's day. Moreover, the measure of that change is not so much the landmark decisions on church and state (for example the recent *School-Prayer Cases*[12]) as it is the stark irrelevance of the laws of God—be they enunciated in the Old or New Testament, the Koran or any other divinely inspired book—to the law we now teach, practice and write about. And, of course, we regard ourselves as having advanced beyond monkish, medieval lawyers, fanatical Puritan theocrats, and pious "do-good" Victorian lawmakers precisely in that we have become "tough minded"[13] enough to treat law rationally. No longer inhibited by the "transcendental nonsense" which has from time immemorial blinded

---

that "the common law was regarded as binding, only so far as it was expressive of the law of God or of the particular statute of the colony." THE HISTORY OF THE AMERICAN BAR 66 (1913).

[11] MISCELLANEOUS WRITINGS OF JOSEPH STORY 517 (W. Story ed. 1852). In the lecture Story defended the proposition "notwithstanding the specious objection of one of our distinguished statesmen." *Id.* He was referring, of course, to Thomas Jefferson, who had denied the proposition in a published letter addressed to Major Cartwright. In 1824, shortly after Jefferson's letter appeared, Story answered it with a brief but characteristically learned discussion of the Year Book cases relied upon by Jefferson, together with other authorities. *See* 9 THE AM. JURIST 346 (1833).

[12] *E.g.*, Engel v. Vitale, 370 U.S. 421 (1962). It is extraordinary to note the change in the words "liberty" and "freedom" that secularization has brought about. Professor Haskins tells us that the Puritans of Massachusetts sought "liberty," meaning "a freedom to walk in the faith of the Gospel and to serve God through righteousness in conduct and devoutness in worship." G. HASKINS, LAW AND AUTHORITY IN EARLY MASSACHUSETTS 17 (1960).

Likewise the 1662 Book of Common Prayer, which is still generally used in the Church of England, includes a famous prayer which says: "O God who art the author of peace and lover of Concord, in knowledge of whom standeth our eternal life, *Whose service is perfect freedom.* . . ." Today, of course, "freedom" means freedom *from* religion and its restraints.

[13] The phrase 'tough minded,' which is one used with pride by many analytical lawyers today, was apparently first used by Holmes' friend William James in his celebrated LOWELL INSTITUTE LECTURES ON PRAGMATISM (Meridian Books ed. 1955). He distinguished between the "tough minded" and the "tender minded" as follows:

lawyers to the function of law, we are for the first time capable of using law to attain socially determined ends. This new outlook and hope has been the chief effect of rationalism on the law.

The rise of the science of law
Rationalism brought law to earth, but alone it was not enough to bring law to its present state of secularization. This rationalistic outlook had to be conjoined with an equally rationalistic method of analysis before law could be transformed into "legal science."

As late as the eighteenth century the common law was still a rag-bag collection of half-forgotten Anglo-Saxon customs, Norman corruptions, purloined and often imperfectly understood Canon and Roman law doctrines, pedantic procedural points (which, Sir Henry Maine observed, secreted the substantive law), and a chaotic welter of hopelessly botched and irregularly reported decisions.[14]

THE TENDER MINDED:	THE TOUGH MINDED:
Rationalistic (going by "principles")	Empiricist (going by "facts")
Intellectualistic	Sensationalistic
Idealistic	Materialistic
Optimistic	Pessimistic
Religious	Irreligious
Free-willist	Fatalistic
Monistic	Pluralistic
Dogmatical	Sceptical

Id. at 22. The first difference noted by James between "rationalism based on principles" and "Empiricism based on Facts" is precisely the difference (alluded to in note 24 *infra*) between Joseph Story's conception of "the science of Law" and Christopher Langdell's inductive Case Method.

[14] One of the most vivid descriptions of the state of law in the late eighteenth century is found in J. S. Mill's well-known essay on Blackstone's contemporary, Jeremy Bentham. According to Mill, the law had come "to be like the costume of a full-grown man who had never put off the clothes made for him when he first went to school. Band after band had burst, and, as the rent widened, then, without removing anything except what might drop off of itself, the hole was darned, or patches of fresh law were brought from the nearest shop and stuck on." J. MILL, BENTHAM AND COLERIDGE 76 (F. Leavis ed. 1950).

The extent to which this was true, and not a mere figure of speech, is gleaned by the fact that in 1829 a body of commissioners was appointed to examine the law relating to real property. They reported that no general revision of that branch of law had been undertaken since the reign of Edward I—who was king from 1272 to 1307. *See* C. CARR, A VICTORIAN LAW REFORMER'S CORRESPONDENCE 5 (Seldon Soc. Pub. 1955). Over five hundred years of history, without comprehensive revision, could not fail to create a state of absolute chaos from which we are only now gradually extricating ourselves.

This mass of undigested, unorganized and indeed unexplored material, together with a wilderness of statutes, ad hoc authorities and unwritten conventions, was made over into a science at roughly the same time that the physical sciences were coming into being, and at approximately the same pace that the "scientific method" itself was developing. 15

[15] This is not the place, and I am not competent, to give a detailed account of the development of the scientific method, an immense subject that has, in recent years, become established as a separate academic discipline, the "History of Science." We might however point out a few parallels between the secularization of law, as described in the text, and the rise of science itself.

In the Middle Ages, during which the profession and practice of law were enshrouded in ritual and mystical overtones, science made very little progress. A distinguished economic historian and lifelong medievalist, Professor M. M. Postan, explained this curious lack of progress in "the absence in medieval life of what I should be inclined to call scientific incentives." He continued:

> The Middle Ages were the age of faith, and to that extent they were unfashionable to scientific speculation. It is not that scientists as such were proscribed. For on the whole the persecution of men for their scientific ideas was very rare: rare because men with dangerous ideas, or indeed with any scientific ideas at all, were themselves very rare; and it is indeed surprising that there were any at all. This does not mean that there were no intellectual giants. All it means is that in an age of faith, men of intellect and spirit found the calls of faith itself—its elucidation, its controversies, and its conquests—a task sufficient to absorb them, to put it simply, there was no time for occupation like science.

M. POSTAN, *Why Was Science Backward in the Middle Ages?* in A SHORT HISTORY OF SCIENCE 11, 12–13 (Anchor Books ed. 1959).

Moreover, Professor Postan concluded that a contributing factor was the "spirit of protection" that led the several guilds to treat their methods and techniques as strict secrets. Among the medieval guilds were the Inns of Court; and they, no less than the others, strove to keep their techniques secret—a factor, as we have pointed out, that accounts for much of the mysticism and ritual in earlier law and, in its remnant form, the belief that law is explicable only to "the legal mind."

The spread of rationalism, which manifested itself initially in the demise of the Inns of Court as guilds and culminated in Blackstone's effort to reduce the laws of England to a rational system, coincides with the period 1500–1800 described by Professor A. R. Hall as "The Formation of the Modern Scientific Attitude." Though some of the greatest names in science belong to that period—such as Copernicus, Galileo, and Newton—it was, Professor Hall tells us, only a period "of preparation, [while] that since 1800 [has been] one of accomplishment." A. HALL, *The Scientific Revolution, 1500–1800* xii (2d ed. 1962). And if Blackstone's science of law fell short of pure reason, so also did science of this period (Newton possessed a black box full of data about magic, Robert Boyle believed in witches, and Joseph Priestly was said to have exorcised a demon with an electrical machine.)

The era of legal science—which begins with Blackstone and the legal scholar-

The science of law, as we know it, passed through four rather distinct stages in attaining its present state of secularization. First the mighty morass had to be put into some semblance of order (1750–1800); secondly, a sizable body of factual and theoretical data about the law itself had to be gathered (1800–1870); thirdly, the principles underlying this data had to be deduced and the science of law reconstructed on truly scientific foundations (1870–1930); and finally—to speak of the stage at which we have now arrived—the science of law had to be integrated into a still evolving and only dimly perceived "science of sciences."

I shall say a word about each of these stages of development in

---

ship he inspired, culminating in Langdell's inductive case method—coincides with the period during which science came of age, when William Whewell coined the term "scientist," and (to quote A. N. Whitehead) "the greatest invention . . . was the invention of the method of invention." A. WHITEHEAD, *Science and the Modern World 98* (Mentor Books ed. 1948). The age of the scientific method was begun.

The following period—roughly 1870 to 1930—during which laissez faire (according to Twiss) came to the Supreme Court and the legal profession became infinitely more professional (the "Cravath system," actually started by James S. Carter, dates from this period as does the first million dollar fee collected by William N. Cromwell in the Panama Canal affair). At the same time science also languished. So robust and dynamic throughout the earlier parts of the nineteenth century ("every day," Goncourt had written in the 1860's, "science takes another bite out of God") Whitehead says, speaking of the last quarter of the century:

> Then, almost suddenly, a pause occurred; and in its last twenty years the century closed with one of the dullest stages of thought since the time of the First Crusade. It was an echo of the eighteenth century, lacking Voltaire and the reckless grace of the French aristocrats. The period was efficient, dull, and half-hearted. It celebrated the triumph of the professional men.

Id. at 103.

During this curious period of quiescence and professionalization of both law and science the "scientific method" took its most dogmatic, and popular, form. During the period when Herbert Spencer and Thomas Huxley were aggrandizing its virtues in the physical and social sciences, Langdell was applying it to the law, and his followers were spreading it throughout the nation's law schools.

The post-1930 period, during which the Legal Realists began to rebel, and to undermine seriously the authority of the ultra-scientific case method, corresponds to a period during which modern scientists began to retreat from the dogmatism of the earlier forms of the "scientific method." Thus, for example, in 1947 one scientist—referring to Karl Piersons's *Grammar of Science,* published in 1892—wrote:

> I am inclined to think that, on the whole, the popularization of the philosophical analysis of science and its methods has led not to a greater understanding but to a great deal of misunderstanding about science.

J. CONANT, ON UNDERSTANDING SCIENCE 28 (1947).

the science of law as background to the more specific effect of all this on legal education. However, I shall reserve comment upon the last stage until later, for it merges into, and becomes a part of, the third propensity of secularization, that of developing a technology for applying science to practical problems.

Stage one: from chaos to order (1750–1800) Blackstone was the Hercules of the first stage. Though he borrowed directly from Sir Matthew Hale, and his effort was anticipated by Wood and Viner, more than any other single man he familiarized lawyers with the simplest and yet most fundamental scheme for classifying laws. All of the laws of England, he pointed out, either protected "rights" or prohibited "wrongs." Protected rights were classified as rights of persons and the rights of things; while prohibited wrongs likewise fell into two categories, wrongs against private persons and wrongs against the State.[16]

Thus with a single master stroke Blackstone gave the common law a framework with finite limits; he separated the substantive law from the slippery entanglements of procedure; and he identified, in varying degrees of detail, the component parts of the several categories and demonstrated their relationships to each other. In a word, with this epic performance, Blackstone, though himself not a notable rationalist,[17] put the chaos of law into a semblance of order. By so doing he cleared the way for the second stage in the development of the "science of law."

Stage two: creating a critical literature of law (1800–1870) Almost as soon as the *Commentaries* was published lawyers and judges of a bookish bent began disputing Blackstone's conclusions and, more importantly, trying to improve upon his effort. Thus law, partially freed of the oppressive, somewhat mystical tyranny of Lyttleton and Coke,[18] became intellectually challenging in a sense that it had not been for many generations. Speculation and interest soared as an astonishing number of lawbooks of all descrip-

---

[16] *See* BLACKSTONE, COMMENTARIES.

[17] Jeremy Bentham was so disgusted by Blackstone's "unmeaning," as he called it, that he wrote a long and splenetic *Comment on the Commentaries*. For a general discussion of the various elements of unreason going into Blackstone's great works, see D. BOORSTIN, THE MYSTERIOUS SCIENCE OF LAW (1941).

[18] For a collection of vivid illustrations of the Lyttleton-Coke influence, see C. BOWEN, THE LION AND THE THRONE 513–15 (1957).

tions cascaded forth. Some writers, like Kent, Tucker and Sharswood, aspired to adapt the *Commentaries* to this country; or, like Serjeant Stephen and Hammond, to keep it current.[19] Others undertook to systematize particular branches of law as Blackstone had done the whole.[20] At the same time, still others gave their attention to reforming the haphazard method of reporting cases. Even though as early as 1785 one state (Connecticut) had made

[19] The various editions of Blackstone are themselves marvelous records of the growth of the law during the nineteenth century. The extent to which both law and governmental activities expanded is spectacularly illustrated by Serjeant Stephen's decision in 1841 to reject Blackstone's format and to adopt his own. Among his reasons he noted that the original format

> leaves, in fact, out of consideration, or gives but an awkward and incongruous place for the consideration of, a great and increasingly important branch of the law—that, namely, which concerns the social, as distinguished from the political, institution of the country: e.g., the laws relating to the poor and to highways are treated by Blackstone . . . as mere incidents respectively to the offices of parish overseer and of parish surveyor.

H. STEPHEN, NEW COMMENTARIES ON THE LAWS OF ENGLAND v (12th ed. 1895).

Many learned books have been written about the traumatic upheavals and changes wrought during the nineteenth century. None, however, demonstrate more convincingly—and, because of Serjeant Stephen's carefully worded, somewhat ponderous reasoning, more eloquently—how the role of the state in dealing with what Carlyle called "The Condition of England Question" had in fact been changed.

[20] In many ways the nineteenth century was the era of law based upon treatise. Though courts had the power of ultimate decision, they relied often with the profoundest deference upon the words of a text writer. Story's influence (along with Lord Stowell's) on admiralty, conflict of laws (a field he is sometimes said to have invented), and American equity are well-known cases in point. We may give one more example, both to illustrate the influence of the treatise and the towering certitude and self-confidence of the treatise-writer, a remark appearing in Joel Bishop's introduction to his treatise on criminal procedure. In defending the proposition that the law should be amended and improved by text books rather than by codification (a method he deemed more appropriate to periods of national "decline and death"), Bishop wrote:

> . . . as I long ago believed, and claim now to have demonstrated, text books written on the plan above detailed, by competent men, . . . may simplify the law, . . . diminish litigation, . . . produce uniformity of opinion and decision in the courts, . . . augment, not diminish, the usefulness of legal studies as an educator. . . . The reader will not expect me further to show this in the present brief space, but only to tell him where the demonstration can be found. Let him then carefully examine the books on marriage and divorce, and the decision of the Courts as they were before the present author wrote. He will learn that there has never been a legal subject upon which our tribunals have been in so much confusion and conflict. . . . Let him then follow down the decisions of our courts to the present time. He will find that as often as the views of [my] book were seen and *understood,* they were adopted by the courts; and that not only is the rule, but to it there is no exception. . . . The result disclosed will be that, today,

provision for a permanent record of Supreme Court decisions, the system, or lack of system, of private reporters continued to prevail in both this country and England throughout much of the nineteenth century. As a result of agitation by reformers such as C. Watkins, W. T. S. Daniel and Lord Westbury, and private societies such as the Verulam Society and the Law Amendment Society, the method of reporting case law was vastly improved.[21] In addition, a number of digests of cases (for example, Cox's *Digest of Criminal Cases,* Angell's *Cases on Watercourses,*[22] and Smith's *Leading Cases*) carried forward and vastly improved the earlier, more ambitious digests of Bacon, Viner and Comyns.

The formidable body of systematic knowledge amassed over the incredibly brief span of five to six decades changed law from an insular form of pedantry wrapped in mystery into a volatile field of intellectual enquiry. As a result, the standards of the bar were considerably elevated as points of substantive law increasingly took precedence over procedural niceties; and a widespread, general interest was stimulated in the possibilities and limitations of the new "science." The second stage in the development of the science of law ended with a generation of incipient lawyers seeking (to quote the title of a student's manual published in 1872) *A Systematic View of the Science of Law.*[23]

---

the law of our Courts on marriage and divorce is more harmonious than on any other topic. Most, and perhaps all, of the few differences remaining would have been avoided had the book been looked into.
Preface to J. Bishop, Criminal Procedure (1880).

In undertaking to apply the same method to criminal law, Bishop admitted that "The undertaking would have been deemed fit only for eminence and consummate abilities"—a hurdle that he has now disposed of to his satisfaction.

For a general discussion of legal literature and its influences in nineteenth century England, see 15. W. Holdsworth, A History of English Law, ch. 6 (Goodhart & Hanbury ed. 1965).

[21] For discussions of the reform in law reporting in England, see W. Holdsworth, *supra* note 20, ch. 5.

[22] Reference is made especially to Angell's *Cases on Watercourses,* published in 1824, because, according to Charles Warren, it was the first American case book. On the recommendation of Joseph Story 246 pages of cases were added to ninety-six pages of text. *See* C. Warren, A History of the American Bar (1913).

[23] The book cited in the text was by Sheldon Amos, Professor of Jurisprudence at University College, London. Amos not only held the chair formerly occupied by John Austin, he did much to popularize the Austinian conception of the law that became so influential at the end of the nineteenth century—long after Austin, bitter, unrecognized and defeated, had passed away.

Stage three: making law an academic science (1870–1930) During the last half of the nineteenth century the secularization of law took a new form as the emphasis shifted from the gathering of new data and further exposition of particular aspects of law by isolated scholars to a systematic search for first principles by institutionally trained and based legal "scientists."[24] The chief impetus to this development was Langdell's "case method." The precepts of the case method were as simple as Blackstone's formulation of legal categories, but they were also as fraught with implications and ramifications.

The scientists of law at the beginning of this century—Langdell, Ames, Pollock and Holland—assumed like Blackstone before them that law could be broken down into component parts, and that the principles underlying each part could be arrived at only by reading all the relevant adjudicated cases. The very heart of the case method was the assumption that the cases, once they were sorted out and properly classified, would themselves fall into patterns suggesting the true underlying principles. Undoubtedly the best statement and explanation of the method was made by Langdell himself:

> Law, considered as a science, consists of certain principles or doctrines
> . . . the growth [of which] is to be traced in the main through a series
> of cases; and much the shortest and best, if not the only, way of
> mastering the doctrine effectively is by studying the cases in which it
> is embodied. But the cases which are useful and necessary for this
> purpose at the present day bear an exceedingly small proportion to any
> that have been reported. The vast majority are useless, or worse than
> useless, for any purpose of systematic study. . . . It seems to me,
> therefore, to be possible to take such a branch of law as Contracts, for
> example, and without exceeding comparatively moderate limits, to
> select, classify or arrange all the cases which had contributed in any

[24] Throughout this article I have touted Langdell as the champion of "legal science." Story was no less so. As indicated, however, the difference was between an "inductive science" based on principles derived from cases and a "deductive science" based on principles derived from truth, be it found in cases, Christianity, Judaism, Roman law or wherever. Story's attitude was perhaps best illustrated by his remarks in the moot court room at Harvard:
> Gentlemen, this is the High Court of Errors and Appeals from all other courts in the world. Tell me not of the last case cited having overruled any great principle—not at all. Give me the *principle,* even if you find it laid down in the Institutes of Hindu Law.

Keener, 1 YALE L.J. 146 (1892).

important degree to the growth, development or establishment of any of its essential doctrines.[25]

Thus the proper function of the legal scientist-scholar was to identify the principles, and to state them correctly. Then the judges, assisted by lawyers properly trained in this scientific method, could apply them correctly. In this way, cases would be decided on true principles of law, and the science of law would be brought even closer to a perfectly rational system.[26]

---

[25] *Preface* to C. LANGDELL, A SELECTION OF CASES OF THE LAW OF CONTRACTS (1870). In this Article I have tended to equate Langdell with the case method. To do so is perhaps to give him more credit than he deserves. For the development and ultimate spread of the system is very probably more attributable to the efforts of others, especially Ames.

In a tribute to Ames we find the following suggestive remark:

> It is a curious fact that Langdell, who was a great logician, taught a doctrine through its historical development; Ames, a great historian, sought to teach the law chiefly as a philosophical system. Ames's way was far better adapted to the needs of the student, and by use of it succeeded in building up in his pupils, "the legal mind." Ames gave the system its success as a method of teaching. . . .
>
> Langdell is entitled to the great honor of a discoverer; but Ames put the discovery to practical use.

Memoir of James Barr Ames, in LECTURES ON LEGAL HISTORY 3, 8–9 (1913).

In the same vein, another commentator noted:

> It was Ames who really fixed the type of case book in American law schools. His decisions were chosen, not with a purpose of tracing by slow steps the historical development of legal ideas, but with the design, through the selection of striking facts and vivid opinions, of stimulating the thought of the student, and leading his mind on by one step after another until he had become familiar with the fundamental principles of the subject and the reasons for them. Ames himself worked out one or two foundation principles in each topic, guided the class in its discussion to the adoption of these principles, and then used them for the solution of every problem that arose. His method became, at least for his pupils, the typical method of teaching by cases. . . .

THE CENTENNIAL HISTORY OF THE HARVARD LAW SCHOOL, *1817–1917* at 81 (1918).

[26] Perhaps the best (and most optimistic) exposition of the possibilities of case law becoming perfected through the spread of scientific views is found in Sir Frederick Pollock's essay on *The Science of Case Law,* reprinted in JURISPRUDENCE AND LEGAL ESSAYS BY SIR FREDERICK POLLOCK 169 (Goodhart ed. 1961).

Pollock looked forward to the times when parties would be "moved by pure zeal for the advancement of legal science to make a point of carrying [important] cases to an ultimate appeal." Recognizing, however, that the parties always have interests that conflict with those of science, he suggested the possibility of making appeal compulsory in such cases or, again, making it

In other words, to Langdell and his disciples law was an inductive science, the cases being the data from which the true legal principles could be derived. "Under this system," wrote the disciple who carried the torch to Columbia, "the student must look upon the law as a science consisting of a body of principles to be found in the adjudged cases, the cases being to him what the specimen is to the geologist."[27]

It can be seen that Langdell and his followers regarded students as fellow-scientists who had to be trained to do the type of research and analysis that their professors did. Thus the modern law school —a distinct American phenomenon—became of central importance, not so much for training lawyers, as for furthering the science of law.[28] And it is to be noted that the law school's greater influence in America than in England is at least partially a reflection of the fact that the process of secularization has progressed further in this country since 1870.

Be that as it may, down to about 1930 the science of law meant the science of law based on the analysis of the cases. And some of the greatest names in Anglo-American law, such as Pollock, Ames, Williston, Scott and Prosser, are scholars who implicitly or otherwise adopted this conception of law.

"somebody's business to call the attention of the Court of Appeals to difficulties of this kind from time to time, and to submit cases to it for the purpose of obtaining judicial opinions, which should be of the same authority as the actual judgments of the court." For this latter purpose he suggested the creation of "a Ministry of Justice, Legal Department, or what else it may be called." *Id.* at 172.

[27] *Preface* to 1 W. KEENER, A SELECTION OF CASES ON THE LAW OF QUASI-CONTRACTS (1888). For an interesting discussion of the dramatic split the case method precipitated at Columbia, see J. GOEBEL, A HISTORY OF THE SCHOOL OF LAW, COLUMBIA UNIVERSITY, pt. 3 (1955).

[28] In a singularly suggestive essay on the history of the Harvard Law School, Dean Pound pointed out:

> For a century the single professed aim [of the Law School] was to conduct what is called a "national" school, seeking to prepare students to practice in any jurisdiction whose institutions are based upon the English common law. From 1871 to 1928 the statement in the catalogue spoke only of "such a training in the fundamental principles of English and American law as will constitute the best preparation for the practice of the profession in any place where that system of law prevails." Since 1928 the announced purpose of the school has included this with two other aims: to train law teachers, and to investigate problems of legal adjustment of human relations and discover how to meet them effectively.

Pound, *The Law School,* in THE DEVELOPMENT OF HARVARD UNIVERSITY, *1869–1929,* at 472, 476–77 (S. Morison ed. 1930).

The highwater mark of the science of law idea came with the establishment of the American Law Institute in 1920. Its aim was to "restate" the case law in a clear and logical form, the fear being that the large number of jurisdictions in this country created unnecessary confusion about the true principles of the law.[29] Using law professors (legal scientists) as reporters, the A.L.I. purported to have true scientific detachment: when conflicts of opinion developed, the reporters were to note the conflict and step aside. Only in the *Restatement, Second,* which has appeared during the period of what we term a new stage of the secularization of law, have reporters ventured to assert their own opinions on controversial issues rather than simply to report the conflict.[30]

We can see that by 1930, law, at least American law, was firmly established as a science. A hundred and fifty years earlier, in Blackstone's day, law had been a wilderness of confusion and ignorance. In the intervening years lawyers and legal scholars, demonstrating the propensity to subject chaos to reason, and to systematize the results, had succeeded in totally changing the prevailing conceptions of law, its sources, and, of course, its teaching. And if the optimism of the scientific lawyers of the Langdell-Ames era has palled in the light of reality—that is, if legal science has failed to discover the "first principles" of law or if, as seems more likely, the principles it has discovered somehow seem every day a little less relevant—we must recall that even so, the science of law is only following the pattern of the natural and physical sciences. Since the days of Spencer, Huxley and John Ficke, contemporaries of Langdell and Ames, pure scientists have also lost some of their optimism and dogmatism.[31] The widespread

---

[29] See generally H. GOODRICH & P. WOLKIN, THE STORY OF THE AMERICAN LAW INSTITUTE, *1923–1961* (1961).

[30] See the criticism levelled at Dean Prosser, the Reporter for the Restatement on Torts, for restating his own views, rather than the case law, in § 402A, which virtually imposes strict liability upon manufacturers for all manufactured products.

[31] A scientist, writing in 1933, made the following observation:

> Science has become self-conscious and comparatively humble. We are no longer taught that the scientific method of approach is the only valid method of acquiring knowledge about reality. Eminent men of science are insisting, with what seems a strange enthusiasm, on the fact that science gives us but a partial knowledge of reality, and we are no longer required to regard as illusory everything that science finds itself able to ignore.
> . . .
> This change in the scientific outlook seems to have taken place suddenly.

retreat from the certitude of scientific principles after about 1930 brings to a conclusion the third stage of the scientification of law.

Modern legal technology — making the science of law useful
Secularization, we have said, carries with it more than the notion of rationalism and scientific method; it also carries with it a strong urge or proclivity to make scientific knowledge useful.

By 1930 the science of law, meaning the analysis of cases, had developed to such a point that certain hard-headed men of the world began to challenge its usefulness. Their reaction was well expressed by Thurmond Arnold, who wrote a stinging, sarcastic reply to Dean Goodrich's spirited defense of the *Restatement:*

> When the writer was in law school, Williston's treatment of contracts was in one volume which seemed adequately to state the general dialectic of that general subject. There were only eighteen American law school reviews. Immediately after the war Williston had increased to five volumes, and there were twenty-four law school reviews. Then followed the Restatement of Contracts. Today Williston's new edition has increased to eight volumes and there are over sixty law reviews published in America, and about 250 current Anglo-American legal periodicals. The Restatement is as perfect as scholarship can make it. Williston on Contracts is certainly a very necessary addition to the perfection of the Restatement or he would not have published it. And the law reviews are known to contain the very pearls of the law. Yet the whole is beginning to be a great burden, particularly when it is repeated in all the other so-called legal fields. And the only thing that can stop it is a complete change of attitude which will produce a different and simpler type of legal literature.[32]

The so-called American Legal Realist movement began to set the tone of learned discussion of law in the thirties; and in the years following, most of the better American law schools reflected, at least in part, the Realist philosophy of law. That philosophy, if it

It is not yet sixty years since Tyndall, in his Belfast Address, claimed that science alone was competent to deal with all man's major problems. . . .
J. SULLIVAN, THE LIMITATIONS OF SCIENCE 138–39 (Mentor Book ed. 1952).
   Tyndall, of course, was a contemporary of Langdell and his faith in science is matched by Langdell's faith in the inductively derived principles of law — just, indeed, as Sullivan's doubts and lack of dogmatism about science corresponded both in time, and import, to the retreat of the legal realists from the scientific case method.
[32] Arnold, *Institute Priests and Yale Observers — A Reply to Dean Goodrich,* 84 U. PA. L. REV. 811, 822 (1936).

can be called philosophy,[33] was simply to make the law—the
science of law—more useful.[34] Dean Leon Green, writing in 1928,
expressed, perhaps as clearly as anyone, the common bond of
agreement shared by an essentially eclectic group:

> [A]ny science of law, is, at bottom, the science of the administra-
> tion of law. . . . Hence 'law' as here conceived is the power of pass-
> ing judgment through formal political agencies for securing social
> control.[35]

Unlike a true legal scientist of the Langdellian ilk, Dean Green was
quite willing to dismiss as inexplicable the scholarly (and indeed
epistemological) problem of the source of law. Like a technician,
however, he focused his attention on the practical aspects of the
problem. Insofar as the sources of law are apparent, he added,
"they are found in the judgment of individuals who are intrusted
with the power to pass those judgments."[36] Hence, he concluded,
the real problems of law were to contrive a language technique, a
judging technique, and a statistical technique whereby, in short,

---

[33] The skepticism about the philosophy underlying the legal realist movement is
based on a facetious remark by Arnold—and yet was it really facetious?
> Most of the literature of jurisprudence, to paraphrase William James, is
> tedious, not as hard subjects like physics and mathematics are tedious,
> but as throwing feathers, endlessly, hour after hour, is tedious. Therefore
> it has been the habit of more red-blooded students at Yale to ignore the
> subject.
Id. at 811.

[34] For a recent sympathetic discussion of the Legal Realists, see E. ROSTOW,
American Legal Realism and the Sense of the Profession, in THE SOVEREIGN
PREROGATIVE—THE SUPREME COURT AND THE QUEST OF THE LAW 3 (1962).
It is necessary to stress the "American" in legal realists, for some continental
legal writers have developed quite independently of Americans a school of
realism. *See, e.g.,* K. OLIVECRONA, LAW AS FACT (1939) (an analysis of force
as the reality of the legal system by a distinguished Swedish scholar).

[35] Green, *The Duty Problem in Negligence Cases,* 28 COLUM. L. REV. 1014–1016
(1928).

[36] *Id.* at 1014. Compare Dean Green's modern statement with the following
remark by a worldly eighteenth century clergyman, Benjamen Hoadley, Bishop
of Bangor:
> . . . whoever hath an *absolute authority* to *interpret* any written or spoken
> law it is he who is truly the Law Giver to all intents and purposes, and not
> the Person who first wrote and spoke them."
B. HOADLEY, SERMONS PREACHED BEFORE THE KING 12 (15th ed. 1717).
The Bishop's Sermon, preached on the text "my kingdom is not of this world,"
sought to establish that the visible Church had no divine authority. It excited

the science of law could be put to practical use solving solvable problems.[37]

The efforts of legal scholars since the Second World War have been precisely of this pragmatic, technological nature. Thus in a recent discussion of strikes by public employees, we find the President of the University of Michigan saying:

> It's not important whether, as a matter of theory, these strikes are legal. That is a purely academic question. . . . What must be realized is that, legal or not, they are occurring, and the lawyer's challenge is to find some means of dealing effectively with the strikes when they do occur.[38]

This statement, with its rather conscious lack of concern about "legality" is, I think, most extraordinary. I do not believe any lawyer in any century prior to the present one could have made such a statement, yet none could be more characteristic of the present. As stated at the outset, this type of statement is the third manifestation of the impact of secularization of the law.

The Development of Legal Education

So far we have tried to indicate, without critical comment, the long-term effects of secularization on the law. We have done so to provide a general background to the current debate on legal education, for with that background in mind we can readily see that the modern law school is in fact an admixture of the various tendencies we have already mentioned: rationalism, scientific method, and technology. Moreover it also retains, despite the long, searching process of secularization, some remnants of the mystical aspect of the law—corners which remain unilluminated by the clear light of reason.

We shall consider each of these several elements as they manifest themselves in, and play a part in the curricula of, the law schools of today. First, however, we shall offer a few general remarks about

one of the bitterest controversies of the age, the so-called "Bangorian Controversy"—just, indeed, as did the Legal Realists in the twentieth century with their no-nonsense attitude towards law. See N. SYKES, CHURCH AND STATE IN XVIIITH CENTURY 332–62 (1934).

[37] *See* Green, *supra* note 35, at 1014.

[38] President R. W. Fleming was quoted in a University of Michigan publication, 12 LAW QUAD. NOTES 2 (1967).

the influence of secularization on legal education itself. Though legal education is obviously a part of the broad notion of law, and as such has been subjected to the same general influences we have already discussed, it nevertheless has had its own peculiar reactions and responses to secularization.

Broadly speaking, secularization has produced two main reactions in legal education. First, the law taught to and learned by law students has drastically changed in form and content. Secondly, the types and qualifications of persons teaching law have undergone similar change.

In the early days of the common law, when the mystical aura of the law was an overpowering reality and the Inns of Court were de facto guilds, students were trained as apprentices. Learning the law itself was scarcely separable from learning to be a lawyer, a distinct way of life rigidly governed by the rules and regulations of the Brotherhood:

> Long habituation, both to the subject matter discussed and to the *ex parte* handling which they met with in the various exercises conducted in the Inns of Chancery and Inns of Court, tended to saturate the legal minds of those days in a remarkable degree with the learning of their profession.[39]

In short, law was like the priesthood—a way of life as well as a vocation.

Beginning sometime in the sixteenth century, the Inns of Court fell into gradual decay, and after about 1650 they ceased to function as teaching institutions.[40] Except for a few fitful unsuccessful experiments in the eighteenth and nineteenth centuries, they ceased altogether to teach young lawyers, though they retained monopolistic control over admission to the Bar.[41] The once proud apprenticing

[39] P. SMITH, A HISTORY OF EDUCATION FOR THE ENGLISH BAR 39–40 (1860).
[40] For a discussion of the causes of the collapse of the Inns of Court as teaching institutions, see 6 W. HOLDSWORTH, *supra* note 20, at 490.
[41] The depths to which the Inns fell is indicated by the following testimony given before a commission on legal education in 1854, by one who had read law at Lincoln's Inn.
> When I was a Student, I used to be marched up to the Barristers' table, with a paper in my hand, and I said, "I hold the widow—" the Barrister made a bow, and I went away; and the next man said, "I hold the widow shall not—" and the Barrister made a bow, and he went off; and that was the remnant of performing the Exercises.
ROYAL COMMISSION APPOINTED TO ENQUIRE INTO THE ARRANGEMENTS IN

system, touted as "England's third University," fell victim to the same secularizing forces that demolished such kindred institutions as the trade guilds and church monasteries. As a result, law students were literally thrown upon their own resources.[42] They tended either to read in law offices, thus being exposed to the narrowest, most technical attitude towards law conceivable, or to pursue the general course of reading prescribed by well-known lawyers and judges.[43]

This uninstitutionalized system of legal education which prevailed in England, and probably in this country as well, down to the middle of the nineteenth century has come under more or less constant fire of criticism by legal historians and others; but it may not be amiss to remind modern readers, who are perhaps overly inclined to put faith in institutional reforms, that though this system, or lack of system, produced many narrow-minded lawyers, it also produced some of the most civilized and learned

---

THE INNS OF COURT AND CHANCERY FOR PROMOTING THE STUDY OF LAW AND JURISPRUDENCE, 1854–1855 PARL. PAPERS 54 (testimony of William Whateley).

[42] The lack of institutional education was one (but only one) of Blackstone's motives for giving his lectures at Oxford. Thus he lamented, in a letter written long before he himself became the great Commentator on the law:

> We may appeal to the experience of every sensible lawyer, whether anything can be more hazardous or discouraging than the usual entrance on the study of the law. A raw and inexperienced youth, in the most dangerous season of life, is transplanted on a sudden into the midst of allurements to pleasure, without any restraint or check but what his own prudence can suggest; with no public direction in what course to pursue his enquiries, no private assistance to remove the distress and difficulties which will always embarrass a beginner. In this situation he is expected to sequester himself from the world and by a tedious, long, lonely process to extract the theory of law from a mass of undigested learning. . . .

Letter from William Blackstone, Jan. 28, 1745, in L. WARDEN, THE LIFE OF BLACKSTONE 56–57 (1938). Blackstone's other, perhaps more compelling, reason for giving his lectures was a strong desire to reach Oxford students who, as gentlemen of property, would one day be members of the squirearchy which controlled England. That such students should be ignorant of the law they would one day administer he thought atrocious. 1 BLACKSTONE, COMMENTARIES *8–10 (1770). For a modern historian's interpretation of Blackstone's political motives in this reform see Lucas, *Blackstone and the Reform of the Legal Profession,* 77 ENG. HIST. REV. 456 (1962).

[43] Fulbeck's *A Director or Preparative to the Study of Law,* published in 1599, appears to be the earliest book of this genre; but during the seventeenth and eighteenth centuries the number expanded considerably. Among the better known lawyers and judges preparing such lists and advice were Sir Matthew Hale, Roger North and Lord Mansfield.

lawyers ever to grace the Bar in both England and this country. Indeed, rather paradoxically, the law's claim to being a learned profession dates in many ways from the period 1650 to 1850. For "law student law," not being subject to any institutional definition, was a subject of more or less continual speculation and debate, in which such lofty souls as John Milton felt free to participate.[44] Perhaps only in those circumstances could a judge advise his son: "Nothing is so likely to improve you in that most material qualification for a lawyer, as translating Greek and Latin oration into English."[45] Among the lawyers trained in England without benefit of institutional instruction were Sir William Jones,[46] Blackstone and Bentham. And in this country may be counted almost all of the so-called "Founding Fathers," men who were philosophers of law first and lawyers only second.

We are undoubtedly correct in assuming today that institutionalized learning is necessary, though, as we shall see, we might not all accept the rationale of Langdell's scientific analysis—the force that more than any other made law a university subject. Nevertheless the experience of the eighteenth and early nineteenth centuries, an age of truly heroic thinkers, serves to remind us that though under-institutionalization may be a grave and costly error,

---

[44] See J. MILTON, *Of Education,* in JOHN MILTON: COMPLETE POETRY AND SELECTED PROSE 663, 670–71 (Mod. Lib. ed. 1950).

[45] MEMOIRS OF THE LIFE OF SIR JOHN EARDLEY WILMOT 45. Mr. Fifoot, speaking of the leading law figures of the eighteenth century—the period during which legal education was so frightfully unorganized—said: "Somers was the patron of Locke and Newton, Lord Thurlow had the friendship of Cowper and Johnson and corresponded with Lord Monboddo on the remote, if fascinating, topic of Greek accents, and even Lord Hardwick essayed, not too auspiciously, to emulate the success of Addison and Steele." C. FIFOOT, LORD MANSFIELD 32 (1936).

[46] Sir William Jones (1746–1794) was a High Court Judge in India, who learned Persian, founded the Asiatic Society of Bengal, and became one of the first western scholars to master Sanskrit. Through his studies and translations of that ancient language, he came to be regarded as the "father of comparative philology." 2 J. SANDYS, A HISTORY OF CLASSICAL SCHOLARSHIP 439 (1908). His *Essay on the Law of Bailments* (1796) is one of the most learned law books ever published, the author drawing upon the Hindu, Roman and Greek sources as well as the common law. His advice on becoming a good lawyer is rather typical of the day. "[A]n Englishman's real importance in his country will always be in a compound ratio of his virtue, his knowledge, and his eloquence; without all of which qualities, little real utility can result from either of them apart. . . ." P. SMITH, *supra* note 39, at 122. For a recent study of this great, and too little remembered lawyer and man, see R. MUKHERJEE, SIR WILLIAM JONES (1908).

institutionalization of anything, and especially of education, is done at a price. And the more legal education becomes the private concern of lawyers, the more likely it is to become excessively legalistic and deprived of its more elevated and elevating aspects.

Over-institutionalization can also be detrimental, and there is some evidence that this may be a present problem. The widespread movement among law faculties to remove course requirements, and at the same time increasingly to permit students to take extra-legal course work, is the manifestation of a certain distrust or uneasiness toward the established, institutional definitions of legal education. This uneasiness I take to be a healthy sign. Given the pace of secularization in recent years I believe the definition of "law school law" should be the subject of prolonged debate in order to make legal education comport with the changing attitudes toward law itself. Of course abolishing required courses is a negative act that scarcely resolves the issue, but it serves the practical purpose of removing unnecessary restraints that would otherwise deter the better, more creative students from studying law. I shall return to this point later.

The institutionalization of legal education

Since the late eighteenth century, when legal education was institutionalized for the first time in this country, "law school law" has passed through three distinct stages of development which clearly reflect the process of secularization already described. It has been transformed from a body of "rules," taught *ex cathedra* and learned by rote, to a system of "principles," searched for and inductively ferreted out of cases, and then to a bundle of skills which are to be brought to bear upon relevant data, legal or otherwise, in order to formulate public policy.

In the first stage of institutionalized legal education the professor, usually a retired judge with long experience at the bar, laid down "the law." His lectures, like the treatises that were then being published with such astonishing frequency, usually consisted of a series of rules, together with appropriate statutory and judicial authorities. Students were at great pains to transcribe them as nearly verbatim as possible; and later, when properly bound and annotated, they became the lawyer's Bible. Though the lectures were often published (Blackstone's, Kent's, and Story's treatises were all delivered originally as lectures) most professors kept their lecture notes under lock and key, never allowing students to have access to them. Lectures were to be heard, not read, and classroom discussion was, in the continental fashion, probably almost nonexistent.[47] An exception was John Austin, who apparently urged his students to push him to the wall on every point. After only three years, however, he was forced to give up lecturing because of poor attendance.[48]

The lecture system of rule-teaching and rote-learning continued to dominate American law schools down to the late nineteenth century, the most significant change in the system being the introduction of the idea of a curriculum of distinct law "courses," rather than a series of lectures. In 1846, after Story's death, Harvard divided its law studies into three parts. The first, or elementary, part consisted of a study of Blackstone and Kent; the second part, or "fundamental subjects," consisted of Real Property, Equity, and Constitutional Law; and the third part, the "less fundamental" courses, consisted of Pleading, Bills and Notes, Domestic Relations, Evidence, Shipping and Admiralty, Bailments, Wills, and Partnerships (with Insurance and Agency being offered every second year).[49] Though the courses continued to be rule teaching in lecture form, the division of law studies into distinct courses was an indispensable step in the subsequent development of Langdell's scientific law school.

The result of rule-teaching law can be readily surmised; it produced lawyers who regarded the law as a body of rules, a bar that argued cases in terms of rules, and courts that decided cases on the basis of rules. Naturally, therefore, the greatest premium was put on knowledge of the rules, so it is not surprising that when Justice Bradley of the United States Supreme Court addressed the Law Department of the University of Pennsylvania in 1878, he commended to the students the example of the lawyer who

[47] For an eloquent defense of the continental system of lecturing in the face of overwhelming pressure for the case method, see Tiedeman, *Methods of Legal Education,* 1 YALE L.J. 150 (1892).

[48] Austin's note to himself read: "I . . . entreat you, as the greatest favour you can do me, to demand explanations and ply me with objections—turn me inside out. I ought not to stand here, unless, etc." 1 LECTURES ON JURISPRUDENCE 7 (Austin ed. 1863).

[49] CENTENNIAL HISTORY OF THE HARVARD LAW SCHOOL, *1817–1917,* at 74–75 (1918).

read and reread Blackstone until he had become "a veritable walking Commentary."[50]

Clearly the institutionalization of legal education in lecture form reinforced rule teaching, which in its turn gave "law school law" of that period certain characteristics similar to that of the earlier days of the Inns of Court. The presumed omniscience of the lecturer as a source of authoritative rules,[51] together with learning by rote, produced something of a priestly class of lawyers with a priestly attitude towards the law. Thus in the nineteenth century, during which the idea of science was so influential and the scientific method developed so remarkably, lawyers still learned that law was a body of preexisting rules which they had no power or authority to alter, and under which they had a solemn duty to serve in such a way as to protect and preserve its integrity. These inhibitions, derived from the highest motives and deepest of convictions, resulted in a far reaching policy of laissez faire. It took the Legal Realists, with their Puckish disrespect for "Our Lady, the Law," to shake these inhibitions and free lawyers of their restraints.

The institutionalization of legal education in the nineteenth century thus initially created an attitude toward law that did not comport, and indeed clashed, with the rational, scientific world of which it was a part. There was increasingly in that period a need for law schools and their rule-teaching system to be secularized. The case method met that need.

After 1870, when Langdell's case method was first introduced at Harvard, the lecture system began to give way to the new "scientific" form of legal education. Rather than hand down a set of rules to the student, the professor, often with blistering questions

[50] Justice Bradley's description of the method used by the lawyer (George Wood of the New York Bar) was as follows:

> It was his custom for many years in the earlier part of his professional life, when not over-burthened with business, to read a chapter of Blackstone of a morning and then to take a long walk, and repeat to himself all that he could remember of what he had read, even to the very words and phrases in those parts that were important, such as definitions and the like. If not satisfied with the first trial, he would repeat the process, on the succeeding day, and in this manner, chapter after chapter, he went through the commentaries, until they were so perfectly mastered both in matter and form, that he became almost a walking commentary himself.

J. BRADLEY, LAW, ITS NATURE AND OFFICE AS THE BOND AND BASIS OF CIVIL SOCIETY 39 (1884).

[51] For examples of the adoration inspired by a great lecturer of the law, Theodore Dwight, see J. GOEBEL, *supra* note 27, ch. 2.

and sarcastic retorts, would help the novice to find for himself the principles of law. The "principles," of course, underlay the rules.

The rationale of the system was simple. The professor, who had read all the cases in a given field, could select those most illustrative of the basic principles; and the student, in his innocence, would read the cases precisely as one reads the newspaper, so that the professor, through a line of questions, could lead the student to see the "real" meaning of the case. That is, he forced the student to discover inductively the "principles" of law.

The case method had several built-in assumptions that have never been altogether accepted, though the system itself spread like wildfire after about 1910. Langdell, in one of his few published statements on the method, said:

> [I]f printed books are the ultimate sources of all legal knowledge—if every student who would obtain any mastery of law as a science must resort to these ultimate sources, and if the only assistance which it is possible for the learner to receive is such as can be afforded by teachers who have travelled the same road before him,—then a university, and a university alone, can afford every possible facility for teaching and learning law.[52]

Now this system, based on so many "ifs," has largely ceased to exist, at least in its pure form. This is partially true because of the attacks of the Legal Realists, but more so perhaps because of a "silent revolution" carried out by practical, often quite unphilosophical teachers.

It is not my purpose to debate the merits of the case method as such. No subject has elicited more learned (and not so learned) discussions. And rightly so, for despite the fact that in some circles, especially at Yale, belittling the method has become something of an academic pastime, it remains (and here I express my own opinion) the most creative single contribution that America has made to educational theory. "I do not know if there is anything," wrote James Bryce in 1888, referring to Langdell's Harvard Law School, "in which America has advanced more beyond the mother country than in the provisions she makes for legal education."[53]

---

[52] Address by Professor Langdell, November 5, 1886, *printed in* 3 L. Q. REV. 124, 125 (1887).

[53] L. BRYCE, 2 THE AMERICAN COMMONWEALTH 487 (1888). For Pollock's equally laudatory appraisal of Langdell, see F. POLLOCK, THE EXPANSION OF THE COMMON LAW 6-8 (1904).

And Josef Redlich, an Austrian legal scholar commissioned by the Carnegie Foundation in 1914 to make a study of legal education in the United States, concluded after a study of Germanic thoroughness:

> Whatever judgment may be passed upon the significance and value of this method, one thing is clear at the outset even to the continental observer: it is an entirely original creation of the American mind in the realm of law, and must be comprehended and appraised as such. It is indeed particularly noteworthy that this new creation of instruction in the common law sprang from the thought and individual characteristics of a single man, Christopher C. Langdell, who as the originator of this method, became the reformer of the Harvard Law School, and in this way of American University law schools in general.[54]

The modern American law school owes its present form to the case method.

While, as I have said, I do not wish to debate the merits of the case method, I do want to stress the ways that it marked a distinct stage in the secularization of American legal education, and how at the same time it has in many ways outgrown its usefulness for the present day.

The case method was the *ne plus ultra* of the nineteenth century tendency to convert all forms of learning into "sciences" based on the scientific method. The case method not only applied reason to law, it made law a science; and it not only made law a science, it made it an inductive science.

This last point was of paramount importance, for it placed law on the same footing in the academic world as the burgeoning physical and social sciences, rather than on the level of the lethargic moral sciences, which it had occupied first on the continent and later in England.[55] As a result law became a part of the main

[54] J. REDLICH, THE COMMON LAW AND THE CASE METHOD IN AMERICAN UNIVERSITY LAW SCHOOLS 9 (1914).

[55] The origins of the University of Oxford, and to a less extent the University of Cambridge, are shrouded in mystery and legend giving rise to much scholarly debate. *See, e.g., Preface and notes to ch. 1,* 3 THE UNIVERSITIES OF EUROPE IN THE MIDDLE AGES (F. Powicke & A. Emden eds. 1936). Even so, however, the history of law teaching at these institutions is clear at least in this respect: before the Inns of Court, as common law teaching institutions, had risen to eminence, and indeed before the Royal Courts were situated permanently in Westminster (as demanded by the barons in Magna Carta), the teaching of canon and civil law was firmly entrenched in both Oxford and Cambridge.

stream of modern educational experimentation and development; and as an inductive science, it became a charter member of the new secularized, research-oriented universities coming into being at the end of the nineteenth century. As Redlich observed:

> If one adopts this point of view assumed by the leading American teachers of law, according to which Langdell's mode of instruction is nothing more than the application of the [scientific] method to the study of law, then, certainly, his reform appears no longer as an organically disconnected intrusion into the historically developed system of American legal education, but rather as a natural link in the chain of universal reform which affected all American higher education, and especially the American college, during the last half-century, and most strongly after 1870. . . . Under the pressure of public opinion the old course of study, dominated, and from this point of

---

Indeed in 1271 Roger Bacon complained that "a civil lawyer is more praised in the Church of God, even if he be skilled only in civil law, and ignorant of canon law and theology, than a Master in Theology, and he is sooner chosen for ecclesiastical dignities." Quoted in H. MAXWELL-LYTE, HISTORY OF THE UNIVERSITY OF OXFORD 55 (1886). But the clerical lawyers fell into disfavour at the time of the Reformation. Henry VIII, "stung with the dilatory pleas of the *Canonists at Rome* in point of his marriage, did in revenge destroy their whole Hive throughout the Universities." WORDSWORTH, SCHOLAE ACADEMICAE 137 (1877). But not for long. For the need for civilians to serve as ambassadors and negotiators with foreign countries forced him to establish, in 1540, Regius Professorships of Civil Law at both Universities.

Down to 1758, when Blackstone's Viner Chair was established in Oxford— the first at either University for the study of the common law—all law teaching in both Universities was the responsibility of the Regius professors. Sir George Downing, who died in 1749, left his estate in trust to Cambridge to establish a new college: the will was taken into Chancery, and it was not until 1800 that it was extricated, financially repleted, its grandiose plans considerably compromised; one consequence, however, was the Downing Chair of English laws created in 1800, upon the advice of Blackstone, and filled by Edward Christian, an editor of the *Commentaries*. D. WINSTANLEY, EARLY VICTORIAN CAMBRIDGE, ch. 1 (1955).

Though the most eminent modern historian of Cambridge tells us that "Judged by [prevailing] standards the professors of civil law cut a respectable figure," D. WINSTANLEY, UNREFORMED CAMBRIDGE 125 (1935), it remains nonetheless true that "a harry soph's gown and a law degree continued to be the refuge of the lazy and the dullard." WORDSWORTH, *supra* at 140–41.

In the nineteenth century the Faculties of Law along with the rest of the University were substantially reformed. Of course the Viner Chair remained in Oxford, though it fell considerably in prestige down to 1882 when Dicey was given the appointment just as did the Downing Chair at Cambridge until 1900 when Maitland was appointed. For a discussion of the development of the law faculties (as opposed to the Chairs of law) at Oxford and Cambridge, see generally F. LAWSON, THE OXFORD LAW SCHOOL (1968); D. WINSTANLEY, LATER VICTORIAN CAMBRIDGE (1947).

view deadened, by classical instruction, could no longer remain. It must, rather, adapt itself to the pressure of the modern tendency originating, in all American education, in the unbounded progress of the technical and natural sciences. . . . The method of Langdell and his pupils, taken in connection with the simultaneous appearance of important investigators in legal history, such as Thayer, Bigelow, and others, lifted law schools at one stroke, as it were, to this same level of genuine "science."[56]

Of course the "modern tendency" to which Redlich refers is that which I have described as "secularization;" and no statement could make it clearer that law and legal education have been made over in conformity with the American technological society.

We might add that it was no mere coincidence that Charles W. Eliot, the man who did so much to remake Harvard College in the modern form of Harvard University,[57] appointed Langdell to be a professor and later Dean of the Law School. And the appointment was no routine one. Eliot went to the trouble to dig him out of relative obscurity in a New York law office. "He was so little known by members of the governing boards," Eliot later recalled, "that he was asked to give the names of some New York lawyers who were in a position to answer enquiries as to his qualifications for a law professor."[58]

[56] J. REDLICH, *supra* note 54, at 17.

[57] For a comprehensive survey of Eliot's influence on Harvard see THE DEVELOP-MENT OF HARVARD UNIVERSITY, *1869-1929* (S. Morison ed. 1930). For a more general account of this great educator's work see H. JAMES, CHARLES W. ELIOT (1930).

[58] CENTENNIAL HISTORY OF THE HARVARD LAW SCHOOL, *1817-1917*, at 228 (1918). Eliot's reasons for selecting Langdell were apparently altogether personal. As he put it:

> I remembered that when I was a junior in college, in the year 1851-1852, and used to go often in the early evening to the room of a friend who was in the Divinity School, I there heard a young man who was making the notes to "Parsons on Contracts" talk about law. He was generally eating his supper at the time, standing in front of the fire and eating with a good appetite a bowl of brown bread and milk. I was a mere boy, only eighteen years old; but it was given me to understand that I was listening to a man of genius. In the year 1870 I recalled the remarkable quality of that young man's exposition, sought him in New York, and induced him to become Dane Professor.

Quoted in J. AMES, *Christopher Columbus Langdell,* in LECTURES ON LEGAL HISTORY 464, 473 (1913).

Langdell and his case method thus made legal education what it had never been before, a full-fledged, legitimate part of university learning—a status it scarcely had before 1870 in this country and has attained only recently in England (in 1900 Maitland read a paper entitled *Is There a Place for Law in a University?*—a question he answered, at best, with equivocation).[59] And if a few university faculty members (I almost said "purists") once objected to professional schools being part of a university (in 1921 Thorstein Veblen asserted that "law schools belong in the modern university no more than a school of fencing or dancing"[60]) virtually no one today challenges the propriety of the law school's place in the university. This achievement is Langdell's greatest contribution to both legal education and legal history. It is also the best evidence of the effect of secularization on legal education, for Langdell did not make legal education a part of university learning by "humanizing" it; he made it an inductive science at a time when the idea of a university, and indirectly knowledge itself, was being similarly secularized in terms of the scientific method.

[59] See F. MAITLAND, COLLECTED LEGAL PAPERS (1911). Compare, also, Dicey's remarks in his Introductory Lectures as Vinerian Professor at Oxford in 1883:
> [I]f the question whether English law can be taught at the Universities could be submitted in the form of a case to a body of eminent counsel, there is no doubt whatever as to what would be their answer. They would reply with unanimity and without hesitation that English law must be learned and cannot be taught, and that the only places where it can be learned are the law courts and chambers.

W. HOLDSWORTH, SOME LESSONS FROM OUR LEGAL HISTORY 171 (1928).

[60] T. VEBLEN, THE HIGHER LEARNING IN AMERICA 211 (1918). In making this pungent remark Veblen was obviously ignorant of Fortescue's description of legal education in the Inns of Court during the "Golden Age" of the fourteenth century. Fortescue tells us that
> In these greater inns, indeed, and also in the lesser, there is, besides a school of law, a kind of academy of all the manners that the nobles learn. *There they learn to sing and to exercise themselves in every kind of harmonics. They are also taught there to practice dancing and all games proper for nobles, as those brought up in the King's household are accustomed to practise.* In the vocations most of them apply themselves to the study of legal science, and at festivals to the reading, after the divine services, of Holy Scripture and of chronicles. This is indeed a cultivation of virtues and a banishment of all vice.

J. FORTESQUE, *supra* note 6, at 119 (emphasis added). For a perceptive account of Veblen, his ideas on education, and their effect on law and legal education, see D. RIESMAN, THORSTEIN VEBLEN: A CRITICAL INTERPRETATION (1953).

As Langdell converted legal education into an inductive science, he also brought about a drastic change in the qualifications of those responsible for training law students. Law professors, he insisted, had to be legal scientists—men who had done research into the law as embodied in judicial opinions. He expressed himself with particular clarity on this point in a way that indicated the nature of the change he was bringing about:

> I wish to emphasize the fact that a teacher of law should be a person who accompanies his pupils on a road which is new to them, but with which he is well acquainted from having travelled it before. What qualifies a person, therefore, to teach law is not experience in the work of a lawyer's office, nor experience in dealing with men, nor experience in the trial or argument of cases—not, in short, in using law, but experience in learning law.[61]

The result of this change in professorial qualifications was dramatized by Langdell's appointing James Barr Ames to be assistant professor at the age of twenty-seven, full professor at thirty, and Bussey Professor at thirty-two. The young man had not practiced law for a single day at the time of his appointments.[62] One need only recall the age and background of earlier professors of law, men like Judge Tapping Reeve, Chief Justice Parker (the first Royall Professor at Harvard), Chancellor James Kent, and Justice Joseph Story, to appreciate the magnitude of the innovation. The rationale, of course, was that Ames, though still of tender age and wholly inexperienced at the bar, was an expert in the particular field of law he would teach. Ames had read and analyzed all the cases in the field of torts and scientifically had arrived at principles which were otherwise quite undiscoverable. Hence the youthful teacher was better qualified to teach his subject than all the judges or lawyers at the bar. For, to invert the well-known statement of Holmes, the essence of law school was logic, not experience.[63]

[61] Quoted in J. AMES, *supra* note 58, at 478.

[62] CENTENNIAL HISTORY OF THE HARVARD LAW SCHOOL, *1817–1917*, at 175 (1918).

[63] Though Holmes used the phrase more than once, O. HOLMES, THE COMMON LAW 1 (1881), I think it is significant that he first said, "[t]he life of the law has not been logic: it has been experience" in a review of Langdell's case book on Contracts. 14 AM L. REV. 233, 234 (1880).

Once legal education became the responsibility of academic
lawyers, as it rapidly did with the spread of the case method, the
nature of law school law, and the type of lawyers it produced,
naturally changed. As early as 1914 one commentator observed:

> The undoubtedly increasing influence that American university
> professors of law exert upon the appreciation and treatment of the
> fundamental problems of the legal profession in America, and the
> recognized importance of these professors in the development of the
> entire legal system, should be noted as constituting one of the most
> encouraging features of American public life.[64]

The nature of the change was two-fold. Such purely theoretical
education did become too ivory-towerish, too much a search for
principles that would bring "certainty" to the law, but with too
little concern with "substantial justice."

The second and possibly more significant result of legal education
having come into the hands of academic lawyers was perhaps less
obvious. The reaction to the excessive abstractions of the case
method took place in law schools primarily in the minds of academic lawyers who had no more practical experience than Ames. And,
as might be expected, their reaction expressed itself in academic
terms, as new theories or schools of thought: "legal pragmatism,"
"sociological jurisprudence," "legal realism," or "functionalism."
All of these movements were begun by legal scholars, not practitioners, in protest against a form of legal education that had lost
touch with reality. In a word, they sought a more result-oriented
form of law. "The major tenet of the 'functional approach,' which
they [the American legal realists] have so vigorously espoused,"
wrote Professor McDougal, "is that law is *instrumental* only, a
means to an end, and is to be appraised only in the light of the
ends it achieves."[65]

From our point of view, this meant that lawyers trained as legal
scientists were rebelling against the excessive abstractness of their
science. And when scientists turn from theory and try to make
their science practical and useful, they become "applied scientists"
or "technicians," which is precisely what legal scholars have
increasingly become since 1930. This is my reason for saying that

[64] J. REDLICH, *supra* note 54, at 5.

[65] McDougal, *Fuller v. The American Legal Realist: An Intervention,* 50 YALE
L.J. 827, 834–35 (1941).

legal education has been transformed in the twentieth century, from an inductive science based on the case method, into an applied science based on practical considerations. Such is, I think, the effect of secularization on American law.

REMNANTS BLOCKING THE PATH OF LEGAL REFORM

If, as I have suggested, Anglo-American law and legal education have in fact been secularized, one would expect to find modern law schools primarily concerned with training students to become technicians skilled at wielding the instrument of law to attain socially desirable ends. And they are so concerned—up to a point. Still, it would be a gross exaggeration, if not a simple misstatement, to say this is being done in most law schools today. Though it is probably true as a general rule that the better the law school the more secularized it is likely to be, contemporary legal education is by no means so uniform in content or homogeneous in quality as to make the conclusion true in very many specific cases. The reason is simple: secularization like all long-term developments has not so much destroyed, as built upon, the past; and in the course of such prolonged developments certain practices are sometimes perpetuated by inertia into conventionally accepted truisms that survive long after their reason for being is forgotten. And so it is with modern legal education; two remnants, widely accepted as truisms, contribute heavily to the present unsatisfactory state of legal education by constricting artificially the scope of the debate about its true ends and means.

In the first place, a medieval aura of mystery still surrounds the vaunted "legal mind"—the end product of legal education—in a way that I think is positively harmful to contemporary needs.

Secondly, certain aspects of Langdell's ultra-inductive scientific method continued to be uncritically accepted, even by those who have rejected his reasoning. I shall say a word about each of these remnants in order to show how, together, they deter the process of secularization as well as the full and open debate about the ends and means of legal education.

The cult of the "Legal Mind"

We have already seen how Anglo-American legal education was conceived in the guild-like Inns of Court, nurtured as a part of the ritualistic and ceremonial rites of the Brotherhood of Barristers, and carefully shielded from odious comparison with the uninitiated by extraordinary monopolistic powers. It would be only expected that one legacy of such a heritage would be a fierce pride in the profession itself and the peculiar mentality it engendered. For lawyers from a very early period have taken an almost masochistic pleasure in the peculiar difficulty and abstruseness of their endeavors. Erasmus tells us that of all the learned professions law owed most to Folly. "[N]or," he added, "is there any other class quite so self-satisfied; for while they industriously roll up the stones of Sisyphus by dint of weaving together six hundred laws in the same breath, no matter how little to the purpose, and by dint of piling glosses upon glosses and opinions upon opinions, they contrive to make their profession seem the most difficult of all. What is really tedious commends itself to them as brilliant."[66]

This professional pride in the legal mind stemmed only partly from the guild heritage. Long after the Inns of Court had ceased to be a teaching institution and students were given virtually no institutional initiation in qualifying for the Bar, the idea that the legal mind had distinctive qualities persisted. The transcendental nature of law, like that of theology, made it something rather more than pure reason and distinguished it from other academic and scholarly ventures. Every schoolboy is familiar with the celebrated confrontation between King James I and Lord Coke—in which the noble lord, though he ended by trembling abjectly upon all fours, vindicated the uniqueness of the law and the legal mind. In Coke's words:

> [T]hen the King said, that he thought the law was founded upon reason, and that he and others had reason, as well as the judges: to which it was answered by me, that true it was, that God had endowed His Majesty with excellent science, and great endowments of nature; but His Majesty was not learned in the laws of his realm of England, and causes which concern the life, or inheritance, or goods, or fortunes of his subjects, *are not to be decided by natural reason but by the artificial reason and judgment of law, which law is an art which requires long study and experience, before that a man can attain to the cognizance of it:* and that the law was the golden met-wand and measure to try the causes of the subjects; and which protected His Majesty in safety and peace: with which the King was greatly offended, and said, that then he should be under the law, which was treason to

[66] D. ERASMUS, THE PRAISE OF FOLLY 76 (Hudson transl. 1941).

affirm, as he said; to which I said, that Bracton saith, quod Rex non debet esse sub homine, sed sub Deo et lege.[67]

As Coke affirmed that law was "over" man and the product of a special kind of reasoning, so law students continued to regard studying law as tantamount to taking Holy Orders. Thus when Ferne, the author of the celebrated *Essay on Contingent Remainders,* "resolved to dedicate himself to the study of the law, he burned his profane library and wept over its flames"[68]—just as the poet Gerard Manley Hopkins burned all his poems when he became a Jesuit novitiate.

Though modern law schools rarely stress and indeed often deny the transcendental aspects of the law, Coke's attitude continues today in only slightly less exaggerated form to color legal education. Thus freshmen law students are still treated as initiates who must be taken only gradually into the inner sanctum of law; and many law professors feel duty bound to make the initiation into the fellowship an unforgettable one. The late Professor Warren of Harvard, otherwise known as "Bull," had good reason for publishing a volume entitled *Memoirs of a Spartan Education.*[69] Developing the "legal mind" through close reasoning and hard analysis is still the hallmark of first year law school.

It is not my purpose to decry tradition. Professional pride in a rich heritage is a splendid thing—so long as it serves to maintain high standards and to inspire creative lawyers. Insofar as it deters or is detrimental to these ends it is not so splendid.

And if, as I have suggested, law has been secularized—if, that is, the transcendental nonsense has been replaced by some kind of functionalism—tradition, together with professional pride, may be deterring some very necessary reforms in legal education by perpetuating an obsolete pedagogical separateness.

Law, meaning a social instrument wielded by technicians, has no special claim to transcendental uniqueness. For all the other social sciences also purport to create skills and tools that will enable man to control better his social environment. In a very real

---

[67] 6 *Coke's Reports* 63 (1619) (emphasis added).

[68] Quoted in REMINISCENCES OF CHARLES BUTLER, ESQ. 119 (4th ed. 1824). Butler, one of the most learned conveyancers of the day, was the author of a famous introduction to Coke's edition of Lytlleton.

[69] C. WARREN, MEMOIRS OF A SPARTAN EDUCATION (1943).

sense, secularized law is but one of several tools in the modern social scientist's kit.

While law as an instrument of social reform differs from other social sciences in content it does so only as anthropology, for example, differs from economics. Otherwise, as Holmes long ago prophesied, law has come closer to the social sciences[70] — so close, indeed, that one can legitimately wonder if there is, or should be, any difference between "legal education" for functionalism, and training for the "social sciences." Various experiments of an inter-disciplinary nature appear to have given rise to an uneasy suspicion among some law faculties that the difference is currently exaggerated.

Modern debate about legal education should not, I think, be inhibited by false pride in the uniqueness of the profession or an excessive preoccupation with cultivating the virtues of the "legal mind." To the contrary, it should begin by seriously considering precisely how the legal mind differs from any other well-trained mind; whether those differences, if any, should be accentuated or

---

[70] In the review of Langdell's *Cases on Contracts* I have quoted so often in this article, Holmes expressed himself very clearly about the relationships between law and the social sciences. As he put it:

> No one will ever have a truly philosophic mastery over the law who does not habitually consider the forces outside of it which have made it what it is. More than that, he must remember that as it embodies the story of a nation's development through many centuries, the law finds its philosophy not in self-consistency, which it must always fail in so long as it continues to grow, but in history and the nature of human needs. As a branch of anthropology law is an object of science; the theory of legislation is a scientific study. . . .

14 AM. L. REV. 233, 234 (1880).

In a better known article Holmes elaborated on the point as follows:

> Every lawyer ought to seek an understanding of Economics. The present divorce between the schools of political economy and law seems to me an evidence of how much progress in philosophical study still remains to be made. In the present state of political economy, indeed, we come again upon history on a larger scale, but there we are called on to consider and weigh the ends of legislation, the means of attaining them, and the cost. We learn that for everything we have we give up something else, and we are taught to set the advantage we gain against the other advantage we lose, and to know what we are doing when we elect.

The Path of the Law, in COLLECTED LEGAL PAPERS 195.

We shall consider in the text below whether "the program in philosophical study" has or has not brought law and economics closer together, and if so how. At the moment my purpose is simply to demonstrate that Holmes looked forward to, and anticipated, the present trend to integrate law with the social sciences.

minimized; how legal education might be enriched and broadened by making use of techniques employed by other disciplines; and, above all, to what extent legal education itself should be merged (or "integrated," if you will) into the other social sciences.

The trend of secularization seems to suggest that legal education for the lawyer as a social scientific technician must be as broad as that for the guild apprentice was narrow. The ancient belief in the uniqueness of law—a remnant of the mystical past when law was vested with transcendental overtones—should not prevent us from breaking down guild walls in the interest of improving the quality of legal education and making law more useful to society.

The ultra-inductive science of law

The modern American law schools are enormously indebted to Langdell; and the proudest chapter in the history of American legal education must involve the rise and development of the case method. Still, Langdell's legacy has not been an unqualified good, as the legal realists have amply demonstrated. A considerable part of the current discontent with legal education is attributable to the remarkable grip that his ideas still have on American law schools.

Specifically the case method continues to dominate legal education in three ways. First, the notion of "fundamental" courses, those making up the first year and upon which everything else depends, stems directly from Langdell's scientific conception of law. Secondly, the body of knowledge (law school law) that students are required to master is still found in "casebooks." And thirdly, classes are still conducted in some variation of the socratic method, as if the prime aim of the teacher were to teach the student to extract principles from cases scientifically.

Each of these features of legal education, I must reiterate yet again, has become part of legal education only since 1870 as an adjunct to Langdell's case method. This is not to say that since Langdell and his disciples introduced these ideas they must be replaced by something else. It is, however, to say that the rationale for these three ideas—the "fundamental" first year courses, case-books, and classes conducted along socratic lines—was first provided by the case method, and insofar as that rationale is no longer viable I should think these adjuncts would likewise be suspect, unless they are valid for some reason other than that given by Langdell. They may well be, but I nonetheless suspect that much of the present unrest in law schools stems from the fact that no satisfactory justification for the continuance of this extremely stylized form of legal education has been given to the ever growing number of social science-conscious lawyers.

The rationale of the case method—or the inductive approach to law—has been undermined by three diverse trends that to some extent have been independent of the more vocal attacks by the legal realists. First, many law professors apparently no longer believe, as did Langdell and Ames, that the cases embody the "principles" of law. Indeed it seems probable that Holmes's legal pragmatism has been so effective that many of them (including, I suspect, the present writer) doubt that there are any such principles—in the cases, or anywhere else. I say this partially because of the form the casebooks themselves now take. It will be recalled that Langdell's casebooks contained nothing, absolutely nothing, but cases. The student, with the help of the professor, was supposed to discover inductively the principles of law hidden in them. It was not long before the "pure" casebook began to admit of modification, however. Extraneous materials in the form of law review comment and readings in extra-legal sources, were added to such an extent that by 1940 one review noted:

> In these days, when so-called case-books range from the bizarre to the prosaic, from mere reprints of reported decisions and citations of other opinions to the heterogeneous collections of diverse materials, one may question whether there is such a thing as a typical case book.[71]

And by 1953 Professor Harno could find that:

> The inclusion of extra-legal materials in the casebooks represents a trend in legal education that during the last two or three decades has become ever more apparent. The literal case-law instructor is today a rarity. A new generation of teachers is taking over. The new teacher believes that case instruction is a vital factor in legal education, but he recognizes also that law does not operate in a vacuum.[72]

This tendency to add extra-legal materials to cases suggests a loss of faith in either the proposition that the cases contain the law or that the law is a body of scientifically deducible principles, or

[71] Wilson, Book Review, 25 CORNELL L.Q. 653, 655 (1940).

[72] A. HARNO, LEGAL EDUCATION IN THE UNITED STATES 69 (1953).

perhaps in both. Still the casebook form remains, as does the inductive analysis, despite the demise of the case method's *raison d'être.*

A second indication that the case method has been undermined is the growth of non-common law courses. By his case method Langdell confined the scope of legal education to the judge-made common law. In this respect he was rather like his contemporary and admirer, A. V. Dicey, the author of the first book on English constitutional law, whose respect for the judge-made "rule of law" led to an almost pathological fear of administrative law.[73] Of

---

[73] Langdell's law school had no stouter, or more influential champion than A. V. Dicey, Vinerian Professor of English Law at Oxford from 1882 to 1909. In 1900 Dicey wrote a glowing appraisal of "Teaching of English Law at Harvard" in the *Contemporary Review* (Nov. 1899) [reprinted in 13 HARV. L. REV. 422 (1899)] in which he applauded the fact that "the professors of Harvard have, throughout America, finally dispelled the inveterate delusion that law is a handcraft to be learned only by apprenticeship in chamber or offices; they have convinced the leaders of the Bar that the Common law of England is a science, that rests on valid grounds of reason, which can be so explained by men who have mastered its principles as to be thoroughly understood by students whose aim is success in the practice of law." 13 HARV. L. REV. 422, 423–24 (1899). For a comparison of his appraisal of the attitude of the Bar in England, see note 59 *supra.*

As indicated in the text, Dicey was no less a champion of the common law than Langdell and his colleagues. Whereas the latter expressed their devotion for it by equating "legal education" with the study of (common law) cases, the former expressed his devotion negatively through increased agitation and frustration at the growth of other forms of law by legislation and administrative law, in derogation (as he conceived it) of the judge-made common law. Thus in his *Law and Opinion in England* (1905) (delivered originally as lectures at Harvard and dedicated to Charles W. Eliot) he expressed apprehension — and in his introduction to the second edition a decade later, hysterical fear — of what he called "collectivism." Public opinion, he observed (speaking of the "Social Justice" movement at the turn of the century) increasingly demanded legislation to change the common law so as to solve particular pressing problems; and each enacted statute, in its turn, created a new public opinion giving rise to stronger demands for more — and progressively more radical — legislation. Each statute, in short, started a chain reaction that threatened to destroy by fiat the common law, culminating in a collectivist society in which individual rights were left unprotected.

Likewise, in his *Law of the Constitution* (1885) (the first treatise on English Constitution Law, as opposed to history) Dicey aggrandized the common law by making the English Constitution depend upon "The Rule of Law" (a phrase he brought into modern usage). He asserted that this was based on the common law, built up slowly and silently by numerous fair-minded judges over the centuries, and provided the Englishman's essential safeguards against governmental despotism. Thus his love for the judge-made constitutional freedoms was matched by a no less intense hatred for the then newly emerging field of "administrative law" which he believed to be a systematic evasion by govern-

course in this country the expansion of both legislation and administrative law have, to some extent, dethroned the common law; and this fact of life is recognized in most law schools, though its true significance with respect to the case method's monopoly of legal education is scarcely appreciated. It is to the credit of Harvard that one of the more comprehensive treatments of law to appear in recent years, one embracing legislation, administrative law, and "private ordering," as well as the common law, has come from Langdell's own institution. I refer, of course, to the materials on *The Legal Process* by Professors Hart and Sacks.[74]

Still other evidence of the retreat from the case method is found in the gradual redefinition of "fundamental courses" that has been taking place since Langdell's day. We may take torts as an example. Torts is of course a relatively new academic course. It is well known that the first law book on the subject was not published

---

mental officials of the common law safeguards. To him, therefore, the example of the French "Droit Administratif"—then captivating the imagination of lawyers and scholars—posed a threat to the common law as potent as that of "collectivism" itself.

The history of legal education since the days of Langdell and Dicey has been, in part, a prolonged effort to broaden the base of law school law beyond the common law and to integrate into a system based on the case method a proper appreciation of other forms of law than judge-made law. To Felix Frankfurter must go, I think, much credit for stimulating scholarly interest in both legislative and administrative law in the face of the strictures of Dicey and the dogmatism of the Langdell-Ames group. Frankfurter attacked Dicey's view of administrative law in an article, *The Task of Administrative Law,* 75 U. PA. L. REV. 614 (1927). Moreover, I believe some of the most constructive impetus to reform legal education in this respect has come from his students, by whom I mean Professor Henry Hart, Paul Freund and my colleague Carl McFarland.

For a brief glimpse of Dicey, see W. HOLDSWORTH, THE HISTORIANS OF ANGLO-AMERICAN LAW 91–94 (1927); for a comprehensive survey of his influence, see Professor E. C. S. Wade's *Introduction* to A. DICEY, LAW OF THE CONSTITUTION (9th ed. 1939); for the most searching criticism of him, see I. JENNINGS, LAW AND THE CONSTITUTION (1933); and for an excellent contemporary appraisal of him, see Lawson, *Dicey Revisited,* 6 POL. STUDIES 109, 207 (1959).

[74] H. HART & A. SACKS, LEGAL PROCESS: BASIC PROBLEMS IN THE MAKING AND APPLICATION OF LAW (1958). It is perhaps appropriate that this material, like that of Langdell's first case book, was prepared for use by students in the Harvard Law School only and not for general publication; and it is altogether fitting that despite Professors Hart's and Sacks' Langdellian indifference to publishing it for general circulation, the fame and interest in the material has spread far beyond Cambridge. I have been told that the Hart-Sacks materials are currently used—in mimeographed form—in some twenty-five law schools, including the University of Virginia.

until 1859, when Francis Hilliard, an American, published *The Law of Torts and Private Wrong.* A year later, an Englishman, C. G. Addison, published *A Treatise on the Law of Torts or Wrongs and their Remedies.* And in 1870, when Nicholas St. John Green prepared an abridged version of Addison's treatise to use at Harvard, Holmes in reviewing it uttered one of his most extraordinary judgments. "We are inclined to think," he said, "that Torts is not a proper subject for a law book."[75] Nor, we might add, had the pre-Langdellian professors thought it a proper subject for a law course, for torts was not taught at Harvard until 1870, when Langdell assumed his professional duties. Immediately thereafter the curriculum was totally revamped in order to put certain "basic courses" in the first year. Among these courses was the newcomer, torts. In the words of the *Centennial History of the Harvard Law School:*

> With the advent of Langdell came an entire change in the curriculum, as well as a division between those courses which should be taken in the first year of law study, and those which, being more advanced, should be taken later. . . . Real Property was continued as an elementary course. Pleading became also a first year subject. The other courses in the first year were Contracts and Criminal Law, irregularly taught before, and Torts, which was entirely new. These five courses have constituted the work of the first year, or the greater part of that work, from that day to this.[76]

It seems rather odd that torts, a subject so novel in 1870, should become so basic immediately thereafter. The only explanation I can give to this puzzle is based on my own conjecture.[77] I believe that Langdell knew that torts and contracts were the common law equivalents to two basic categories of private Roman Law, namely

[75] Book Review, 5 AM. L. REV. 340, 341 (1871). This unsigned review is attributed to Holmes by Warren Seavey in his article, *Principles of Torts,* 56 HARV. L. REV. 72 (1942).

[76] CENTENNIAL HISTORY OF THE HARVARD LAW SCHOOL, 1817-1917, at 76.

[77] With respect to my inability to document the speculation set forth in the text, compare two remarks. H. T. Buckle (the great Victorian generalizer without facts) remarked: "How unhandsome it is of mankind to expect authors to give proof of what they assert and how silly it is of authors to give it!" A. HUTH, THE LIFE AND WRITINGS OF HENRY THOMAS BUCKLE 94 (1880). The other—which perhaps answers Buckle—was Bishop Henry Vaughn's dictum: "Where authority ends, influence begins." CUNNINGHAM, WILLIAM CUNNINGHAM 108.

delict and obligations. He knew further that the principles underlying those two categories, and the Roman Law generally, had been
fully developed, elucidated and refined by generations of Roman
lawyers. From these premises Langdell could have concluded, in
Austin's words: "In consequence of this mastery of principles, of
their perfect consistency, 'elegantia' and of the clearness of the
method in which they are arranged, there is no positive system of
law which it is so easy to seize as a whole."[78] If indeed Langdell
did reason this way, we can surmise that he decided to use the
inductive analysis of cases to identify, establish and perpetuate
the equivalent common law principles in the two fields in which
experience had proved that it could be done. Legal education in the
hands of genuine legal scholars could become the agency of system-
atizing the common law. And therein lay the promise — it would be
a de facto code, based upon scientific analysis. If true, this theory
would account for Langdell's own interest in contract and the
interests of his best students (Ames in tort and Keener in quasi-
contract) in "basic" subjects having rather obvious Roman law
equivalents.

Be that as it may, Langdell introduced torts as a basic course in
1870, and so it remains today. Yet the subject, presumably so basic,
has undergone traumatic change. Workmen's compensation cases
were first carved out of it, and now automobile negligence cases are
likely to be removed also. At the same time the law of insurance
has pervaded the subject so extensively, the economics of risk-
sharing have become so important, and concern about such practical aspects as damages and jury control have become so prevalent
that tort principles seem irrelevant even in torts. Moreover, the

---

[78] J. AUSTIN, *The Uses of the Study of Jurisprudence,* in THE PROVINCE OF
JURISPRUDENCE DETERMINED 366, 378 (Library of Ideas ed. 1954). This
whole essay would bear examination as a defense of Roman law as a basis for
modern legal education.

At first glance Austin's point of view appears to be diametrically the opposite
of Langdell's, for he insists that the very last thing a law student should study
is the law of his particular jurisdiction (including presumably the cases).
Rather the student should be first thoroughly grounded in the "principles" of
law as developed by the civilians. Having mastered the principle of law governing the basic legal relationship (which are common to all legal systems) the
student can then, but only then, turn to and master the law of his own, or
indeed any, jurisdiction.

As stated in the text, I believe Langdell sought to achieve the same ends
using specially selected cases, rather than the Pandects of Roman Law, to
inculcate in the novice the fundamental principles common to our American
jurisdictions.

Supreme Court has construed the first amendment so broadly as to make serious inroads into the scope of common law defamation and the right to privacy. Torts, in short, is now about as destitute of "basic principles" as any course could be. Yet it is still regarded today, as it was in Langdell's time, as one of "rocks" upon which legal education must be based.

I find this remarkable, for I have been trying to show how the case method has been undermined. Still, however, Langdell's first year is our first year; his method—briefing cases, analyzing holdings, socratic probing—is our method. In other words, legal education remains in form a kind of Procrustean bed in which all learning for lawyers is forced to lie. I think I know why Langdell and his colleagues made it so. Frankly I do not know why we do, unless it is pure inertia.

For the above reasons, I conclude that though we have more or less thoroughly rejected the philosophy of the case method, like Maitland's forms of action, it still rules us from the grave.

THE CURRENT FRUSTRATION

The reason for the current discontent in American law schools may be stated as follows: attitudes towards the law have become secularized at a faster pace than those towards legal education.

To the majority of law students, professors and alumni there is probably nothing wrong with that or with legal education. After all, the bar is well staffed, corporations are stoutly manned, judicial standards are high, legal scholarship continues to grow apace, and a fair share of the most idealistic reformers are law school graduates. Those who would minimize the discontent would undoubtedly say quite reasonably that secularization has kept legal education current while preserving the best of the past. They would point out that the virtues of the case method are now conjoined with judicious insights from outside the laboratory of the inductive legal science. Thus a modern casebook is not, as in Ames's day, a mere collection of cases, but an anthology of specific examples (cases) illustrating the types of "problems" involved, together with the most learned discussion, legal and otherwise, of those problems. And if the system is not perfect, it is nevertheless quite possibly the best there has ever been. Hence they would conclude that the process of secularization has made legal education ever more enlightened and ever more useful, and that this is precisely as it should be. Such I think is a facsimile of the answer that the great majority of law students and professors and alumni would give to the question today. And, as I say, they might very well be right.

Still, as we have noted, there is considerable discontent, and we must consider how the discontented might respond to the phenomenon of secularization and to what extent it has contributed to their discontent. As might be expected there are two main camps of dissidents: those who believe secularization has gone too far, and those who are frustrated because it has progressed no further.

Those frustrated by secularization having gone too far can likewise be subdivided into two groups: inductive scientists (that is, Langdellians), and idealists. The Langdellians we need discuss no further. Suffice it to say that they share basic convictions about the case method: they believe law is divisible into rather clear-cut fields based on rationally determined "principles"; that those fields (as defined largely since 1870) are inherent in the nature of law itself; and that, accordingly, their bounden duty is to teach, socratically, the students to analyze cases until they have reached the underlying immutable "principles." In the view of law students and professors and alumni of this kind, secularization has produced a group of woolly-minded, policy-oriented sociologists who now pass themselves off as lawyers; and the chief problem of secularization is to vindicate the integrity of law and to safeguard legal education from both their good intentions and their ignorance.

The other group of dissidents who believe secularization has gone too far are the idealists. These are not idealists in the technical, philosophical sense,[79] but in their general feeling that legal educa-

---

[79] Holmes regarded Langdell's case method as a form of abstraction very close to philosophical idealism.

> If Mr. Langdell could be suspected of ever having troubled himself about Hegel, we might call him a Hegelian in disguise, so entirely is he interested in the formal connection of things, or logic, as distinguished from the feelings which make the content of logic and which have actually shaped the substance of the law.

Book Review, 14 AM. L. REV. 233, 234 (1880). I confess to an inability to distinguish between philosophical idealists, natural lawyers, and legal positivists. Bentham and Austin, who were both revolted by Blackstone's natural law, have been called natural law devotees because they were committed to "the greatest happiness" principle; and Professors Lasswell and McDougal (who abhor no less intensely Professor Kelsen's positivism) have been also called natural lawyers because they posit the values of a free, democratic society and human dignity as the ends to which the legal system must aspire.

New directions in legal education

tion has somehow been debased by the very "functionalism" and result-oriented juristics that saved law from scholasticism. Law, they will tell you, is more than functionalism, more than policy, more indeed than the ends ascribed to it by value analysts such as Professors McDougal and Lasswell. And whatever more law may be than all this it is certainly greater than man himself. Among the idealists of this camp (and I include myself among them) may be counted Professor Fuller, whose faith in the morality of law is quite unshakable,[80] and Professor d'Entreve whose reassertion of natural law in an age of relativism is no less remarkable.[81]

To the secularized observer, however, these defenders of the ideals of law are evidence—yet more evidence—of secularization itself. For the process of secularization carries with it, as M. Eliade, the distinguished French anthropologist, has pointed out, a built-in source of frustration: the loss of the security of the myths of our past.[82] However rational we may become, he points out, we still have, as part of our heritage, a long past in which irrational mysticism in various forms of the "sacred" played a capital role. And though we may reason ourselves out of the past we cannot psychologically forget it. The memory, the yearning for forgotten myths, he tells us, is the source of frustration and friction.

[80] *See, e.g.,* L. FULLER, THE MORALITY OF LAW (1964).

[81] The reference is to A. D'ENTREVES, NATURAL LAW (1951), a warm, humane, eminently civilized discussion of the role of and need for some form of natural law in the modern world of scientific law. The present writer vividly recalls the occasion of a paper being read by Professor d'Entreves to the Faculty of the Yale Law School. His eloquent plea for some supra-rational standard of "legitimacy" to measure "legality" was kindly and courteously received by that group of "tough-minded" social science-oriented lawyers; but one still felt that many of them regarded the message as hopelessly irrelevant. The paper referred to was subsequently published under the title of *Legitimacy and the Law.*

[82] M. ELIADE, THE SACRED AND THE PROFANE: THE NATURE OF RELIGION 8–18 (1959).
  I find this book enormously suggestive because it seems to be as relevant to the law, and indeed to modern society generally, as it is to religion itself. Thus M. Eliade states his purpose to be
    to show in what ways religious man attempts to remain as long as possible in a sacred universe, and hence what his total experience of life proves to be in comparison with the experience of the man without religious feeling, of the man who lives, or wishes to live, in a desacralized world.
  Id. at 83.
  As the reader will have gathered from the earlier parts of this paper, I do think the laws have been as "desacralized" as religion itself. "Desacralization" as M. Eliade defines it, is in fact the negative reciprocal—or more simply, the cost—of a "secularization" as I have defined it.

M. Eliade calls this inevitable companion to secularization "desacralization." And it is, I suggest, the basis of the idealists' discontent with the secularization of the law, for M. Eliade's description of modern nonreligious man comports almost exactly with modern secularized law as we have described it:

> Modern nonreligious man regards himself solely as the subject and agent of history, and he refuses all appeals to transcendence. In other words he accepts no model for humanity outside the human condition as it can be seen in the various historical situations. Man *makes himself* and he only makes himself completely in proportion as he desacralizes himself and the world. The sacred is the prime obstacle to his freedom. He will become himself only when he is totally demysticized. He will not be truly free until he has killed the last God.[83]

One cannot read this passage without thinking of the leading movements of twentieth century legal philosophy — sociological jurisprudence, legal pragmatism, and American legal realism — and their struggle to replace "transcendental nonsense" with a "functional approach" to the law. For as we have already noted, the one point of agreement among those various schools was and is the firm conviction that law, whatever it might be, is neither a body of divinely conceived "rules" nor a system of logically discoverable, scientifically deducible "principles." And increasingly in the better law schools there is a consensus that law, at least that which forms the substance of legal education, is in fact an expression of societal preferences. This widely acclaimed, enlightened point of view is, as I say, but an application of M. Eliade's definition of the beliefs of desacralized man to the law. Modern legal educators are really teaching their students (to paraphrase M. Eliade's remarks quoted above) that as man makes himself, so lawyers make the law; but they do so only in the same degree as they desacralize both themselves and the law, for the prime obstacle to the true legal reform (which will bring about true freedom) is their lingering belief in the mysticism in themselves and the law.

If M. Eliade is right, it would seem that the only frustration presented by the growth of secularization is an unconscious and irrational clinging to and yearning for the past. And in this sense the discontent of the idealists is inevitable, one of the costs of progress. At the same time it is perhaps a warning of hard times

[83] *Id.* at 203.

which will come in the form of growing dissatisfaction and disaffection with law and the secularized world, unless we can somehow reconcile our mystical past with our ultrarationalistic scientific present.

The remaining category of malcontents are those who wholly endorse the functional approach to the law. To them the process of secularization has been tantamount to the spread of enlightenment, and their only lament is that secularization has not gone far enough. Thus their frustration stems from disappointment, the capital problem of modern legal education being in their opinion to contrive new ways to make the applied science, or technology, of law more useful.

This group—and it includes proportionally perhaps more students than it does faculty members—encounters two types of resistance: that of the "Old Guard" and that of newness. The "Old Guard," described above, tends to equate legal education with that which Langdell and Ames put together between 1870 and 1910—a first year based on fundamental courses which deal with the cases embodying the principles of our legal system, tort, contract, property, public law (criminal and constitutional law) and procedure; a commitment to "casebooks" as the basic source of legal knowledge; and some variation of the socratic teaching method calculated to sharpen analytical skills, rather than to convey positive knowledge in the manner of the still older lecture system.

To students and professors whose aim is to make the instrument of law ever more useful in a world rife with international tension, racial conflict, urban difficulties, monetary exchange problems, and burgeoning crime rates, this traditional world of legal education seems appallingly irrelevant and very possibly harmful, for it fails to prepare adequately those who as lawyers must deal with such problems. Specifically it teaches them to put too much faith in only one form of law, the common law; it places too high a premium on only one of many needed skills, analysis; and it is too devoid of the positive knowledge necessary to understand even the language of the social sciences which are more directly relevant to such quasi-legal problems. Thus when these "functionalists," who are eager to promote educational experiments to remedy these shortcomings, encounter a wall of unyielding and unsympathetic resistance from their tradition-oriented Langdellian colleagues, they can only become bitter.

If such bitterness is the cause of some of the present discontent with American legal education, it is not so major a cause as some would have us believe. At least in the better law schools "functionalists" and "realists" are no longer lonely aliens in a hostile world. In truth they probably outweigh in influence, if not in number, the Langdellians. Holmes, Pound, Jerome Frank, Lleweleyn, Lasswell and McDougal have fought and won the battle for recognition. Now the problem is simply one of fulfillment. The door is open, and the way is clear to those who wish to make law an instrument of social policy. All they have to do is to do it.

In other words, the problem that frustrates so many students and professors today is a deep dissatisfaction with the prevailing system of legal education, coupled with an inability even to envision the improvements they all sense are necessary. The fact that Langdell and his disciples are no longer realistic targets of abuse only adds to their frustration.

In Conclusion

We have tried to show how, broadly speaking, the society-wide trend toward secularization is the culmination of a centuries-long development that has transformed the Law from a "brooding omnipresence in the sky" into a down-to-earth instrument of social reform and, at the same time, translated (to use a Canonical term) the lawyer from a quasi-priestly figure into a social engineer. Legal education, we have also insisted, has both reflected and contributed to this long-term trend. "Law school law" has undergone a corresponding evolution from an apprenticeship for a ritualistic medieval guild, characterized by an awesome preoccupation with forms of action or other procedural points, to university training for inductive scientists, or applied scientists, which is consciously concerned with formulating social policy.

Any discussion of contemporary legal education, I have said, should take into account the phenomenon of secularization and its long-term effects; for secularization is, I am convinced, the underlying cause of much of the most agonizing discontent in American law schools and indeed in American society.

Conceding (as hopefully some readers will) the merit of the foregoing assertion, still many readers will complain that it scarcely justifies the prolonged peregrination into the past. For it leaves us, after all, precisely where we started—with all the problems of the present bearing down upon us and all the perplexities of the future looming before us. The reader has a right to expect that the writer, having gone so far into the past, will venture at least a little way into the future. And this I shall try to do briefly, bearing in mind the historian's occupational danger of (to use Mrs. Malaprop's rather splendid phrase) "anticipating the past." We shall consider both the negative and positive aspects of secularization in legal education and offer a few concrete suggestions as to the future.

The negative aspects of secularization

The most obvious effect of secularization has been the pressure to relate law and legal education more closely to our collective experience and to the solution of social problems. Put in this way, the effect is laudatory. As with most things, however, secularization has an evil as well as a good side, and its evil side is evil indeed.

As we have indicated, the process by which law is made more functional inevitably conjures up from the subliminal depths certain irrational yearnings for the certitude and omniscience afforded by the no longer rationally tenable forms of transcendental or suprahuman law. And though yearnings of themselves usually need not bother us, these yearnings for mystical forms of law are dangerous because they inevitably lead members of society to compare the rather shabby, mundane, faltering course of man-made law with the glory of Divine Law or Natural Law or simply the "Law of Laws." In a specialized system the comparison cannot fail to be odious. For social engineers, however highly motivated, can never match the inspiration of prophets; functionalism, however enlightened, still bears the unforgivable, if irradicable, taint of man himself. Secularization thus torments the souls of men while it gratifies their minds.

The current manifestation of this inner conflict is a paradoxical loss of respect for "legality" as a social sanction at the very time that the law, because of its humanitarian and egalitarian aims, deserves great esteem. Modern man, no longer *sub deo et sub legi,* feels himself morally free of the demands of externally imposed law that clash with his own innermost convictions. Predictably, the result is a generation of law teachers who find it difficult to believe — by this I mean profoundly believe — in the existence of law beyond what fallible courts say it is; a generation of law students who consequently do not learn to be restrained in any essential way by the law; and a generation of laymen who are markedly uninhibited by, and indeed contemptuous of, the sanctions of law. The appeal to a "Rule of Law" under such circumstances is rather pathetic and almost hopeless.

All this, I say, is attributable, at least in part, to the secularization and desacralization of law. And rational men, understandably proud of the progress made in replacing transcendental nonsense with functionalism, are puzzled and frustrated by the untoward consequences of enlightenment. What good is a tool, however potent, and an army of scientist-technicians, however skilled, if men neither recognize nor defer to law?

The most important question raised by the secularization of law with which modern legal education must contend, then, is this: granting that the "functional" approach to law is more adept at problem-solving than ever was the brooding transcendental form of law, does it follow that it is also as effective as an ideal for commanding the respect of the people? And if not, is *any* problem-solving technique or *any* group of legal technicians worth the cost which we have paid for functionalism? Worse still, does the functional approach not teach all manner of men to look to law as an instrument for *their* private or personal disposal? Surely no "social problem" could be so critical, or chronic, as that of people regarding law first as a means of gratifying their own wants, and only incidentally as imposing upon them responsibilities towards their fellow men and their society.

The pessimist, taking in at a glance both the lawlessness around him and the profusion of modern, policy-oriented, legal education, is likely to find a causal connection between the two and to blame the irreverent and jeering Legal Realists of the thirties and their uncritical followers for the unhappy result of secularization. Though few can state the point as eloquently as E. M. Forster, many must look back upon their efforts with the same sense of quiet cynicism as he did on the course of Twentieth Century reform generally.

> Fifty years ago, when I was young, the idea of a Problem was exhilarating. The nineteenth century had emphasized Progress. The early twentieth century, while not rejecting Progress, felt itself more realistic if it approached progress through problems. The problems lay about like sheets torn out of Euclid, all waiting to be solved and posed with

impeccable clarity. "Here is a completely new problem," a statesman would enthusiastically exclaim. And though people occasionally remarked that one problem often led to another, no one realized how sinister the remark was. With proper attention and adequate commercial resourcefulness all problems would be solved and God's great Q.E.D. peal out.

This attitude was scotched rather than killed by the First World War. . . . Disillusionment and distrust of problems began back in the 'twenties — the most clear sighted decade in our half-century. It realized that nothing had been solved, and so-called solutions were hydras who produced more heads than had been decapitated.[84]

History teaches us, however, that the problem of enforcing a law detached from divine or moral sanction is neither the original creation of twentieth century reformers nor the unique product of our present state of secularization. To the contrary, it has been, in one form or another, a perennial threat to all societies. Thus it was that a worldly Eighteenth Century prelate posed with singular clarity the problem confronting legal education today. Writing in 1750, Bishop Thomas Sherlock said:

Infidelity and immorality are too nearly allied to be separated; and though some have pretended to preserve a sense of Virtue without the aid of Religion, yet Experience has shewed that people who have neither Hope nor Fear with Respect to another World, will soon abuse *this* by indulging the worst of their Passions, and will not regard Man, when once they learn to disregard God.[85]

The problem of the mid-Twentieth Century is, therefore, the same as that of the Eighteenth or any other century: how to make godless men obey the law? With us the sanction of religion — the threat of Eternal Damnation — is lost. But because we can no longer rely upon fire and brimstone does not mean all is lost. Nor does it mean our problem is any easier. It simply means that a greater burden falls upon law, or the sanction of law, to preserve peace and harmony among men. For law is the most reasonable (or reasoned) of all societal sanctions. In a secularized world, society must rely more heavily upon it than upon religion. This is the challenge to legal education. And this is the shortcoming of

[84] E. M. FORSTER, quoted in London Times Literary Supplement (1964).
[85] T. SHERLOCK, SERMONS 8–9 (1750).

Functionalism: it is simply too limited in outlook. However enlightened and highly motivated, it is too result-oriented to transcend the particular and too worldly to inspire in the abstract. Its chief aspiration comes from an excessive devotion to—and this should never be forgotten—the ideal of "Justice" at a time when transcendental forms of law were themselves tied down and hidebound by legality.

The positive aspects of secularization
If, as we have said, secularization has undermined the influence of religion and discredited legality as social sanction, our world must indeed be in great danger of annihilation—as indeed it probably is. But secularization has not only destroyed; it has also created. And we must not forget this positive side of the centuries-long development we have described. It has exalted the ideal of Justice, and the course of secularization has been led, almost without exception, by men seeking substantial justice. And therein lies the clue—a straw in the wind—for modern law schools. In a world populated by ultra-rational men, Law must find its strength in Justice, not Legality.

Law schools must rid themselves of the vestiges of mysticism that, in days past, held laymen in awe of law and legality; and students must be trained to regard themselves as agents of justice as well as officers of the court. More important, they must be shown precisely what this responsibility entails. And establishing a course of instruction that will serve this purpose should be the great issue in legal education today.

Without purporting to show how to resolve this issue, I shall offer a few observations on the subject. The legal education of the future must be governed by a combination of two maxims. First, within the House of the Law there are many mansions—in which practitioners of all kinds, counsellors, judges, public servants, scholars and philosophers work in their several ways to further the course of, and to implement, Justice. Second, legal education, as an adjunct of Justice, must start with the proposition that the greater includes the lesser, the higher the lower, and not *vice versa*. That is, law schools must assume, as their basic premise, that the man who first understands his obligations to Justice will be better able to fulfill his legal "function," whatever it might be. Justice, in a word, must take precedence over law.

With this premise in mind we can see that the law school curriculum should promote justice in three ways: first, by serving the needs of private individuals (the "practical aspect"); second, by dealing with problems too complicated or too far reaching to be resolved on a piecemeal basis (the "collective aspect"); and third, by encouraging speculation about the nature and role of law in any of its variegated forms (the "philosophical, or theoretical, aspect"). Of these three aspects, only the third speaks for itself. Thus I shall say a word about the first two.

By the "practical aspect" of Justice I mean that which involves, and can be attained through satisfying, the claims and demands of private parties. Such law office inventions as the "chattel mortgage" and the "sale and lease-back" have been notable contributions to Justice in this sense. In legal education, the "practical aspect" is effectuated by training lawyers to provide individuals with the legal means to accomplish their legitimate aims, and, perhaps more importantly, by training both lawyers and judges to participate intelligently and equitably in the resolution of private disputes. The law office and the court room are the chief foci in the process of "practical" Justice, and the Legal Realists, with their concern for the factors which influence judicial decision-making, have done much to advance this aspect of Justice.

The "collective aspect" of Justice concerns those problems which must be dealt with not in terms of individuals but rather "in the lump." I refer specifically to such so-called "structural" problems as poverty, slum conditions, economic depression, and racial discrimination. Legislation and to a lesser extent administrative orders, rather than judge-made law, are the chief means by which the "collective aspect" of Justice is and must be attained. In a law school curriculum dealing primarily with the problems of private parties before the courts, these broader collective issues are likely to be ignored or dealt with inadequately.

Traditionally most legal education has concentrated on the first (the "practical") and the third (the "theoretical") of these aspects. Continental law faculties have stressed the third; American law schools, especially those employing the case method, have stressed the first. The second has generally been neglected, and lamentably so. For it has forced law schools to emphasize—overemphasize, I should say—the judge as the means of attaining justice through legal reform. And as in the case of Lord Mansfield's gallant, but futile, efforts to incorporate the *lex mercatoria* into the common law, there are real limits on the most enlightened judges as innovators.

The role of the judge has been overemphasized, and the collective aspect of justice neglected, because there has never been an adequate means of dealing with collective problems. There was, of course, legislation. But legislation without knowledge is at best dangerous. Now, as a result of fifty years of social scientific research, we have for the first time a body of knowledge on virtually all subjects. And this knowledge, properly used, gives us power to deal with complex social problems in ways simply unknown to the past.

What we require now is access to all this knowledge. We need a force capable of organizing the several social sciences into a single comprehensive body of knowledge.

In medieval universities theology was the queen of the sciences. In the modern university such unity is lacking, but justice is sought. The logical heir to theology in the multiversity is Law—the Queen of the Social Sciences.

The claim is not farfetched. Historically the oldest of the social sciences, economics, had close connections with law. Originally Moral Philosophy, it was transformed into Political Economy at the end of the Eighteenth Century. And the early political scientists were almost uniformly concerned with law. Adam Smith lectured on "Law and Police" as well as the laws governing the wealth of nations; Jeremy Bentham gravitated from law, which he hated, to political economy, which he came to worship; and James Mill, J. R. McCulloch and J. S. Mill all included chapters on "Jurisprudence" in their treatises on political economy. Indeed, Walter Bagehot even compared Ricardo's treatment of political economy with Austin's treatment of jurisprudence.[86] It was not until the 1890's, with the development of marginal analysis in economic theory, that the "Political" was dissociated from the "Economy" and law and economics went their separate academic ways.

Now economic theory, as economics, has long since become a separate discipline. But it is one that lawyers need, not only to serve the private but especially to serve the collective aspect of justice. The two disciplines must be brought together again, as

[86] The first major work to reflect the changes in the title of the discipline was Alfred Marshall's PRINCIPLES OF ECONOMICS (1st ed. 1890). It is somewhat paradoxical that in 1879—just as the "Politics was being taken out of 'Economics'" and a new pedagogical subject was coming into being—Holmes should have been deploring "the present divorce between the schools of political economy and law" and looking forward to a time when the two would be brought closer together. See note 70, *supra.*

must law and sociology, law and political science, law and psychology, and law and all the other social sciences. How they are to be
reunited is of course the question. It does not matter that as law
teachers we do not yet have a satisfactory answer to this question.
As law teachers we can insure at least that lawyers will answer it —
lawyers who are educated to be agents of justice and make of their
subject what theology was to Newton's Ideal of the University.

*This book was set in Vladimir by University Graphics, Inc.
It was printed on acid-free, long-life paper and bound by The
Maple Press Company. The designers were Elliot Epstein and
Edward Butler. The editors were Nancy Tressel and Cheryl
Allen for McGraw-Hill Book Company and Verne A. Stadtman and
Terry Y. Allen for the Carnegie Commission on Higher Education.
Alice Cohen supervised the production.*